The Interpersonal Communication Book

The Interpersonal Communication Book

Joseph A. DeVito

Queens College

Harper & Row, Publishers
New York/Hagerstown/San Francisco/London

Sponsoring Editor: Michael E. Brown
Project Editor: Karla B. Philip
Designer: Emily Harste
Production Supervisor: Francis X. Giordano
Compositor: V & M Typographical, Inc.
Printer and Binder: The Murray Printing Company
Art Studio: Danmark & Michaels Inc.

**The Interpersonal
Communication Book**

Library of Congress Cataloging in Publication Data

DeVito, Joseph A   1938-
     The interpersonal communication book.

     Includes index.
     1. Communication—Psychological aspects.   I. Title.
BF637.C45D49   301.14   75-25595
ISBN 0-06-041658-0

Contents

Contents in Detail   vii
Preface to the Student and Teacher   xv

PART ONE   **COMMUNICATIONS AND COMMUNICATORS**   **1**

Unit 1 Introduction to Interpersonal Communication 3
Unit 2 Communication Concepts 9
Unit 3 Communication Models 20
Unit 4 Forms, Functions, and Styles of Communication 30
Unit 5 Characteristics of Effective Interpersonal
         Communication 43
Unit 6 Some Axioms of Interpersonal Communication 52
Unit 7 The Self: Structures and Functions 63
Unit 8 Intrapersonal Awareness 80
Unit 9 Self-Disclosure 91
Unit 10 The Self in Transaction 101
Unit 11 Interpersonal Credibility 128
Unit 12 Communication Practices 147
Unit 13 Communication Techniques 165
Unit 14 Systems of Ethics 181

PART TWO   **MESSAGES AND MESSAGE RECEPTION**   **189**

Unit 15 Interpersonal Perceptual Judgments 191
Unit 16 Interpersonal Perceptual Processes 205
Unit 17 Interpersonal Listening 217
Unit 18 Effective Interpersonal Listening 224
Unit 19 Universals of Language 233
Unit 20 Sublanguages 242
Unit 21 Universals of Verbal Interaction 252

Unit 22 Meaning 262
Unit 23 Barriers to Verbal Interaction 283
Unit 24 Supportive and Defensive Interaction 298
Unit 25 Some Principles of Nonverbal Communication 305
Unit 26 Body Communication 313
Unit 27 Spatial Communication 323
Unit 28 Territoriality and Tactile Communication 333
Unit 29 Physical Characteristics as Communication 341
Unit 30 Esthetic, Color, and Time Communication 349
Unit 31 Paralanguage 358

PART THREE INTERPERSONAL INTERACTIONS AND EFFECTS   **365**

Unit 32 Interpersonal Attraction 367
Unit 33 Cooperating and Competing 379
Unit 34 Conflict and Accommodation 390
Unit 35 Loving and Trusting 401
Unit 36 Attitudes in Interpersonal Communication 412
Unit 37 Machiavellianism and Dogmatism 426
Unit 38 Conditioning and Attitude Change 435
Unit 39 Cognitive Balance and Attitude Change 446
Unit 40 Interpersonal Communication Effects 457
Unit 41 Types and Limits of Interpersonal
        Communication Effects 468
Unit 42 Measuring the Effects of Interpersonal
        Communication 480

Glossary 491
Index 503

Contents in Detail

Contents   v
Preface to the Student and Teacher   xv

PART ONE   **COMMUNICATIONS AND COMMUNICATORS**   **1**

Unit 1 Introduction to Interpersonal Communication   **3**
Characteristics of Interpersonal Communication   4
Purposes of the Text   5
Preview of the Text   6
    Male and Female   8

Unit 2 Communication Concepts   **9**
Communication Context   11
Sources and Receivers   12
Messages   13
Noise   13
Encoding and Decoding   13
Competence and Performance   14
Feedback   15
Field of Experience   16
Communication Effect   16
A Note on Ethics   16
    Communication with Strangers   18
    Interpersonal Communication Concepts   19

Unit 3 Communication Models   **20**
Functions of Communication Models   21
Representative Models of Communication   21
    General Models of Communication   27
    Specific Models of Communication   28

Unit 4 Forms, Functions, and Styles of Communication   30
Forms of Communication   30
Functions of Communication   34
Styles of Communication   36
    Communication Channels   39
    Mass and Mini Communication   41

**Unit 5 Characteristics of Effective Interpersonal
      Communication   43**
Openness   44
Empathy   45
Supportiveness   45
Positiveness   45
Equality   46
A Note on Homophily-Heterophily   46
    Effective Interpersonal Interaction   49

Unit 6 Some Axioms of Interpersonal Communication   52
We Cannot Not Communicate   53
All Communications Have a Content and a Relationship
    Dimension   54
A Relationship Is Defined, in Part, by the
    Punctuation of Communication Sequences   56
Human Communication Is Both Digital and Analogic   56
All Communication Interactions May Be Viewed as
    Either Symmetrical or Complementary   58
    Analyzing an Interpersonal Interaction   60

Unit 7 The Self: Structures and Functions   63
A Model of the Self   64
Principles of the Model   68
    Self-Concept: Part I   73
    Goals of Self and Others   75
    Values and Communication   78

Unit 8 Intrapersonal Awareness   80
The Open Self   81
The Blind Self   82
The Hidden Self   84
The Unknown Self   86
    Self-Awareness   87
    I'd Prefer to Be   88

Unit 9 Self-Disclosure   91
The Rewards of Self-Disclosure 92
Sources of Resistance to Self-Disclosure 94
Contexts for Self-Disclosure 95
    Self-Disclosure Questionnaire 98
    Disclosing the Hidden Self 98

Unit 10 The Self in Transaction   101
Ego States 102
Transactions 104
Life Positions 108
    PAC Communications 112
    Mapping Transactions 117
    Communications of Different Life Positions 121

Unit 11 Interpersonal Credibility   128
Types of Credibility 130
Dimensions of Credibility 132
Variations in Credibility Perception 134
A Note on Intrapersonal Credibility 134
    Interpersonal Credibility 137
    Communicator Credibility 140
    Quintilian College 144

Unit 12 Communication Practices   147
Censorship 148
Ghostwriting 151
Data Bank Record Keeping 153
Academic Freedom 155
    Communication Practices: Questions of Ethics 159

Unit 13 Communication Techniques   165
Fear Appeals 166
Conditioning—As Persuasion, As Therapy 168
Emotional Appeals 171
The Prevention of Interaction 172
Communication Techniques: Questions of Ethics 175

Unit 14 Systems of Ethics   181
Wallace's Ethical Basis of Communication 182
McCroskey's Ethical Obligations 183
Keller and Brown's Interpersonal Ethic for
  Communication 184

Weinberg's Effective Time-Binder 185
A Tentative Theory of Interpersonal
    Communication Ethics 188

PART TWO   MESSAGES AND MESSAGE RECEPTION   189

Unit 15 Interpersonal Perceptual Judgments   191
Types of Judgments 191
Three Principles of Perception 192
Bases for Judgments 194
Accuracy in International Perception 196
    Perceiving Others 199
    Perceiving a Stranger 200

Unit 16 Interpersonal Perceptual Processes   205
Primacy-Recency 206
Self-Fulfilling Prophecy 207
Perceptual Accentuation 207
Implicit Personality Theory 208
Consistency 209
Stereotyping 209
    Perception and the Self: A Model of
        Perceptual Space 211
    Perception and Significant Others: Interpersonal
        Perceptual Processes in Operation 214

Unit 17 Interpersonal Listening   217
The Nature and Importance of Listening 217
Listening and Feedback 219
    Feedback in Communication 222

Unit 18 Effective Interpersonal Listening   224
Obstacles to Effective Listening 224
Guides to Effective Listening 227
    Sequential Communication 231

Unit 19 Universals of Language   233
Vocal-Auditory Channel 234
Broadcast Transmission and Directional Reception 234
Specialization 235
Semanticity 235
Rapid Fading 235

Interchangeability 235
Arbitrariness 236
Duality of Patterning 236
Total Feedback 236
Discreteness 237
Displacement 237
Productivity 237
Cultural or Traditional Transmission 237
Reflexiveness 238
Prevarication 238
Learnability 238
    Human and Nonhuman "Language" Systems 240
    Word Coinage 240

Unit 20 Sublanguages   **242**
Language as a Social Institution 242
Functions of Sublanguages 243
Kinds of Sublanguages 245
    Five Sublanguages 247
    Forms of Address 250

Unit 21 Universals of Verbal Interaction   **252**
The Principle of Immanent Reference 253
The Principle of Determinism 254
The Principle of Recurrence 254
The Principle of Contrast and the Working Principle of
    Reasonable Alternatives 255
The Principle of Relativity of Signal and Noise 255
The Principle of Reinforcement/Packaging 256
The Principle of Adjustment 256
The Principle of the Priority of Interaction 256
The Principle of the Forest and the Trees 257
    The Case of *Waldon* v. *Martin and Company* 258

Unit 22 Meaning   **262**
The Triangle of Meaning 262
Denotation and Connotation 264
Measuring Meaning 266
    I, You, and He and She Talk 271
    Meanings in People 275
    Classification 279
    Association 280

Unit 23 Barriers to Verbal Interaction   **283**
Polarization 283

Intensional Orientation 285
Fact-Inference Confusion 287
Allness 289
Static Evaluation 290
Indiscrimination 292
    Reflections on Words and Things 294
    E-Prime 295
    Facts and Inferences 297

Unit 24 Supportive and Defensive Interaction   **298**
Description and Evaluation 299
Problem Orientation and Control 299
Spontaneity and Strategy 299
Empathy and Neutrality 300
Equality and Superiority 300
Provisionalism and Certainty 301
    The Case of Francis Bacon College 303

Unit 25 Some Principles of Nonverbal Communication   **305**
Nonverbal Communication Occurs in a Context 306
Nonverbal Behavior in an Interactional Situation
    Always Communicates 307
Nonverbal Behavior Is Highly Believable 308
Nonverbal Behavior Is Frequently Metacommunicational 309
    Breaking Nonverbal Rules 311

Unit 26 Body Communication   **313**
Area of Kinesics 313
Types of Movements 315
    Instructing Nonverbally 320
    Control by Nonverbal Communication 321

Unit 27 Spatial Communication   **323**
Proxemic Dimensions 324
Proxemic Distances 325
    Spatial Relationships—Part I 329
    Spatial Relationships—Part II 330

Unit 28 Territoriality and Tactile Communication   **333**
Territoriality 333
Tactile Communication 335
    Touch Communication 338

Unit 29 Physical Characteristics as Communication   **341**
Body Type 341

Hair   343
Skin Color   345
Odor   345
   Body Type   347

Unit 30 Esthetic, Color, and Time Communication   **349**
Esthetic Surroundings   349
Color   351
Time   352
   Esthetic, Color, and Time Communication   357

Unit 31 Paralanguage   **358**
The Structure of Paralanguage   359
Judgments Based on Paralanguage   360
   Paralanguage Communication   363

PART THREE INTERPERSONAL INTERACTIONS AND EFFECTS   **365**

Unit 32 Interpersonal Attraction   **367**
   The Qualities of Interpersonal Attraction: Part I   368
Attractiveness   370
Proximity   371
Reinforcement   373
Similarity   374
Complementarity   375
   The Qualities of Interpersonal Attraction: Part II   377

Unit 33 Cooperating and Competing   **379**
Cooperating   379
Competing   381
Cooperation and Competition   383
Red and Blue Game   385
Orange and Green Game   387

Unit 34 Conflict and Accommodation   **390**
Conflict   390
Accommodation   392
   Sandy   396
   The Case of Michael Mannix   397

Unit 35 Loving and Trusting   **401**
Loving   401
Trusting   405
   Roommate Preference   410

Unit 36 Attitudes in Interpersonal Communication   **412**
Attitude, A Definition   413
Related Concepts   414
Dimensions of Attitudes   416
Functions of Attitudes   418
    The Attitude Game   422
    The Attitudes and Values Game   423

Unit 37 Machiavellianism and Dogmatism   **426**
Machiavellianism   426
Dogmatism   428
    Individual and Group Decision Making   431

Unit 38 Conditioning and Attitude Change   **435**
The Operation of Conditioning   435
Principles of Behavior Control   438
    Conditioning Behavior   443

Unit 39 Cognitive Balance and Attitude Change   **446**
The Nature of Cognitive Balance   447
Cognitive Dissonance   449
    The Related Attitudes Game   455

Unit 40 Interpersonal Communication Effects   **457**
Importance of Communication Effects   457
Difficulties in Determining Effects and Causes   460
    Self-Concept: Part II   463
    Positive Words   465

**Unit 41 Types and Limits of Interpersonal
      Communication Effects**   **468**
Types of Effects   469
Limiting Variables   473
    Effects of the Course   478

**Unit 42 Measuring the Effects of Interpersonal
      Communication**   **480**
Reliability and Validity   480
Observing the Behavior   482
Rating the Behavior   484
    Measuring Interpersonal Communication Effects   488

Glossary   491
Index   503

Preface to the Student and Teacher

When I began teaching eleven years ago I was determined to write an introductory text to interpersonal communication that would be both relevant and interesting. I wanted to write a book that would enable students to enjoyably learn the theories of communication and, at the same time, apply what they learn to their own behavior—ultimately to better understand and control their communicative behaviors.

I realized rather quickly that I would need a great deal more knowledge and experience before I could actually write such a book—a book that would make a meaningful contribution to the students who read it and to the field of interpersonal communication. I also realized that I had to learn more about students. And so I started to listen to what they were saying. I tried to find out what a student knows and what a student does not know; what a student wants out of college and, particularly, what a student wants out of an introductory interpersonal communication course; and what a student needs to function effectively now and in the future. In other words, I wanted to find out what students should learn that would help them tomorrow as well as today and what I could do to encourage such learning. The students had many good things to say and so I kept listening. What was learned from students, from educational theorists, from other writers in the field, and from my own successes and failures has been incorporated into this book. I wanted to write a text that college students would find interesting, so I wrote in such a style and about such things that I thought would be of interest to students.

Right now there are about ten other interpersonal communication texts available. A logical question is "Why write another one?" Why should I put in years of time to write another text? The logical answer, and it seems the only legitimate answer, is that this book is different, this book is better.

It is written as I would talk with my students. The jargon that characterizes so many texts has been eliminated. Where technical terms are used, they are defined as clearly and as concretely as possible. A glossary is also included at the end of the text to further clarify any new or difficult terms.

I tried to eliminate all common gender masculine pronouns as well as the use of *man* to mean human beings or the human race. You may find that some of the sentences may not read as smoothly as they would had the masculine pronoun been used, but, this is only because we are not used to it; five, ten, or twenty years from now the use of *he* to mean both he and she will seem awkward. Although the entire manuscript was read and reread by four different people, *he, his, him,* and the like remained in a few instances even after type had been set. Our conditioning, it seems, has been so successful that we hardly notice the use of these terms, so expected are they. In ninety-nine percent of the cases, however, the masculine pronoun as a common gender pronoun has not been used.

This book reflects what I think are the central dimensions of interpersonal communication or, as noted in the text, the *universals* of interpersonal communication. Universals of interpersonal communication are those concepts or principles that need to be understood in order to understand interpersonal communication. That is, they are the essentials of interpersonal communication, the aspects which are common to all and every interpersonal communication interaction. I did not try to include all possible areas of communication, only those aspects which I felt were essential for an adequate understanding of interpersonal communication. I integrated these concepts and principles with the latest thinking in the related fields of psychology, linguistics, anthropology, psycholinguistics, and the like.

Throughout the text, and even in the Experiential Vehicles, I have emphasized the relationship between certain dimensions of interpersonal communication and other forms of communication by using examples from the other forms of communication and by discussing the principles of interpersonal communication as they apply to intrapersonal, public, and mass communication.

This book is a complete learning package. Prefaced to each unit is a series of objectives, a set of goals that should be read before reading the unit and reread upon completion of the unit so that students can determine if they have accomplished the objectives. If the objectives have not been accomplished, the unit should be reread.

Following each unit is a brief paragraph listing of sources. This listing seemed preferable to the use of long and frequent footnotes at the bottoms of pages. These sources are acknowledgments of my indebtedness to other writers and are guides to further reading. Of course, I realize that any author who assumes that students are going to do extra reading is generally judged overly optimistic, but I hope that in this case the situation will be different—that students will want to explore the area in more detail, in other sources and in other experiences.

Concluding each unit is what I call Experiential Vehicles, the exercises. This combination of reading and experience is designed to enable students to both learn the theories of interpersonal communication and also to test its applications and examine its relevance to real-life situations. The Experiential Vehicles, with perhaps two or three exceptons, were all written especially for this book; they grew out of the concepts and principles discussed in the text and are now an integral part of it.

Unlike other texts in interpersonal communication, I have included a thorough discussion of the ethical issues of communication. All communication acts (including but not limited to interpersonal communication) involve consequences for both the speaker, the listener, and, many times, third parties, and because of this the rightness or wrongness of any given communication act must be taken into consideration. Rather than attempt to impose any one system of ethics on you or on the area of interpersonal communication, I have raised questions of ethics about significant issues and tried to stimulate you to develop your own system of ethics as applied to interpersonal communication.

You will notice, as you review the text, that the book consists of short units rather than the traditional long chapters. There are forty-two units in all, each of which covers an essential dimension of interpersonal communication. This system of short units will make the book easier to read and, since each unit is self-contained, will enable the units to be read in any sequence. The units may be arranged to suit any number of different purposes.

Short units rather than long chapters serve a second purpose. Most of a student's studying today is done in relatively short periods of time. He or she reads on the bus or train, during the half hour before dinner, while on a class break, and in similar short intervals. When students set aside longer blocks of time for study, any one course generally receives only one fourth to one sixth of the alloted time; and this percentage does not generally amount to a great deal. Fortunately, students also learn best when they study in relatively short intervals. Textbooks with long chapters create problems for this type of study situation and hinder productivity. With long chapters reading is broken off and later returned to, continuity is lost, and the student-reader is forced to retrace his or her steps if what is now being read is to make any sense. More often than not this retracing is not done and the student reads on but comprehension is reduced. With the short units provided here, students will be able to read one or two units in their entirety in any normally or typically used study period. At the same time, the units are sufficiently long to enable the student to get a sense of having learned something, of having mastered some whole. The result is both efficient learning and a sense of accomplishment.

In fact, I would urge students to read no more than one or, at the most, two units at any one time. After this reading the student should attempt to digest and internalize what was read, relate it to everyday experiences, and in effect make the material his or her own rather than simply words in a text.

I was especially fortunate to have been able to class-test both the Experiential Vehicles and the textual material. The comments from both students and teachers resulted in a number of improvements and in the necessary and pleasant personal reinforcement.

I have tried to write this book so that you will come to see the area of interpersonal communication as fascinating and as significant as I do. I hope you do.

I want to thank the many people who helped me in the writing of this book. My colleagues and Boo assisted me by allowing me the opportunity to test and clarify my ideas about interpersonal communication and by providing me with a stimulating and challenging atmosphere in which to teach and write.

My students, especially those in my interpersonal communication course who used the first draft of this book and the graduate students who adopted my office as theirs, helped a great deal by contributing numerous insights into interpersonal communication and by rewarding my teaching and writing.

The people at Harper & Row all helped in the transition from disordered, poorly typed manuscript to book. Michael Brown, communication editor, got me and Harper & Row together and encouraged me at every stage of development. Michael provided just the right mixture of guidance and freedom I needed to develop, refine, and express the ideas presented here. Karla Philip, project editor, ably and pleasantly helped me clarify what I wanted to say through deft editing, provided logical and coherent format for the book, and made final editing and proofreading almost enjoyable tasks. Emily Harste conceptualized the attractive design for the text, and Elaine Feigenbaum cheerfully and efficiently supervised all efforts to produce the book, seeing that all went on schedule, a schedule we at first thought impossible to follow.

Harper & Row gave me a second home so that all efforts could be coordinated and the book produced as we all wanted. Together Harper and I were determined to produce *the* book in interpersonal communication as reflected by the title—*The Interpersonal Communication Book*—and I think we succeeded.

Lastly, to Maggie, my friends, and those I love who put up with my long hours at the typewriter, at the library, and at the office, I owe everything.

Joseph A. DeVito

PART ONE
COMMUNICATIONS AND COMMUNICATORS

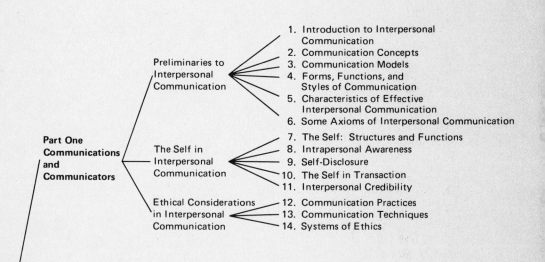

Part One Communications and Communicators

- Preliminaries to Interpersonal Communication
  1. Introduction to Interpersonal Communication
  2. Communication Concepts
  3. Communication Models
  4. Forms, Functions, and Styles of Communication
  5. Characteristics of Effective Interpersonal Communication
  6. Some Axioms of Interpersonal Communication

- The Self in Interpersonal Communication
  7. The Self: Structures and Functions
  8. Intrapersonal Awareness
  9. Self-Disclosure
  10. The Self in Transaction
  11. Interpersonal Credibility

- Ethical Considerations in Interpersonal Communication
  12. Communication Practices
  13. Communication Techniques
  14. Systems of Ethics

INTERPERSONAL COMMUNICATION

unit 1

Introduction to Interpersonal Communication

Characteristics of Interpersonal Communication
Purposes of the Text
Preview of the Text
  Male and Female

Objectives

Upon completion of this unit, you should be able to:

1. cite examples of interpersonal communication from your own observations and experiences
2. define *interpersonal communication*
3. define *message* and *feedback*
4. explain the relationship between theory and application in interpersonal communication

You enter your sociology class and spot a person you would like to date. You get the person's phone number from a mutual friend and call that evening. A previous engagement prevents this person from saying yes, and you decide to call next week. At the same time, you wonder if this "previous engagement" was merely another way of saying no.

You are sitting on a bus reading a book when a person who smells of cigar smoke sits next to you. The odor is so strong that you change your seat.

You are on a basketball team and are discussing strategy for the next quarter with the other members. The captain wants to do certain things while other members want to do something else. The members argue and fight.

You are having dinner with your family and the conversation covers a variety of topics—what each person did during the day, the accident that happened down the street, the plans for tomorrow, and so on.

These and thousands of similar examples are interpersonal communication situations. More formally, we might define *interpersonal communication* as the sending of messages by one person and the receiving of messages by another person, or small group of persons, with some effect and some immediate feedback. Some of these characteristics should be clarified.

CHARACTERISTICS OF INTERPERSONAL COMMUNICATION

Messages

In order for interpersonal communication to exist, messages—signals that serve as stimuli for a receiver—must be sent and received, and they must have created some effect. These messages may be auditory, visual, tactile, olfactory, gustatory, or any combination of these. It is particularly important to note that interpersonal communication does not have to be oral. We can communicate by gestures, touch, smell, or taste, as well as by sounds. We should further note that interpersonal communication does not have to occur face-to-face. Rather, it can occur over the telephone, through prison cell walls, or through videophone hookups. Lastly, note that the messages need not have been sent intentionally. Through slips of the tongue, a lingering body odor, or a nervous twitch we also communicate, though of course not intentionally.

Persons

Interpersonal communication involves at least two persons (a source and a receiver) but may involve a small group of persons. It is important to note a number of related issues here. First, interpersonal communication cannot occur with oneself. Communication with oneself is termed *intra*personal communication. It is essential to understand intrapersonal communication if we are to fully understand interpersonal communication. Yet, it is best to keep these two forms of communication separate. Second, interpersonal communication deals with people, human beings. Communication by or with animals, machines, plants, pictures, and the like are not interpersonal communication situations. It will perhaps be necessary to revise this definition if we discover intelligent beings on other planets. Captain Kirk of the Starship *Enterprise*, of course, was engaging in interpersonal communication whether it was with Mr. Spock, Dr. McCoy, or Scott, or with the Tryskillions or Tholians. But—at least for now —we are not so fortunate. The specification of humans in the definition, therefore, seems reasonable enough today. Third, interpersonal communication occurs between two people or a small group of people. It excludes, however, mass communication and public speaking situations in which there is a large audience and a message goes from speaker to audience but not from audience to speaker.

Reception

In order for interpersonal communication to occur the messages must be received. This is perhaps an obvious point, but one that warrants clarification. The situation in which a parent talks to his or her child when that child is equipped with stereo headphones is not an interpersonal communication situation simply because the messages are not being received.

Effect

If a situation is to involve interpersonal communication there must be some effect. Effects may, of course, range from total agreement to total disagreement, from total understanding to total confusion. Without an effect there can be no interpersonal communication. The receiver must be affected in some way by the message sent. This is not to say that the effects need be overt and observable. Most often they are covert and non-observable. Yet, for interpersonal communication to exist, the receiver must be somehow different as a result of receiving the message.

Feedback

Feedback is the message sent by the receiver—intentionally or not—back to the source. It is crucial to interpersonal communication and often distinguishes this form of communication from other forms. In interpersonal communication there must be some relatively immediate feedback. In a face-to-face situation the feedback may come in words and sentences, eye movements, smiles and frowns, nodding and shaking the head, and so on. As we speak we get relatively immediate feedback from the receiver. In a telephone situation the feedback is exclusively vocal. If there is no opportunity for immediate feedback, the situation did not involve interpersonal communication. Consider television, public speaking, newspapers, magazines, and the like. Here there is little opportunity for relatively immediate feedback. On this basis, such communication forms are excluded from what we call interpersonal communication.

PURPOSES OF THE TEXT

We each spend a great deal of time and energy engaging in interpersonal communication—certainly the greater part of our waking day. Most of the interpersonal communication that goes on, however, seems less effective than it might be. This book is designed to correct that. More specifically, it is designed to enable us to utilize interpersonal communication as an effective means for relating to each other. We sit in a college class for an entire semester, for example, and may never say a word to half the students in the class. We thus lose a great deal, I think. This book will enable us to effectively establish more meaningful dialogue with our fellows. The superficial conversations we hear every day should be enough evidence to demonstrate the need for communication that is more meaningful, less superficial. This book is designed to enable us to better listen to what others are saying, to better understand what they mean.

Interpersonal communication here includes both theory and application. Thus the text has two major aims. First, it attempts to explain the theories and research relevant to interpersonal communication. Put differently, it covers the ideas and evidence about interpersonal communication that are significant and relevant. Second, it attempts to provide the means for becoming a better interpersonal communicator, as source, as receiver, and as analyst or critic.

Unlike other texts, this is a complete learning package which should make learning about interpersonal communication easier, more effective, and more enjoyable and interesting. Both the theory and the application of each major concept in interpersonal communication is covered in both the text and in the experiential vehicles. For example, the concept of self-disclosure in interpersonal communication is covered in the text where the different aspects of self-disclosure are discussed. In the experiential vehicles, actual self-disclosures are dealt with and your own self-disclosing behavior is analyzed.

PREVIEW OF THE TEXT

Part One begins with Five units that focus on the nature of communication generally and on interpersonal communication in particular. These units are designed to provide insight into the structures and functions of communication and the principles by which interpersonal communication is made effective. These principles, or characteristics, of effective interpersonal communication (openness, empathy, supportiveness, positiveness, and equality) should also underlie the communication about communication which takes place in class.

With this as a general background we next consider the self, as source and as receiver. Without an adequate understanding of the self, it is impossible to understand the structures or functions of interpersonal communication or the processes by which one person interacts with another. The reason for this is simple: To the extent that we know ourselves, we can predict our behavior and control ourselves; to the extent that we are strangers to ourselves, we cannot predict and control ourselves. Although we are here focusing on communication behavior, the relationship of self-understanding to the control of the self holds for any type of behavior.

The three unit discussion of questions of ethics in interpersonal communication is based on the assumption that any communication which has an effect has an ethical dimension to it. That is, if our communication has an effect on another person, then we need to deal with questions of right and wrong.

Having received a general background into the nature of communication, the self, and ethics, we will consider messages.

Part Two contains seventeen units devoted to messages and message reception. Perception and listening, the processes by which messages are received are discussed. Under perception we consider the ways in which we perceive and judge people and the processes we use in formulating these judgments. The nature and importance of listening, its relationship to feedback, and the dos and don'ts of effective listening are also considered. Next, we explore verbal and nonverbal messages. Here we deal with some universals of language and verbal interaction, sublanguages, body communication, spatial communication, tactile communication, supportive and defensive language, and various other dimensions of messages. The more we understand about messages, the more effectively we will be able to deal with both verbal and nonverbal messages—as senders, as receivers, and as analysts.

Part Three covers interpersonal interactions and effects. It focuses on interactions between speakers and hearers (attraction, competition, cooperation, loving, trusting, accommodation, and conflict), attitudes and the ways in which attitudes may be changed, and the effects of interpersonal communications and how we might analyze these effects.

As previously mentioned, each unit consists of two parts. The first part is devoted to the theories of interpersonal communication, the second to the experiential vehicles that will allow you to actively deal with and test the implications of the theories in relation to your own communication behaviors. Neither part is complete without the other. Similarly, as a student of interpersonal communication you need to involve yourself in both the theory and the application of interpersonal communication if your exposure to this field is to be a meaningful one.

Sources

The nature of interpersonal communication is surveyed in a number of excellent sources. See, for example, Gerald Miller and Mark Steinberg, *Between People* (Chicago: Science Research Associates, 1975); Kenneth Sereno and Edward Bodaken, *Trans-Per: Understanding Human Communication* (Boston: Houghton Mifflin, 1975); and the articles in R. Wayne Pace, Brent D. Peterson, and Terrence R. Radcliffs, *Communicating Interpersonally: A Reader* (Columbus, Ohio: Merrill, 1973).

Experiential Vehicle

MALE AND FEMALE

This exercise is designed to increase awareness of those matters which may prevent meaningful interpersonal communication between the sexes. It is also designed to encourage meaningful dialogue among class members.

The women and the men are separated; one group goes into another classroom and one group stays in the original room. The task of each group is to write on the board all the things that they dislike having the other sex think, believe, do, and/or say about them. The women should write on the board all the things that men think, believe, say, or do in reference to women which they dislike and which prevents meaningful interpersonal communication from taking place. The men do likewise.

After this is completed, the groups change rooms. The men go into the room in which the women have written their dislikes and the women go into the room in which the men have written their dislikes. The men discuss what the women have written and the women discuss what the men have written. After satisfactory discussion has taken place the groups should get together in the original room. Discussion might center on the following:

1. Were there any surprises?
2. Were there any disagreements? That is, did the men (or women) write anything that the women (or men) argued they do not believe, think, do, or say?
3. How do you suppose the ideas about the other sex got started?
4. Is there any reliable evidence in support of the beliefs of the men about the women or the women about the men?
5. What is the basis for the things that are disliked? Put differently, why was each statement written on the blackboard?
6. What kind of education or training program (if any) do you feel is needed to eliminate these problems?
7. Specifically, in what ways do these beliefs, thoughts, actions, and statements prevent meaningful interpersonal communication?
8. How do you feel now that these matters have been discussed?

unit 2

Communication Concepts

Communication Context
Sources and Receivers
Messages
Noise
Encoding and Decoding
Competence and Performance
Feedback
Field of Experience
Communication Effect
A Note on Ethics
    Communication with Strangers
    Interpersonal Communication Concepts

Objectives

Upon completion of this unit, you should be able to:

1. discuss the nature of the universals of interpersonal communication (and its four dimensions)
2. define the following terms: *communication context, sources* and *receivers, messages, competence* and *performance, encoding* and *decoding, noise, feedback, field of experience, communication effect, ethics,* and *process*
3. explain the transactional nature of interpersonal communication
4. diagram the model of communication presented in this unit, labeling all its parts
5. construct an original model of communication which incorporates the following: context, source, receiver, message, encoding, decoding, noise, feedback, and field of experience

The elements and processes noted in the definition of interpersonal communication, as well as a number of others to be discussed here, may be considered universals of interpersonal communication. A universal of interpersonal communication is a characteristic that is integral to any and all interpersonal communication encounters.

Universals may be treated as existing on a number of different levels. At the most general level, the universals of interpersonal communication would include, for example, source, receiver, message, context, noise, effect, and ethics. We might also discuss universals of interpersonal communication at more specific levels; we might consider those universals which would be included in each of the general universals. For example, the universals included in the general universal of source would include self-awareness, self-disclosure, credibility, attitudes, and so on.

The universals of interpersonal communication are the characteristics or the concepts relevant to all forms of interpersonal communication. These are the concepts of dyadic communication (communication between two people) and the concepts of small group communication. Con-

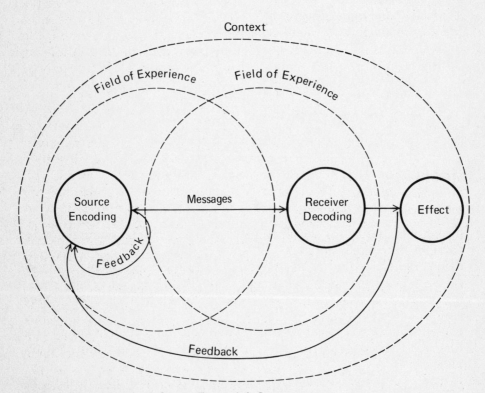

Figure 2.1 *A Model of Some Essential Components in Interpersonal Communication*

sequently, there are no separate units on dyadic or small group communication because the entire book deals with these forms of communication.

Before discussing the specifics of interpersonal communication, the universals of the communication process in general need to be considered. Figure 2.1 illustrates some of the essential components and processes (that is, universals) involved in the communication act.

Interpersonal communication is a process; it is ongoing, and it is forever in motion. For the sake of convenience we may talk about interpersonal communication elements such as source, context, and message as if they were static and discrete elements existing apart from their role in the total act of communication. But this is simply a technique for explaining and illustrating the various elements. In actual fact, these elements exist in interaction with the other elements. Thus, we should keep in mind the process nature of each of these elements even though the discussion may make them seem static.

Interpersonal communication is best viewed as transactional. Sources and receivers are in constant transaction with each other and with the context—in fact, they are in constant transaction with each element in the total communication act. The source influences the receiver; at the same time, the receiver influences the source and the context influences both source and receiver. In turn, the context is influenced by both the source and the receiver and their interactions. This may be a confusing way of saying that each element in the communication act influences and is influenced by each other element.

COMMUNICATION CONTEXT

Communication always takes place within a context. At times this context is not obvious or intrusive; it seems to be so natural that it is ignored, like background music. At other times, the context stands out, and the ways in which it restricts or stimulates our communications are obvious. Compare, for example, the differences in communicating in a funeral home, a football stadium, a quiet restaurant, and a rock concert.

The context of communication has at least four dimensions: physical, social, psychological, and temporal. The room or hallway or park—that is, the tangible or concrete environment—in which communication takes place is the *physical context*. This physical context, whatever it is, exerts some influence on the content as well as the form of our messages. The *social dimension* of context includes, for example, the status relationships among the participants, the roles and the games that people play, and the norms and cultural mores of the society in which they are communicating. The *psychological context* would consist of such aspects as the friendliness or unfriendliness of the situation, the formality or informality, and the seriousness or humorousness of the situation. Communications are permitted at a graduation party that would not be permitted at a funeral or in a hospital. The *temporal dimension* includes the time of day as well as the time in history in which the communication act takes place. For many people the morning is not a time for communication; for others, the morning is ideal. Some interpersonal communication behaviors, for example, sexual relations, seem to many to be more appropriate at night than in the morning or afternoon. Time in history would be particularly important for the communication researcher since the messages —their appropriateness, their importance, their insightfulness—depend in great part on the times in which they were uttered. Consider how difficult it would be to evaluate messages on sexual attitudes and values if we did not know the time in which these messages were communicated.

These four dimensions of context interact with each other; each influences and is influenced by the others. If, for example, the temperature in a room becomes extremely hot (a physical change), it would probably lead to changes in the social and psychological dimensions as well. General discomfort seems to make people friendlier, as many have witnessed when a subway train or bus gets stuck. Change in the context, then, may be brought about in any of three general ways: 1) from outside influences, for example, a train failure; 2) from a change in one of the basic dimensions, for example, time change or temperature change; or 3) from the interaction among the dimensions, for example, friendliness increasing as a result of a train breakdown. The context in the communication model is depicted by a broken line to illustrate that the context is changing rather than static.

SOURCES AND RECEIVERS

In the model, communication is illustrated as taking place between two persons. If we wanted the diagram to illustrate *intra*personal communication, we would view the two circles designating two participants as two roles or functions of the same person.

But regardless of whether there is one person (as in intrapersonal communication), two persons (as in interpersonal communication), or a mass of people (as in mass communication), communication, by definition, demands that someone send signals and someone receive them. One person, of course, might send and receive his or her own signals, as in talking to yourself.

Who people are, what they know, what they believe in, what they value, what they want, what they were told, how intelligent they are, what their attitudes are, and so on all influence what they say and how they say it, what messages they receive and how they receive them. A rich, pampered, well-educated child and a poor, neglected, uneducated child do not talk about the same things, or in the same way. Nor, of course, will they receive messages of the same content in the same way or in the same form or style.

MESSAGES

The messages that are sent and received in interpersonal communication may be of any form. Although we customarily think of communication messages as being verbal (oral or written), these are not the only kinds of messages that communicate interpersonally. We also communicate nonverbally. For example, the clothes we wear communicate something to other people and, in fact, probably communicate to us as well. The way we walk communicates as does the way we shake hands or the way we cock our heads or the way we comb our hair or the way we sit or the way we smile or frown. In fact, everything about us communicates. All of this information constitutes our interpersonal communication messages.

NOISE

Noise may enter into any communication system. Noise is anything that distorts or interferes with the message. Put differently, noise is present in a communication system to the extent that the message sent differs from the message received. The screeching of passing cars, the hum of an air conditioner, the lisp of the speaker, the sunglasses a person wears, may all be regarded as noise since they interfere with the effective and efficient transmission of messages from sender to receiver. (Noise is also present in written communication. Such noise would include blurred type, the print that shows through from the back page, creases in the paper, and anything that prevents a reader from getting the message sent by the writer.)

The concept of noise might also refer to psychological interference and would include biases and prejudices in senders and receivers which lead to distortions in processing information, and closed-mindedness, which is perhaps the classic example of noise preventing information from being received.

ENCODING AND DECODING

In communication theory the processes of speaking or writing and understanding or comprehending are referred to as *encoding* and *decoding*. The act of producing messages, for example speaking or writing, is termed encoding. By putting our ideas into sound waves we are putting these ideas into a code, hence *en*coding. By translating sound waves into ideas we are taking them out of the code they are in, hence *de*coding. Thus we may refer to speakers or writers as encoders and to listeners or readers as decoders.

If further discrimination among the various communicative components is necessary, the idea-generating aspect (that is, the brain) and the message-producing aspect (such as the vocal mechanism) may be distinguished. The idea-generating component would be referred to as the source, while the signal- or message-producing aspect would be referred to as the encoder. Or, if one were talking on a telephone, the source would be the speaker and the vocal mechanism (and the telephone mouthpiece) would be the encoder. Conversely, in listening the brain would be the receiver while the auditory mechanism would be the decoder. The listener in a telephone conversation would be the receiver while the auditory mechanism (and the earpiece of the telephone) would be the decoder.

COMPETENCE AND PERFORMANCE

The concepts of competence and performance are essential to an understanding of encoding and decoding. Consider the "simple" act of speaking. Verbal messages are formed with no real problems; we open our mouths and will certain things to be said. Without any difficulty, they are said. At times we make an error and perhaps say what we did not want to say; but for the most part the vocal mechanism seems a most obedient servant. Similarly, when we listen to the words of others we have no difficulty understanding them, at least most of the time.

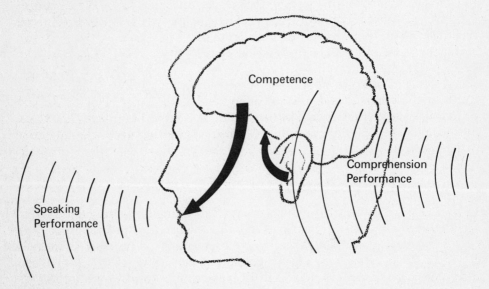

Figure 2.2 *Competence and Performance*

We are able to perform these linguistic feats without any problems because we have, among other things, what is called *linguistic competence*. We know the rules of the language (competence) and therefore can formulate and understand sentences (performance) (Figure 2.2). We are able to produce and understand sentences because we have a set of linguistic rules which in effect tell us that these sounds, structured together in this way, mean something specific. This set of linguistic rules—which we know but cannot necessarily verbalize—is our language competence. When we recognize an error in grammar, for example, we do this by matching up what was said with a rule that is part of our competence. Our competence, then, is a somewhat abstract set of grammatical rules that pairs or matches sound with meaning. Our actual speaking and comprehending are performance aspects of language.

Competence and performance differ in an important way. Competence is knowledge of language, which is uninfluenced by any psychological or physical processes. Performance, on the other hand, is influenced not only by competence but also by such factors as fatigue, anxiety, boredom, attention span, and interest. When we fail to understand what someone says, it may be due to our competence. More likely, however, it is due to our failing to attend to what was said or perhaps to our lack of interest —that is, to performance.

FEEDBACK

Another type of message is that of *feedback*. When we send a message, say in speaking to another person, we also hear ourselves. We get feedback from our own messages—we hear what we say, we feel the way we move, we see what we write, and so on. On the basis of this information we may correct ourselves, rephrase something, or perhaps smile at the clever turn of phrase. Even more important than this self-feedback is the feedback we get from others. In speaking with another individual, not only are we constantly sending messages, but we are also constantly receiving messages. Both parties are sending and receiving messages at the same time. The receiver's messages (sent in response to the source's messages) are termed *feedback*. This feedback, like other messages, can be in many forms: auditory, tactile, visual, gustatory, or olfactory. A frown or a smile, a yea or a nay, a pat on the back or a shot in the mouth are all feedback.

Feedback may be positive or negative. Positive feedback tells the source that everything is fine and that one should continue as one has been going. Negative feedback tells the source that all is not well and that a reassessment of one's communication behavior is necessary. Negative feedback serves a corrective function by informing the communicator that something needs changing, something needs adjustment. Effectiveness in interpersonal communication seems largely due to the ability of the communicator to respond appropriately to feedback. Teaching effectiveness may also be seen in the same way. Effective teachers seem to be those who can read the responses of their students accurately and adjust their messages accordingly. Ineffective teachers seem oblivious to how students are responding and just carry on as always.

FIELD OF EXPERIENCE

The overlapping circles in Figure 2.1 refer to what is called a *field of experience*. The assumption here is that communication can only take place to the extent that the participants share the same experiences. Communication is impossible or ineffective to the extent that the participants have not shared the same experiences. Parents have difficulty communicating with their children, in this view, because the children cannot share the parental experience and because the parents have forgotten what it is like to be a child. When management forgets what it is like to be labor and when labor does not share any of management's experiences, communication becomes extremely difficult, if not impossible. Differences among people serve to make communication more and more difficult; the larger the differences the more difficult communication becomes. Although many differences cannot be eliminated, communication is still not hopeless. While we cannot, for example, share the same experiences of our parents, we can perhaps attempt to role play what it is like being a parent and perhaps in that way better extend the field of experience.

COMMUNICATION EFFECT

Communication always has some effect. For every communication act there is some consequence. The effect may be on the source or on the receiver or on both. When communication affects the environment or context, this is done through people. The effects of communication are, then, first on people; they are always personal. Even when we cannot observe an effect (which is perhaps most of the time) we assume that for every interpersonal communication act there is an effect. As students of communication, part of our task is to determine what these effects are. But that, as we shall see, is a most difficult, though important, undertaking.

A NOTE ON ETHICS

To the degree that communication has an effect, it also has an ethical dimension. Because communication has consequences there is a rightness-wrongness aspect to any communication act. Unlike principles of effective communication, principles of ethical communication are difficult if not impossible to formulate. We can observe the effect of communication and on the basis of the observations formulate what might be principles of effective communication. But we cannot observe the rightness or wrongness of a communication act. The ethical dimension of communication is further complicated by the fact that it is so interwoven with one's personal philosophy of life that it is difficult to propose universal guidelines.

Given these difficulties, we nevertheless include ethical considerations as being integral to any communication act. The decisions that we make concerning communication must be guided by considerations of ethics as well as effectiveness.

Sources

Communication concepts are considered in most of the available texts in communication. My reader, *Communication: Concepts and Processes*, revised and enlarged ed. (Englewood Cliffs, N.J.: Prentice-Hall, 1976), or that by Jean Civikly, *Messages: A Reader in Human Communication* (New York: Random House, 1974) would be good starting places. A brief introduction to the entire area is provided by Gerald Miller, *An Introduction to Speech Communication*, 2d ed. (Indianapolis: Bobbs-Merrill, 1973). An excellent introduction to communication terminology is provided by Wilbur Schramm in his recent *Men, Messages, and Media: A Look at Human Communication* (New York: Harper & Row, 1973).

Experiential Vehicles

COMMUNICATION WITH STRANGERS

For this exercise each member of the class should talk with a stranger for at least ten minutes and report back to the class on what transpired. Here are a number of guidelines that should be followed.

1. Play it safe. It is probably unwise to go up to a stranger on a dark street in a deserted area and attempt to communicate. When in doubt select another person.
2. Do this exercise alone. Do not do it with a group. The other person should not feel that he or she is being studied.
3. Do not tell the person that this is an exercise for an interpersonal communication course. You may tell the person after the conversation but do not tell him or her before.
4. Do not interview the person. "Just" communicate.
5. Select a stranger with whom you would not normally communicate. The person should be different from you on at least one significant variable, for example, age, race, educational background, or social status.

Discussion should center on at least the following:

1. Describe the following:
   a. the person with whom you communicated
   b. the communication context (physical, social, psychological, temporal)
   c. the types of feedback received
   d. the kinds of noise that interfered with communication
   e. the respective fields of experience
   f. the possible effects (on you, on the stranger)

2. How did you open the conversation? Describe the stranger's initial responses.
3. Who did most of the talking? Explain.
4. What did you talk about? Why do you suppose this topic was used?

5. Was the conversation at all worthwhile? If not, why not? If it was worthwhile, explain why.

INTERPERSONAL COMMUNICATION CONCEPTS

The following concepts are generally considered as essential ingredients in even the most basic model of interpersonal communication. Read over the terms and their definitions (in this unit and/or in the Glossary) and construct an original visual representation of the process of interpersonal communication which includes (as a minimum) the concepts noted below.

source
encoder
message
decoder
receiver
channel
context
noise
feedback
effect
field of experience

When each student has completed the model, groups of five or six should be formed so that members may pool their insights in order to construct one improved model of communication. After this is completed all models should be shared with the entire class.

unit 3

Communication Models

Functions of Communication Models
Representative Models of Communication
  General Models of Communication
  Specific Models of Communication

Objectives

Upon completion of this unit, you should be able to:

1. identify and explain the four functions of models
2. reproduce and explain at least two of the communication models developed by Lasswell, Gerbner, Berlo, Shannon and Weaver, and Johnson
3. construct a model of communication that visually represents one or more of the definitions of communication provided here

Communication in general and interpersonal communication in particular are extremely complex processes. Because of the tremendous complexity and the fact that in communication everything is constantly changing, we need to simplify and generalize the essential elements and processes so that we may better explain and understand the structure and function of interpersonal communication. Communication models are perhaps the best way to accomplish this simplification.

The model presented in Figure 2.1, for example, was designed to illustrate some of the essential concepts as developed in this text. However, communication models have been developed for other purposes. A few of the more popular models are presented here so that the broad spectrum of communication might be observed. First, however, some of the major purposes of such models should be noted.

FUNCTIONS OF COMMUNICATION MODELS

Communication models are visualizations of the communication process. In one sense they are basic theories concerning the elements of communication and how these elements operate and interact. More specifically, models of communication may serve any or all of the following four general functions. We here follow Karl Deutsch's general outline.

First, models serve to *organize* the various elements and processes of the communication act. Of course, no model can organize all the data pertaining to communication, but we can expect a reasonably good model to organize at least some of the data in a meaningful and interesting way.

Second, models aid in the discovery of new facts about communication; that is, they serve a heuristic function. The model should generate questions concerning communication that can be researched and hopefully answered, even if only in part.

Third, models enable us to *make predictions* concerning communication. They should help us to predict what will happen under certain conditions.

Fourth, models might provide a means of *measuring the elements and processes involved in communication.* For example, such a model might contain explicit statements concerning the relative importance of different communication channels and the means by which the information each transmits could be measured. This function is a particularly sophisticated one, and most models of communication do not even attempt to serve it. The models presented here attempt or organize the elements and processes, to propose some questions, and to offer certain predictions about communication processes and elements.

REPRESENTATIVE MODELS OF COMMUNICATION

Perhaps the earliest systematic model of communication was presented by Aristotle, the Greek philosopher, in his *Rhetoric*, completed some 2300 years ago. The model is extremely simple, as one can be seen in Figure 3.1.

Aristotle included five essential elements of communication; the speaker, the speech or message, the audience, the occasion, and the effect. In his *Rhetoric*, Aristotle advises the speaker on constructing a speech for different audiences on different occasions for different effects. (This model is actually more applicable to public speaking than it is to interpersonal communication.)

The models devised by both Lasswell and Gerbner, presented in Tables 3.1 and 3.2 attempt to explain the essential elements in communication and the areas of study concerned with them. The Gerbner model expands on the five general components originally defined by Lasswell. Notice

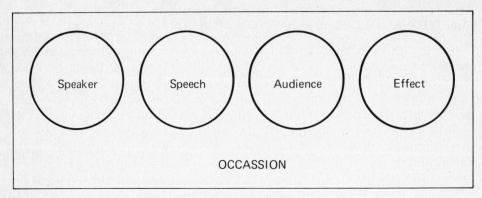

Figure 3.1 *Aristotle's Model of Communication*

that the Lasswell model is not very different from that proposed by Aristotle some 2300 years ago.

David Berlo's model of communication attempts to explain the various components in the communication process (Table 3.3). The four basic components are: source, message, channel, and receiver. For each of these four components there are five elements that need to be considered. The source and receiver are treated in essentially the same way. To study either we need to consider their communication skills (speaking and writing for the source, and listening and reading for the receiver), their attitudes, their knowledge, the social system of which they are a part, and the culture in which they operate. The message consists of both elements and structure, each of which may be broken down into content, treatment, and code. For the channel, Berlo lists the five senses, emphasizing that messages may be sent and received through any and all of the senses.

Perhaps the most famous of all the models of communication is that proposed by Claude Shannon and Warren Weaver, termed the Mathe-

Table 3.1 *Lasswell's Model of Communication*

Communication Component	Research Area
Who	Control Analysis
Says What	Content Analysis
In What Channel	Media Analysis
To Whom	Audience Analysis
With What Effect	Effect Analysis

Source: Harold D. Lasswell, "The Structure and Function of Communication in Society," in Lyman Bryson, ed., *The Communication of Ideas* (New York: Harper & Row, 1948), p. 37.

Table 3.2 *Gerbner's Model of Communication*

Communication Component	Research Area
Someone	Communicator/Audience Research
Perceives an Event	Perception Research and Theory
And Reacts	Effectiveness Measurement
In a Situation	Physical/Social Setting Research
Through Some Means	Media Investigation
To Make Available Materials	Administration; Distribution
In Some Form	Structure; Organization; Style
And Context	Communicative Setting
Conveying Content	Content Analysis; Study of Meaning
Of Some Consequence	Overall Changes Study

Source: George Gerbner, "Toward a General Model of Communication," *Audio-Visual Communication Review,* 4 (1956): 173.

matical Theory of Communication (Figure 3.2). Communication, according to this model, follows a simple left to right process. The information source, let's say a speaker, selects a desired message from all the possible messages. The message is sent through a transmitter, for example, a microphone, and is changed into signals. In telephone communication these signals would be electrical impulses and would be sent over a communication channel such as a wire. The signals are received by a receiver, for example, an earphone of some kind, changed back into a message and given over to the destination, a listener. In the process of transmission certain distortions are added to the signal which were not part of the message sent by the source, and these we call noise.

One of the most insightful models and clearly a model of interpersonal communication is that proposed by Wendell Johnson (Figure 3.3). Although it may seem complex, the model is actually rather simple when compared to the really complex process of communication. The sur-

Table 3.3 *Berlo's Model of Communication*

Source	Message	Channel	Receiver
Communication Skills	Elements	Seeing	Communication Skills
Attitudes	Structure	Hearing	Attitudes
Knowledge	Content	Touching	Knowledge
Social System	Treatment	Smelling	Social System
Culture	Code	Tasting	Culture

Source: David Berlo, *The Process of Communication* (New York: Holt, Rinehart and Winston, 1960), p. 72.

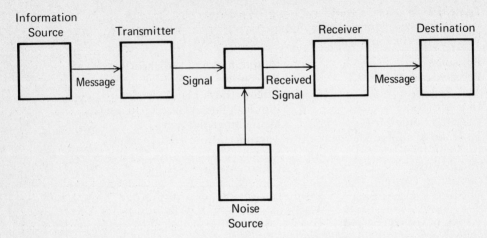

Figure 3.2 *Shannon and Weaver's Model of Communication* (*Source*: Claude E. Shannon and Warren Weaver, *The Mathematical Theory of Communication* [Urbana, Ill., University of Illinois Press, 1949], p. 5.)

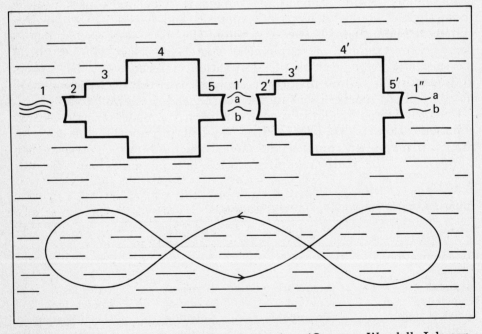

Figure 3.3 *Johnson's Model of Communication* (*Source*: Wendell Johnson, "The Spoken Word and the Great Unsaid," *Quarterly Journal of Speech* 37 [1951]:421.)

rounding rectangle indicates that communication takes place in a context which is external to both speaker and listener and to the communication process as well. The curved loop indicates that the various stages of communication are actually interrelated and interdependent.

The actual communication process begins at 1 which represents the occurrence of an event, anything that can be perceived. This event is the stimulus. Although not all communication occurs with reference to such external stimuli, communication makes sense, Johnson argues, only when it does in some way relate to the external world. At stage 2 the observer is stimulated through one or more sensory channels. The opening at 2 is purposely illustrated as relatively small to emphasize that out of all the possible stimuli in the world, only a small part of these actually stimulate the observer. At stage 3 organismic evaluations occur. Here nerve impulses travel from the sense organs to the brain which effect certain bodily changes in, for example, muscular tension. At 4 the feelings which were aroused at 3 are beginning to be translated into words, a process which takes place in accordance with the individual's unique language habits. At stage 5, from all the possible linguistic symbols, certain one are selected and arranged into some pattern.

At 1', the words that the speaker utters, by means of sound waves, or the words that are written, by means of light waves, serve as stimulation for the hearer, much as the outside event at 1 served as stimulation for the speaker. At 2' the hearer is stimulated, at 3' there are organismic evaluations, at 4' feelings are beginning to be translated into words, at 5' certain of these symbols are selected and arranged, and at 1" these symbols, in the form of sound and/or light waves, are emitted and serve as stimulation for another hearer. The process is a continuous one.

These models are certainly not complete explanations of communication. Rather, they are attempts to picture some of the most essential elements and processes and the relevant relationships which make up the communication act. These models should clarify some of the components and interactions that exist in interpersonal communication. At the same time, they provide a kind of framework into which the more specific details of interpersonal communication, to be discussed throughout the remainder of the text, may be fit. Finally, these models should serve to introduce a basic vocabulary of interpersonal communication.

Sources

For communication models see the summaries by DeVito, *The Psychology of Speech and Language: An Introduction to Psycholinguistics* (New York: Random House, 1970), from which much of the present discussion was drawn; David Mortensen, *Communication: The Study of Human In-*

teraction (New York: McGraw-Hill, 1972); or Ron Smith's article in Larry L. Barker and Robert J. Kibler, eds., *Speech Communication Behavior: Perspectives and Principles* (Englewood Cliffs, N.J.: Prentice-Hall, 1971). References to specific models may be found in any of these sources. For a more extended treatment of the functions of models see Karl Deutsch, "On Communication Models in the Social Sciences," *Public Opinion Quarterly*, 16 (1952). More sophisticated treatments of the theory and model of communication are presented by Leonard C. Hawes in "Elements of a Model for Communication Processes," *Quarterly Journal of Speech*, 59 (1973) and *Pragmatics of Analoguing: Theory and Model Construction in Communication* (Reading, Mass.: Addison-Wesley, 1975).

Experiential Vehicles

GENERAL MODELS OF COMMUNICATION

Below are presented several definitions of communication. Each of these definitions presents a somewhat different view of the nature and function of communication. After reading each of these definitions select the one that seems most meaningful to you and construct a model of communication based on that definition—that is, construct a visual representation of communication as viewed by the definition selected.

After completing this model the class should separate into groups based on the definition chosen. Each group should then discuss the several visual representations and attempt to formulate a composite model that incorporates the best of the individual models.

These composite models should then be presented to the class as a whole in order to emphasize the many different ways in which communication may be viewed and in order to introduce some of the essential concepts and processes of communication.

Definitions

1. "A word that describes the process of transferring meaning from one individual to another." (Robert S. Cathcart, *Post Communication: Criticism and Evaluation* [Indianapolis: Bobbs-Merrill, 1966], p. 1.)
2. "A process involving the selection, production, and transmission of signs in such a way as to help a receiver perceive a meaning similar to that in the mind of the communicator." (Wallace C. Fotheringham, *Perspectives on Persuasion* [Boston: Allyn and Bacon, 1966], p. 254.)
3. "Communication means that information is passed from one place to another." (George A. Miller, *Language and Communication* [New York: McGraw-Hill, 1951], p. 6.)
4. "The discriminatory response of an organism to a stimulus." (S. S. Stevens, "Introduction: A Definition of Communication," *Journal of the Acoustical Society of America,* 22 [1950]: 689.)

5. "All behavior in an interactional situation has message value, i.e., is communication. . . ." (P. Watzlawick, J. H. Beavin, and D. D. Jackson, *Pragmatics of Human Communication* [New York: Norton, 1967], p. 48.)
6. "A process whereby a source elicits a response in a receiver through the transmission of a message, be it sign or symbol, verbal or nonverbal." (Andrea L. Rich, *Interracial Communication* [New York: Harper & Row, 1974], p. 4.)
7. "Communication occurs whenever persons attribute significance to message-related behavior." (C. David Mortensen, *Communication: The Study of Human Interaction* [New York: McGraw-Hill, 1972], p. 14.)

SPECIFIC MODELS OF COMMUNICATION

In groups of five or six construct a diagrammatic model of the essential elements and processes involved in one of the following communication situations. This model's primary function should be to describe what elements are involved and what processes are operative in the specific situation chosen. (It may be useful to define the situation chosen in more detail before constructing the model.)

1. Sitting silently on a bus
2. Thinking
3. Asking for a date on the phone
4. Conversing with a very close friend
5. Talking with three or four acquaintances
6. Delivering a lecture to a class
7. Watching television
8. Participating in a formal group discussion
9. Writing a speech for a political candidate
10. Reading a newspaper
11. Performing in a movie
12. Acting a role in a play
13. Arguing with your instructor
14. Selling insurance door-to-door
15. Persuading an angry crowd to disband

Each group should share their models with the rest of the class. Discussion might center on the following:

1. How adequately do the models explain the processes which they are supposed to represent? Do they incorporate all the essential elements and processes? Are the relationships among the elements and processes clear?
2. What insight into the actual processes of communication do these models provide? What new ideas or information may be found in these models?

3. What elements and processes included here might also be included in the general models of communication discussed in the unit?
4. What functions do these models serve? Explain. (Respond to this question with specific reference to the functions of models presented by Deutsch.)
5. Which of the fifteen situations are interpersonal communication ones? Explain.

unit 4

Forms, Functions, and Styles of Communication

Forms of Communication
Functions of Communication
Styles of Communication
  Communication Channels
  Mass and Mini Communication

Objectives

Upon completion of this unit, you should be able to:

1. define the major forms of communication
2. explain the major differences between intrapersonal, dyadic, small group, public, and mass communication
3. explain the operation of feedback in the five forms of communication discussed here
4. define the six functions of language proposed by Roman Jakobson
5. explain the six functions of communication in terms of the six functions of language
6. explain the five styles of communication

Communication exists in many different forms, has many different functions, and is actualized in a number of different styles. These forms, functions, and styles of communication as a whole need to be understood before interpersonal communication can be fully appreciated.

FORMS OF COMMUNICATION

Communication exists in many different forms, on many different levels. Here five such forms or levels are distinguished (Figure 4.1).

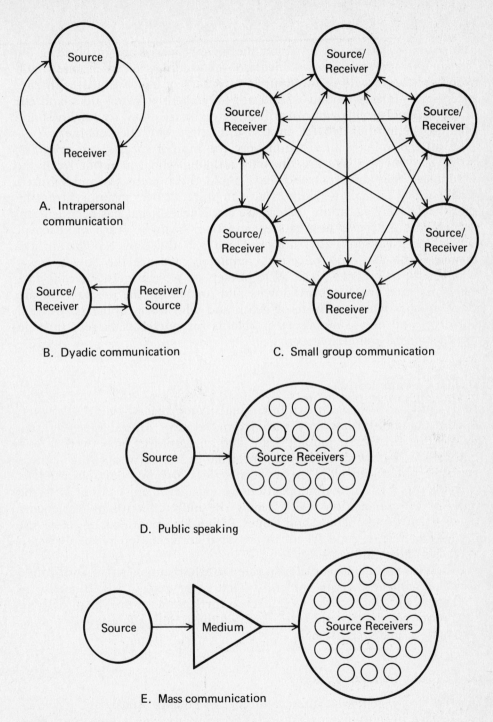

Figure 4.1 *Five Forms of Communication*

Intrapersonal

The communication act in which the fewest people are involved is obviously *intrapersonal communication*—communication with one's self. Whether we are willing to admit it to others or not, we all—with rare exceptions—talk to ourselves. And not only silently. When alone and out of the reach of prying ears we will often verbalize aloud to ourselves and even engage in brief debates, first assuming one side then another.

Of all the animals in creation only the human species can progress, grow, and develop. We are the only animals who can profit from the wisdom of our ancestors and learn from their successes and failures. Unlike other animals we do not have to start all over again, reinventing the wheel each generation. Instead we can learn all that has been learned since we as a species first existed and then begin to learn or discover new things. Paradoxically, however, we are the only animals in the universe who can fool ourselves completely; we are the only animals who can lie to others as well as to ourselves. We can quite literally talk ourselves into nervous breakdowns and among all the animals we are the only ones who are aware of death and who worry about it. We fool ourselves and create numerous problems for ourselves largely through intrapersonal communication.

Dyadic Communication

In *dyadic communication* two individuals communicate with each other. Dyadic communication may vary from the very formal type of communication between a job applicant and an employer or between a witness and a trial lawyer to the very informal communication which occurs between parent and child or between lovers. Dyadic communication is perhaps the form of communication we engage in most often. It is the form of communication which seems the most effective in influencing opinions, attitudes, beliefs, and values. Although a politician on television has some effect, a good friend in personal conversation probably has a great deal more influence.

Dyadic communication can also refer to what some writers have called *serial* or *sequential communication*. That is, A speaks to B, B speaks to C, C speaks to D, D speaks to E, and so forth. A never speaks directly to C, C never speaks directly to E. Each of these units, however, is a dyad and may be analyzed as such.

Small Group Communication

In *small group communication* a number of people, usually about five to ten, engage in mutual conversation. The word *mutual* is important here because it rules out gatherings of people where individual conversations go on but no group communication takes place. Because people are in proximity with each other does not mean that they are engaging in group communication. Like dyadic communication, small group communication may be formal as in the case of a colloquium or panel discussion or it may be informal as when a number of people have dinner together and communicate as a group.

Small group communication is not simply a number of dyadic communication situations going on at once; the whole here is not equal to the sum of its parts. The small group communication (the whole) is a lot more than the sum of its parts. It includes the sum of its parts plus all the interactions among the parts.

Public Speaking

In *public speaking* one speaker addresses a large or relatively large audience. Here the communication is essentially one way, from speaker to audience, although the audience responds with feedback and perhaps with questions, comments, and the like. For the most part, however, the communication messages are sent by the speaker and received by a mass of people.

Public speaking by its nature is almost always formal. There are some situations where public speaking is somewhat informal, but for the most part formality characterizes most public speaking. The formality is often related to the degree to which the message of the speaker is planned in advance. In the very formal situation the speech is planned word for word, and the speaker reads from manuscript. At other times the speech is not planned at all but is impromptu; this usually is the most informal type of public speaking.

Public speaking situations vary from the classroom situation in most college courses to comedians playing before a Las Vegas audience to a speaker at a rally addressing thousands of people to the President addressing Congress.

Mass Communication

Mass communication differs from the other forms of communication in that there is an intermediary between source and receiver. We do not see or hear or read the communicator directly but only through some medium such as television, radio, film, newspapers, and magazines. Another important difference is in the immediacy of the feedback from the listeners. In dyadic, small group, and to some extent in public speaking, the feedback is immediate. Speakers can immediately ascertain what effect their message is having on the receivers. In mass communication this is not possible. The feedback received—in the form of letters to the editor or box office sales—is delayed. By the time that this feedback is received the message has already been completed and consequently there is no opportunity for speakers to adjust the message on the basis of the feedback. This is one reason why so many plays have tryouts in small towns and why television shows are sold on the basis of actual pilots. In this way the feedback can be evaluated and utilized to develop a more effective or more appealing message. Still another difference between mass communication and the other forms is the cost. The amount of money that time in the mass media costs makes it extremely difficult for the average person to communicate. A letter to the editor hardly has the same effect as a 60 second commercial or a full-page ad.

In this text we are concerned with interpersonal communication, which is used here to include intrapersonal communication, dyadic communication, and, to some extent, small group communication. Although it shares much with public speaking and mass communication, it excludes these for the most part.

FUNCTIONS OF COMMUNICATION

Communication is such a complex act that it is probably impossible to list or define in any complete way the purposes or functions it serves. Any given communication, upon close analysis, may have a number of different purposes, some of which the speaker may be consciously aware of and some of which may function below the level of awareness.

Throughout the history of communication, theorists have sought to define and delimit the various functions of communication. At times their objective was to gain insight into the nature of language, at other times into the nature of the mind, and at other times into the nature of persuasion.

Aristotle, for example, in his *Rhetoric*, distinguished three general purposes. Political speaking was concerned with "establishing the expediency or the harmfulness of a proposed course of action." Forensic or legal speaking aimed at "establishing the justice or injustice of some action." Lastly, the epideictic or ceremonial speaker praised or attacked a person and aimed at "proving him worthy of honor or the reverse."

The classification of communication functions which seems most complete is that proposed by the linguist Roman Jakobson. Jakobson defines communication functions in terms of a basic and general communication model consisting of six components: source, channel, message, code, referent, and receiver. Any given communication, according to this conception, may be viewed as being oriented primarily to one of these components.

When language is oriented to the source or speaker it serves an *emotive* purpose or function; it tells us something about the speaker. This is what psychiatrists focus on in interviews with patients. The psychiatrist would examine the communication for the information it may reveal about the speaker or patient. Catharsis, the verbal expression of emotional problems, is perhaps the clearest example of language serving an emotive function.

Communications oriented to the channel serve primarily a *phatic* function. Phatic language, a term coined by the cultural anthropologist Bronislaw Malinowski, refers to communication that creates "ties of union" between the parties involved in the communication act. It does not communicate information about the outside world but conveys a desire on the part of the speaker for mutual interaction and mutual communication. "Hello," "How are you," and "What's happening," are examples of phatic communication; their function is to open up the channels of communication. It is the "small talk" that oils the communication machinery and prepares the way for the "big talk."

That language which functions to give beauty or a certain distinctiveness to a message serves a *poetic* function and is oriented primarily to the message. Poetic language is primarily stylistic and refers to the form of the message rather than to its content.

The *metalingual* function of communication is oriented to the code or grammar of the language. It is language which refers not to the outside world but to language itself; it is a higher order or a more abstract kind of language. When we define a term, for example, we are using metalanguage—that is, language which refers to language. In the expression "never say never" the first "never" is in metalanguage; it refers not to the real world but to language, specifically to the second "never." Expanded, this phrase would read, "Never use the word 'never' in referring to people, objects, and events in the world."

Language that is oriented to the referent or real world of people, objects, events, and relationships is *informative* or *referential* communication. Basically, the function of informative communication is to communicate to another what he or she does not already know. If I were to tell you that Lincoln was the sixteenth president of the United States I would not be using informative language since I did not communicate something new; you already knew this. On the other hand, if I were to say, "The longest continuous speech delivered in the United States Senate was given by Senator Wayne Morse of Oregon in 1953 on the Tidelands Oil Bill when he spoke for 22 hours and 26 minutes," this would probably be informative since it is likely that you did not know this bit of information before. It is important to stress that in informative or referential communication the information communicated need not be useful or interesting or even true. The only criterion is that it is not already known. Of course, if the information is useless, boring, and generally false you will soon find yourself without a listener.

Language oriented to the receiver is called *directive* or, more commonly, *persuasive;* it is communication that serves to direct the receiver in some way toward some end. We can, with relatively little difficulty, subdivide this function into various and numerous categories. For example:

to stimulate thought
to provoke questions
to entertain
to reinforce attitudes
to change attitudes
to change behavior

The important thing to note here is that all of these purposes or functions call for some kind of persuasion or direction. To stimulate thought it is necessary to persuade the individual to think in a particular way, to entertain it is necessary to persuade the persons to laugh or smile or relax and so on.

Any given communication, then, may be viewed as emphasizing one of these purposes. At the same time, however, it is probable that many of these functions will be incorporated into any specific message. The lecture that persuades us to change our attitudes toward our foreign policy must also have informed us about the nature of that foreign policy and must also have opened the channels of communication. This lecture, then, served a persuasive, informative, and phatic function at the same time. In short, messages are multipurpose.

STYLES OF COMMUNICATION

It should be clear that each of the forms of communication covered earlier may serve any or all of the functions considered here. Furthermore, it should be clear that we do not communicate in the same style when engaging in different forms and when pursuing different functions. The way we communicate will depend on the form of the communication and on the function of the communication.

We might here distinguish five major styles of communicating, following linguist Martin Joos in *The Five Clocks:* frozen, formal, consultative, casual, and intimate.

Frozen style is the style of written prose and of social strangers. There is no participation by the addressee here. The speaker speaks and the listeners listen; in fact, the speaker is hardly aware of the listeners' presence and in any case does nothing to alter his or her style on the basis of listener reactions.

Formal style, also not participated in by the listener, serves primarily an information function and is the style generally used in addressing a large audience. When used with only one listener it signals distance between speaker and hearer. At times the distance is one of deference and at other times it is one of contempt. When formal style is used where casual style would be expected it signifies that something is wrong in the relationship. If a mother calls *"John David Smith"* when *"Johnny"* is the usual name she calls, the child knows that something is wrong and consequently modifies his response. The formal style signals distance or nonimmediacy. The speaker addresses the audience with a cohesive, carefully planned, and well-constructed talk. Sentences are varied and grammatical and the vocabulary is extensive; repetitions, sentence fragments, slang, and "in group" expressions are avoided.

Consultative style, the style of business talks and small-group discussions, does involve participation by the addressee. Here the speaker supplies background information, the amount and kind of which is regulated by the listener. By his participation the addressee insures that the speaker does not provide unnecessary or already known information and that he does provide information which is essential to their interaction. In consultative style there is no extensive planning of what will be said or how it will be expressed. The continuous participation by the addressee makes such planning unnecessary and, in fact, impossible. Because of this lack of planning there will be a number of grammatical "errors," for example, run-on sentences, the use of *can* instead of *may* to indicate permission, and the "overuse" of certain terms such as *and*, *well*, and *on*.

Casual style is the style in which friends and "insiders" speak. Background information and continuous participation by the addressee are absent; both are unnecessary in casual style and, in fact, might be insulting since they imply that speaker and listener do not share the same information. Casual style is characterized by the frequent occurrence of terms used in special senses and by ellipsis (the omission of various unstressed words or certain sounds). For example, in casual style *"The coffee is cold"* would be rendered *"Coffee's cold"* and *can* as *"c'n."* Other casual expressions include *"Don't care"* for *"I don't care,"* *"Got a flat?"* for *"Have you got a flat?"* and *"Want to come?"* for *"Do you want to come?"* Determiners and auxiliaries, being unnecessary for communicating meaning, are omitted. Ellipsis, of course, does not occur in the first three styles.

Intimate style is characterized by the use of the private and relatively permanent language code of the group and by extraction. In extraction some minimum pattern taken from a casual utterance serves as the entire sentence, for example, *"Coffee's cold"* would be said as *"Cold."* In contrast to formal style which serves to inform the addressee about the outside world, intimate style serves to convey feelings, that is, to inform about the world inside the speaker's skin. One particularly interesting feature of this style is that language itself can never be a topic of conversation. Any mention of grammar automatically removes the conversation from intimate style.

Interpersonal communication utilizes only three of the five styles. Consultative, casual, and intimate styles are interpersonal styles whereas frozen and formal are styles reserved for public speaking or mass communication. One of the most important differences among these styles and the one which is most relevant to interpersonal communication is the role of the listener. In frozen and formal styles the listener does not participate in the communication. In consultative, casual, and intimate styles, however, the roles of speaker and listener are constantly being reversed, where the speaker becomes the listener and the listener becomes the speaker. This constant reversal of speaker and listener roles is one of the defining characteristics of interpersonal communication.

Sources

Other introductory texts cover essentially that which is covered here under forms of communication. For greater insight into the various forms and levels of communication, consult specialized works in each of the areas. For example, select a book on interviewing, one on small group communication, one on public speaking, and one on mass media and compare the various topics and perspectives. (There does not seem to be a book devoted entirely to intrapersonal communication though any number of the various "self-help" books might be considered to deal with this area.) For Roman Jakobson's model of language and communication see his "Closing Statement: Linguistics and Poetics," in *Style in Language,* edited by Thomas A. Sebeok (Cambridge, Mass.: M.I.T. Press, 1960) and my "Style and Stylistics: An Attempt at Definition," *Quarterly Journal of Speech* 53 (1967). Martin Joos' five styles are presented in his "The Five Clocks," *International Journal of American Linguistics* 28, no. 2 (1962). Henry Gleason's discussion and modification of these styles is presented in his *Linguistics and English Grammar* (New York: Holt, Rinehart, and Winston, 1965). One of the best presentations of style in communication is that of Jane Blankenship, *A Sense of Style* (Belmont, Cal.: Dickerson, 1968).

Experiential Vehicles

COMMUNICATION CHANNELS

In this exercise we attempt to explore the efficiency and satisfaction of communication in different channel patterns.

Five groups of equal numbers are formed according to the following patterns:

Circle   Wheel   Y

Chain   All channel

Arrows connecting two individuals indicate that communication may take place between them. Individuals not connected by arrows may not communicate directly but only indirectly through the individual(s) with whom they are connected.

The problem is the same for all groups. Each group is to reach *unanimous* agreement on how many squares are contained in the following diagram:

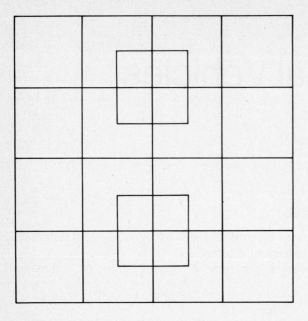

All messages are to be written on individual pieces of paper. Members may pass to other members only those messages that they themselves have written. Thus, if members receive a message they wish to pass on to another member, they must rewrite the message.

Efficiency and Satisfaction Indexes

The efficiency of the groups should be indexed in at least two ways. First, the time necessary for completion should be carefully noted. Second, the messages sent should be saved and counted. Efficiency will thus be indexed by the time it took to arrive at the correct answer and by the number of messages needed for communicating.

The satisfaction of the group members should be indexed by responses on the following scales.

Task Participation

Rate your participation in the task on the following scales:

interesting ____:____:____:____:____:____:____ boring
enjoyable ____:____:____:____:____:____:____ unenjoyable
dynamic ____:____:____:____:____:____:____ static
useful ____:____:____:____:____:____:____ useless
good ____:____:____:____:____:____:____ bad

Compute your mean score for these scales as follows: 1) number the scales from 7 to 1 from left to right; 2) total the scores from all five scales (this number should range from 5 to 35), and 3) divide by five to get your mean score.

Each group should then compute the group mean score by totaling the individual mean scores and dividing the sum by the number of participants.

Efficiency and Satisfaction Scores

Channel Patterns	Efficiency		Satisfaction
	Time	Number of Messages	Group Mean Scores
circle	——	——	——
wheel	——	——	——
"Y"	——	——	——
chain	——	——	——
all channel	——	——	——

For Discussion

1. On what basis do you account for the differences in efficiency and satisfaction among the groups?
2. Are there realistic counterparts to these five communication structures? Do we find these communication structures and patterns in the "real world?" Where? What are some of the consequences of these various communication patterns?
3. How does structure influence function? Examine your own group situation and consider how the structure of the group (the positioning of the members for example) influenced the functions the members played. Does this have a realistic counterpart? In what ways do you function differently as a result of the structure in which you find yourself?
4. What implications would you be willing to draw from this experience for improved communication in the classroom?

MASS AND MINI COMMUNICATIONS

The objectives of this exercise are

1. to become acquainted with some of the diverse media of mass and mini communication
2. to become aware of some of the differences and similarities between these two media
3. to become familiar with some audience variables

4. to obtain some practice in audience analysis
5. to provide some experience in discovering communication
6. to become acquainted with some of the effects of mass and mini communications

Instructions

1. Select an example of a print medium of mass communication, for example, a newspaper or magazine addressed to a large audience.
2. Select an example of a print medium of mini communication, for example, a newspaper or magazine addressed to a relatively small audience.
3. Analyze the audience of each of these publications. Consider, for example, the following factors: age, sex, educational level, status, occupation, political persuasion, religion, income, marital status, ethnic background, special interests. In this analysis point out both the similarities and the differences between the audiences of these two media.

    Clues for this analysis may be found throughout the publication, for example, in the educational policy, in the advertisements, in the articles and authors, in the special features, in the pictures, in the letters to the editor, and so forth.

    This audience analysis may take any number of different forms. For example, you may construct a profile of the typical reader of each publication. This would take the form of a listing of the characteristics common to most of the readers. Or you may construct your analysis on predicted percentages, for example, 75 percent of the readers are male, 90 percent are unmarried, 15 percent are college professors, and so forth. Support your inferences with specific references to the publications analyzed. For example, if you say that the typical reader is male, give your reasons for making this inference. What is contained in the publication that leads you to this conclusion?
4. On the basis of your analyses state *one* principle of communication that you feel these communicators (publishers, editors, or advertisers) are following. What is your reasoning-evidence for this conclusion?
5. On the basis of your review of these publications state what you feel are some of the effects of these media on the readers. Do these publications also have effects on nonreaders? Explain.

Notes

1. Bring these publications to class so that everyone can examine them.
2. Be prepared to discuss your findings with the class.

unit 5

Characteristics of Effective Interpersonal Communication

Openness
Empathy
Supportiveness
Positiveness
Equality
A Note on Homophily-Heterophily
   Effective Interpersonal Interaction

Objectives

Upon completion of this unit, you should be able to:

1. define *openness* and identify the two aspects of interpersonal communication to which it refers
2. define *empathy* and distinguish it from sympathy
3. define *supportiveness*
4. define *positiveness* and explain the three aspects of interpersonal communication to which it refers
5. define *equality* as it relates to interpersonal communication
6. identify the presence of these qualities (openness, empathy, supportiveness, positiveness, and equality) in interpersonal interactions

Interpersonal communication, like any form of behavior, can vary from being extremely effective to extremely ineffective. Probably no interper-

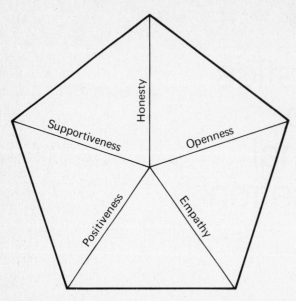

Figure 5.1 *Effective Interpersonal Communication*

sonal encounter is a total success or a total failure; it could have been better, but it could have been worse. Here we attempt to characterize effective interpersonal communication, recognizing that each communicative act is different and that principles or rules must be applied judiciously with a full recognition of the uniqueness of communication events.

Effective interpersonal communication seems to be characterized by at least the following five qualities: openness, empathy, supportiveness, positiveness, and equality (Figure 5.1).

OPENNESS

The quality of *openness* refers to at least two aspects of interpersonal communication. First, and perhaps most obvious, is that effective interpersonal communicators must be willing to open up to the other people with whom they are interacting. This does not mean that we should immediately pour forth our entire life history. Interesting as that may be, it is not usually very helpful to the communication or interesting to the other individuals. By openness is simply meant a willingness to self-disclose, to reveal information about oneself which might normally be kept hidden but which is relevant to the interpersonal encounter.

The other aspect of openness refers to the willingness of a communicator to react honestly to incoming stimuli. Silent, uncritical, and immovable psychiatrists may be of some help in a clinical situation, but they are generally boring conversationalists. We want (and have a right to expect) people to react openly to what we say. Nothing seems worse than indifference; even disagreement seems more welcome. Of course there are extremes here too.

EMPATHY

Perhaps the most difficult of all the communication qualities to achieve is the ability to *empathize* with another individual. By empathizing is meant a feeling with the individual; to empathize with someone is to feel as that person does. To sympathize, on the other hand, is to feel for the individual, to be sorry for the person, for example. To empathize is to feel as the individual feels, to be in the same shoes, to feel the same feelings in the same way. If we are able to empathize with people, we are then in a position to understand where they are coming from, where they are now, and where they are going. Also, we are less likely to judge their behaviors or attitudes as being right or wrong.

SUPPORTIVENESS

An effective interpersonal relationship is one which is *supportive*. Open and empathetic interpersonal communication cannot survive in a threatening atmosphere. If participants feel that what they say will be criticized or attacked, for example, they may be reluctant to open up or to reveal themselves in any meaningful way.

In a supportive environment silence does not take on a negative value. Rather, silence is seen as a positive aspect of communication; an opportunity for relating nonverbally.

POSITIVENESS

Positiveness in interpersonal communication refers to at least three different aspects or elements. First, interpersonal communication is fostered if there is a certain positive regard for the self. The persons who feel negative about themselves will invariably communicate these feelings to others, who in turn will probably develop similar negative feelings. On the other hand, people who feel positive about themselves will convey this feeling for themselves to others, who in turn are likely to return the positive regard.

Second, interpersonal communication will be fostered if a positive feeling for the other person is communicated. This obviously will make the other person feel better and will encourage more active participation on a more meaningful level. One will, for example, be more likely to self-disclose.

Third, a positive feeling for the general communication situation is important for effective interaction. Nothing is more unpleasant than communicating with someone who does not enjoy the exchange or does not respond favorably to the situation or context. A negative response to the situation makes one feel almost as if one is intruding and communication seems sure to quickly break down.

EQUALITY

Equality is a peculiar characteristic. In any situation there is probably going to be some inequality. One person will be smarter, richer, better looking, or a better athlete. Never are two people absolutely equal in all respects. Even identical twins would be unequal in some ways. Despite this inequality, interpersonal communication is generally more effective when the atmosphere is one of equality. This does not mean that unequals cannot communicate. Certainly they can. Yet their communication, if it is to be effective, should recognize the equality of personalities. By this is meant that there should be a tacit recognition that both parties are valuable and worthwhile human beings and that each has something important to contribute.

Equality should also characterize interpersonal communication in terms of speaking versus listening. If one participant speaks all the time while the other listens all the time, effective interpersonal communication becomes difficult if not impossible. There should be an attempt at achieving an equality of sending versus receiving. Depending on the situation, one person will normally speak more than the other person, but this should be a function of the situation and not of the fact that one person is a "talker" and another person is a "listener."

People in varied occupations often develop a certain snobbishness about communication. The professor may not feel it worthwhile to communicate with a salesperson in an atmosphere of equality. The college graduate may feel it worthless to communicate equally with high school dropouts. The truck driver may feel it useless to communicate with a scientist as an equal. All in their way are interpersonal communication snobs. All assume that they have nothing to gain from such interactions and that time is better spent talking to "equals." This is a particularly harmful attitude since it prevents each from learning what the other person has to offer. But perhaps we have to experience the rewards from such communications before we can believe that they are in fact enjoyable, profitable, and generally rewarding.

A NOTE ON HOMOPHILY-HETEROPHILY

These five characteristics of effective interpersonal communication are qualities that can be learned, and so it seems important that they be singled out for discussion. We should, however, make note here of the concepts of homophily and heterophily. *Homophily* refers to the degree of similarity between the parties engaged in interpersonal communication and *heterophily* refers to the degree of difference between the parties. The similarity and difference may refer to just about any characteristic—age, religion, political leaning, financial status, educational level, and so forth.

Generally, research has shown that interpersonal communication is more effective when the parties are homophilous. James McCroskey, Carl Larson, and Mark Knapp, for example, state: "More effective communication occurs when source and receiver are homophilous. The more nearly alike the people in a communication transaction, the more likely they will share meanings." We will, according to this principle, communicate best with people who are most like ourselves. Butchers will communicate best with butchers, Texans will communicate best with Texans, and college students will communicate best with college students.

Because of the contribution which homophily-heterophily makes to the study of interpersonal communication it needs to be discussed in relation to the five characteristics of effective interpersonal communication. The more homophilous individuals are the more open they will be with each other. This seems to follow since we seem to be most comfortable with those who are like us. Consequently, we are more apt to reveal ourselves and to self-disclose to people like ourselves. We feel perhaps that they would reveal themselves and disclose to us. And so by being open we do not risk as much as we would in a heterophilous situation.

Empathy is greatest when people are homophilous and least when people are heterophilous. We can more easily feel as other people do (which is the essence of empathy) when we are like them to begin with. There is little distance to travel in order to empathize when we are similar to the individuals but much distance when they are not like us. Consider the difficulty a poor person would have empathizing with the disappointment of a rich one because he or she must give up the second car, or the difficulty a rich person would have in empathizing with a poor person's hunger.

It seems that we all want to support people who are like us more than people who are very different from us. By supporting homophilous people we are in effect supporting ourselves. People like us, we may feel, will be supportive to us and so we respond in kind and support them. We can be silent with people who are like us and not be uncomfortable. We do not feel we have to impress them with our knowledge or intelligence.

When we are with people who are homophilous we feel more positive toward ourselves because we are not made to feel inferior as we might be made to feel if we were with heterophilous people. We generally enjoy the act of communicating in a homophilous situation more than we would in a heterophilous one. Of course, we generally like people who are like us more than we like people who are unlike us. In a sense, being with homophilous individuals provides a kind of confirmation of self.

Perhaps the most obvious relationship that exists with homophilous people is that of equality. By definition, homophilous people are equal to us, neither inferior nor superior. Hence there is more likely to be an atmosphere of equality, a free give and take of ideas, and an awareness that both participants have something to contribute.

Although communication is most effective when the individuals are homophilous, we should note that change is often brought about when the parties involved are "optimally heterophilous" in regard to the subject under discussion. According to McCroskey, Larson, and Knapp, if the two people are homophilous in regard to the subject matter then neither will be competent enough to change the attitudes, beliefs, or behaviors of the other. Also, when the individuals are too far apart in their competence on a subject, the more competent one will obviously not be changed by the less competent one, and the less competent one will probably have difficulty in understanding the other. Consequently, no change will take place here either. But when one party is optimally heterophilous, optimally more competent than the other, he or she will be better able to effect change in the other.

Sources

For this unit I relied (sometimes consciously and at other times subconsciously) on the work of Jack Gibb, particularly his most insightful "Defensive Communication," *Journal of Communication* 11 (1961):141–148. This article has been reprinted in a number of different places, for example, in the readers by DeVito and Civikly, cited in Unit Two. For an overview of homophily and heterophily see James C. McCroskey, Carl E. Larson, and Mark L. Knapp, *An Introduction to Interpersonal Communication* (Englewood Cliffs, N.J.: Prentice-Hall, 1971). For a more extensive treatment see E. M. Rogers and F. F. Shoemaker, *Communication of Innovations* (New York: Free Press, 1971). See Mark I. Alpert and W. Thomas Anderson, Jr., "Optimal Heterophily and Communication Effectiveness: Some Empirical Findings," *Journal of Communication* 23(September 1973):328–343 for a recent review of relevant findings and an example of an experimental study on this question. A book which provides an excellent transition between the characteristics of effective interpersonal communication and the self is Edmond G. Addeo and Robert E. Burger, *Egospeak: Why No One Listens To You* (New York: Bantam, 1973).

Experiential Vehicle

EFFECTIVE INTERPERSONAL INTERACTION

In order to see the characteristics of effective interpersonal communication in actual operation, the following role playing situations have been designed. The procedures are as follows:

1. Participants should be selected (hopefully from volunteers) to role play the characters in the situations described below.
2. Participants should act out the parts, developing their roles and the interactions as seems logical at the time.
3. In these role-playing situations the participants will either closely follow the characteristics of effective interpersonal communication or clearly violate the characteristics as they are instructed by the group leader or instructor.
4. The remainder of the class should monitor the role playing, observing how closely the participants are following or violating the characteristics of effective interpersonal communication. Two general procedures have been found useful for this monitoring:

   a. The observers may stop the role-playing session as soon as any member fails to follow his or her instructions. The person who stops the role playing should naturally explain why he or she felt that the participants were not following instructions. After essential discussion the role playing should resume to be stopped again when any role player fails to follow instructions. *Note:* If this procedure is used, it is best not to stop the role playing during the first three minutes. This will allow the members an opportunity to begin to feel the characters they are playing.
   b. The observers may take notes during the role playing, reserving all discussion of the characteristics of effective interpersonal communication until the role playing session is completed. If this procedure is followed it is generally useful to first ask the role players how closely they felt they were following the instructions.

Role-Playing Situations

Any or all of the following situations may be used to illustrate 1) following the characteristics of effective interpersonal communication or 2) violating the characteristics. It is recommended that at least one of the situations be used to illustrate following and one violating the characteristics so that the differences between the two interactions may be more easily noted.

1. *Participants:*

   Joan Davis (college sophomore)
   Homer Davis (Joan's father)
   Ann Davis (Joan's mother)

   Situation:

   Joan wants to go away for the weekend with her boyfriend and use the family car. Homer and Ann are totally against this. First, they thoroughly detest Joan's boyfriend. Second, they disapprove of unmarried couples spending weekends together. Third, they want to use the car themselves.

2. *Participants:*

   Chris Martin (Diane's husband)
   Diane Martin (Chris' wife)
   Marlene Jason (Diane's mother)

   Situation:

   Diane and her mother have just gone to purchase new furniture for the Martins' home. They have picked out extremely expensive furniture which Chris and Diane cannot afford. Upon hearing of this Chris becomes angry and demands that different furniture (which they can afford) be selected. Marlene says that she will pay for the furniture since she wants her daughter to have the best. Chris argues that what comes into the house should be bought by Diane and himself and that they should not accept such gifts since there will inevitably be strings attached as there have been in the past.

3. *Participants:*

   James and Thelma (married couple)
   Frank and Carol (married couple)

   Situation:

   James and Frank want to go bowling alone. Thelma and Carol want to go to dinner and the movies with their husbands. The husbands feel that this is their one day out a week and that their desire to spend it bowling does not seem unreasonable. The wives argue that this, too, is their only chance to go out and that they have a right to this outing.

4. *Participants:*

   Dr. Mary James (professor)
   Michell Russo (student)
   Daniel Miller (student)
   Ronald Kennedy (student)

   Situation:

   Michell, Daniel, and Ronald have just received their grades for their Introduction to Communication course and have gone to complain to Dr. Mary James. Michell received a C+, Daniel received an F, and Ronald received a D. All three students feel that they deserved better grades. Dr. James feels that the grades the students received—based on their class performance and their examination scores—were fair.

5. *Participants:*

   Dr. Michael Craeman (professor)
   Joan Mitchell (student)
   Danny Santos (student)
   Molly McCoy (student)
   Dr. Joseph Bartlett (professor)

   Situation:

   Joan, Danny, and Molly have written a letter of complaint against Dr. Michael Craeman and submitted it to Dr. Bartlett, chairperson of the Sociology Department. The students claim that Dr. Craeman's classes are dull, that he is often late to class, that his tests are impossible to pass, and that they are not learning anything.

unit 6
Some Axioms of Interpersonal Communication

We Cannot Not Communicate
All Communications Have a Content and a Relationship Dimension
A Relationship Is Defined, in Part, by the Punctuation
    of Communication Sequences
Human Communication Is Both Digital and Analogic
All Communication Interactions May Be Viewed as Either
    Symmetrical or Complementary
    Analyzing an Interpersonal Interaction

Objectives

Upon completion of this unit, you should be able to:

1. explain the importance of the statement "we cannot not communicate"
2. identify the alternatives available when one does not wish to communicate but another person does
3. distinguish between the content and the relationship dimension of communication
4. distinguish among *confirmation, rejection,* and *disconfirmation* in interpersonal communication
5. explain the concept of punctuation in interpersonal communication
6. distinguish between *digital* and *analogic communication*
7. distinguish between *symmetrical* and *complementary interactions*

In *Pragmatics of Human Communication: A Study of Interactional Patterns, Pathologies, and Paradoxes,* Paul Watzlawick, Janet Beavin, and Don Jackson present an analysis of the behavioral effects of communication derived from the study of behavior disorders. Perhaps the most essential part of their analysis of human communication is the five axioms of communication, propositions that are essential to an understanding of communication in all its forms and functions.

WE CANNOT NOT COMMUNICATE

Often we think of communication as being intentional, purposeful, and consciously motivated. In many instances it is. But in other instances we are communicating even though we might not think we are or might not even want to communicate. Take, for example, the student sitting in the back of the room with an expressionless face, perhaps staring at the front of the room, perhaps staring out the window. Although the student might say that he or she is not communicating with the teacher or with the other students, that student is obviously communicating a great deal —perhaps disinterest, perhaps boredom, perhaps a concern for something else, perhaps a desire for the class to be over with as soon as possible. In any event, the student is communicating whether he or she wishes to or not; we cannot not communicate.

Further, when we are in an interactional situation with this person we must respond in some way. Even if we do not actively or overtly respond, that lack of response is itself a response and communicates. Like the student's silence, our silence in response also communicates.

Watzlawick, Beavin, and Jackson give the example of two strangers on a plane; one wishes to communicate while the other does not. When we do not wish to communicate we have four general alternatives which may be employed.

1. We may simply and explicitly state the desire not to communicate. We may do this nonverbally which is perhaps the less socially offensive way or we may do this verbally. This expression of not wishing to communicate, whether verbal or nonverbal, obviously does not follow communication etiquette. Despite the fact that the person next to us is a complete bore and that we might want just to daydream, we are under social pressure not to ignore anyone. Yet the option to say we do not wish to communicate is still open to us.

2. We may simply give in and communicate. This, it seems, is the alternative that many people take, and it seems to be the road of least effort. In fact, it may take more psychic energy to tell this person that you do not wish to communicate than to communicate. And we can still hope that the person will soon tire and go away.

3. We may disqualify our communications in various ways. For example, we may contradict ourselves, speak in incomplete sentences, or change the subject without any apparent motivation. In all of these cases the intent is to get the other person bored or confused so that he or she

will then go away. Of course it often happens that the person becomes all the more interested in figuring us out and consequently seems to stay with us for what seems like forever.

4. Perhaps the most ingenious way is to pretend to want to talk but to also pretend that something is preventing us from doing so. For example, we might say that we would like to talk but we are just so sleepy that we cannot keep our eyes open and then doze off. Or perhaps we feign a toothache which makes speaking difficult. Or we might pretend to be drunk or sick or deaf. At times, of course, the other person is aware that we are pretending. Yet this is a more socially acceptable manner of getting out of talking than honestly stating that we do not want to communicate.

Notice that regardless of what we do or do not do we are still communicating. All behavior is communication; all behavior has message value.

ALL COMMUNICATIONS HAVE A CONTENT AND A RELATIONSHIP DIMENSION

Communications, to a certain extent at least, refer to the real world or to something external to both speaker and hearer. At the same time, however, communications also refer to the relationship between the parties. For example, a teacher may say to a student, "See me after class." This simple message has a content aspect, which refers to the behavioral responses expected—namely that the student see the teacher after class—and a relationship aspect, which tells us how the communication is to be dealt with. Even the use of the simple command states that there is a status difference between the two parties such that the teacher can command the student. This is perhaps seen most clearly when we visualize this command being made by the student to the teacher. It appears awkward and out of place simply because it violates the normal relationship between teacher and student.

In any communication the content dimension may be the same but the relationship aspect different or the relationship aspect may be the same with the content different. For example, the teacher could say to the student, "You had better see me after class," or he or she could say, "May I please see you after class?" In each case the content is essentially the same; that is, the message being communicated about the behavioral responses expected is about the same in both cases. But the relationship dimension is very different. In the first it signifies a very definite superior-inferior relationship and even a put-down of the student, but in the second a more equal relationship is signaled and a respect for the student is shown. Similarly, at times the content may be different but the relationship essentially the same. For example, a son might say to his parents, "May I go away this weekend?" and "May I use the car tonight?" The content is clearly very different in each case and yet the relationship dimension is essentially the same. It is clearly a superior-inferior relationship where permission to do certain things must be secured.

Thus on the relationship level we communicate, not about the outside world of content, but about the relationship between the communicators. In such communications we offer a definition of ourselves. When we so offer this definition of self the other person may make any of three general responses, according to Watzlawick, Beavin, and Jackson. In *confirmation* the other person verifies the individual's self-definition. The student who responds to the teacher's, "You had better see me after class" with "Yes, sir" confirms the teacher's definition of himself. In *rejection* the other person rejects the individual's self-view. Such rejection may be constructive as when a therapist rejects a patient's self-definition. The student who responds to the teacher's, "You had better see me after class," with "No, I don't feel like it," is rejecting the teacher's definition of self. Lastly, in *disconfirmation* the other person ignores or denies the right of the individual to even define himself or herself. The student who ignores the teacher's command is disconfirming the teacher's definition of self.

Many problems between people are caused by the failure to recognize the distinction between the content and the relationship levels of communication. For example, consider the engaged couple arguing over the fact that the woman made plans to study during the weekend with her friends without first asking her boyfriend if that would be alright. Probably both would have agreed that to study over the weekend was the right choice to make; thus the argument is not at all related to the content level. The argument centers on the relationship level; the man expected to be consulted about plans for the weekend whereas the woman, in not doing this, rejected this definition or relationship. Similar situations exist among married couples when one person will buy something or make dinner plans or invite a guest to dinner, as in an example given by Watzlawick, Beavin, and Jackson, without asking the other person first. Even though the other person would have agreed with the decision made, they argue over it because of the message communicated on the relationship level.

This is not to say that the relationship level is often discussed or even that it should be explicitly discussed by both parties. In fact, Watzlawick, Beavin, and Jackson argue the contrary: "It seems that the more spontaneous and 'healthy' a relationship, the more the relationship aspect of communication recedes into the background. Conversely, 'sick' relationships are characterized by a constant struggle about the nature of the relationship, with the content aspect of communication becoming less and less important."

We might also note that arguments over the content dimension are relatively easy to resolve. Generally, we may look something up in a book or ask someone what actually took place or perhaps see the movie again. It is relatively easy to verify facts that are disputed. Arguments on the relationship level, however, are much more difficult to resolve in part because we seldom recognize that the argument is in fact a relationship one.

A RELATIONSHIP IS DEFINED, IN PART, BY THE PUNCTUATION OF COMMUNICATION SEQUENCES

Communication events are continuous transactions. They are broken up into short sequences only for purposes of convenience. What is stimulus and what is response is not very easy to determine when we, as analysts of communication, enter after the communication transaction is under way. Consider, for example, the following incident. A couple is at a party. The wife is flirting with the other men and the husband is drinking; both are scowling at each other and are obviously in a deep nonverbal argument with each other. In explaining the situation the wife might recall the events by observing that the husband drank and so she flirted with the sober men. The more he drank the more she flirted. The only reason for her behavior was her anger over his drinking. Notice that she sees her behavior as the response to his behavior; his behavior came first and was the cause of her behavior.

In recalling the "same" incident the husband might say that he drank when she started flirting. The more she flirted, the more he drank. He had no intention of drinking until she started flirting. To him, her behavior · was the stimulus and his was the response; she caused his behavior. Thus she sees the behavior as going from drinking to flirting, and he sees it as going from flirting to drinking.

This tendency to divide up the various communication transactions into sequences of stimuli and responses is referred to by Watzlawick, Beavin, and Jackson as the punctuation of the sequences of events. They do not argue that punctuation is wrong; obviously, it is a very useful technique in providing some organization for thinking about and talking about communication transactions. At the same time, because we each see things differently, we each punctuate events differently. To the extent that these differences are significant, the possibility for a communication breakdown exists.

HUMAN COMMUNICATION IS BOTH DIGITAL AND ANALOGIC

In human communication we make use of both *digital* and *analogic* information and utilize both digital and analogic communication systems.

These two kinds of systems are actually quite simple to distinguish, although when we attempt to translate messages from one system to another we run into problems.

Digital systems are those that deal with discrete rather than continuous elements; they are systems that work on the all-or-none principle. For example, a light switch is a digital system; the light is either on or off. A calculator is a digital system; it gives answers in discrete numbers.

Analogic systems are those that are continuous rather than discrete; they are systems that work on the more-or-less principle. For example, a rheostat or dimmer is an analogic system; the light's intensity can be varied to different degrees of brightness. A slide rule is an analogic system; unlike the calculator the slide rule gives us an approximate rather than a discrete and exact answer.

Human communication makes use of both digital and analogic systems. Our verbal communication system, consisting of words and sentences, is digital; our words and sentences are discrete entities. On the other hand, most of our nonverbal system, for example, the loudness of our voice or the degree of our smile, is analogic and is more like the rheostat than the on-off light switch.

Watzlawick, Beavin, and Jackson note that the digital system is more likely to communicate the content message and that the analogic system is more likely to communicate the relationship message. We will verbalize about the outside world but our relationship to another person will more likely be communicated through nonverbal means; eye contact, touching behavior, the way we stand, and so on.

Watzlawick, Beavin, and Jackson also note that digital messages may be more complex and more abstract than analogic messages. It would be difficult, for example, to communicate highly complex and abstract notions nonverbally (or analogically) but we can easily talk about them in words and sentences (or digitally). Analogic messages are subject to greater ambiguity than are digital messages. Although digital messages may be ambiguous, there seems to be greater ambiguity or room for misinterpretation with analogic messages. As Waltzawick, Beavin, and Jackson point out we can cry and shed tears of both joy and sorrow; we can smile to convey both sympathy and contempt; we can appear reticent to convey both tact and indifference.

In translating analogic messages into digital messages we often run into problems. Consider, for example, how many times in attempting to write a message expressing deep emotions and thought one has wished to be able to say the message instead. In speaking we would have the use of the analogic communication system as well, but in the written message we have only the digital system. Similarly, as Watzlawick, Beavin, and Jackson point out, giving a gift is an analogic message. But when the receiver attempts to translate it into a digital message, he or she may consider it a sign of affection, a conscience present, or perhaps a bribe.

We also run into problems when we attempt to show people that we really understand how they feel and attempt to put their nonverbal or analogic messages into verbal or digital messages. At times we can do it with satisfaction but most often, it seems, we cannot. We fail, not necessarily because we are not insightful or cannot accurately read the nonverbal cues, but rather because one system does not translate into another system very easily. There are no one-to-one equivalencies between analogic and digital messages.

ALL COMMUNICATION INTERACTIONS MAY BE VIEWED AS EITHER SYMMETRICAL OR COMPLEMENTARY

Symmetrical and *complementary* relationships are not good or bad in themselves. Both are usually present in normal, healthy relationships.

In a symmetrical relationship the two individuals mirror each other's behavior. The behavior of one party is reflected in the behavior of the other party. If one member nags, the other member responds in kind. If one member expresses jealousy, the other member expresses jealousy. If one member is passive, the other member is passive. The relationship is one of equality with the emphasis on minimizing the differences between the two individuals.

In a complementary relationship the two individuals engage in different behaviors, with the behavior of one serving as the stimulus for the complementary behavior in the other. In complementary relationships the differences between the parties are maximized. It is necessary in a complementary relationship for both parties to occupy different positions, one being the superior and one being the inferior, one being passive and one being active, one being strong and one being weak. At times such relationships are established by the culture as, for example, the complementary relationship existing between teacher and student or between employer and employee. Perhaps the classic complementary relationship would be between the sadist and the masochist, where the sadistic behavior of the sadist serves to stimulate the masochistic behavior of the masochist and vice versa.

Problems may arise in both symmetrical and complementary relationships. In the symmetrical relationship it is easy to appreciate that two individuals who mirror each other's jealousy will find very little security. The jealous behavior is likely to escalate to the point where one or both parties will quit from exhaustion. As Watzlawick, Beavin, and Jackson put it, "In marital conflict, for instance, it is easy to observe how the spouses go through an escalation pattern of frustration until they eventually stop from sheer physical or emotional exhaustion and maintain an uneasy truce until they have recovered enough for the next round."

Perhaps the classic example of problems created in complementary relationships, familiar to many college students, is that of rigid complementarity. Whereas the complementary relationship between mother and child was at one time vital and essential to the life of the child, that same relationship when the child is older "becomes a severe handicap for his further development, if adequate change is not allowed to take place in the relationship."

These five axioms as set forth by Watzlawick, Beavin, and Jackson seem essential to any introductory or advanced analysis of interpersonal communication. They provide us with insight into the nature and function of human communication as well as into the intricacies of human interpersonal relationships and interactions.

Sources

For this unit I relied on Paul Watzlawick, Janet Helmick Beavin, and Don D. Jackson, *Pragmatics of Human Communication: A Study of Interactional Patterns, Pathologies, and Paradoxes* (New York: Norton, 1967). Another useful work in this area is Jurgen Ruesch and Gregory Bateson, *Communication: The Social Matrix of Psychiatry* (New York: Norton, 1951). Many of the ideas set forth in *Pragmatics* may be found in the work of Bateson. For a useful collection of Bateson's writings, see *Steps to an Ecology of Mind* (New York: Ballantine, 1972).

Experiential Vehicle

ANALYZING AN INTERPERSONAL INTERACTION

The five axioms of human communication proposed by Watzlawick, Beavin, and Jackson and discussed in this unit should prove useful in analyzing any interpersonal interaction. To better understand these axioms and to obtain some practice in applying them to an actual interaction, a summary of Tennessee Williams' *Cat on a Hot Tin Roof* is presented. Ideally, all students would read the entire play or see the movie and then apply the five axioms to the interpersonal interactions that take place. The brief summary is presented, then, more in the nature of a "mental refresher." (Note that the original play as it has been published differs from the film, particularly in the last act. The film version of the play is somewhat more positive. The summary presented here is from the original stage play, the version Williams prefers.)

Big Daddy and Big Mama Pollitt, owners of a huge estate, have two sons: Brick (married to Maggie, the cat), an ex-football player who has now turned to drink; and Gooper (married to Mae), a lawyer and father of five children with one on the way. All are gathered together to celebrate Big Daddy's sixty-fifth birthday. The occasion is marred by news that Big Daddy may have cancer for which there is no hope of a cure. A false report is given to Big Mama and Big Daddy stating that the test proved negative and that all that is wrong is a spastic colon—a sometimes painful but not fatal illness. It appears, to Maggie and perhaps to others as well, that Gooper and Mae are really here to claim their share of the inheritance.

The desire to assume control of Big Daddy's fortune (estimated at some $10 million and 28,000 acres "of the richest land this side of the valley Nile") has created considerable conflict between Gooper and Mae on the one hand and Maggie on the other. Brick, it appears, does not care about his possible inheritance.

Throughout the play there is conflict between Brick and Maggie. Brick refuses to go to bed with Maggie although Maggie desperately wants him. This fact is known by everyone since Mae and Gooper have the adjoining room and hear everything that goes on between Brick and Maggie. The cause of this conflict between Brick and Maggie goes back to Brick's relations with Skipper, his best friend. Brick and Skipper were football players on the same team and did just about everything together. So close were they that rumors about their love for each other began to spread. While Brick is in the hospital with a football injury Maggie confronts Skipper and begs that he either stop loving Brick or tell him of his love. In an attempt to prove Maggie wrong Skipper goes to bed with her but fails and as a result takes to drinking and drugs. Maggie repeatedly attempts to thrash this out with Brick but he refuses to talk about it or even to listen to Maggie. All he wants to do is drink—waiting for the little click in his head that tells him he can stop.

In a confrontation with Big Daddy, Brick talks of his disgust with lying and his using liquor to forget all the lies around him. Under pressure from Big Daddy, Brick admits that Skipper called to make a drunken confession after his attempted relationship with Maggie but that Brick hung up and refused to listen. It was then that Skipper committed suicide. And this, it appears, is what Brick uses alcohol to forget. In his anger Brick tells Big Daddy that he is dying of cancer.

Gooper and Mae confront Big Mama with the news that Big Daddy has cancer and attempt to get Big Mama to sign some papers concerning the disposition of the property now that Big Daddy has not much longer to live. Perhaps Gooper and Mae's major argument is that they are responsible (as shown by their five children), while Brick and Maggie are not responsible (as shown by Brick's drinking and by his refusal to sleep with Maggie and have a child, something Big Daddy wants very much). At this point Maggie announces that she is pregnant. Big Mama is overjoyed and seems to be the only one who believes her. This, Big Mama reasons, will solve all problems, even the problem of Brick's drinking. Brick of course knows that Maggie is lying but says nothing to betray her.

In the final scene Maggie locks up all the liquor and pressures Brick into going to bed with her in order to make her lie about her pregnancy become truth. Afterwards she promises to unlock the liquor so that they may both get drunk. She sobs that she really loves Brick while Brick thinks if only that were true.

After reading the play or viewing the film, identify instances of and explain the importance of:

1. the impossibility of not communicating
    a. What alternatives does Brick use in attempting to avoid communicating with Maggie?
    b. What alternatives does Brick use in attempting to avoid communicating with Big Daddy?

2. content and relationship dimensions of specific messages
    a. How does Brick deal with the self-definitions of Maggie and Big Daddy?
    b. How does Big Daddy deal with Big Mama's definition of herself?
    c. Are any problems caused by the failure to recognize the distinction between the content and the relationship levels of communication?

3. different punctuation of the sequences of events

   a. How do Maggie and Brick differ in their punctuation of the events?
   b. Why do they punctuate the sequences differently?

4. digital and analogic messages

   a. Are any problems caused by attempting to translate analogic into digital messages? (Look specifically at Maggie's interpretation of Brick's communications and Brick's interpretation of Maggie's communications and of Big Daddy's communications. Also look at Big Mama's interpretation of Big Daddy's messages toward her.)
   b. From what can be constructed of Skipper's communications, how were they interpreted in digital versus analogic terms?

5. symmetrical and complementary relationships

   a. What type of relationship existed between Brick and Maggie, Gooper and Mae, Big Daddy and Big Mama, Big Daddy and Brick, Big Daddy and Gooper, Maggie and Mae?

unit 7

The Self: Structures and Functions

A Model of the Self
Principles of the Model
   Self-Concept: Part I
   Goals of Self and Others
   Values and Communication

Objectives

Upon completion of this unit, you should be able to:

1. diagram and explain the model of the semantic reactor
2. distinguish among and give examples of electrochemical, self-moving, feeling, and thinking activities
3. state three corollaries of the semantic reactor model
4. discuss critically Bois' semantic reactor model
5. explain the relevance of Bois' model to your own intra- and interpersonal interactions
6. prepare an original model of the self

What is the self? Of what does it consist? How does it function? These are not easy questions to answer. Yet, we need to at least attempt it because an understanding of the self is a prerequisite to an understanding of interpersonal communication. This is true for a number of reasons. First, if we are to understand any process we need to understand its parts; the self is a part—perhaps the most important part—of the interpersonal communication process. Second, the messages generated and received are in large part a function of the self; to understand the messages we need to understand the self. Third, the effectiveness of our interpersonal communications is related to the effectiveness of the self generally. If we are to understand effective communication we must understand the effective self. Fourth, intrapersonal communication, a prerequisite to the understanding of interpersonal communication, is totally dependent upon a knowledge of the self.

The self, obviously the most important single element in the interpersonal communication process, is best approached through a general model of its essential components and relationships. Although there are numerous models to choose from, the one proposed by J. S. Bois seems to be the most useful and the most insightful for interpersonal communication.

The self, in this view, is referred to as a "semantic reactor," meaning that the self responds to stimuli as a whole. "We call this complex reaction of the whole organism," says Bois, "a *semantic reaction;* that is, a reaction that is determined by what the actual situation—the outside event, the word that is spoken, the thought that occurs, the hope that emerges—means to the individual at the moment."

A MODEL OF THE SELF

Bois' model of the semantic reaction is presented in Figure 7.1. Focus first on the four activities in the center of the model.

Electrochemical Activities

Electrochemical activities refer to the bodily movements which begin with the operation of DNA and RNA in the genes and include neuronal activity, bodily reactions to drugs, the effects of uppers and downers, of LSD, of birth control pills, and the like. Such bodily activities are revealed through laboratory analyses of blood and tissue and through electrocardiograms and electroencephalograms.

Self-Moving Activities

Self-moving activities include the autonomic movements of the various bodily organs, such as the heart, lungs, and intestines, as well as the consciously controlled movements of the hands, legs, and head. The activities labeled "self-moving" would include anything from the tapping of the heart to the skilled movements of the surgeon or artist. Also included here would be the movements involved in marching, singing, flag waving, playing basketball, and boxing.

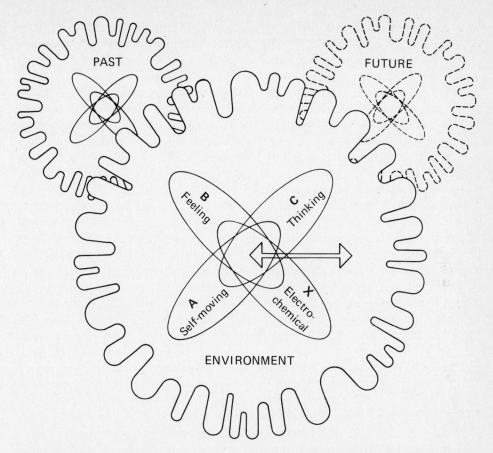

Figure 7.1 *Semantic Reactor* (*Source*: J. Samuel Bois, *The Art of Awareness: A Text on General Semantics and Epistemics*, 2d ed. [Dubuque, Iowa: Brown, 1973], p. 20.)

Feeling Activities

Feeling activities include the operation of needs and drives, wants and fears, hopes and ambitions. This group of activities, more uniquely human than the first two, would include love and hate, commitment and indifference, trust and distrust, happiness and sorrow, contentment and frustration.

Thinking Activities

Thinking activities include all those functions that involve symbolic processes such as the mathematical operations of adding and subtracting, conceptualizing and abstracting, speaking and writing, listening and reading, asking and answering questions, decision making, and strategy formulation. Thinking activities may vary from the writing of a short note to conceptualizing the plans for building a skyscraper.

The way in which these four activities are represented in the diagram attempts to emphasize that each activity is related to each of the other activities. No activity is separate or distinct from any other activity; rather all activities are closely related and mutually dependent. They are all aspects or dimensions of the self-as-a-whole, of the self as a semantic reactor. For example, if we attempt to solve a very difficult mathematical problem, this activity is not limited solely to the thinking aspect of the self. It also influences and is influenced by our feeling activities; witness how angry we become when we fail to solve a problem and how difficult it is to think clearly when emotionally upset. In this problem-solving experience our self-moving and electrochemical activities are likewise involved. Our heart rate might increase and the energizer we took to stay awake would further influence our responses. One of the exercises suggested by William Schutz in *Joy* is to pound a pillow, taking out all your frustration on this mass of foam rubber. If you do this for two or three minutes you would quickly note that what began as a purely self-moving activity has also greatly influenced your electrochemical, feeling, and thinking activities. If you participate in a ceremony of some sort—for example, a religious ceremony—you will probably emerge with a more sympathetic attitude than if you had not participated. Demagogues have long known that one of the best ways to persuade people is to elicit an overt expression of agreement. When this happens (on the surface a purely self-moving activity not involving any original conceptualization) the individual's attitude almost always moves in the direction of his or her verbal advocacy. This seems to be true even if the person is aware that he or she is only participating in an experiment or exercise.

The human organism is designed to function as a whole; inconsistencies seem fiercely resisted. Psychologically it is uncomfortable for an individual to say one thing and believe another. For example, it is uncomfortable for a person to physically participate in a ritual without believing at least partly in the purpose of the experience.

Thus the self must be viewed as a unit that acts and reacts as a whole and that cannot have its parts separated and dissected, all going off in different directions, without causing psychological discomfort at best and a breakdown at worst. Although we may *describe* a person's activities in terms of these four areas of activity, it should always be recognized that these four activities operate in a mutually dependent fashion.

The environment is indicated in the model as uneven and indefinite. This is to illustrate that at times the environment presses close to the individual and greatly limits the range of possible behaviors; at other times it stretches far and does not exert great influence. Nevertheless, the environment is always present and always exerts some influence. The self is never alone; it always operates within a context.

The context influences the self and the behaviors in which the self engages. Similarly, however, the self also influences the context or environment. The environment that we were born into is not the same environment that exists now. People have changed it. And, of course, the environment that we leave when we die will be still different, in part because of what we have done. Whereas at one time people were simply concerned with getting as much out of the environment as possible, they are now concerned with putting back into the environment at least what they have taken out and perhaps something of a bonus as well. And so if we cut down a tree we plant one or possibly two to take its place.

The environment or context as viewed here should be seen as consisting of a number of different aspects or dimensions. It has a physical dimension (the specific place we are in, such as a room or building), a social dimension (the type of function we are attending, whether a funeral or a wedding or a union meeting), a psychological dimension (the atmosphere of the context, whether friendly or hostile), and a cultural dimension (the prevailing value systems or the unwritten codes of acceptable and unacceptable behaviors). These four dimensions are not the only ones that could be singled out. Yet they seem to be four of the more important aspects. The self's interaction with the environment is signified in the model by the double arrow connecting the center of the interrelated ellipses with the environment.

The self also functions in relation to time. The self lives not only in space but also in a world defined by time. The self operates in the present but always with some reference to the past and to the future. Present actions of the self are greatly influenced by its past experience and by the future it envisions. That the past influences the self is obvious; this seems to be acknowledged since recorded history and almost universally since Freud. We do things in part because of some past experience, insight, reward, or punishment. How much we are influenced by past experiences cannot be stated. Some theorists would argue that we are influenced by the past very little while others would claim that the past influences us completely. The way we envision the future, the way we plan for it, and the way in which we see ourselves 10 or 20 years from now also influence what we do or think or feel in the present. You are now, for example, in college. This is the present. Yet you are here largely because of the future. Perhaps you anticipate getting a better job with a college degree, or you anticipate financial or social rewards. Or you may be in school because of some past situation, such as a promise to a parent or an unspoken expectation that you would simply go to college.

This, then, is the self—not the whole self, not the complete explanation. But it does seem to represent some of the significant dimensions of the self that are especially pertinent to interpersonal communication. This model or point of view would define a human being, to use Bois' terms, as a "thinking, feeling, self-moving, electrochemical organism in continuous transaction with a space-time environment."

Some sources of possible misunderstanding should first be pointed out. The title of the model, "semantic reactor," can be misleading. The title does not mean to imply that a person simply *re*acts; we act as well as react; we are initiators as well as responders. We are self-actuators and self-starters as well as *re*actors. The term "semantic reactor," as indicated earlier, signifies the self's *total* reaction to a *total* environment. Second, the diagram should not be taken to imply that we and the environment are in clear-cut contrast. Rather, they should be seen in more fluid interaction. Third, and most important, it should be noted that the self is constantly moving, constantly changing, constantly reorganizing; the diagram is of necessity static.

PRINCIPLES OF THE MODEL

Bois has suggested a number of corollaries that might be derived from the model. Here we look at a few of those that are especially relevant to understanding our specific selves and ourselves as intrapersonal and interpersonal communicators.

The larger frame, that of the present, is the center of the diagram and of gravity. If the future or the past becomes too large they will physically unbalance the model, pulling it to the right or to the left. Psychologically, the same principle seems to operate when we place too much emphasis on the past or on the future. The model becomes unbalanced and the self becomes disoriented; it has difficulty functioning effectively and efficiently in the present. And the present is, of course, the only reality the self ever really knows.

We are probably all familiar with people who live their entire lives in the past; they recall the old days, the good old days when beer was a nickle a glass and when a satisfying dinner cost less than a dollar. They remember when there was clean air, no traffic jams, and low taxes. Remembering such details poses no real problem. A problem is caused, however, when all one does is remember the past. We are living in the present and our primary attention must be on it. If we force ourselves to live in the past we unbalance the self. People also live in the past when they carry attitudes and values from the past and attempt to apply them uncritically to the present. "Women belong in the home," is perhaps the now classic example.

Then there is the individual who lives entirely for the future. This person refuses to enjoy anything now, refuses to spend a penny, and would never engage in any activity that will not bring rewards in the future. This person's problem is that the future never comes. To such an individual the future is always tomorrow. He or she saves for the future but never sets a date for actually spending what is saved and so throughout life does nothing but save, eventually to die wealthy.

The effective self seems to live in the present with a recognition of (though not a reverence for) the past and the future. Present experiences are enjoyed as experiences and not merely as steps to some future goal. Put more concretely, this individual does not sit in college classes merely to obtain the bachelor's degree because of the desire to be an accountant, because of the desire to earn a lot of money, because one's brother went to college, because one wants to own one's own house, because of being promised a new car, because one wants to buy a boat, and so on. Rather, one should sit in a college class because the class is in itself an experience from which one can benefit now and in the future.

Encounter groups, transcendental meditation, awareness sessions, Zen Buddhism, and the like are currently enjoying considerable popularity among college students. The reason, or at least part of the reason, seems to be that they are all attempts to get us to focus on the present, to experience ourselves and our environments, to live in the here-and-now. It seems that we may have to be explicitly taught how to live in the present or how to unlearn living in the past or the future.

Just as damaging as overemphasizing the past or the future seems to be totally neglecting them. We are in part a product of our past and a product of our imagined and planned-for future. Consequently, we cannot ignore these aspects of the self. They are part of the self and exert influence on what the self is, what it does, and what it becomes.

Persons who roll along without any consideration for the future are soon going to have problems, as rainy days do sometimes come. Similarly, individuals who think they can get along without any regard for yesterday soon find that the past has helped to make them what they are and that their past mistakes as well as successes are still a part of them and a part of others' perceptions of them.

Much as there is a tendency for the model to balance itself in terms of time, it also tends to balance itself in terms of the various dimensions of the self. The four activities have a tendency to stay in balance, and if there is excessive emphasis on one to the total or near exclusion of the others, the model will become unbalanced. This again has its realistic counterpart in the individual who attempts to be solely intellectual, to be devoid of feelings and emotions, to be in full control. This excessive emphasis on the thinking activities will surely unbalance the model. Excessive emphasis on the feeling or emotional activities likewise creates problems. Excessive emphasis on drugs (on electrochemical activities) or on self-moving activities (caricatured in the superjock) likewise leads to unbalancing.

This is not to say that these four activities are evenly distributed at all times of our lives. Certainly they are not. At times the thinking activities are emphasized, at times the feeling activites, and so on. This is natural and productive. The problem seems to arise when one aspect is neglected to the point where it is never emphasized or when it is emphasized to the point where it becomes the central and only focus.

The semantic reactor is always in process; it is forever moving, changing, transforming. Its seven aspects are interacting with each other and are all in part formed from unique experiences and expectations. Because of the complex and dynamic qualities of the self it is impossible for any two semantic reactors to be identical. One implication of this is that no two people can ever perceive the same event in the same way or react to the same person in the same way. We are each unique individuals (our semantic reactor dimensions are never the same as any one else's); each sees the world and each reacts to the world in somewhat different ways.

Much as no two people can have the same semantic reactions, no one person can have the same semantic reaction on two different occasions. This must be true since the model is in a constant state of change and one's semantic reactor model of today must be different from one's semantic reactor model of tomorrow and of even ten minutes from now. No reaction, therefore, can ever be repeated. No two perceptions, no two evaluations, no two conceptualizations can ever be exactly the same.

The implication here is that we should not, contrary to much of what we have been taught, assume that we should be extremely consistent in our behavior and in our evaluations. We are changing human beings and we should not hold ourselves responsible tomorrow for an evaluation we made today. All our reactions are made or should be made on the best evidence we can assemble at the time. We should not assume that other evidence will not arise tomorrow. We should have an open mind and not lock ourselves into responding in a certain way just to maintain some semblance of consistency that someone somewhere told us was a good thing and something to admire.

Our reactions, whether to people or objects or events or ideas, are always reactions of the organism-as-a-whole and are never totally logical or totally emotional or totally self-moving or totally electrochemical. Whether we are conscious of it or not, we react as a whole and not in parts with our logic part responding to a math problem and our feeling part responding to a naked body. Feeling is involved in the math problem and logic in our response to the naked body. Consequently, solving a mathematical problem which may be primarily logical may be aided or hindered by changes in the feeling, self-moving, or electrochemical aspects of the self. Our ability to solve a difficult problem will be greatly influenced by pills, by a previous fight with a friend, by financial worries, by a sprained back, and so on.

In this view we look at communication not as a transfer of some abstract idea from one head to another or of some words from one person's mouth to another person's ear, but rather as an exchange of semantic reactions. For the most meaningful communication—communication in its idealized form—we would have an interchange of semantic reactions. If you were to fully understand what I was trying to say right now you would not only be participating in my thoughts but would be feeling what I am feeling emotionally and physically and electrochemically. You would experience my past and my anticipated future as I do so that you would know more completely what my present semantic reactions are. Obviously most people do not even come close to this kind of communication; most people seem content to hear the words and respond with other more or less appropriate words which in turn are responded to with another group of more or less appropriate words and so on. Rarely are attempts made to empathize with one another, to feel what the other person is feeling, to exchange semantic reactions. But hopefully this book and this course will improve your present communication behaviors.

This model does not explain completely how and why the self operates as it does. Yet it does explain some of the important dimensions and some of the important relationships of the self. In considering the various approaches to the self that follow, we should recognize a self such as that presented here. For example, when we consider self-disclosure—revealing ourselves to others—it should be clear that this interaction is an electrochemical, self-moving, feeling, and thinking activity, that our past and envisioned future as well as our space-time environment influences and is influenced by the self-disclosure. Whenever we talk of the self we should visualize a semantic reactor.

Sources

The model and related insights presented in this unit are based on J. S. Bois, *The Art of Awareness: A Textbook on General Semantics and Epistemics*, 2d ed. (Dubuque, Iowa: Brown Co., 1973). A book from a totally different perspective and yet one that deals with many of the same concepts is Albert Ellis and Robert A. Harper, *A Guide to Rational Living* (No. Hollywood, California: Wilshire, 1969). A readable and insightful discussion of the self and its functions may be found in Jess Lair's *I Ain't*

Much, Baby—But I'm All I've Got (New York: Doubleday, 1972). An interesting study of the self-concept of students is Carolyn B. Smith and Larry R. Judd, "A Study of Variables Influencing Self-Concept and Ideal Self-Concept Among Students in the Basic Speech Course," *Speech Teacher* 23 (1974).

Experiential Vehicles

SELF CONCEPT: PART I

Every experience we engage in should change us in some way, hopefully for the better but sometimes for the worse. In order to determine whether this course and everything else that happens between the beginning and the end of the semester has any effect on the way in which we view ourselves, complete the following series of bi-polar scales according to the way you see yourself now. Ideally, the responses should be dated and placed in a sealed envelope and deposited with the instructor. At the end of the course you should fill out an identical set of scales and examine the differences.

A number of the exercises in this text make use of semantic differential scales such as these. The instructions given here should be followed whenever semantic differential scales are used.

Instructions for Completing Semantic Differential Scales
Taking the kind-cruel scale as an example, the seven positions should be interpreted as follows. If you feel that the concept being rated is *extremely* kind or *extremely* cruel mark the end positions as follows:

kind __X__:____:____:____:____:____:____ cruel

or

kind ____:____:____:____:____:____:_X__ cruel

If you feel that the concept is *quite* kind or *quite* cruel mark the scale as follows:

kind ____:_X__:____:____:____:____:____ cruel

or

kind ____:____:____:____:____:_X__:____ cruel

If you feel that the concept is *slightly* kind or *slightly* cruel mark the scale as follows:

kind ____:____:__X__:____:____:____:____ cruel

or

kind ____:____:____:____:__X__:____:____ cruel

If you feel that the concept is neutral in regard to kind-cruel mark the scale in the middle position, that is,

kind ____:____:____:__X__:____:____:____ cruel

Note: Mark each scale in order; do not omit any scales. Mark each scale only once. Mark each scale on one of the seven scale positions; do not put a mark between positions.

ME

Happy	____:____:____:____:____:____:____	Sad
Positive	____:____:____:____:____:____:____	Negative
Healthy	____:____:____:____:____:____:____	Sick
Strong	____:____:____:____:____:____:____	Weak
Beautiful	____:____:____:____:____:____:____	Ugly
Honest	____:____:____:____:____:____:____	Dishonest
Good	____:____:____:____:____:____:____	Bad
Self-Confident	____:____:____:____:____:____:____	Not Self-Confident
Active	____:____:____:____:____:____:____	Passive
Interesting	____:____:____:____:____:____:____	Boring
Graceful	____:____:____:____:____:____:____	Awkward
Elegant	____:____:____:____:____:____:____	Uncouth
Pleasant	____:____:____:____:____:____:____	Unpleasant
Powerful	____:____:____:____:____:____:____	Powerless
Fast	____:____:____:____:____:____:____	Slow
Up	____:____:____:____:____:____:____	Down
Clean	____:____:____:____:____:____:____	Dirty
Kind	____:____:____:____:____:____:____	Cruel
Successful	____:____:____:____:____:____:____	Unsuccessful
Sociable	____:____:____:____:____:____:____	Unsociable
Moral	____:____:____:____:____:____:____	Immoral
Realistic	____:____:____:____:____:____:____	Unrealistic
Optimistic	____:____:____:____:____:____:____	Pessimistic
Brave	____:____:____:____:____:____:____	Cowardly
Organized	____:____:____:____:____:____:____	Disorganized

GOALS OF SELF AND OTHERS

1. Working in dyads, on Form 1 rank these twelve goals in order of their importance to you at this time in your life. Use 1 for the most important, 2 for the next most important, and so on, using 12 for the least important.
2. On Form 2 rank these goals in order of their importance to your partner. That is, attempt to predict how your partner will rank these goals.
3. Exchange Form 2 with your partner so that both of you now have your own rankings and the rankings your partner gave you. Compute an error score by subtracting your own rankings from the rankings your partner gave you, disregarding sign (whether + or −). For example, if you ranked emotional security 4 and your partner gave you a ranking of 7 then there would be 3 error points. Note that since signs are disregarded there would also be 3 error points if your partner had given you a rank of 1 for emotional security. Do this for all 12 items.
4. Discuss with your partner the predictions each of you made. Consider, for example, the following:

   a. the basis for the predictions, that is, what cues were used for making the various predictions
   b. the certainty or uncertainty you felt in making them
   c. the implications of your predictions for interpersonal communication between the two of you
   d. the social constraints influencing your predictions
   e. the possible reasons for the accurate/inaccurate predictions
   f. whatever else may seem relevant to your interpersonal communica-cation behavior

Note: It may be useful to use those items for which there was a large error score as take-off points for discussion.

FORM 1 (SELF)

____ Emotional Security
____ Sexual Love
____ Independence
____ Knowledge
____ Family Love
____ Financial Security
____ Friendship
____ Self-Regard
____ Work
____ Excitement
____ Beauty
____ Creative Self-Expression

FORM 2 (OTHER)

_____ Emotional Security
_____ Sexual Love
_____ Independence
_____ Knowledge
_____ Family Love
_____ Financial Security
_____ Friendship
_____ Self-Regard
_____ Work
_____ Excitement
_____ Beauty
_____ Creative Self-Expression

VALUES AND COMMUNICATION

The class is divided into groups of approximately five or six members each. Each group is charged with the same basic task, but each discharges its task from a different perspective. The general task is to select those objects that best reflect American values.

By "values" we mean those objects or ideas that people regard as positive or negative, beautiful or ugly, clean or dirty, pleasant or unpleasant, valuable or worthless, moral or immoral, just or unjust, true or false, and so forth, and those objects or ideas that influence the judgments and decisions people make.

The only limitations or restrictions are that 1) five objects be selected —no more and no less; size, weight, and cost are of no consequence and should not influence your decisions, and that 2) the objects be in existence at the present time in the same form they will be in when chosen; that is, you may not construct objects specifically for selection nor combine several objects and count them as one.

Each group is to select objects representing American values as seen from the point of view of one of the following groups:

1. the previous generation
2. the current generation
3. the next generation
4. males
5. females
6. the poor
7. the rich
8. the middle class
9. hippies
10. hard hats
11. college students
12. professors
13. blacks
14. whites
15. American Indians

Each group then reports to the entire class the selections made and the specific values each selection represents. Discussion may then focus on any number of communication related issues such as:

1. the accuracy with which each group represented the values of the group it was assigned
2. the difficulty of communication across generations, sex, economic class, race, and so forth

3. the degrees of stereotyping evidenced by the objects and values selected
4. the degree to which the members' own values influenced their selections of values for the group assigned
5. the role of values in influencing communication generally and of divergent values in hindering communication
6. the ways in which communication might be facilitated when basic values differ

unit 8

Intrapersonal Awareness

The Open Self
The Blind Self
The Hidden Self
The Unknown Self
  Self-Awareness
  I'd Prefer to Be

Objectives

Upon completion of this unit, you should be able to:

1. explain the structure and general function of the Johari window
2. define the *open, blind, hidden,* and *unknown selves*
3. provide examples of information that might be contained in each of the four selves

If we had to list some of the qualities we wanted to possess, that of self-awareness would surely rank high. We all wish to know ourselves better. The reason is that we are in control of our thoughts and our behaviors only to the extent that we understand ourselves, only to the extent that we are aware of ourselves.

This concept of self-awareness is basic to an understanding of intrapersonal and interpersonal communication and is best explained by the Johari Window, presented in Figure 8.1. The window is broken up into four basic areas or quadrants, each of which contains a somewhat different self.

Open Self known to self known to others	**Blind Self** not known to self known to others
Hidden Self known to self not known to others	**Unknown Self** not known to self not known to others

Figure 8.1 *The Johari Window* (*Source*: Joseph Luft, *Group Processes: An Introduction to Group Dynamics* [Palo Alto, Cal.: National Press Books, 1970], p. 11.)

THE OPEN SELF

The open self, quadrant 1, represents all the information, behaviors, attitudes, feelings, desires, motivations, ideas, and so on that are known to the self and also known to others. The type of information included here might vary from one's name, skin color, and sex to one's age, political and religious affiliation, and batting average. Each individual's open self will vary in size depending upon the time and upon the individuals he or she is dealing with. At some times we are more likely to open ourselves up than at other times. If, for example, we opened ourselves and got hurt because of it, we might then close up a bit more than usual. Similarly, some people make us feel comfortable and support us; to them, we open ourselves wide, but to others we prefer to leave most of ourselves closed.

In some instances the size of the open self seems directly related to the degree of closeness with the individual: We might reveal most to those we are closest to and least to those we are least close to. Yet it seems that some of our most important desires or motivations often concern the people we are closest to. Thus we might not want them to learn such information. Should our need to open ourselves become too strong we might disclose our feelings to a stranger or relative stranger or at least to someone not closely involved with our daily life, for example, a religious counselor or a therapist of some sort. Sometimes a student will select a teacher or an athletic coach to confide in. Despite this variation each person has a "modal area," a kind of average which defines how open one will generally be.

The size of the open self also varies greatly from one individual to another. Some people are prone to reveal their innermost desires and feelings while others prefer to remain silent about both the significant and the insignificant things in their lives. Most of us, however, open ourselves to some people about some things at some times.

"The smaller the first quadrant," says Luft, "the poorer the communication." Communication is dependent upon the degree to which we open ourselves to others and to ourself. If we do not allow others to know us, (that is, if we keep the open self small) communication between them and us becomes extremely difficult if not impossible. We can communicate meaningfully only to the extent that we know each other and to the extent that we know ourselves. To improve communication, we have to work first on enlarging the open self.

We should also note that a change in the open area—in any of the quadrants—will bring about a change in the other quadrants. We might visualize the window as a whole as being of constant size but with each pane of glass as being variable, sometimes small, sometimes large. As one pane becomes smaller, one or more of the others must become larger. Similarly, as one pane becomes larger, one or more of the others must become smaller. For example, if we enlarge the open self this will shrink the hidden self. Further, this revelation or disclosure in turn will function to lead others to decrease the size of the blind self by revealing to us what they know and we do not know. Thus these several selves are not separate and distinct selves but interacting selves, each one dependent upon the other.

THE BLIND SELF

The blind self represents all those things about ourselves which others know but of which we are ignorant. This may vary from the relatively insignificant habit of saying "you know" or of rubbing your nose when you get angry or of a peculiar body odor, to something as significant as defense mechanisms or fight strategies or repressed past experiences.

Some people have a very large blind self and seem to be totally oblivious to their own faults and sometimes (though not as often) their own virtues. Others seem overly concerned with having a small blind self.

They seek therapy at every turn and join every encounter group. Some are even convinced that they know everything there is to know about themselves, that they have reduced the blind self to zero. Still others only pretend to want to reduce the size of the blind self. Verbally they profess a total willingness to hear all about themselves. But when confronted with the first negative feature the defenses and denials go up with amazing speed. In between these extremes lie most of us.

Interpersonal communication depends in great part on both parties sharing the same basic information about each other. To the extent that blind areas exist communication will be made difficult. Yet blind areas will always exist for each of us. Although we may be able to shrink our blind areas we can never totally eliminate them. If, however, we recognize that we do in fact have blind areas, that we can never know everything that others know about us, this recognition will help greatly in dealing with this most difficult and elusive self and with our other selves as well.

The only way to decrease the size of the blind self is to seek out information which others have and which we do not have. In everyday interactions, we influence how much of the blind area will be made open by others. This need not be done directly although at times it is, as when we ask someone's honest opinion about our appearance or our speech or our home. Most often, however, it is done indirectly; in fact, it is a consequence of everything we do. In any interaction with another person we invariably reveal how much of ourselves we want to know about, how much we prefer not to know, which aspects we want to know about, and which aspects we prefer to leave hidden. We also reveal in these interactions how we will react to such revelations. In some contexts we would react defensively, in other contexts openly. Throughout our interactions we give cues as to how we will react in future situations, and we in effect enable others to accurately predict our future behaviors. Generally, if we are open about ourselves and reveal our inner selves to others, others in turn will reveal what is contained in the blind area more readily than they would if we did not engage in any self-disclosure.

Although communication and interpersonal relations are generally enhanced as the blind area becomes smaller, it should not be assumed that people should therefore be forced to see themselves as we see them or to find out everything we know about them. Forcing people to see what we see may cause serious trauma. Such a revelation might cause a breakdown in defenses; it might force people to see their own masochism or jealousy or prejudice when they are not psychologically ready to deal with such information. It is important to recognize that such revelations, since they may cause problems, might best be dealt with in the company of trained personnel.

THE HIDDEN SELF

The hidden self contains all that you know of yourself and of others but which you keep to yourself. This area includes all your successfully kept secrets about yourself and others. In any interaction this area includes what is relevant or irrelevant to the conversation but which you do not want to reveal.

At the extremes we have the overdisclosers and the underdisclosers. The overdisclosers tell all. They keep nothing hidden about themselves or others. They will tell you their family history, their sexual problems, their marital difficulties, their children's problems, their financial status, their strategies for rising to the top, their goals, their failures and successes, and just about everything else. For them this area is very small and had they sufficient time and others sufficient patience it would be reduced to near zero. The problem with these overdisclosers is that they do not discriminate. They do not distinguish between those to whom such information should be disclosed and those to whom it should not be disclosed. Nor do they distinguish among the various types of information which should be disclosed and which should not be disclosed. To discuss one's wife's or husband's sexual relationships with co-workers might not be the wisest thing to do, and yet they do it.

The underdisclosers tell nothing. You get the feeling that they know a great deal about themselves but simply refuse to say anything. They will talk about you but not about themselves. Depending upon one's relationship with these underdisclosers we might feel that they are afraid to tell anyone anything for fear of being laughed at or rejected. Or we may feel somewhat rejected for their refusal to trust us. To never reveal anything about yourself comments on what you think of the people with whom you are interacting. On one level, at least, it is saying, "I don't trust you enough to reveal myself to you."

The vast majority of us are somewhere between these two extremes. We keep certain things hidden and we disclose certain things. We disclose to some people and we do not disclose to others. We are, in effect, selective disclosers.

At other times, however, it seems that we must carefully weigh the pros and cons because the consequences are so great. Consider, for example, the sociology professor. She is married with three school-age children. She recently received her Ph.D., had her first book published, and is now teaching a course in criminology. In discussing drugs and present laws part of her wants to disclose that as a graduate student she was busted on drug charges and served two years in jail. But the other part of her, the practical part, wants to remain silent for fear of losing her job and therefore causing problems for her family. This is not at all a rare situation. In fact, such a decision-making process seems to occur with amazing frequency. All of us, it seems, hide something. But this takes energy—a fact that we probably do not appreciate as fully as we should. We are forced to expend great amounts of energy to keep parts of ourselves hidden. Hiding some aspects of ourselves is not a passive but an active process at which we must constantly work if we are to succeed. This principle seems to have been recently recognized by many homosexuals who have found that keeping their homosexuality hidden cost them a great deal in psychic energy and that once they moved this information from the hidden to the open area they have felt freer and less burdened.

Although it is comforting to tell ourselves that the information we disclose to others will be treated confidentially we cannot always be sure that it will. The teacher who confidentially tells her class about her criminal record may have a very sympathetic audience that day. But after a rough mid-term she may lose some of her "friends" who may no longer wish to be "burdened" by this "secret."

As potential disclosers we should also recognize that we impose a burden upon the person to whom we disclose. In disclosing anything significant we are in effect saying, "I know you will be supportive and not reveal this to anyone else." But at times people cannot be supportive and at times people cannot or simply do not remember that this bit of information is to be classified as a secret.

When dealing with our feelings, especially our present feelings, self-disclosure is especially useful, helpful, and conducive to meaningful dialogue. Last year, for example, on the first day of an interpersonal communication course I was teaching I became extremely nervous. I was not sure of the reason, but I was nervous. At that point I had three basic options open to me. One was to withdraw from the situation, for example, by saying I was not feeling well or that I had forgotten something and just walk out. Second, I could have attempted to hide the nervousness, hoping that it would subside as the class progressed. The third option and the one I chose (although I did not go through these options consciously at the time) was simply to tell the class that I was nervous and did not understand why. The class was most supportive, telling me I had nothing to be nervous about and that I should not worry. They revealed that they were the ones who felt anxious; for many, this was their first college class. I in turn assured them that they should not be nervous. After this very simple exchange, all of which happened without any conscious planning or strategy, as an expression of what our feelings were at the time, we worked together closely and warmly for the rest of the semester. This incident was not in itself responsible for the success of the course, yet it helped greatly to set the tone for an open and supportive atmosphere.

THE UNKNOWN SELF

The unknown self represents all that exists but which neither we nor others know about. One could legitimately argue that if neither we nor any one else knows what is in this area, we cannot know that it exists at all. Actually, we do not *know* that it exists but rather we *infer* that it exists.

We infer its existence from a number of different sources. Sometimes this area is revealed to us through temporary changes brought about by drug experiences or through special experimental conditions such as hypnosis or sensory deprivation. Sometimes this area is revealed by various projective tests or dreams. There seem to be sufficient instances of such revelations to justify our including this unknown area as part of the self.

Although we cannot easily manipulate this area we should recognize that it does exist and that there are things about ourselves and about others that we simply do not and will not know.

Sources

The Johari model is most thoroughly discussed in the works of Joseph Luft, particularly *Group Processes: An Introduction to Group Dynamics,* 2d ed. (Palo Alto, Cal.: Mayfield Publishing Company, 1970) and *Of Human Interaction* (Palo Alto, Cal.: Mayfield Publishing Company, 1969). Ronald B. Levy's books cover this area but in a more elementary fashion: *Self Revelation Through Relationships* (Englewood Cliffs, N.J.: Prentice-Hall, 1972) and *I Can Only Touch You Now* (Englewood Cliffs, N.J.: Prentice-Hall, 1973). John Powell's *Why Am I Afraid to Tell You Who I Am?* (Niles, Ill.: Argus Communications, 1969) and *Why Am I Afraid to Love?* (Niles, Ill.: Argus Communications, 1972) and *The Secret of Staying in Love* (Niles, Ill.: Argus Communications 1974) are three of the most interesting and perceptive works in this area. They are deceptively simple so do not dismiss them if they appear too elementary. Nathaniel Branden's *The Psychology of Self Esteem* (New York: Bantam, 1969) and *The Disowned Self* (New York: Bantam, 1971) and Henry Clay Lindgren's *How to Live With Yourself and Like It* (Greenwich, Conn.: Fawcett, 1953) are useful for understanding ourselves. Patricia Niles Middlebrook in her *Social Psychology and Modern Life* (New York: Knopf, 1974) provides a thorough overview of the social psychological dimensions of the self.

Experiential Vehicles

SELF-AWARENESS

Presented below is a model of the Johari window. With specific reference to the four selves represented by the model, discuss in a small group of five or six what you see to be 1) the selves of someone you most admire and 2) the selves of someone you least admire.

Open Self known to self known to others	**Blind Self** not known to self known to others
Hidden Self known to self not known to others	**Unknown Self** not known to self not known to others

What do the most admired persons seem to have in common? What do the least admired persons seem to have in common? What insights can you derive from the discussion which might be pertinent to your own model of awareness? What general principles might you derive that are pertinent to interpersonal communication?

I'D PREFER TO BE

This exercise should enable members of the class to get to know each other better and at the same time get to know themselves better. The questions asked here should encourage each individual to think about and increase awareness of some facet(s) of his or her thoughts or behaviors.

Rules of the Game
The "I'd Prefer To Be" game is played in a group of four to six people with general procedures as follows:

1. Each member individually rank orders each of the twenty groupings using 1 for the most preferred and 3 for the least preferred choice.
2. The group then considers each of the twenty categories in turn, with each member giving his or her rank order.
3. Members may refuse to reveal their rankings for any category by saying, "I pass." The group is not permitted to question the reasons for any member's passing.
4. When a member has revealed his or her rankings for a category the group members may ask questions relevant to that category. These questions may be asked after any individual member's account or may be reserved until all members have given their rankings for a particular category.
5. In addition to these general procedures, the group may establish any additional rules it wishes, for example, appointing a leader, chairman, establishing time limits, and so forth.

Areas for Discussion
Some of the areas for discussion which might prove of value are:

1. What are the reasons for the individual choices? Note that the reasons for the least preferred choice may often be as important or even more important than the reasons for the most preferred choice.
2. What do the choices reveal about the individual? Can persons be differentiated on the basis of their choices to these and similar alternatives?
3. What is the homogeneity/heterogeneity of the group as a whole? Do the members evidence relatively similar choices or wide differences? What does this mean in terms of the members' ability to communicate with each other?
4. Do the members accept/reject the choices of other members? Are some members disturbed by the choices other members make? If so, why? Are some apathetic? Why? Did hearing the choices of one or more members make you want to get to know them better?

5. Did any of the choices make you aware of preferences you were not aware of before?

6. Are members reluctant to share their preferences with the group? Why?

"I'D PREFER TO BE"

1. ____ intelligent
   ____ wealthy
   ____ handsome

2. ____ movie star
   ____ senator
   ____ successful businessman

3. ____ blind
   ____ deaf
   ____ mute

4. ____ on a date
   ____ reading a good book
   ____ watching television

5. ____ loved
   ____ feared
   ____ respected

6. ____ alone
   ____ in a crowd
   ____ with one person

7. ____ brave
   ____ reliable
   ____ insightful

8. ____ adventurous
   ____ scholarly
   ____ creative

9. ____ in a large city
   ____ in a small town
   ____ in an uncharted wilderness

10. ____ handsome but unintelligent
    ____ intelligent but not handsome
    ____ average in looks and brains

11. ____ a professional athlete
    ____ a professional chess player
    ____ a professional actor

12. _____ at a large urban college
    _____ at a small rural college
    _____ at an Ivy League college

13. _____ a famous brain surgeon
    _____ a famous cartoonist
    _____ a famous philosopher

14. _____ traveling in China
    _____ traveling in England
    _____ traveling in the United States

15. _____ the loved
    _____ the lover
    _____ the onlooker

16. _____ left alone
    _____ the center of attraction
    _____ the average type

17. _____ a tree
    _____ a rock
    _____ a flower

18. _____ the sun
    _____ the wind
    _____ the waters

19. _____ a leader
    _____ a follower
    _____ a loner

20. _____ married
    _____ single
    _____ living with someone but unmarried

unit 9

Self-Disclosure

The Rewards of Self-Disclosure
Sources of Resistance to Self-Disclosure
Contexts for Self-Disclosure
   Self-Disclosure Questionnaire
   Disclosing the Hidden Self

Objectives

Upon completion of this unit, you should be able to:

1. define *self-disclosure*
2. distinguish between *history* and *story*
3. explain at least three rewards of self-disclosure
4. explain at least three sources of resistance to self-disclosure
5. explain the contexts of self-disclosure
6. explain the differences in self-disclosure in terms of topic, sex, and age

Along with the recent interest in encounter groups, integrity groups, and intra- and interpersonal communication generally, has come great interest in the concept of *self-disclosure*. In terms of the Johari window discussed in the previous unit, self-disclosure consists of revealing information about yourself that is in the hidden area—that is, it is a process of moving information from the hidden area to the open area. More formally, we may define self-disclosure as a type of communication in which information about the self is communicated to another person. Special note should be taken of several aspects of this elementary definition.

   Self-disclosure is a type of communication. Thus overt statements pertaining to the self as well as slips of the tongue, unconscious nonverbal movements, written confessions, and public confessions would all be classified as self-disclosing communications.

Self-disclosure is information, in the information theory sense, meaning something previously unknown by the receiver. Information is new knowledge. To tell someone something he or she already knew would not be self-disclosure; in order to be self-disclosure some new knowledge would have to be communicated.

Self-disclosure involves at least one other individual. In order to self-disclose, the communication act must involve at least two persons; it cannot be an *intra*personal communication act. Nor can we, as some people attempt, "disclose" in a manner that makes it impossible for another person to understand. This is not a disclosure at all. Nor can we write in diaries that no one reads and call this self-disclosure. To be self-disclosure the information must be received and understood by another individual.

Gerard Egan, in *Encounter*, makes another distinction that may prove useful. He distinguishes between "history" which he calls "the mode of noninvolvement" and "story" which he calls "the mode of involvement." History is a manner of revealing the self that is only pseudo–self-disclosure. It is an approach that details some facts of the individual's life but does not really invite involvement from listeners. From a person's history we may learn what the individual did or what happened to him or her throughout that person's life, but somehow we really do not get to know the person.

Story, on the other hand, is authentic self-disclosure. In story individuals communicate their inner selves to others and look for some human response rather than just simple feedback. The speaker takes a risk, puts himself or herself on the line, and reveals something significant about who he or she is and not merely what he or she has done.

THE REWARDS OF SELF-DISCLOSURE

The obvious question when the topic of self-disclosure arises is *why*. Why should anyone self-disclose to anyone else? What is it about this type of communication that merits its being singled out and discussed at length? There is no clear-cut answer to these very legitimate questions. There is no great body of statistical research findings that attests to the usefulness or importance of self-disclosure. Yet there is evidence in the form of testimony, observational reports, and the like which have led a number of researchers and theorists to argue that self-disclosure is perhaps the most important form of communication in which anyone could engage.

One argument is that we cannot know ourselves as fully as possible if we do not self-disclose to at least one other individual. It is assumed that by self-disclosing to another we gain a new perspective on ourselves, a deeper understanding of our own behavior. In therapy, for example, very often the insight does not come directly from the therapist; while the individual is self-disclosing, he or she realizes some facet of behavior or some relationship that had not been known before. Through self-disclosure then we may come to understand ourselves more thoroughly. Sidney M. Jourard in his *The Transparent Self* notes that self-disclosure is an important factor in counseling and psychotherapy and argues that people may need such help because they have not disclosed significantly to other people.

Closely related is the argument that we will be better able to deal with our problems, especially our guilt, through self-disclosure. One of the great fears that many people have is that they will not be accepted because of some deep dark secret, because of something they have done, or because of some feeling or attitude they might have. Because we feel these things as a basis for rejection, we develop guilt. If, for example, you do not love—or perhaps you hate—one of your parents, you might fear being rejected if you were to self-disclose such a feeling; thus a sense of guilt develops over this. By self-disclosing such a feeling, and by being supported rather than rejected, we are better prepared to deal with the guilt and perhaps reduce or even eliminate it. Even self-acceptance is difficult without self-disclosure. We accept ourselves largely through the eyes of others. If we feel that others would reject us we are apt to reject ourselves as well. Through self-disclosure and subsequent support we are in a better position to see the positive responses to us and are more likely to respond by developing a positive self-concept.

Keeping our various secrets to ourselves and not revealing who we are to others takes a great deal of energy and leaves us with that much less energy for other things. We must be constantly on guard, for example, lest someone see in our behavior what we consider to be a deviant orientation, or attitude or behavior pattern. We might avoid certain people for fear that they will be able to tell this awful thing about us, or avoid situations or places because if we are seen there others will know how terrible we really are. By self-disclosing we rid ourselves of the false masks that otherwise must be worn. Jourard puts this most clearly:

> Every maladjusted person is a person who has not made himself known to another human being and in consequence does not know himself. Nor can he be himself. More than that, he struggles actively to avoid becoming known by another human being. He works at it ceaselessly, twenty-four hours daily, and it is work! In the effort to avoid becoming known, a person provides for himself a cancerous kind of stress which is subtle and unrecognized, but none the less effective in producing not only the assorted patterns of unhealthy personality which psychiatry talks about, but also the wide array of physical ills that have come to be recognized as the province of psychosomatic medicine.

Self-disclosure is also helpful in improving communication efficiency. It seems reasonable to assume that we understand the messages of others largely to the extent that we understand the other individuals—that is, we can understand what an individual says better if we know the individual well. We can tell what certain nuances mean, when the person is serious and when joking, when the person is being sarcastic out of fear and when out of resentment, and so on. Self-disclosure is an essential condition for getting to know another individual. You might study a person's behavior or even live together with another for years, but if that person never self-discloses, you are far from understanding that individual as a complete person.

Perhaps the main reason why self-disclosure is important is that it is necessary if a meaningful relationship is to be established between two people. Without self-disclosure meaningful relationships seem impossible to develop. There are, it is true, relationships that have lasted for ten, twenty, thirty, and forty years without self-disclosure. Many married couples would fall into this category as would colleagues working in the same office or factory or people living in the same neighborhood or apartment house. Without self-disclosure, however, these relationships are probably not terribly meaningful or at least they are not as meaningful as they might be. By self-disclosing we are in effect saying to other individuals that we trust them, that we respect them, that we care enough about them and about our relationship to reveal ourselves to them. This leads the other individual to self-disclose in return. This is at least the start of a meaningful relationship, a relationship that is honest and open and one that goes beyond the surface trivialities.

SOURCES OF RESISTANCE TO SELF-DISCLOSURE

For all its advantages and importance, self-disclosure is a form of communication that is often fiercely resisted. Some of the possible reasons for its resistance should be examined so that we may better understand our own reluctance to enter into this type of communication experience.

Perhaps the most obvious reason—and some would argue the only reason—for our reluctance to self-disclose, according to Gerard Egan, is that there is a societal bias against it, and we have internalized this bias. We have been conditioned against self-disclosure by the society in which we live. The hero in American folklore is strong but also silent; he bears responsibilities, burdens, and problems without letting others even be aware of them. He is self-reliant and does not need the assistance of anyone. Males have internalized this folk hero, it seems, at least to some extent. Women are a bit more fortunate than men. They are allowed the luxury of self-disclosure; they are allowed to tell their troubles to someone, to pour out their feelings, to talk about themselves. Men are more restricted. Women are allowed greater freedom in expressing emotions, to verbalize love and affection; men are somehow conditioned to avoid such expressions. These, men have been taught, are signs of weakness rather than strength.

Although it is difficult to admit, many people resist self-disclosing because of a fear of punishment, generally rejection. We may vividly picture other people laughing at us or whispering about us or condemning us if we self-disclose. These mental pictures help to convince us that self-disclosure is not the most expedient course of action. We rationalize and say it is not necessary to tell anyone anything about ourselves. We are fine as we are, or so we tell ourselves.

We may also fear punishment in the form of tangible or concrete manifestations, such as the loss of a job, the loss of some office, or of some "friends." At times this does happen. The ex-convict who self-discloses his or her past record may find himself or herself without a job or out of political office. Generally, however, these fears are overblown. These fears are often in the nature of excuses which allow us to rest content without self-disclosing.

Gerard Egan, in *Encounter*, points out that this fear of rejection operates like a reverse halo effect. A halo effect refers to the generalizing of virtue from one area to another. For example, your communication teacher may know a great deal about communication and may be perceived as highly credible in that field. The halo effect operates to generalize that perceived credibility to other fields as well, and so when he or she talks about politics or economics or psychology we are more apt to see him or her as credible and knowledgeable in these areas too. The reverse halo effect operates in a similar manner. We wrongly assume that if we tell others something negative about ourselves their negative responses will generalize to other aspects of our behavior and they will see us as generally negative, much as we may see the teacher of one field as competent in other fields.

Another possible reason why we resist self-disclosure is what Egan calls fear of self-knowledge. We may have built up a beautiful, rationalized picture of ourselves—emphasizing the positive and eliminating or minimizing the negative aspects. Self-disclosure often allows us to see through the rationalizations. We see those positive aspects for what they are, and we see the negative aspects that were previously hidden.

CONTEXTS FOR SELF-DISCLOSURE

As a particular form of communication, self-disclosure occurs more readily under certain circumstances than under others. Generally, self-disclosure is reciprocal. In any interaction self-disclosure by A is more likely to take place if B engages in self-disclosure than if B does not.

This seems quite obvious and predictable. Yet its consequences are interesting. It implies that a kind of spiral effect operates here, with each person's self-disclosure serving as the stimulus for additional self-disclosure by the other person which in turn serves as the stimulus for self-disclosure by the other person and on and on.

Self-disclosure, perhaps because of the numerous fears we have about revealing ourselves, is more likely to occur in small groups than in large groups. Dyads are perhaps the most frequent situations in which self-disclosure seems to take place. This seems true for any number of reasons. A dyad seems more suitable because it is easier for the self-discloser to deal with one person's reactions and responses than with the reactions of a group of three or four or five. The self-discloser can attend to the responses quite carefully and on the basis of the support or lack of support monitor the disclosures, continuing if the situation is supportive and stopping if it is not supportive. With more than one listener such monitoring is impossible since the responses are sure to vary among the listeners. Another possible reason is that when the group is larger than two the self-disclosure takes on aspects of exhibitionism and public exposure. It is no longer a confidential matter; now it is one about which many people know. From a more practical point of view it is often difficult to assemble in one place at one time only those people to whom we would want to self-disclose.

Research has not been able to identify fully the kind of person with whom self-disclosure is likely to take place. There seems a great deal of individual variation here. Some studies have found that we disclose more often to those people who are close to us, for example, our spouses, our family, our close friends. Other studies claim that we disclose to persons we like and not disclose to persons we dislike regardless of how close they are to us. Thus an individual may disclose to a well-liked teacher even though they are not particularly close and yet not dislose to a brother or sister with whom he or she is close but who is not liked very much. Other studies claim that a lasting relationship between people increases the likelihood of self-disclosure while still others claim that self-disclosure is more likely to occur in temporary relationships, for example, between prostitute and client or even between strangers on a train.

According to Jourard there are topic, sex, and age differences in self-disclosure communications. Certain areas are more likely to be self-disclosed than others. For example, we would be more likely to self-disclose information about our jobs or hobbies than about our sex lives or about our financial situation. Male college students are more likely to disclose to a close friend than to either of their parents, but college females will disclose about equally to their mothers and to their best friends but will not disclose very much to their fathers or to their boyfriends. There are even differences in the amount of self-disclosure in different age groups. Self-disclosure to a spouse or to an opposite sex friend increases from the age of about seventeen to about fifty and then drops off. As might be expected, husbands and wives self-disclose to each other more than they do to any other person or group of persons. "This confirms the view," says Jourard in *The Transparent Self,* "that marriage is the 'closest' relationship one can enter, and it may help us the better to understand why some people avoid it like the plague. Anyone who is reluctant to be known by another person and to know another person—sexually and cognitively—will find the prospective intimacy of marriage somewhat terrifying."

Sources

On self-disclosure see Sidney M. Jourard's *Disclosing Man to Himself* (New York: D. Van Nostrand Reinhold, 1968) and *The Transparent Self,* rev. ed. (New York: Reinhold, 1971). In writing this unit I relied heavily on the insights of Gerard Egan. See especially his *Encounter: Group Processes for Interpersonal Growth* (Belmont, Cal.: Brooks/Cole, 1970) or, if you prefer a shorter version, *Face to Face: The Small-Group Experience and Interpersonal Growth* (Belmont, Cal.: Brooks/Cole, 1973). An overview of self-disclosure in communication is provided by W. Barnett Pearce and Stewart M. Sharp, "Self-Disclosing Communication," *Journal of Communication* 23 (December 1973): 409–425. This article also provides an excellent review of the research on self-disclosure and communication. Sam Keen and Anne Valley Fox's *Telling Your Story: A Guide to Who You Are and Who You Can Be* (New York: New American Library, 1973) provides some interesting insights on self disclosure.

Experiential Vehicles

SELF-DISCLOSURE QUESTIONNAIRE

Complete the following questionnaire by indicating in the appropriate spaces your willingness-unwillingness to self-disclose these matters to members of a group of students chosen at random from those in this class.

In a group of five or six persons discuss the questionnaires, self-disclosing what you wish to self-disclose and not disclosing what you do not wish to disclose. Consider at least the following:

1. Are there any discrepancies between what you indicated you would self-disclose and what you were actually willing to self-disclose?
2. What areas were people most unwilling to self-disclose? Why? Discuss these reasons in terms of conditioning.
3. After the group got going and a number of people self-disclosed, did you feel more willing to self-disclose? Explain your feelings.
4. Were negative qualities (or perceived negative qualities) more likely to remain undisclosed? Why?
5. How would the results of your questionnaire have differed if this information was to be disclosed to your parents, a stranger you would never see again, a counselor, and a best friend? Would the results differ depending on the sex of the individual to whom the disclosures were to be made? Explain the reasons why.

DISCLOSING THE HIDDEN SELF

General Discussion of Model

How might the information in the hidden self area, if not disclosed, prevent meaningful communication? How might this information, if disclosed, foster meaningful interaction? How might nondisclosure and disclosure work in reverse? What positive effects might self disclosure have on the individual? Negative effects? What positive and/or negative effects might self-disclosure have on interpersonal interaction? In any decision pertaining to self-disclosure, what audience factors should the individual take into

	Would definitely self-disclose	Would probably self-disclose	Don't know	Would probably not self-disclose	Would definitely not self-disclose
1. My religious beliefs					
2. My attitudes toward other religions					
3. My attitudes toward different nationalities and races					
4. My political beliefs					
5. My economic status					
6. My views on abortion					
7. My views on pornography					
8. My views on premarital relations					
9. My major pastime					
10. My parents' attitudes toward other religions					
11. My parents' attitudes toward different nationalities and races					
12. My parents' political beliefs					
13. My parents' economic status					
14. My relationship with my parents					
15. My sexual fantasies					
16. My past sexual experiences					
17. My perceived sexual attractiveness					
18. My desired physical attractiveness					
19. My most negative physical attribute					
20. My physical condition or health					
21. My ideal mate					
22. My drinking behavior					
23. My drug behavior					
24. My gambling behavior					
25. My personal goals					
26. My most embarrassing moment					
27. My unfulfilled desires					
28. My major weaknesses					
29. My major worry					
30. My major strengths					
31. My present happiness-unhappiness					
32. My major mistakes					
33. My general attractiveness					
34. My general self-concept					
35. My general adequacy					

Open Self	Blind Self
Hidden Self	Unknown Self

The Johari Window

consideration? That is, what variables of the audience might influence an individual's decision to disclose or not disclose?

On an index card write a statement of information that is currently in the hidden self. Do not put your names on these cards; the statements are to be dealt with anonymously. These cards will be collected and read aloud to the entire group.[1]

Discussion of Statements and Model

1. Classify the statements into categories, for example, sexual problems, attitudes toward family, self doubts, and so forth.
2. Why do you suppose this type of information is kept to the hidden self? What advantages might hiding this information have? What disadvantages?
3. How would you react to people who disclosed such statements to you? For example, what difference, if any, would it make in your interpersonal relationship?
4. What type of person is likely to have a large hidden self and a small open self? A large open self and a small hidden self.
5. In relation to the other group members would your open self be larger? Smaller? The same size? Would your hidden self be larger? Smaller? The same size?

[1]The general idea for this exercise comes from Gerard Egan, *Encounter* (Belmont, Cal.: Brooks/Cole, 1970).

unit 10

The Self
in Transaction

Ego States
Transactions
Life Positions
   PAC Communications
   Mapping Transactions
   Communications of Different Life Positions

Objectives

Upon completion of this unit, you should be able to:

1. identify and define the three *ego states*
2. list the common verbal and nonverbal behaviors of each ego state
3. create dialogues that illustrate the way people in the different ego states would react in different situations
4. distinguish among and define *complementary, crossed,* and *ulterior transactions*
5. create dialogues that illustrate the three kinds of transactions and identify the type of transaction when given the dialogues
6. diagram the three types of transactions and identify the type of transaction when given the diagrams
7. explain the way people see themselves and others and the way they react in different situations when in the four life positions

One of the most insightful and certainly one of the most popular approaches to understanding the self is that of *transactional analysis* (TA), a rather forbidding term for a relatively simple set of principles. Transactional analysis, popularized by Eric Berne in *Games People Play* and *What Do You Say After You Say Hello?*, and by Thomas Harris in *I'm*

O.K.—You're O.K., is an approach to or a means for analyzing and improving transactions between people.

The approach discussed here for understanding the self is not an alternative to the approaches considered earlier; rather, it is supplementary. Transactional analysis focuses on understanding the self through an analysis of interactions with others.

Some of the basic assumptions and principles of transactional analysis are presented here with two goals in mind: 1) to provide insight for better understanding ourselves and others, and 2) to provide a means for understanding and analyzing interpersonal encounters. To this end we consider the TA concepts of ego states, transactions, and life positions.

The *ego state* is a more or less stable pattern of feeling which corresponds to a pattern of behavior. In transactional analysis three such states are defined: Parent, Adult, and Child. *Transactions* refer to the patterns of interaction between two people. Complementary, crossed, and ulterior transactions are here distinguished. The *life positions* are the scripts or set of directions by which we live our lives. Four such scripts are considered here: I'm not O.K., You're O.K.; I'm not O.K., You're not O.K.; I'm O.K., You're not O.K.; and I'm O.K., You're O.K.

EGO STATES

In transactional analysis distinctions are made among three ego states, which are defined as relatively consistent patterns of feelings that are or can be related to a corresponding consistent pattern of behavior. The three ego states are used in TA to describe the behaviors of people as they interact with each other. At any given time, individuals exhibit the behaviors characteristic of one of these ego states, although they may (and often do) shift from one ego state to another. The three ego states identified in TA are Parent, Adult, and Child. These ego states bear no relationship to the chronological age of the individual—a child may act as an Adult and an adult as a Child. (Note that the ego states are capitalized to distinguish them from actual parents, adults, and children.)

Parent

The ego state of Parent is one which is borrowed from one's real or substitute parents and may take the form of "mothering" or controlling. When in the ego state of Parent the individual acts and speaks like a real parent; verbally and nonverbally he or she assumes the role of the parent. The Parent makes frequent use of such expressions as "don't," "should," "shouldn't," "Don't touch," "Be good," "Eat this," "I'll do it," "You'll get hurt," "Don't bother me now," "I'll get it," "Stop that," "Don't move from here," "Don't worry," "I'll fix everything," and so on. The Parent is especially evaluative and frequently uses such labels as good and bad, beautiful and ugly, healthy and sick, and similar terms to define an individual or group of individuals. Nonverbally, the Parent uses his or her body to supplement the words and makes frequent use of the accusing finger, the tapping foot (indicating impatience), the head nod (indicating "no"), the disapproving arms folded in front of the abdomen, the consoling arm on the shoulder, the approving cheek pinch, and so on.

Adult

In the ego state of Adult the individual is oriented to the world as it is, not as it is talked about. The Adult is logical rather than emotional, calm rather than excitable, inquiring rather than accusatory. The Adult is particularly oriented to accumulating and processing relevant information and to estimating the probabilities in any given situation. The Adult questions a great deal, asking "how," "what," "why," "when," and "where" (rather like the good reporter), "What can we learn from this situation?" "What do the statistics say?" "What might we predict based on the probabilities?" Nonverbally, the Adult's body communicates interest and attention. This individual stands straight (but not rigid) and engages the attention of the other individuals by maintaining appropriate eye contact and physical distance and by moving close to the speaker to hear and see better.

Child

The ego state of Child may be either the Adapted Child State or the Natural Child State. In the Adapted Child State, individuals obey the directives of their parents, modify their behavior on the basis of the commands of the parents, do what the parents order or want, and perhaps even become what the parents want them to become when they get older. This Child may also adapt to the parents by withdrawing, crying, or having a temper tantrum. The Natural Child, on the other hand, is spontaneous, creative, intuitive, and rebellious. This Child does what he or she wants to do—and that is to have fun, play games, have sex, and otherwise please one's various appetites. This Child wants to explore new things and go to new places. The Child will frequently use such expressions as "can't," "don't want to," "Is this O.K.?" "Let's play," "You don't love me," "Doesn't everybody love me?" "This is mine," "Don't hit me." Nonverbally, the Child cries and screams and maintains an uninhibited posture regardless of the social situation. The Child bites his or her nails and picks his or her nose whenever the urge presents itself.

Any individual in any interaction may be analyzed as operating in one of these three ego states. Transactional analysis provides a method for analyzing transactions in terms of these ego states. Whether the communication continues or is broken and what the outcome of the communication interaction will be is largely determined by the ego states of the individuals and by the type of transaction formed.

TRANSACTIONS

There are three basic types of transactions: *complementary, crossed,* and *ulterior.*

Complementary Transactions

Complementary transactions may be defined as those involving messages that are sent and received by the same ego state for each of the participants. That is, A's messages are sent by the same ego state that B is addressing, and B's messages are sent by the same ego state that A is addressing. Put differently and more simply, complementary transactions are those involving only two ego states.

In Type I complementary transaction we have the same ego states communicating with each other. This may be diagramed as follows:

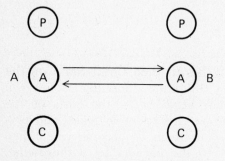

A dialogue representative of this kind of communication transaction might go something like this:

Spouse A: This is great furniture; too bad we can't afford it.
Spouse B: Yes, let's go downstairs; they're having a sale on floor samples and we might be able to get some good buys.

In Type II complementary transactions each person is in a different ego state but each addresses his or her messages to the other's appropriate ego state. One such pattern is diagrammed as follows:

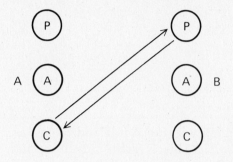

In this example, A's Child is addressing B's Parent, and B's Parent is addressing A's Child. This type of transaction might be identified from a dialogue such as the following:

Spouse A: Let's go on the town and get drunk.
Spouse B: Now, you know you get sick when you drink. There's more to life than just having fun.

Here A is in the Child state and wants to have fun, to play. B assumes the Parent state and restrains the Child.

In complementary transactions communication is productive and may continue indefinitely. In the Type I example, as long as the couple remain as two Adults communication will continue with little chance of breaking down. In the Type II example the same holds true. As long as A remains in the Child state and B in the Parent state, no barriers will be established and communication will continue.

Crossed Transactions

Trouble enters when one individual slips out of the ego state he or she is in and into one that creates what is called a *crossed transaction*. Again there are two general types. In Type I the communication—to use the most common pattern—begins as Adult to Adult. That is, A as Adult says to B, also as Adult, "This is great furniture; too bad we can't afford it." But B does not respond as Adult, nor does B address the message to A's Adult. Rather, B responds as a Child to a Parent and says, for example, "Let's buy it anyway. I want it. Buy it for me." This transaction might be diagramed as follows:

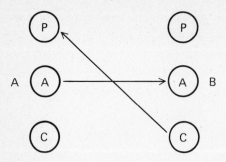

In Type II the transaction again begins with an Adult addressing an Adult, saying, to keep the same example, "This is great furniture; too bad we can't afford it." Here, however, B responds as a Parent to a Child saying, for example, "Now you know you can't afford it so why waste your time and mine looking at it." This dialogue, we might diagram as follows:

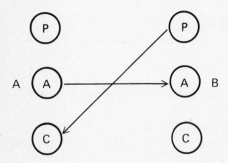

As you can see, it is with crossed transactions that problems in interpersonal communication arise. For example, in Type I-crossed, A (as Adult) may try to reason with B (as Child) but success will be almost impossible since A's arguments presuppose that B is in the Adult state, which B is not. Or A might switch to the Parent state and answer B as a parent would: "I told you we can't afford it and that finishes that." This may end the conversation but it does not clear up the communication breakdown. In Type II-crossed, A is again presented with a serious breakdown. A could attempt to reason with B and say something to the effect that A was just looking and did realize that there was not enough money and so on. But this kind of approach would only have an effect on someone in the Adult ego state.

We may generalize from these situations and note that communication has broken down largely because messages were addressed to inappropriate ego states.

Ulterior Transactions

A third class of transactions, somewhat more complex than the previous two, is that of *ulterior transactions*. In ulterior transactions more than two ego states are involved at the same time. Here there is an unspoken or hidden agenda, which is generally communicated nonverbally. Consider, for example, the following dialogue:

> *Student:* (Handing the teacher a term paper while looking at the floor and speaking too softly) This is the best writing I could do on this extremely difficult topic you assigned me.
> *Teacher:* (Accepting paper though with an expression of annoyance) Well, I'll read it and let you know.

On the surface the student's message is Adult to Adult, but the ulterior message is Child to Parent (I've been a bad student). The teacher responds on the surface as Adult but the ulterior and nonverbal message (the expression of annoyance) is from Parent to Child and punishes the student.

We might diagram this transaction as follows (dotted lines are generally used for ulterior transactions):

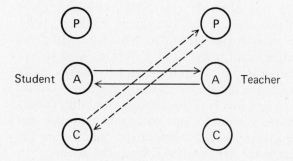

These ulterior transactions are the substance of game behavior. The problem with such games in terms of interpersonal relationships is that it is often difficult to tell when one is playing a game and when one is not playing. At times we may respond to someone as if that person was serious, only to find that a game was being played. And of course the reverse is just as much a problem, when we assume that someone is playing a game but later discover he or she was serious. The person who says, "My jacket is ugly," may mean it and may be simply stating an opinion. On the other hand, this person may be looking for reassurances that it is not ugly and that indeed it looks particularly attractive. When we know the individual involved we are in a better position to respond appropriately, but even here there is much room for error.

Some people play such games constantly; they are always "on." We are forever forced to look for hidden meanings in what they say and somehow feel that their real selves never come through. In the example of the student and teacher, the student is playing the game of "kick me," according to Berne's *Games People Play*. The student is, in effect, asking to be punished. In this example the teacher played too and "kicked" as the student asked.

Although individuals play games to win, the players are not winners in the usual sense. More often they are losers. "Games," note Muriel James and Dorothy Jongeward in *Born to Win* "prevent honest, intimate, and open relationships between the players. Yet people play them because they fill up time, provoke attention, reinforce early opinions about self and others, and fulfill a sense of destiny."

LIFE POSITIONS

One of the basic tenets of transactional analysis is that we live our lives largely according to "scripts." These scripts are very similar to dramatic scripts, complete with a list of characters and roles, stage directions, dialogue, and plot.

Our culture provides us with one kind of script. This cultural script provides us with guides to proper dress; rules for sexual conduct; roles for men and women; a value system pertaining to marriage, children, money, and education; the concepts of success and failure; and so on. Families provide another kind of script. Family scripts contain more specific instructions for each of the family members—the boys should go into politics, the girls should get involved in social work, this family will always have its own business, "we may not earn much money but we will always have adequate insurance," the oldest son takes over the father's business, the oldest daughter gets married first, and so on.

From out of all our early experiences, particularly from the messages—both verbal and nonverbal—received from our parents, we develop a psychological script for ourselves and, for the most part, follow this throughout our lives.

Individual scripts are generally "written" by the age of three; they provide us with specific directions for functioning within the larger cultural script. Should we play the victim or the persecutor, the slave or the master, the clown or the intellectual?

Some children, for example, are told that they will be successes. Non-verbally, they are given love and affection; verbally, they are reinforced for numerous actions. Other children have been told they will never succeed. Statements such as, "No matter what you do, you'll be a success," as well as statements such as, "You'll never amount to anything," are extremely important in determining the script the child will assume in later life. Generally, people follow the scripts their parents have written for them. But such scripts can be broken. We do *not* have to follow the script written for us by our parents. One of the major purposes of transactional analysis is to break the negative and unproductive scripts and to substitute positive and productive scripts in their place. TA is used to prevent destructive messages from getting written into the script.

These scripts, which we all have, are the bases from which we develop what are called "life positions." In TA there are four basic life positions.

I'm Not O.K., You're O.K.

This person sees others as being well-adjusted and generally effective (you're O.K.) but sees himself or herself as maladjusted and ineffective (I'm not O.K.). This is, acording to Harris, the first position we develop as very young children. This is the position of the child who sees himself or herself as helpless and dirty and sees the adult as all-powerful and all-knowing. This person feels helpless and powerless in comparison to others and withdraws from confrontations rather than compete. This kind of life position leads one to live off others, to make others pay for their being O.K. (and oneself being not O.K.). Such people are frequently depressed; at times they isolate themselves, lamenting, "If only . . ." or "I should have been . . ."

I'm Not O.K., You're Not O.K.

People in this category think badly of themselves (I'm not O.K.) as well as of other people (you're not O.K.). They have no real acceptance of either themselves or others. They give themselves no support (because they are not O.K.) and they accept no support from others (because others are not O.K.). These people have given up. To them, nothing seems worthwhile and so they withdraw. Interpersonal communication is extremely difficult since they put down both themselves and others and intrapersonal communication does not seem particularly satisfying either. Attempts to give such people help are generally met with refusals since the would-be helpers are seen as "not O.K."

Such people seem to have lost interest in themselves, in others, and in the world generally. Living seems a drag. In the extreme they are the suicides and homicides, the autistics and pathologicals.

I'm O.K., You're Not O.K.

Persons in this position view themselves as generally effective (I'm O.K.) but see others as ineffective (you're not O.K.); "I am good, you are bad." These people have little or no respect for others and easily and frequently find fault with both friends and enemies. They are supportive of themselves but do not accept support from others. They are independent and seem to derive some satisfaction from *intra*personal communication but reject *inter*personal interaction and involvement. Literally and figuratively they need space, elbow room; they resent being crowded by those "not O.K." others. Criminals are drawn with disproportional frequency from this class, as are the paranoids who feel persecuted and who blame others for their problems.

I'm O.K., You're O.K.

This is the adult, normal, healthy position. This, says Berne in *What Do You Say After You Say Hello?*, is "the position of genuine heroes and princes, and heroines and princesses." These people approach and solve problems constructively. They have valid expectations about themselves and others and accept themselves and others as basically good, worthy, and significant human beings. These people feel free to develop and progress as individuals. They enter freely into meaningful relationships with other people and do not fear involvements. They feel neither inferior nor superior to others. Rather, they are worthy and others are worthy. This is the position of winners.

It is impossible to say how many people are in each class. Many pass through the "I'm not o.k., you're o.k." position. Few arrive at the "I'm o.k., you're o.k." position; few people are winners in this sense. Very probably the vast majority of people are in the "I'm not o.k., you're o.k." and "I'm o.k., you're not o.k." positions. It should be clear, of course, that these are general classes and that human beings resist each classification. Thus these four positions should be looked at as areas on a continuum, none of which have clear-cut boundaries and yet all of which are different.

Transactional analysis is perhaps the most effective means for understanding interactions among people and for making clear when and why interactions are effective and when and why interactions break down. It is an approach that enables us to look at our own communications and understand the ego state we are in; at the same time, it makes us aware of the effects our ego state has on others. Perhaps most important is that TA helps to bring to consciousness our own life positions so that we may change them to a more effective alternative.

It seems that these insights are prerequisite to understanding ourselves and our interpersonal communications—ultimately to make them more effective.

Sources

This unit is based on the theory of transactional analysis. When you read this, new books on TA will probably be on the best-seller list. Most of the popular works on TA cover essentially the same basics but apply them to different areas. In writing this unit I made most use of Thomas A. Harris, *I'm O.K., You're O.K.* (New York: Harper & Row, 1969) which I wholeheartedly recommend to any college student. Also useful are Muriel James and Dorothy Jongeward's *Born to Win: Transactional Analysis with Gestalt Experiments* (Reading, Mass.: Addison-Wesley, 1971) and Eric Berne's *Games People Play* (New York: Grove Press, 1964). Berne's book, I should mention, was a best seller for an extremely long time and apparently had considerable appeal; yet I found it dull, ponderous, and extremely difficult to stick with. A more simplified account of transactional analysis is *Success Through Transactional Analysis* by Jut Meininger (New York: New American Library, 1973).

Experiential Vehicles

PAC COMMUNICATIONS

These ten brief situations should be role played so that the differences among Parent (P), Adult (A), and Child (C) may be more easily seen. Three persons should be chosen for each situation, one to portray P, one to portray A, and one to portray C. After a neutral party or the instructor announces the general situation, for example, "A fellow employee enters the office crying," the three members interact in response to this situation according to the ego state each is to portray.

After this brief role playing members of the class should discuss the faithfulness of the roles to the ego state, offering other possible alternative ways of acting. Record in the spaces provided what you feel are "ideal" responses for each ego state.

As a variation, three members may interact according to the situation without telling the class who is playing what role. Discussion may then center on the reasons for the ease or difficulty in identifying the roles.

Consider also how you would react in these situations (without attempting to respond as would an Adult. Can you identify any influences that would lead you to respond as you would? Be as specific as possible.

1. A fellow employee enters the office crying.

   P

   A

C

2. A student fails a course and tells his friends.

P

A

C

3. A relative has just died.

P

A

C

4. A friend is to be married to a person of another race.

P

A

C

5. A beggar asks for a dime.

P

A

C

6. One's teenage son is arrested on drug charges.

P

A

C

7. A local politician is found to have been taking graft.

P

A

C

8. An auto accident occurs in the neighborhood.

P

A

C

9. A favorite teacher on campus is fired.

P

A

C

10. A close friend dies.

P

A

C

MAPPING TRANSACTIONS

For this exercise dyads should be formed with a third person being the transactional analyst. The analyst selects a brief situation with some initial dialogue (one of the ten presented below or one that does not appear here) and the two parties role play the situation in accordance with the initial dialogue they have been given. After this brief role playing, the analyst maps the transaction and all three members discuss the type of transaction it was and the effectiveness-ineffectiveness of the communications. "Map" the transaction by drawing arrows connecting the appropriate ego states expressed in the dialogue.

This exercise may also be done with two persons interacting and the rest of the class serving as analysts.

1. *Jim:* I wish you would stop drinking. You know this is not the place to get drunk.
   Sara: Have a drink with me. Come on, let's have some fun.

   Jim (P) (A) (C)   (P) (A) (C) Sara

2. *Ronald:* I didn't finish my term paper. I just didn't know where to begin and couldn't seem to get it started.
   Dr. Hill: Now, don't worry. We'll talk about it and I'm sure you'll be able to do it once the directions are made clear.

   Ronald (P) (A) (C)   (P) (A) (C) Dr. Hill

3. *Husband:* Why the hell aren't the kids in bed yet? I have to have some time to relax in quiet.
   Wife: (crying) Stop yelling at me; can't you see I'm already upset.

   Husband (P) (A) (C)   (P) (A) (C) Wife

4. *Husband:* Can't you get a better job and make more money like everyone else?
Wife: If you weren't so ignorant of the economic conditions today you
wouldn't ask such a stupid question.

Husband (P) (A) (C)   Wife (P) (A) (C)

5. *Son:* I'm going to watch some television.
Mother: O.K.

Son (P) (A) (C)   Mother (P) (A) (C)

6. *Son:* I'm going to watch some television.
Mother: You're always watching television. Isn't there anything else
you can do? You're going to grow up just like your father.

Son (P) (A) (C)   Mother (P) (A) (C)

7. *Employer:* I'm sorry but we are going to have to lay you off for at least the next six months.
   Employee: This company should fall apart.

Employer (P) (A) (C)   (P) (A) (C) Employee

8. *Student:* Why is it that every teacher is so critical of everything I do. Don't I ever do anything right?
   Teacher: I'm sure they don't criticize everything. I'm sure they are just trying to be helpful.

Student (P) (A) (C)   (P) (A) (C) Teacher

9. *Teenage boy:* How about going to a movie tonight?
   Teenage girl: Aren't you every going to grow up and ask me out to some sophisticated place? I'm almost seventeen!

Boy (P) (A) (C)   (P) (A) (C) Girl

10. *Son:* Let's play in the sand.
    Father: O.K. Let's go.

COMMUNICATIONS OF DIFFERENT LIFE POSITIONS

How would you respond to each of the following situations? Indicate here what you think your initial response(s) would be.

1. Being offered a promotion to a position of responsibility

2. Being fired from a job held for the past five years

3. Being asked out on a date

4. Being robbed

5. Being designated leader in a small group situation

6. Being complimented for something you made

7. Being criticized for something you did

8. Being asked a favor which will take about an hour of your time

9. Being assigned an unpleasant job which will last about a month

10. Being given the opportunity to vote for or against the promotion of your interpersonal communication instructor

   After you have completed all ten, respond to the following ten situations, but this time determine how each of the four life positions would respond in the same situation.

1. Being offered a promotion to a position of responsibility

    a. I'm not O.K., You're O.K.

    b. I'm not O.K., You're not O.K.

    c. I'm O.K., You're not O.K.

    d. I'm O.K., You're O.K.

2. Being fired from a job held for the past five years
    a. I'm not O.K., You're O.K.

    b. I'm not O.K., You're not O.K.

    c. I'm O.K., You're not O.K.

    d. I'm O.K., You're O.K.

3. Being asked out on a date
    a. I'm not O.K., You're O.K.

    b. I'm not O.K., You're not O.K.

c. I'm O.K., You're not O.K.

d. I'm O.K., You're O.K.

4. Being robbed
   a. I'm not O.K., You're O.K.

   b. I'm not O.K., You're not O.K.

   c. I'm O.K., You're not O.K.

   d. I'm O.K., You're O.K.

5. Being designated the leader in a small group situation
   a. I'm not O.K., You're O.K.

   b. I'm not O.K., You're not O.K.

c. I'm O.K., You're not O.K.

d. I'm O.K., You're O.K.

6. Being complimented for something you made

    a. I'm not O.K., You're O.K.

    b. I'm not O.K., You're not O.K.

    c. I'm O.K., You're not O.K.

    d. I'm O.K., You're O.K.

7. Being criticized for something you did

    a. I'm not O.K., You're O.K.

    b. I'm not O.K., You're not O.K.

c. I'm O.K., You're not O.K.

d. I'm O.K., You're O.K.

8. Being asked a favor which will take about an hour of your time
   a. I'm not O.K., You're O.K.

   b. I'm not O.K., You're not O.K.

   c. I'm O.K., You're not O.K.

   d. I'm O.K., You're O.K.

9. Being assigned an unpleasant job which will last about a month
   a. I'm not O.K., You're O.K.

   b. I'm not O.K., You're not O.K.

   c. I'm O.K., You're not O.K.

   d. I'm O.K., You're O.K.

10. Being given the opportunity to vote for or against the promotion of your interpersonal communication instructor

   a. I'm not O.K., You're O.K.

   b. I'm not O.K., You're not O.K.

   c. I'm O.K., You're not O.K.

   d. I'm O.K., You're O.K.

Analyze your own responses in terms of the four life positions. Do you see any patterns in your responses? How would these responses influence your day-to-day experiences?

As an alternative, this exercise may be conducted by having the forms on which each person indicates how he or she would respond collected (without names). The instructor or some member of the class would read the responses aloud and the class would attempt to classify these into the four life positions. More important than classification, would be a discussion of what these responses mean in terms of our views of ourselves and of others.

unit 11

Interpersonal Credibility

Types of Credibility
Dimensions of Credibility
Variations in Credibility Perception
A Note on Intrapersonal Credibility
  Interpersonal Credibility
  Communicator Credibility
  Quintilian College

Objectives

Upon completion of this unit, you should be able to:

1. define *credibility*
2. define the three major types of credibility
3. define the dimensions of credibility and explain at least one way in which each may be established or communicated to a receiver
4. explain some of the ways in which the perception of credibility may vary
5. define *intrapersonal credibility*
6. recognize and identify credibility references when presented with excerpts from communications

We have probably all had the experience of speaking or listening to someone and as a result of who the person was or what that person said or how it was said, believing that person. Similarly, we must have also had the experience of disbelieving someone after speaking or listening to him or her. When teachers or researchers, for example, present their conclusions on a topic, some people believe them and others do not. And of course when we speak some people believe us and some people do not believe us.

The question we should now consider is what leads us to believe some people and to disbelieve others? What is there about a person that makes him or her believable? This question, generally called *speaker credibility*, has been discussed and investigated for at least 2500 years and perhaps longer. Some 2300 years ago Aristotle, in his *Rhetoric*, said:

> Persuasion is achieved by the speaker's personal character when the speech is so spoken as to make us think him credible. We believe good men more fully and more readily than others; this is true generally whatever the question is, and absolutely true where exact certainty is impossible and opinions are divided.

> There are three things which inspire confidence in the orator's own character—the three, namely, that induce us to believe a thing apart from any proof of it: good sense, good moral character, and goodwill.

Although Aristotle was talking about the formal speech delivered in a court of law, a political meeting, or at some formal ceremony, the characteristics noted as contributing to persuasion—namely, good sense, good moral character, and goodwill—are essentially the same qualities stressed by modern theorists as being applicable to all forms of communication, whether they be formal public-speaking type situations or informal, interpersonal situations.

Hadley Cantril, in his study *The Invasion from Mars*, for example, concluded:

> It is a well known fact to the social psychologist, the advertiser, and the propagandist that an idea or a product has a better chance of being accepted if it can be endorsed by, or if it emanates from, some well known person whose character, ability, or status is highly valued.

Basically, there are two ways to examine credibility. One way is to examine effective versus ineffective individuals and explore the differences between them, specifically asking what makes one person effective and another person ineffective. Why is one person believed when the other person is disbelieved? The second way is to conduct controlled experiments. The typical design involves setting up two different but similar groups, say two sections of a college course in interpersonal communication. One group is presented with a speaker, introduced as a person who runs a barber shop, whose topic is foreign policy. The other group hears the same speaker and the same speech but this time the person is introduced as a political science professor. The students are then tested on the extent to which they agreed or disagreed with the speaker. Invariably, the group that heard the speaker introduced as a political science professor evidences more agreement than the group hearing the speaker introduced as a barber. In other instances speakers may deliver essentially the same speech, but in one there might be references to noted and respected philosophers and in the other there would be no such references. Again, the references to philosophers give the speaker a much higher credibility rating. Elaborating on these basic procedures, researchers have discovered a great deal about this important dimension of interpersonal communication.

TYPES OF CREDIBILITY

For our purposes, we should distinguish three general types of credibility: *initial*, *derived*, and *terminal*.

Initial Credibility

Initial or *extrinsic credibility* is that which the communicator is seen to have before the actual communication begins. Regardless of who we talk to or who we read or listen to, the source is seen as possessing or lacking some degree of credibility. Often this initial credibility is a function of the individual's title or position. Thus in the first day of class, the person who walks in the room to teach begins with some initial credibility by virtue of the position of teacher. If there is a "Dr." or "Professor" in front of his or her name, then that person's credibility is perhaps higher than if no such title appeared.

Derived Credibility

During any communication we naturally talk about ourselves, whether explicitly or implicitly. The topics we talk about, the vocal emphasis we give them, our facial expression as we talk about them, the degree of conviction we express, and so on all say something about ourselves. *Derived credibility* is the credibility that a listener perceives based on what takes place during the interpersonal encounter. All communication is self-reflexive; all communication says something about the speaker or source. Consequently, all communications relate, directly or indirectly, to the speaker's credibility. Inevitably, in our communications we convey impressions of our intelligence, our morals, or our goodwill toward others.

Note, for example, how our impressions change when a person mispronounces a word we think he or she should know or when some kind of grammatical mistake is made. When this happens we tend to think less of the individual's intelligence or competence and perhaps would be less likely to believe what the person is saying. Conversely, if a person is able to cite obscure facts or quote famous philosophers or do complicated mathematical operations, the credibility that person is seen to possess is likely to increase.

In many instances specific and direct attempts are made to change the perceived credibility of a particular individual. For example, when politicians are confronted with some wrong they have done or unpopular decision they have made, they quickly attempt to rebuild their credibility by stressing that they did this based on facts and figures not available to the general public (knowledge), that they are good people and would never do anything immoral (high moral character), or that they would only do what is right for the rest of the state or country and that the people's interests were really paramount (goodwill).

Teachers will often intersperse their lectures or discussions with credibility-building references. They may, for example, "casually" note that their new book will be out soon or that an article they have written will clarify important questions, or they may note how thorough their own education was. In all of these instances the teacher (knowingly or not) is building credibility or at least making an attempt to do so.

More specifically, we should ask what factors influence the perception of credibility in listeners. That is, what does a communicator do that enhances or detracts from his or her credibility? A great deal of research has been directed at discovering the various means of achieving high credibility.

The way in which the message is presented and constructed influences credibility a great deal. If a person communicates haltingly, with poor grammar, with numerous hesitations, and with an uneasiness, we would probably perceive that person to be of low credibility and not readily believe him or her. Conversely, the speaker who speaks with assurance, who speaks in accordance with the rules of grammar, and who appears self-confident seems to have a much better chance of being perceived as credible. Thus the words we choose in speaking, the way in which we arrange those words, the way in which we organize our arguments, questions, or responses, influences our credibility.

The fairness with which one presents oneself seems also to influence the perception of credibility. If we feel that people have some kind of ulterior motive then we would be less likely to believe them. On the other hand, speakers who present themselves honestly seem to be believed more readily.

Generally, we perceive as believable people who are like ourselves. The more similar people are to our own backgrounds, attitudes and beliefs, goals and ambitions, the more likely it is that they will be perceived as credible. Closely related to this is the issue of "common ground." When people align themselves with what we align ourselves, they establish common ground with us and are generally perceived as more believable than people who do not establish this common ground. In the movie *Gypsy*, Rose carries around with her a collection of pins and buttons for various societies. If she meets an Elk she puts on the Elk pin; if she meets a Moose she dons the Moose pin. In this way she establishes common ground and stands a better chance of being believed. I guess we do not like to think that people who are like us would be anything but knowledgeable, of good character, and of good will.

Terminal Credibility

Terminal credibility is that which the communicator is seen to possess after the interpersonal interaction is completed. This terminal credibility is a product of the interaction of initial and derived credibility. Based on the initial credibility and the derived credibility a terminal credibility image is formed. At times this is higher than the initial credibility, and at times it is lower. But it is always a product of the interaction of the before or initial and the during or derived credibility. After the job interview, after the teacher and students finish the last discussion of the course, after the lovers kiss goodnight, there is some terminal credibility picture that is formed in the mind of each person about the other person.

DIMENSIONS OF CREDIBILITY

Lovers, entertainers, educators, salespersons, and in fact everyone who wishes to influence attitudes, opinions, beliefs, and behaviors is concerned with the components or dimensions of credibility. They are concerned with what goes into making a person appear believable or credible. Although various writers put their emphases in different places, most agree with McCroskey who defines five major dimensions: *competence, character, intention, personality,* and *dynamism.*

Competence

The more intelligent and knowledgeable a person is thought to be, the more that person will be perceived as credible, the more likely it is that he or she will be believed. The teacher, for example, is believed to the extent that he or she is thought knowledgeable about the subject. Similarly, the textbook writer is thought credible to the extent that he or she is thought competent.

Competence is logically subject-specific. A person may be competent in one subject and totally incompetent in another subject. However, people often do not make the distinction between areas of competence. Thus a person who is thought competent in politics will often be thought competent in general and will thus be perceived as credible when talking on health or physical education.

Character

We will perceive someone as credible if we perceive that person as having what Aristotle referred to as a high moral character. Here we would be concerned with the individual's honesty and basic nature. We would want to know if we could trust that person. A person who can be trusted is apt to be believed; a person who cannot be trusted is apt not to be believed.

Intention

An individual's motives or intentions are particularly important in determining credibility. The salesperson who says all the right things about a product is often doubted because his or her intentions are perceived as selfish; credibility is therefore low. The salesperson is less believable than a consumer advocate who evaluates a product with no motives of personal gain. Of course it is extremely difficult to judge when individuals are concerned with our good or with theirs. But when we can make the distinction, it greatly influences our perception of credibility.

Personality

Generally, we perceive as credible or believable people we like rather than people we do not like. And, it seems, we like people who have what we commonly refer to as a "pleasing personality." We believe people who are friendly and pleasant rather than people who are unfriendly and unpleasant. Positive and forward-looking people are seen as more credible than negative and backward-looking people. Perhaps we reason that they have gotten themselves together and so are in a better position to know what is right and what is wrong. We would be leery of accepting marital advice from an unhappily married couple, perhaps for a similar reason. If they cannot solve their own problems, we reasonably doubt their ability to help us.

Dynamism

The shy, introverted, soft-spoken individual is generally perceived as less credible than the aggressive, extroverted, and forceful individual. The great leaders in history have generally been dynamic people. They were aggressive and empathic. Of course, we may still have the stereotype of the shy, withdrawn college professor who, though not very dynamic, is nevertheless credible. Generally, however, the more dynamic, the more credible the person is perceived to be. Perhaps it is because we feel that the dynamic person is open and honest in presenting himself or herself whereas the shy, introverted individual may be seen as hiding something.

In short, the person who is seen as competent, of good character, of legitimate intention, of pleasant personality and dynamic, will be perceived as credible. That person's credibility will decrease as any one of these five qualities decreases; his or her credibility will increase as any one of these five qualities increases.

VARIATIONS IN CREDIBILITY PERCEPTION

The answers about credibility are somewhat more complex when we attempt to examine the relative importance of these qualities. One of the reasons for the complexity is that the perception of credibility varies with the individual doing the evaluating and with the subject matter. To some people the most credible person is the most competent person, and issues such as personality and dynamism are relatively unimportant. To other people, a good character is the most important attribute; a person is thought credible if he or she is thought to be of good character. Similarly, the perception of credibility depends on the subject under consideration. When evaluating surgeons or physicians we would probably be most concerned with their competence. If they are perceived as competent they will be thought credible and believed. It would be an added bonus if they were of high character, pleasant, forceful, and so on but these would clearly be of minor importance. In thinking about a husband or wife, character may be more important than competence and personality more important than dynamism.

There are also differences among people in evaluating each of the five qualities. For example, one individual may be perceived by some people as pleasant but by others as unpleasant. Some teachers are perceived as friendly by some students and as unfriendly by others. Similarly, some people may like aggressiveness, whereas others may dislike it. A minister may be perceived as highly credible by his congregation but as not credible by atheists or agnostics, for example. A colleague of mine sees fortune tellers and astrologers as highly credible whereas many others find these people to be of low credibility.

We might all agree that a person with a Ph.D. in nuclear physics from Harvard knows something about nuclear physics and is therefore credible in this area. Similarly, we might agree that the average high school freshman does not know much about nuclear physics and is therefore not credible. With these extremes there is seldom any difficulty in securing agreement as to the degree of credibility to be attributed. But in the middle there are many difficulties. Consequently, we cannot point to an individual and say that that person is credible and that this other one is not credible. Credibility is not intrinsic; it is in our perceptions. My friend sees Madame Xenovia, the fortune teller, as highly credible. Madame Xenovia herself is neither credible nor not credible. Whatever credibility she has is in the perceptions of others.

A NOTE ON INTRAPERSONAL CREDIBILITY

As viewed in this unit, and by most other writers, credibility is considered an interpersonal communication component; that is, credibility is seen as being perceived by one person about another person. But there is also an *intra*personal credibility which should be explored. We all have images of ourselves. We all see ourselves as being competent or incompetent to some degree. We all see ourselves as having particular character traits. This view of ourselves leads us to react in certain ways and not in others, much as our view of others leads us to react in particular ways.

For example, consider the student who in taking an examination puts down one answer, sees that another student has put down a different answer, and changes his or her answer to conform with that of the other student. The students who change their answers are, in doing so, saying something about their perception of their own credibility, as well as about the credibility of the other students. The relative faith we have in our own decisions is largely a matter of the degree of credibility we perceive ourselves to have. People who view themselves as being of low credibility (and we all know such people) will constantly seek the advice of others who are of higher credibility before making any move at all.

The way in which we react to others, based on our perception of their credibility, seems very similar to the way in which we react to ourselves, based on our perception of our own credibility. We see ourselves much as we see other people. We evaluate their competence, character, and so on and we evaluate our own competence, character, and so on. On the basis of this credibility rating we believe or disbelieve others and believe or disbelieve ourselves. For example, given a task to accomplish, based on our credibility, we may believe or disbelieve that we could accomplish it.

It should be apparent that the degree to which we appear credible to others is greatly dependent upon the degree to which we appear credible to ourselves. People who do not believe in themselves are rarely going to find others who believe in them. If we think ourselves incompetent we can be fairly certain that others will agree with us. The comforting aspect of this is that it also works in reverse.

Sources

A summary of the experimental research on credibility through the 1960s is provided in Kenneth Andersen and Theodore Clevenger Jr., "A Summary of Experimental Research in Ethos," *Speech Monographs* 30 (1963):59–78. More up-to-date treatments may be found in Kenneth Andersen, *Persuasion: Theory and Practice* (Boston: Allyn and Bacon, 1971), James C. McCroskey, *An Introduction to Rhetorical Communication*, 2d ed. (Englewood Cliffs, N.J.: Prentice-Hall, 1972), and Stephen W. King, *Communication and Social Influence* (Reading, Mass.: Addison-Wesley, 1975).

A study which presents somewhat different dimensions of credibility is Christopher J. S. Tuppen, "Dimensions of Credibility: An Oblique Solution," *Speech Monographs* 41 (1974) An interesting study pertinent to this class is James C. McCroskey, William E. Holdridge, and J. Keven Toomb, "An Instrument for Measuring the Source Credibility of Basic Speech Communication Instructors," *Speech Teacher* 23 (1974).

Experiential Vehicles

INTERPERSONAL CREDIBILITY

Below are a series of semantic differential scales designed to measure credibility. These particular scales, designed by Berlo, Lemert, and Mertz, measure three dimensions or aspects of credibility, namely trustworthiness, expertness, and personal dynamism.

Instructions

1. On Form A rate yourself as you feel you really are. (If necessary, reread the instructions in Unit 7 for completing the scales.)
2. On Form B rate yourself as you feel others see you.
3. On Form C have someone who knows you fairly well rate you.

FORM A

kind	____:____:____:____:____:____	cruel
friendly	____:____:____:____:____:____	unfriendly
honest	____:____:____:____:____:____	dishonest
experienced	____:____:____:____:____:____	inexperienced
informed	____:____:____:____:____:____	uninformed
skilled	____:____:____:____:____:____	unskilled
aggressive	____:____:____:____:____:____	meek
emphatic	____:____:____:____:____:____	hesitant
bold	____:____:____:____:____:____	timid
active	____:____:____:____:____:____	passive

FORM B

kind	____:____:____:____:____:____:____	cruel
friendly	____:____:____:____:____:____:____	unfriendly
honest	____:____:____:____:____:____:____	dishonest
experienced	____:____:____:____:____:____:____	inexperienced
informed	____:____:____:____:____:____:____	uninformed
skilled	____:____:____:____:____:____:____	unskilled
aggressive	____:____:____:____:____:____:____	meek
emphatic	____:____:____:____:____:____:____	hesitant
bold	____:____:____:____:____:____:____	timid
active	____:____:____:____:____:____:____	passive

FORM C

kind	____:____:____:____:____:____:____	cruel
friendly	____:____:____:____:____:____:____	unfriendly
honest	____:____:____:____:____:____:____	dishonest
experienced	____:____:____:____:____:____:____	inexperienced
informed	____:____:____:____:____:____:____	uninformed
skilled	____:____:____:____:____:____:____	unskilled
aggressive	____:____:____:____:____:____:____	meek
emphatic	____:____:____:____:____:____:____	hesitant
bold	____:____:____:____:____:____:____	timid
active	____:____:____:____:____:____:____	passive

Credibility Analysis

Scoring

1. Number all scale positions 1 to 7, from left to right, for example,

            1   2   3   4   5   6   7

trustworthy ____:____:____:____:____:____:____ untrustworthy

2. Determine your scores and enter them on the Credibility Analysis Form.
3. Total the scores for each of the three forms. Enter these totals at the bottom of the analysis form.
4. Enter the average for each scale in the appropriate place, that is, the average for kind-cruel, for friendly-unfriendly, and so forth.

Credibility Analysis Form

Scale	Form A	Form B	Form C	Average
Kind-cruel				
Friendly-unfriendly				
Honest-dishonest				
Experienced-inexperienced				
Informed-uninformed				
Skilled-unskilled				
Aggressive-meak				
Emphatic-hesitant				
Bold-timid				
Active-passive				
Total				

Discussion

In dyads or small groups consider the following:
1. What does a low score on a form mean? A high score? An average score?
2. On which form is your score highest? Does this come as a surprise? Explain.
3. What do these scores tell you about the way you see yourself? About the way you think others see you? About the way others see you?
4. What do low difference scores among Forms A, B, and C mean? High difference scores?

5. What do you think accounts for the differences between the first two sets of scales (between Form A and B)? (Try to think in terms of overt behaviors.)
6. What do you think accounts for the differences between Forms B and C? (Try to think in terms of overt behaviors.)
7. For which scales were there the largest differences? How might you account for this?
8. Do you think the ratings on Form C are typical of the ratings you would get from other people? Explain.

COMMUNICATOR CREDIBILITY

Each of the following excerpts are examples of attempts by communicators to establish their credibility. Examine each with special reference to the dimensions of credibility discussed in this unit and record, in the space following each excerpt, the specific means used by each of the speakers to establish their credibility. The time span of some two thousand years illustrates, I think, that the techniques for establishing credibility have not changed very much.

1. I shall not think much of my pains in this cause, as I engaged in it from principle. I was solicited to argue this cause as advocate general; and because I would not, I have been charged with desertion from my office. To this charge I can give a very sufficient answer. I renounced that office, and I argue this cause, from the same principle; and I argue it with the greater pleasure, as it is in favor of British liberty, at a time when we hear the greatest monarch upon earth declaring from his throne that he glories in the name of Briton, and that the privileges of his people are dearer to him than the most valuable prerogatives of his crown; and as it is in opposition to a kind of power, the exercise of which, in former periods of English history, cost one King of England his head, and another his throne.

   I have taken more pains in this cause than I ever will take again, although my engaging in this and another popular cause has raised much resentment. But I think I can sincerely declare that I cheerfully submit myself to every odious name for conscience sake; and from my soul I despise all those whose guilt, malice, or folly has made them my foes.

   Let the consequences be what they will, I am determined to proceed. The only principles of public conduct, that are worthy of a gentleman, or a man, are to sacrifice estate, ease, health, and applause, and even life, to the sacred calls of his country. These manly sentiments, in private life, make the good citizen; in public life, the patriot and the hero. I do not say, that when brought to the test, I shall be invincible. I pray God I may never be brought to the melancholy trial; but if ever I should, it will be then known how far I can reduce to practice principles which I know to be founded in truth. In the meantime I will proceed to the subject of this writ.
   —James Otis, Speech against the Writs of Assistance

2. For my own part, I consider it as nothing less than a question of freedom or slavery; and in proportion to the magnitude of the subject ought to be the freedom of the debate. It is only in this way that we can hope to arrive at truth, and fulfill the great responsibility which we hold to God and our country. Should I keep back my opinions at such a time, through fear of giving offense, I should consider myself as guilty of treason towards my country, and of an act of disloyalty toward the Majesty of Heaven, which I revere above all earthly kings.
   —Patrick Henry

3. I am certain that my fellow Americans expect that on my induction into the Presidency I will address them with a candor and a decision which the present situation of our Nation impels. This is preeminently the time to speak the truth, the whole truth, frankly and boldly. Nor need we shrink from honestly facing conditions in our country today. This great Nation will endure as it has endured, will revive and will prosper. So, first of all, let me assert my firm belief that the only thing we have to fear is fear itself—nameless, unreasoning, unjustified terror which paralyzes needed efforts to convert retreat into advance. In every dark hour of our national life a leadership of frankness and vigor has met with that understanding and support of the people themselves which is essential to victory. I am convinced that you will again give that support to leadership in these critical days.
   —Franklin Delano Roosevelt, First Inaugural Address

4. I continue to offer counsel, by which I sink below others in your regard; but you, if you followed it, would be exalted. . . . I consider it not the part of an honest citizen, to devise measures by which I shall speedily become the first among you, and you the last among nations; with the measures of good citizens the advancement of their country should keep pace: their counsel should still be the salutary, rather than the agreeable; to the latter will nature

herself incline; to the former a good citizen must direct by argument and instruction.

—Demosthenes, On the Chersonese

5. Mr. Chairman and Gentlemen of the Convention: I would be presumptuous, indeed, to present myself against the distinguished gentlemen to whom you have listened if this were a mere measuring of abilities; but this is not a contest between persons. The humblest citizen in all the land, when clad in the armor of a righteous cause, is stronger than all the hosts of error. I come to speak to you in defense of a cause as holy as the cause of liberty—the cause of humanity.

—William Jennings Bryan, The Cross of Gold Speech

6. Those of us—and they are most of us—who are more Americans than we are Democrats or Republicans, count some things more important than the winning or losing of elections.

There is a peace still to be won, an economy which needs some attention, some freedoms to be secured, an atom to be controlled—all through the delicate, sensitive and indispensable processes of democracy—processes which demand, at the least, that people's vision be clear, that they be told the truth, and that they respect one another.

—Adlai Stevenson, Address to the Southeastern Democratic Conference

7. It is known to Senators who have served with me here, that I have for many years advocated, as an essential attribute of State sovereignty, the right of a State to secede from the Union. Therefore, if I had not believed there was justifiable cause; if I had thought that Mississippi was acting without sufficient provocation, or without an existing necessity, I should still, under my theory of the government, because of my allegiance to the State of which I am a citizen, have been bound by her action. I, however, may be permitted to say

that I do think that she has justifiable cause, and I approve of her act. I conferred with her people before that act was taken, counselled them then that if the state of things which they apprehended should exist when the convention met, they should take the action which they have now adopted.

—Jefferson Davis, On withdrawal from the Union, Secessionist Opinion

8. Mr. Commander Bertinatti: I am free to confess that the United States have in the course of the last three years encountered vicissitudes and been involved in controversies which have tried the friendship and even the forbearance of other nations, but at no stage in this unhappy fraternal war in which we are only endeavoring to save and strengthen the foundations of our national unity has the king or the people of Italy faltered in addressing to us the language of respect, confidence, and friendship. We have tried you, Mr. Bertinatti, as a charge d'affaires and as a minister resident, and in both of these characters we have found you always sincerely and earnestly interpreting the loyal sentiments of your sovereign. At the same time I am sure that no minister here has more faithfully maintained and advanced the interests with which he was charged by his government. I desire that your countrymen may know that I think you have well deserved the elevation to which I owe the pleasure of the present interview.

—Abraham Lincoln, On amity with Italy

9. The unmistakable outbreaks of zeal which occur all around me show that you are earnest men—and such a man am I. Let us, therefore, at least for a time, pass all secondary and collateral questions, whether of a personal or of a general nature, and consider the main subject of the present canvass. The Democratic party, or, to speak more accurately, the party which wears that attractive name—is in possession of the federal government. The Republicans propose to dislodge that party, and dismiss it from its high trust.

The main subject, then, is whether the Democratic party deserves to retain the confidence of the American people. In attempting to prove it unworthy, I think that I am not actuated by prejudices against that party, or by prepossessions in favor of its adversary; for I have learned, by some experience, that virtue and patriotism, vice and selfishness, are found in all parties, and that they differ less in their motives than in the policies they pursue.

—William Henry Seward, On the Irrepressible Conflict

10. Mr. Toastmaster, President LaRoche, members of the Football Hall of Fame, gentlemen of the gridiron: No honor I have ever received moved me as deeply as this one.

    Perhaps this is because no honor I have ever received is less deserved by me.

    Many among you undoubtedly more fully merit this award, but none among you could possibly more fully appreciate it.

    I can accept it only as symbolic of those unnamed thousands who through the years have loyally supported this great national sport.

    Unhappily, President LaRouche, I possess neither that eloquence of diction, that poetry of imagination, nor that brilliance of metaphor, to say adequately what I feel. I can only express my gratitude, sir, in a very simple, but very heartfelt—Thank You.
    —Douglas MacArthur, On accepting the National Football Foundation's Gold Medal Award

QUINTILIAN COLLEGE

The purpose of this exercise is to explore the perception of credibility of others on the basis of their background and previous experiences.

Each student should read the directions and profiles and then rank the candidates in order of merit, using 1 for the first choice, 2 for the second choice, and so on. After these rankings are completed, groups of five or six students should be formed. The task of each group is to agree on a group ranking of the candidates, again using 1 for the group's first choice, 2 for the group's second choice, and so on.

After these rankings are completed, the groups should share their rankings with each other. Attention should be directed to at least the following:

1. the reasons for the rankings
2. the dimensions of credibility each group perceived in each candidate
3. the variations in the perception of credibility and the reasons for these (the variations among the individual students and the variations among the several groups)

The College and the Job

Quintilian College is a private midwestern coeducational institution with a student body of approximately 15,000. It is a four-year liberal arts college that wishes to be known for its progressiveness and responsiveness to the needs of the surrounding communities.

For the most part the students come from the surrounding towns and cities, although some come from other states and even from other countries. The student body is approximately 70 percent white, 20 percent black, and 10 percent Spanish and Mexican. Most of these students are from middle-class families. The tuition is approximately $1500 per semester.

Quintilian has been undergoing a number of problems, the major one being financial. The school has an annual deficit of over $1 million. Because of these financial problems it has cut back on a number of its academic programs and is now in danger of losing accreditation. The college is not, however, in serious danger of bankruptcy since it does own large areas of land. It has been reluctant to sell this land for the needed funds because the value of the land is increasing at approximately 20 percent per year.

The current president is retiring at the end of this year. A committee has been appointed to search for a new president and has submitted the names of the following candidates along with some information they think might be pertinent to the final selection. All candidates have indicated an eagerness to serve as President.

Profiles of the Candidates

HENRY BENSON, white, male, forty-five years old, married with two children, both college students. Currently, Professor of Classics. Author of numerous articles and books on Greek and Latin and currently working on a monograph on the phonological structure of irregular verbs of early Latin. Benson is a Danish citizen but has indicated that he would become a citizen of the United States if offered the presidency.

MARTHA WALLACE, white, female, forty-three years old, single. Currently, Professor of Economics. President of state chapter of Women's Liberation and author of articles and books on economics and women's liberation. Adviser to and a charter member of local group, Lesbian Liberation, and frequent speaker at gay liberation meetings.

JOHN RUSSELL, black, male, thirty-five years old, married, no children. Currently, Professor of Biological Sciences. Author of several monographs on the biological bases of language and cognitive processes. Academic adviser to several conservative black organizations.

ANDREW WILCOX, white, male, forty-six years old, single. Currently, vice-president of a large electronics corporation and former Professor of Linguistics.

Author of numerous articles and books on computer languages and computational linguistics. An avowed supporter of black militancy and a frequent contributor to militant/radical papers and magazines.

MICHEL ANGUS, white, female, forty years old, divorced three times and now married with no children. Recently retired from a large investment firm which she founded and where she served as president. Received a B.B.A. degree from a correspondence school some ten years ago. She has been extremely success-ful in business (largely through her own investments) and is now a multimillionaire.

MARTIN TORES, white, male, sixty years old, Catholic priest. Currently, president of St. Thomas University and former Professor of Philosophy. Author of several widely used philosophy texts and editor of a leading philosophy journal. A leading spokesman for the Spanish and Mexican-American cause. He has been jailed twice for his involvement in demonstrations against discrimination in employment and housing and school segregation.

unit 12
Communication Practices

Censorship
Ghostwriting
Data Bank Record Keeping
Academic Freedom
    Communication Practices: Questions of Ethics

Objectives

Upon completion of this unit, you should be able to:

1. state some of the arguments relating to censorship, ghostwriting, databank record keeping, and academic freedom
2. make predictions as to the state of censorship, ghostwriting, databank record keeping, and academic freedom in the next fifty or sixty years
3. take a tentative stand on issues relating to censorship, ghostwriting, databank record keeping, and academic freedom

Censorship, ghostwriting, academic freedom, and databank record keeping are practices which at times we take for granted as being integral parts of our society. At other times, we question and debate their merits, wondering if they do not lead to more problems than the ones they were instituted to solve.

Here we consider four common communication practices. The purpose here is not to convince anyone of a particular point of view in regard to these issues, but rather to raise the questions and leave you to find your own answers. As a result of considering these four issues, their ramifications and implications, we should be in a better position to analyze related issues that raise similar questions.

CENSORSHIP

Recently the Supreme Court ruled in favor of a most rigid censorship law. Essentially, this law holds that the individual communities and local governments have the right to determine when an article, book, film, play, or other public communication appeals to "prurient interests" and should therefore be censored.

This decision has raised a number of important issues relative to free speech and more generally, to the human right to information. Shortly after the decision was made, numerous movies were banned by local communities—not only the X-rated films, such as *Deep Throat* or *The Devil in Miss Jones*, but also films such as *Carnal Knowledge* and *Paper Moon*. The reasons given for banning such movies have generally centered on the claim that these films offend community standards of morality.

Some people would agree that the community as a whole should have the right to determine what comes into the community, specifically what movies are shown in the local theatres, what programs appear on television, and what books are made available at the local libraries or assigned in schools. Still more people would agree to grant these rights to the community if that community was unanimous in its decisions. If every citizen in the community did not wish to have a picture shown in the local movie house then a strong argument could be made for it not being shown, that is, for it being banned. But what about decisions made by fewer than all of the people? Clearly these would include all the decisions or at least 99 percent of the decisions normally made on such issues. We might extend the argument and ask what if only one person wanted to read a particular book? Should the library make the book available? What if 10 percent of the people wanted to read it? Twenty percent? Forty-nine percent?

One of the many paradoxes that censorship laws have created concerns "the public will." It is argued that the local community should set the standards for what is pornographic and what is not pornographic and that the local community has the right to censor that which it considers pornographic. Given this situation we are compelled to wonder how theatres that show films considered to be pornographic by the "community"—and therefore subject to censorship—can manage to make a profit. Any theatre owner interested in making a profit would be a fool to schedule films that the members of the community are not going to see. But, of course, the theatre owner does make a profit; members of the community clearly do want to see such films. Yet throughout the country films are being ruled pornographic and banned on the basis of the argument that the community does not want to see them.

It is relatively easy to go back into history and find numerous works of literature which were at one time banned as pornographic. Where once people could not read *Lady Chatterly's Lover,* today many students are required to read it as part of some college course in English. Should we wonder if *Deep Throat* will become required viewing in film courses ten or twenty years from now? Will the writings of Linda Lovelace or Xaveria Hollander become required reading in sex education courses? Such a situation probably seems absurd. But then so did the idea that the works of D. H. Lawrence might one day be required reading seem absurd not so many years ago.

We must recognize that morality and definitions of pornography are time bound as well as culture bound (at least according to most systems of ethics). What is considered pornographic in one culture and at one time may not be considered pornographic in another culture or at another time. However, the changing definitions that we have witnessed over time do not seem to be governed by any logic; they appear totally unpredictable.

Still another issue in regard to pornography and its regulation is that it is taken as an axiom that it is the obligation of those who would attempt to depict sexual activities to prove that such depictions are worthy of redeeming social significance. Underlying this notion seems to be the assumption that somehow sex is evil and is therefore to be hidden from public view. Most persons do not object to depictions of theft, murder, and war, and yet they do object to depictions of sexual activity.

It somehow seems to be assumed, though the line of reasoning seems a bit tenuous, that sexually oriented communications have undersirable effects on the persons viewing them. Although there seems little evidence to support this, it is nevertheless an empirical question and one which should be answered by evidence. Yet it is paradoxical that in the absence of such evidence the filmmaker, photographer, and writer must prove their innocence—contrary to the normal system where innocence is assumed and guilt must be proven.

Another assumption underlying these provisions seems to be that the effects of such communications can be predicted with a fair degree of accuracy. But this hardly seems the case. When *West Side Story* was shown on television some years ago, it apparently helped to reactivate gangs and gang wars in New York City and perhaps elsewhere as well. Should *West Side Story* have been banned?

There are other issues—which get at the interpersonal dimension more directly—that we need to consider under the heading of censorship. As citizens we all have the right to make our voices heard. The Constitution grants us that right. Each of us has the right (some would say the obligation) to voice our opinions and our beliefs when they do not endanger the lives or safety of others. Clearly we do not have the right to ruin someone's reputation with lies or yell "fire" in a theatre since this might endanger the lives of others. Yet, we do have the right to speak out for or against a particular way of life or political philosophy or economic policy. But as average citizens how can we do this? To speak and to have our voices heard today is an extremely expensive undertaking. The communications systems throughout the country and the world are too expensive for us to engage for even a single minute. If we wished, for example, to advertise in favor of one of our political views or in support of something we wish to defend, rather like the large corporations do, and we chose to run this ad in *Playboy* it would cost us at least a few years' salary. It is interesting (yet frightening), for example, to reflect on the fact that Bell Telephone can use our money to advertise to millions of people how hard they are working to bring us the best service at the least possible cost but we, who use the phones everyday, cannot advertise to tell these same people of the difficulties we encounter in dealing with them. Of course, this problem is not limited to Bell Telephone, nor was it created by them. Could we purchase one minute of the "Tonight Show" to air our views? Clearly we could not, and yet this is exactly what we would have to do if we were to have an effective voice in influencing public opinion. The days of individuals in their basements with an old printing press, cranking out handbills to distribute in front of the local church, are gone foreever. Such a procedure today would be ludicrous and ineffective.

Are we not effectively censored from communicating our views because we are not millionaires and only have access to interpersonal communication channels? Although there have been some efforts made to require television stations to allot a certain amount of time to the presentation of opposing views, it seems clear that the size of one's voice and hence influence are largely determined by the size of one's bank account.

This problem of expense has been discussed perhaps most often in connection with political campaigning. Without a substantial financial backing it seems impossible to get elected to any high public office. A potential candidate without any money would not be able to advertise, would not be able to buy air time, would not be able to travel to deliver speeches, would not be able to have posters printed and circulated, and so on. And so (if one is at all serious about running for political office) one must obtain this financial backing. And we are well aware that one does not obtain substantial financial backing without giving something in return. And this "something in return" is often given at the expense of the very people who will eventually elect this candidate.

At the same time that we may see dangers in censorship it seems equally clear that some restrictions may be helpful and useful. Most would probably agree that people with access to military information should not be allowed to reveal certain facts which might prove damaging to national security. We might also agree that restrictions on the basis of age might be legitimate. Perhaps certain information, on subjects such as alcohol and cigarettes, should be restricted to "adults," however we might define that term. And so while we might agree that certain lines may be useful to draw, we seem far from agreeing on exactly where the lines should be.

GHOSTWRITING

One of the perennial topics raised in any discussion of communication is that of ghostwriting. Ghostwriting, broadly conceived, refers to the practice of employing professional writers to prepare one's speeches or articles and then presenting them as if they were one's own.

The most familiar example of this practice is among politicians who invariably employ a staff of writers to prepare their speeches. But the practice is much more widespread and certainly is not limited to politics and politicians. Broadly viewed, ghostwriting would include, for example, 1) the student who turns in a term paper or delivers a speech obtained from the fraternity file, from *Reader's Digest,* or from some agency that specializes in preparing such compositions for college students; 2) the student who pays to have his thesis or dissertation written by a professional writer; 3) the college teacher who "demands" or "accepts" coauthorship for an article or book actually written and researched by a graduate student; 4) the news reporter who reads the news copy prepared by another individual; and, of course 5) the politician who presents a speech written by his speech staff.

Clearly there are differences among these several examples of ghostwriting; yet each of them raises significant questions.

We might sympathize with the politician on any number of bases. There is not enough time for the politician to prepare all the speeches, especially when campaigning throughout the country The speeches, if they are to be at all effective, must be individualized for perhaps hundreds of different audiences and must resemble interpersonal communications as much as possible. No one person could possibly have the time necessary for such a monumental undertaking. Certainly the President does not have the time to prepare relatively polished speeches to present over television or at various conferences and conventions. We might further argue that since everyone knows that the politicians are not writing their own speeches, no one is really deceived by the practice. Should one politician attempt to write his or her own speeches, such speeches would surely not be as effective as those of the opponent. Thus by not employing such writers one is, in effect, practically giving up all chances for election.

We might also note that numerous politicians—Franklin D. Roosevelt and Adlai Stevenson are perhaps the clearest examples—guide the speech-writing process of their ghostwriters very carefully. On this basis we might argue, as many have done, that these were really their speeches and not those of their staff.

These are at least some of the familiar arguments used to show that ghostwriting—at least among politicians—should be accepted. But are we or should we be willing to accept this practice? Does practical necessity make a practice acceptable?

When we are attempting to make up our minds regarding the qualifications of several opposing political candidates, is it fair that none of the candidates is actually delivering campaign speeches which he or she has written? Is it fair that politicians would have us listen to a humorous and enlightening speech on, for example, educational reform, when they in fact know nothing about educational reform and are themselves totally humorless? Does the fact that a practice is universal mean we should accept it? Does the fact that everyone is doing it make it right and justified?

Consider the case of the student handing in a term paper or delivering a speech as his or her own when in fact it was obtained from someone else—perhaps a friend, a magazine, or a professional agency. If the student gets caught there is little that can save the student from failing the course or at least the assignment. Most instructors would state without reservation that the student's behavior is unethical.

Yet consider the case of the college instructor who is pressured to publish scholarly articles. A bright graduate student comes along and produces a term paper worthy of publication. This much the instructor knows. So a few suggestions for improvement are made along with some stylistic suggestions, and the instructor offers to have it published with the student as co-author. The assumption when two names appear on an article or a book is that both persons shared in producing the work, but it seems that this instructor did little—certainly not half. And yet the professor's name appears on the article as co-author. If this instructor gets enough good graduate students he or she may become widely known on the basis of a number of articles with which he or she actually had little to do. Students may even enroll in this instructor's classes or attend the school at which the instructor is teaching because of this reputation. Yet, in fact, this instructor may know very little and may not have had anything significant to do with the publications responsible for this wide reputation. (This situation, I should add, is actually not at all exaggerated. There are many instructors in all disciplines who make this type of thing a common practice.)

We might argue that the instructor has provided the stimulation necessary for this kind of work and that the value of this stimulation is surely half the work. Further, the student would not have known enough about procedures to get the article published alone. Also, the instructor did make some changes in the paper and who can say that these changes were not the very thing that led to the paper's acceptance for publication? Are these arguments sufficient to justify this widespread practice?

Take the case in which the graduate student, pleased with the guidance received from the instructor, asks the instructor to co-author the paper. Is the instructor justified in accepting this? Has the instructor a right to pose to the academic world as an expert on a topic he or she may know very little about? And again, is the widespread nature of this practice sufficient to justify it, to make it acceptable? Like the busy politician who must prepare and present several speeches a week, the college instructor must publish—otherwise the instructor does not get promoted and is not granted tenure. But is need enough to justify practice?

This system is similar to that of news reporters who do not prepare their own news reports. A staff of reporters assemble the facts, professional writers write up the copy, and "news reporters" simply present it to the public. Their qualifications may be nothing more than a pleasant voice and a handsome face. Surely we would rather look at a handsome face than an ugly one and would want to hear a pleasant voice rather than a harsh and rasping one. Who would turn on the news to listen to an unpleasant individual? The ratings would drop to near zero and advertisers would cancel. And so the practice is justified for purely economic reasons. The problem with this is that, like instructors who gain reputations for being experts in fields they know nothing about, these attractive people with pleasant voices get reputations for being authorities on world events when in fact they may know nothing and care less about the politics of the world.

Because these several practices are so widespread there is an increasing need not for passive acceptance but for active and thorough evaluation. We need to ask if we are doing ourselves an injustice and if we are actually fostering deception by accepting such practices.

DATA BANK RECORD KEEPING

That information is power is something we all know or at least should know. It is something governments and business organizations have long known. The more information one has about an individual the greater are one's chances for controlling that individual. It is perhaps with this concept in mind that there is today large-scale record keeping maintained by governments and big business. Information on one's credit ratings, criminal records, hospital admissions, education, political activities, and the like are conveniently stored so that interested parties may obtain information on significant personalities within hours.

No one seems to know exactly how many person's records are maintained or exactly what these records contain. But we do know that the practice of storing information on perhaps millions of people is increasing rapidly.

As a society becomes increasingly complex and as the number of its citizens increases it becomes essential that accurate and thorough information on various individuals be readily available. If a person applies for government service it may be necessary that the person's history be reviewed before relevant employment decisions are made. Similarly, it seems that a bank or credit company offering a loan has a right to know something about the credit risk of an individual.

Yet there are many questions that are not so easy to put aside. We would want to know just how much information should be permitted to be stored. Is all possible information legitimate to include? If the issue is credit from a bank, for example, an individual's sexual or political experiences seem immaterial: Should a bank be able to refuse a loan on the basis of one's sexual or political experiences?

In most instances people are not even aware that information on them has been completed and stored in these databanks. If government or business starts a file on you, should you not have the right to know that it exists and what it contains? What if incorrect or false information was somehow put into this file? If you do not have the right to see it then how can you possibly correct it? And, do you not have the right to face your accusers? Do you not have the right to be assumed innocent until proven guilty? With the widespread use of databanks, apparently these rights are being bent if not completely twisted.

There are a number of large organizations which have as their sole business the investigation of individuals and the compilation of these personal records. These records are then sold to some other organization which is, say, planning to hire someone for a job. What methods and what means these organizations use to obtain this information is not easily discovered. And yet they apparently do a thorough job since they are still in business and apparently doing a fairly lucrative business at that.

The central issue raised by this practice is that of the right of privacy. The Fourth Amendment to the Constitution states: "The right of the people to be secure in their persons, houses, papers, and effects, against unreasonable searches and seizures, shall not be violated." Does the practice of maintaining files of personal records without the knowledge of the individual constitute "unreasonable search" and violate this guarantee provided by the Constitution?

Further, what about the concept of change and rehabilitation? If a person was committed to a mental hospital some ten years ago, for example, should this information be relevant now? Does the individual have the right to keep this information private? In the popular mind this kind of stigma is something that remains with an individual throughout life. And yet is it fair to institutionalize this kind of prejudice by having it punched out on computer cards? Should an individual be barred from employment as a teacher or government employee, for example, because he or she was in a mental institution? Should a person be prevented from seeking a position in government service if time was served in prison? Currently, individuals are so prevented if the crime was a felony. But the relevant question is whether they should be.

Again, these are not easy questions to answer. But it is important to raise the questions. The practice is clearly expanding, ultimately to the point where there would be a personal file detailing every individual's activities, interests, preferences, experiences, and so on. But do we want this to happen? Are we willing to accept passively this kind of procedure? Or do we see this kind of practice as a positive good? Are the use of these databanks actually protections for business, government, and the average, innocent citizen?

ACADEMIC FREEDOM

Currently, college teachers enjoy considerable freedom of expression in this country and in many others as well. For the most part they may say what they want when they want and not have to worry about whether they are going to be called to answer for their actions. Periodically, however, instances occur in which a teacher is fired or given a hard time ostensibly for some breach of contract. But there is frequently the suspicion that such action was taken because of something the teacher said or some position that was advocated which may have been unpopular.

Ideally, one of the functions of the college classroom is to prepare students for complete, responsible citizenship. Students must be presented with as many points of view as possible, with the tools for critical analysis and evaluation, and with the freedom necessary to make their own decisions without fear of reprisal. To accomplish this end, it would seem that complete freedom of expression must be allowed. If limitations are imposed on what the teacher may say, we would run into problems in determining where these limits should be imposed and who is to impose them.

On the other hand, college classrooms consist of captive—or relatively captive—audiences. Students are attending classes largely because they want to obtain a college degree and thus be better prepared for the job market and ideally because they want to learn. Given this state of affairs should the college teacher have the right to take advantage of the situation? Does the mathematics professor have the right to use class time for political issues and specifically for the purpose of expressing and advocating his or her personal views?

There is another issue here that merits attention. We know from our own experience as well as from numerous research studies that the effects of credibility generalize very rapidly. Most persons—college students included—do not make distinctions in terms of areas of expertise. When a person is perceived as an expert in one field, this perceived expertise generalizes to other fields. So the perceived expertness of the mathematics professor will generalize in the minds of the listeners beyond mathematics to politics, sociology, economics, and so on. Because of this we may want to ask if it is fair for this mathematics professor to utilize this credibility (logically dependent solely on expertise in mathematics) to persuade college students in favor of a particular political or economic philosophy. If we say, as many have said, that college teachers should "stick to their subject" we run into additional problems. Any subject currently taught in college can be broadened to include political or social or economic issues. Lines of this nature are not easy to draw.

We would also want to ask if college teachers—regardless of subject matter—do not have an obligation to teach students what they feel is important and right. Would teachers not be abandoning responsibility if they never went outside the assigned textbook?

A certain level of audience sophistication must be assumed when it comes to issues of this nature. And yet, there are examples to indicate that this cannot always be assumed. Perhaps an example will suffice. Not so many years ago a teacher was attempting to illustrate the relationship between symbols and reality. The point this teacher was attempting to make was that symbols are not the things for which they stand. Symbols only have meaning when we give them meaning; they do not contain meaning in and of themselves. The color purple may be a symbol of mourning but there is nothing inherent in purple that gives it that meaning. *We* give it that meaning and we can just as well assign the concept of mourning to blue or green or orange. This was a simple enough point to make. But this teacher wanted the students to *feel* rather than to simply intellectualize the distinction between the world of reality and the world of symbols. And so, as an illustration, the American flag was placed on the floor and stepped on, making the point that this act said nothing about anyone's feelings about the country. The act was merely attempting to show that the flag (a symbol) has no inherent meaning; it was simply an agreed upon symbol of the country. Some students in the class did not see it that way and told their parents. A suit was promptly filed and the teacher fired. Although it was clearly stated that stepping on the flag was not a political act but a semantic one (an attempt to illustrate the arbitrary relationship between symbols and things) the teacher lost the job.

But the issue does not stop here. We might also ask whether the teacher should have had the right to step on the flag even if this act was politically motivated. That is, if the illustration was to serve a political rather than a semantic purpose should the teacher have been allowed to make it?

We are currently seeing a great deal of pressure being brought to bear on teachers of sex education. In many schools and in many courses sex education is now given at least some consideration. One of the major problems confronting the institution of sex education courses is defining the limits to be placed on the teacher. Most seem to agree that students should be taught the basic principles of human physiology and hygiene, although even here considerable debate has raged over the proper age at which to teach this material. But few persons seem to agree on other sex-related topics, for example, birth control, abortion, extramarital relations, and venereal diseases and their prevention.

The objection raised to complete teacher freedom is that these and many related topics have a moral dimension and that this is the parents' and not the teachers' responsibility. The issue is perhaps raised in its most provocative form in any discussion of the so-called sexual deviations. In most courses on sex education, the heterosexual role is presented as the one to be followed. But what about the bisexual role? What about the bisexual teacher and student? Should he or she not be allowed to teach that bisexuality and homosexuality are other options open to members of society?

We would probably not even consider the possibility of restricting history teachers from talking about the War of 1812 or the Spanish-American War or the Korean War. Nor would we consider restricting economics teachers from talking about inflation or devaluation or recession. But many do wish to restrict sex education teachers from teaching about certain aspects of sex.

The question at issue in all of these cases is simply the teacher's right to say what he or she wants. Should the teacher be allowed to express personal feelings or should he or she be restricted from teaching what is not included in the syllabus and what is not approved by some local school board?

Clearly the position of the teacher is such an important one that we would want to recognize that with this position comes certain responsibilities. But exactly what these responsibilities (*of* the teacher and *to* the teacher) should be, is not always clear.

These four practices or issues are clearly not the only ones that could have been selected for inclusion here. They are issues that should concern each one of us since the decisions made on these and related issues are surely going to have significant influence on us and on other individuals living in this society.

We should recognize that a decision made today should not necessarily bind us tomorrow. Decisions are means for enabling us to act, and they are not necessarily solutions to problems. Thus it is best to make whatever decisions we do make tentatively, subject to change as we gain new information and new insights.

Sources

On communication practices and ethics see, for example, Thomas R. Nilsen, *Ethics of Speech Communication*, 2d ed. (Indianapolis: Bobbs-Merrill, 1974). For ghostwriting, see especially Ernest G. Bormann, "Ethics of Ghostwritten Speeches," *Quarterly Journal of Speech* 47 (1961):262–267. The discussion in this unit owes much to this Bormann article. Franklyn S. Haiman's "Democratic Ethics and the Hidden Persuaders," *Quarterly Journal of Speech* 44 (1958):385–393 is particularly relevant to this unit. An interesting and relevant discussion of academic freedom is presented in David Rubin's *The Rights of Teachers* (New York: Avon, 1972).

Experiential Vehicle

COMMUNICATION PRACTICES: QUESTIONS OF ETHICS

This exercise and the one in the following unit are designed to raise only a few of the many questions that could be raised concerning the ethics of interpersonal communication and to encourage you to think in concrete terms about some of the relevant issues. The purpose is not to persuade you to a particular point of view but rather to encourage you to formulate your own point of view.

The exercises consist of a series of cases, each raising somewhat different ethical questions. These exercises will probably work best if you respond to each of the cases individually and then discuss your decisions and the implications in groups of five or six. In these small groups simply discuss those cases that you found most interesting. The most interesting cases for small group discussion will probably be those that were the most difficult for you to respond to, that is, those that involved the most internal conflict. A general discussion in which the various groups share their decisions and insights may conclude the session.

As an experience in self-disclosure and perception the group members may attempt to guess what each individual would do in each of these specific situations. Reasons for their choices or guesses would then be considered, for example, what led the group to guess that Person X would act one way rather than another way. Reasons for the accurate and/or inaccurate guesses might then be discussed.

Guidelines

1. Carefully read each of the following cases and write down your responses. By writing your decisions many issues that may be unclear will come to the surface and may then be used as a basis for discussion.
2. Your responses will not be made public, these papers not collected, and your decisions revealed only if you wish to reveal them. If individuals

wish not to reveal their decisions do not attempt to apply any social pressure to get them to make these decisions public.

3. Do not attempt to avoid the issues presented in the various cases by saying, for example, "I'd try other means." For purposes of these exercises other means are ruled out.

4. Focus some attention in the small group discussions on the origin of the various values implicit in your decisions. You might, as a starting point, consider how your parents would respond to these cases. Would their decisions be similar or different from yours? Do not settle for "conditioning" as an answer. If you wish to discuss the development of these values in terms of conditioning, focus on specific reinforcement contingencies, the rewards and punishments received which may have led to the development of these various values.

5. Devote some attention to the concept of change. Would you have responded in similar fashion five years ago? If not, what has led to the change? Would you predict similar responses five or ten years from now? Why? Why not?

    This concept of change is also significant in another respect. Focus attention on the changes or possible changes that might occur as a result of your acting in accordance with any of the decisions. That is, is the student who sells drugs the same individual he or she was before doing this? Can this student ever be the same individual again? How is the student different? If we accept the notion, even in part, that how we act or behave influences what we are, how does this relate to the decisions we make on these issues?

6. Consider the concept of acceptance. How willing is each group member to accept the decisions of others? Are you accepting of your own decisions? Why? Why not? Would you be pleased if your children would respond in the same way you did?

7. Note that there are two questions posed after each case: What *should* you do? and What *would* you do? The distinction between the two questions is crucial and is particularly significant when your answers for the two questions are different. When answers for the *should* and the *would* questions differ, try to analyze the intrapersonal dynamics. How do you account for the difference? Is there intrapersonal conflict? Are these differences the result of changes you are going through? How pleased/displeased are you with the differences in answers?

INTERPERSONAL GHOSTING

You are a capable and proficient writer and speaker and have, for the past three years, worked full time for a large political organization as a ghostwriter. During these three years you have prepared papers for publication and speeches to be delivered by the various officers of the organization. Throughout this time you have been firmly committed to the aims and methods of the organization. Consequently, no problem arose. You were serving your political party by making their appeals and policies more persuasive, in addition to earning an extremely high salary as ghostwriter. Recently, however, the party has decided to endorse a bill which you feel would not be in the public interest. On this issue your attitudes are diametrically opposed to those of the party. As ghostwriter for the organization you are asked to speak in favor of this bill. These informal talks are to be held throughout the state. You realize that if you do not comply you will lose your job. At the time, however, you wonder if you can ethically give persuasive force to a proposal which you feel should not be supported. Not being effective in these interpersonal encounters will not work since you would be fired after one such interaction.

1. What should you do?

2. What would you do?

SELLING DRUGS

While working your way through college you are offered a job selling narcotics to fellow students. You could really use the money, which is extremely good, and you know that if you do not do it someone else will. There are many students, among them some of your close friends, who are anxious to get this job. You will not have to influence people to buy these drugs, instead they will seek you out. There is no chance of getting caught so you have nothing to fear in that respect.

1. What should you do (if this involved only soft drugs)?

2. What should you do (if this involved both hard and soft drugs)?

3. What would you do (if this involved only soft drugs)?

4. What would you do (if this involved both hard and soft drugs)?

BUYING A PAPER

You are presently taking an elective course in anthropology. You need an "A" in this course in order to maintain the average you think you will need to get into graduate school. Although you have done the required work you are running only a "B—" at best. The instructor has told you that he will give you an "A" if you write an extra paper and get an "A" on it. You want to write this paper but are too pressed for time; you need to put what time you do have available into your major courses. You hear about one of these "paper mills" which, for approximately $50, will provide you with a paper which should get you an "A" in the course. You can easily afford the $50 fee.

1. What should you do?

2. What would you do?

COMMUNICATIONS BUREAU

You are in charge of your college's Communications Bureau which arranges for speakers of various persuasions to visit the campus and address students and faculty. The Communications Bureau selects and invites the speakers, pays them an honorarium ranging from $100 to $1500, and arranges a tour of the campus and a luncheon in honor of the speaker. Generally, the Communications Bureau attempts to invite speakers who represent as many different points of view as possible on the significant issues of the day. This year, as president of the Communications Bureau, you face a particularly difficult decision. The selection committee which makes nominations has proposed inviting a speaker from the Nazi Party. This particular speaker has advocated a return to the principles and policies of Hitler's Nazism in all his previous speeches, articles, and books. The selection committee argues that such a speaker is necessary to maintain a balance among the various points of view. At the same time, a number of campus organizations have protested the proposed plans inviting this speaker and have set in motion a student-faculty strike if this speaker is eventually invited. You have full authority concerning all invitations.

1. What should you do?

2. What would you do?

TAPING COMMUNICATIONS

You currently hold an important political position and your chances for an even higher position now look extremely good. You have, however, a number of political enemies intent on destroying you and your career in any way they can. Your adviser has suggested that in order to protect yourself you have your phones tapped so that all incoming and outgoing calls will be taped. In that way, he suggests, you will have a record of any conversation you engage in and will also have these records for use in writing your memoirs. No one calling or being called would be aware that their conversations were being recorded. You do not intend to use these tapes for purposes of destroying the careers of others or even for self-advancement. Rather, you want to use them for defensive purposes should any unfair attacks be made on you.

1. What should you do?

2. What would your do?

POLITICAL PAPERS

You have been working for some time for your state government and have recently come across important papers which implicate high government officials in serious crimes. These papers belong to various government officials but you can, with some effort, get your hands on them. You know that local and even national news services would publish these papers immediately. On the one hand, you want to get these papers and have them made public so that the various injustices may be corrected and the guilty individuals removed from office. On the other hand, since these are personal papers (diaries and personal letters), you are concerned with the right of privacy. Even here, however, you wonder if public officials have a right to privacy when the issues involved are of such great importance. There is no other way to get this information to the public than you personally taking these papers and turning them over to the press.

1. What should you do?

2. What would you do?

unit 13

Communication Techniques

Fear Appeals
Conditioning—As Persuasion, As Therapy
Emotional Appeals
The Prevention of Interaction
   Communication Techniques: Questions of Ethics

Objectives

Upon completion of this unit, you should be able to:

1. state some of the arguments for or against the use of fear appeals
2. define *conditioning, positive reinforcement, negative reinforcement,* and *punishment*
3. identify examples from your own experience that illustrate the operation of conditioning principles
4. state some of the arguments for or against the use of emotional appeals
5. explain the prevention of interaction as an ethical issue
6. take a tentative stand on issues relating to fear appeals, conditioning, emotional appeals, and the prevention of interaction

As agents of influence and change we have at our disposal an arsenal of techniques which are extremely effective. That we would be effective when using these techniques, however, is only half the issue. The other half of the issue is the rightness or wrongness of the techniques.

Here we consider only a small sample of the numerous communication techniques in use today which raise significant questions of ethics. Included here are the use of appeals to fear, conditioning as a technique for changing attitudes and behaviors, the use of emotional or psycho-

logical persuasion, and what we might call—for want of a better term—
the prevention of interaction.

These four topics are related in that they are all concerned with the
freedom of the individual to make his or her own decisions—whether he
or she *is* free and whether he or she *should* be free.

FEAR APPEALS

One of the most potent and widely used sources of persuasion is that of
fear appeals. Consider the mother and father who are afraid that their
child will be molested by some stranger. They warn the child to stay
away from strangers; not to take candy or money from people the child
does not know; and to, at all costs, stay out of cars, hallways, and dark
alleys where strangers might loiter. They attempt to gain compliance by
instilling fear in the child. To the child's natural question, "Why?" they
build elaborate stories about what strangers do to little boys and girls.
Depending upon their originality such stories could range from the im-
position of slavery, to starvation, beating, and death. The real reason, that
they might be sexually molested, is probably never mentioned.

In this type of situation we may side with the mother and father. The
young child is not knowledgeable enough to understand about sexual
molestation, and yet some means is needed to persuade the child to
keep his or her distance from strangers. The use of fear, then, serves
the parents well and hopefully protects the child from various dangers.

The same technique, though in more sophisticated form, is used by
many of the world's religions. We are taught to observe certain rules and
laws lest we be damned either in this life or in the next. Thus in order
to gain compliance with the various rules or laws of the religion, people
are frightened into obedience. This issue, though in much more complicated form than the situation with the parents and the child, involves
many of the same principles.

Depending upon our personal religious beliefs we may accept this
approach or reject it or fall anywhere in between those two extremes.
Assuming that we believe in the laws and rules of a certain religion, we
might be willing to accept the use of such techniques. We might argue
that we need to be persuaded to obey certain rules and that if the fear
technique works, then it is legitimate. If we reject the rules and regulations of a certain religion we would probably resent this type of appeal.
We might say, for example, that there is no afterlife and that to instill
a fear of punishment in individuals is based on false assumptions,
ignores the higher mental processes of logic and reason, and is, therefore, unacceptable.

Now, take the seemingly trivial case of toothpaste manufacturers and
advertisers. The advertiser's task is to persuade us to use one particular

brand of toothpaste. In all probability it is no worse but no better than any of the other available brands. But this particular advertiser is more clever than the others and decides to use fear appeal. In the advertisements gory pictures of diseased and bleeding gums, decayed and rotten teeth, and painful drilling and extractions are shown. Such, we are told, are the consequences of not using this particular brand of toothpaste. Consider the military training films that show the enemy to be cruel and sadistic in their dealings with captured prisoners. The message is also simple: Train harder, avoid capture, and escape all these hardships which are sure to be imposed by the enemy.

This same type of appeal is, of course, also used in more interpersonal situations. Take, for example, the mother who does not want her teenage son or daughter of say, 18 or 19, to move out of the house. Again, depending upon her creativity, her method might focus on instilling fear in the child for his or her own well-being ("Who'll care for you? You won't eat right. You'll get sick") or, more frequently, for the mother's well-being. The caricature of a mother having a heart atack at the first sign of the child's leaving is probably played every day, in various forms, throughout the world. But whether a heart attack or some other gross difficulty which is sure to result should the teenager leave home is used, fear is nevertheless relied on. Obviously no child wants to be the cause of his or her mother's suffering.

It is interesting to note that in our culture the father is not permitted to use his own suffering as an argument. Rather, his task is to show the children how much their leaving home will hurt their mother. Together, parents can make a most effective team. Children now have little chance of getting out on their own—at least not until they get married or somehow manage to work out a more persuasive case.

Parents are actually quite adept at using fear appeals and will use them to discourage anything from smoking (tobacco or grass) to premarital sex to interracial dating. The list—as any young person knows, or, indeed, as any person who has ever been young knows—is endless.

There are a number of related questions involved in the use of fear appeals. The position of the persuader in relation to the person being persuaded needs to be considered. The mother and father instilling a fear of strangers in children, we may say, is acceptable behavior, since children cannot understand and evaluate the possible dangers for themselves. A believer in religion might offer the same argument saying that the obligation of the religious leader is to secure commitment to certain laws and codes of behavior with whatever means possible. When we come to the advertiser, the military, and the parents of the teenager who wants to leave home we run into a somewhat different situation. Here the individuals are supposedly capable of making up their own minds and of evaluating and analyzing the various sides of the issues.

Even here, however, we might argue that these fear appeals are used for the ultimate good of the individual. Even brushing our teeth is for our own good. So what if we have to be frightened into it! The related question, of course, is who is to determine and define "our good." When should individuals be in a position to define what is good for themselves? When does a parent's obligation end and the child's begin? Or when does a parent's obligation to encourage children to make their own decisions begin?

Still another question is that of means and ends. If the end is a good one are any means permissible? If, for example, we are attempting to persuade people to act in a way that is productive and beneficial to them, are we justified in using *any* means to secure that compliance?

If we say no, we are left with the problem of determining what means are to be permitted. If we say yes, we open up entirely new issues concerning conditioning, thought control, brainwashing, and so on. It is to these issues that we need now turn.

CONDITIONING—AS PERSUASION, AS THERAPY

In one of the most widely read, condemned, praised, and generally discussed books of this century, *Beyond Freedom and Dignity*, B. F. Skinner sets forth the case for conditioning—a psychological technique for controlling behavior.

According to Skinner, all learned behavior is learned through a process of conditioning, a process governed by rewards and punishments. Put generally, the "theory" of conditioning states that we will learn and repeat those behaviors that have been rewarded in the past, and we will not learn or not repeat those behaviors that have been unrewarded or punished. Behavior may be rewarded through either of two basic means. Positive reinforcement involves the presentation of some kind of reward after some bit of behavior has been emitted. The result is that this type of behavior is strengthened in frequency and will be more likely to occur in the future under similar circumstances. Negative reinforcement, on the other hand, involves the removal of an aversive or painful stimulus (for example, an unpleasant sound) after some bit of behavior has been emitted. This too results in the behavior being strengthened and in its being more likely to occur under similar circumstances in the future. Behavior that is not reinforced, or that is punished, will not be learned— or, if already learned, will be extinguished or weakened.

According to Skinner all learned human behavior can be explained in essentially this way although there are rather complex types of conditioning schedules to account for the learning of different types of behaviors. But the essence of conditioning is that we learn according to the principles or laws of reinforcement.

Skinner's argument in *Beyond Freedom and Dignity* did not receive so much attention from all segments of the population because it presented a new psychological theory; actually Skinner had presented the same theory decades ago and it can be found in practically every basic psychology textbook. The reason this particular book received so much attention was simply that here Skinner applied the results of laboratory studies to society and denied the existence of what we normally call freedom of choice. We act and behave, according to Skinner, not because we are free to choose, but because of the way in which we have been conditioned. In this work, as well as in his novel *Walden Two*, Skinner portrayed and advocated a society organized on the basis of the principles of conditioning.

This thesis proved particularly disturbing to many people. Skinner's critics argued that society should not be based on such principles and that we would be morally unjustified in establishing a society where certain people were granted the right to reward and punish and thus control the behaviors of its people. Skinner's argument, however, is that we do not have a choice in whether or not we wish to be controlled by conditioning. According to Skinner, we *are* so controlled; that is simply in the nature of being human. And the question then becomes, do we want to organize this process or do we want to leave it to the inconsistent applications, such as we now have.

Admittedly this is a rather disturbing notion. We all want to be free, to think we are free, and to act as if we are free. Yet, Skinner's arguments and evidence are not easy to dismiss. If we accept Skinner's basic assumptions about conditioning, then we are left with two basic choices. Either we accept the present system in which our behaviors are controlled by rewards and punishments, although in a very inconsistent and often illogical manner, or we establish a society in which these rewards and punishments are organized so that the behaviors of the individuals within the society are controlled for the good of the whole. Naturally, there are intermediate positions; but according to Skinner, we do not have the choice of whether or not we want to be controlled by conditioning. We are human and because of that we learn and we behave according to the principles of reinforcement.

It now seems clear that we are influenced greatly (perhaps even "controlled") by conditioning. The questions we should ask concern the use to which such conditioning principles should be put. We are all, according to Skinner, both objects of conditioning and agents of conditioning. Our behavior is controlled by the reinforcements of others and we, in turn, control the behaviors of others by the reinforcements we apply.

In Anthony Burgess' *A Clockwork Orange* we see the protagonist conditioned to the point where he becomes extremely ill when presented with scenes of violence—scenes in which he would have eagerly participated before this conditioning. So thorough is his conditioning that he is powerless to defend himself when attacked. This is perhaps conditioning in its extreme, but we need to examine similar situations and attempt to ferret out the significant issues they raise.

In mental institutions, conditioning is widely applied as a means of behavior control. For example, disruptive and self-destructive behavior may be severely punished in order to reduce it or perhaps eliminate it fully. Small children are at times so self-destructive that they will literally chew huge hunks of flesh out of their arms and legs. Presented with such extreme cases we may be willing to accept the application of conditioning principles to control such behavior. But would we be willing to accept its application in other situations?

One crime that is currently on the books in most states, if not all, is suicide. If an individual attempts to commit suicide he or she is generally judged insane. Such an individual could be conditioned to prevent another suicide attempt. Currently, we grant society this right; that is, we have granted society the right to judge a potential suicide victim insane and to apply whatever treatment it deems effective. But should an individual have the right to take his or her own life? And does society have the right to prevent someone and in effect force someone to learn, through conditioning, contrary behavior patterns?

One of the types of conditioning receiving a great deal of attention is *aversive conditioning.* In this procedure the individual goes through the particular behaviors the therapist wishes to eliminate and is administered some aversive stimulus (for example, an electric shock) while engaging in these behaviors. In relatively short order such behaviors are weakened or eliminated. In one widely publicized case a small child would not keep food in his system. Whatever he was fed, he would throw up. In this case conditioning was used. The infant was wired in such a way so that he would receive a severe electric shock whenever any muscular movements were made in the direction of throwing up after he was fed. Within a matter of days the child stopped throwing up his food and apparently is a healthy young boy today. This same general procedure is used on those who exhibit behavior that society has chosen to condemn (such as homosexuals). At times these individuals will put themselves under the care of such a conditioning therapist and with this we would probably not wish to quarrel. Clearly they have a right to attempt to change their behavior should they wish to. But at times they are not given this choice. In mental hospitals or prisons, people are sometimes forced to submit to such conditioning. And it does not really matter to the issues involved here if they are conditioned by a trained psychologist or by an ignorant prison guard. Both are probably effective in altering the behavior. But the question is whether they should be in the position where such conditioning could be administered without the consent of the individual.

We might argue that such rights are granted to society for its own well-being and, in fact, preservation. This license to alter behavior is then granted for the good of the general population. This argument or reasoning may sound convincing until we recall that in the not so distant past this same argument was used for sterilization of "undesirables" and for the elimination of millions. True, the conditions and times are different now. But are they sufficiently different to risk allocating such great power to a relatively small group?

EMOTIONAL APPEALS

A perennial issue in interpersonal communication is that of the use of emotional appeal in attempting to change attitudes, beliefs, and behaviors. The case of the real estate broker appealing to our desire for status, the friend who wants a favor appealing to our desire for social approval, and the car salesman appealing to our desire for sexual rewards are all familiar examples. The question they all raise is simply, "Is this type of appeal justified?"

There are many arguments that can be adduced for both sides of the issue. The "everyone is doing it" argument is perhaps the most familiar but does not really answer the question of whether or not such appeals are justified. We are a combination of logic and emotion; consequently, we are persuaded by both types of appeals. To be effective, one would have to utilize both types of appeals. Again, however, this does not answer the question of whether or not such emotional appeals are justified. It merely states that they are effective. But we all knew that already.

If our highest achievement is our reasoning ability, then appealing to anything less than this seems an insult to our nature. At least this is how one familiar argument goes. But this is not an argument so much as a definition, and it fails to specify the bases for judgments of right and wrong.

At times we consider the extent of the appeals and their effect on the individuals. One argument says that emotional appeals are justified as long as individuals retain their powers of reasoning. Emotional appeals become unjustified when they short-circuit the reasoning processes. Exactly when people are in possession of such "powers" or when their reasoning is "short-circuited" is, unfortunately, not made clear.

Consider the following incident. A group of teenagers hang out together. A number of them begin to experiment with various drugs. Soon all but one of the group is using drugs with fair regularity. Obviously the one loner is somewhat of an outcast and either must be brought into the group or excluded. Both this member and the group find it difficult to deal with this fence sitting. So the group puts social pressure on this individual to join them. Naturally, the way in which this social pressure is exerted will vary from one region of the country to another and from one time in history to another and on the nature of the group itself. But social pressure seems to be a universal means used by groups to eliminate or change the deviant member's behavior. Although this individual has made the decision not to join the group, the social pressure—the emotional appeal—of the group is too strong to resist and so the person joins them. Or consider the reverse situation. No one in the group uses drugs except for one member. The other members decide to put pressure on this one individual to stop using drugs and eventually the pressure becomes so strong that the individual gives up the use of drugs. We need ask if either group was justified in using this social pressure to change the deviant member's behavior.

Note an important issue involved here. We may be swayed in our decision depending upon our own values regarding the particular topic involved. If we are violently against drugs we might criticize one group for putting this kind of pressure on the nonuser. If we are in favor of drugs we may judge the group innocent and criticize the other group. But our decisions in these matters should not depend on our values regarding the particular topic (in this case, drugs) but rather on the issue of social pressure and emotional appeal.

Many will say that the group is allowed to put pressure on the individual as long as it does not force the individual physically. Here a very tenuous line between the mental and the physical seems to be set up which probably does not exist in reality. According to this position, twisting someone's arm is not permissible but twisting one's mind is permissible.

The central issue regarding emotional appeals seems then to be this: If we live in a world of emotion, it is surely something that is a part of us. It is something we use all the time. Whether we use it to gain a job or to secure some momentary pleasure, we use it daily. And the issue is in what situations and to what extent it is justified to use emotional appeals—to, in fact, short-circuit the reasoning powers of another individual—to gain an end that we want.

THE PREVENTION OF INTERACTION

There are laws in our society—sometimes ignored by the courts and sometimes applied to the letter—that prevent various interactions among adult citizens.

Among the most obvious of these are the laws prohibiting interracial marriage and the laws prohibiting homosexual relations. These laws literally prohibit certain groups of persons from interacting in the manner in which they wish. If an interracial couple wishes to get married, the state in which such a marriage is performed must be chosen carefully. But perhaps more important than the actual laws are the societal codes, which are unwritten but which are prohibitive in a much more insidious way. Interracial couples will run into difficulty in finding housing, employment, and, most significantly, acceptance into a community. Likewise, homosexuals will have difficulty in much the same way, and consequently, many of them are forced to live "straight" lives at least on the surface.

If you run a business, for example, should you have the right to refuse a job to a person because that person is married to an individual of another race or because that person prefers to interact sexually with persons of the same sex? And if you do have the right to choose your employees on the basis of such preferences, do you still retain the rights to protection of the law which the society as a whole has granted to everyone?

Homosexuals are currently prevented from holding jobs as teachers, policemen, firemen, and so forth, in most states. These discriminatory laws are not terribly effective. But this is not the issue. The relative ineffectiveness of such prohibitions should not blind us to the social realities that these laws incorporate. What should be considered is that the homosexual teacher, for example, cannot teach as a homosexual but only as a heterosexual. The teacher is permitted to teach only if he or she —at least on the surface—denies the fact of his or her homosexuality and behaves as a heterosexual would. We do not ask that a black teacher act white—although society once did demand this in often subtle ways. We do not ask a Jew to act like a Christian or a Christian to act like a Jew if he or she wants a job—although, again, some persons do. Yet, we do ask homosexuals that they not reveal their true identity. These persons are only accepted if they act like the majority. But are we being fair when we ask for such concealment of identity?

Take a somewhat different example. A mother of a student recently found birth control pills in her daughter's dresser. The mother was incensed and said, "You don't use these." The young woman confessed that she did, in fact, use them. "No, you don't use them," said the mother, "and I don't ever want to hear about them again." And out of the room she stomped. This act—in somewhat different form—is a frequently occurring one. The mother, because she could not sanction her daughter's behavior, attempted to prevent her sexual interaction.

There are, of course, many different issues which such prohibitions of interactions raise. But I think the central issue they raise is whether any one group—however large and however sanctioned by state or church—has the right to set down rules of behavior for others and to literally prevent them from their own self-actualization. It is no wonder that so many interracial marriages end in divorce, that so many homosexuals are unhappy, and that suicide is one of the major causes of death among college students. In fact, in January 1975 an Associated Press article noted that teenage suicides are now at 30 per day and that more than 50 percent of the patients in psychiatric hospitals are under twenty-one years of age. Is society fostering marital discontent, homosexual unhappiness, and student despair by preventing people from being themselves, from interacting as they wish, from presenting themselves to others as they feel they really are? Lest we all ease our consciences too easily, let us recognize that it is we who constitute this "society," and it is we who give it the power it has—the very power we may deplore as we sit comfortably in the camp of the sanctioned majority.

Sources

On communication techniques see, for example, the articles in Richard L. Johannesen, ed., *Ethics and Persuasion: Selected Readings* (New York: Random House, 1967). For a discussion of ethics as related to efficiency see Robert T. Oliver, "Ethics and Efficiency in Persuasion," *Southern Speech Journal* 26 (1960):10–15. Ethical considerations and how they relate to language is covered in Jane Blankenship, *A Sense of Style* (Belmont, Cal.: Dickenson, 1968). If one article and only one article is to be read it should be Franklyn S. Haiman's "The Rhetoric of the Streets: Some Legal and Ethical Considerations," *Quarterly Journal of Speech* 53 (1967):99–114. Patricia Niles Middlebrook (*Social Psychology and Modern Life* [New York: Knopf, 1974]), in her discussion of the emotional approach to changing attitudes and her thorough treatment of intensive indoctrination, provides a clear analysis of the effectiveness of these techniques. You may wish to read these two discussions with the issues of ethics we raised here in mind.

Experiential Vehicle

COMMUNICATION TECHNIQUES: QUESTIONS OF ETHICS

This exercise is designed to raise only a few of the many questions that could be raised concerning the ethics of interpersonal communication and to encourage you to think in concrete terms about some of the relevant issues. The purpose is not to persuade you to a particular point of view but rather to encourage you to formulate your own point of view.

The exercises consist of a series of cases, each raising somewhat different ethical questions. This exercise will probably work best if you respond to each of the cases individually and then discuss your decisions and the implications in groups of five or six. In these small groups simply discuss those cases which you found most interesting. The most interesting cases for small group discussion will probably be those that were the most difficult for you to respond to, that is, those that involved the most internal conflict. A general discussion in which the various groups share their decisions and insights may conclude the session.

As an experience in self-disclosure and perception the group members may attempt to guess what each individual would do in each of these specific situations. Reasons for their choices or guesses would then be considered, for example, what led the group to guess that Person X would act one way rather than another way. Reasons for the accurate and/or inaccurate guesses might then be discussed.

Guidelines

1. Carefully read each of the following cases and write down your responses. By writing your decisions many issues that may be unclear will come to the surface and may then be used as a basis for discussion.
2. Your responses will not be made public, these papers not collected, and your decisions revealed only if you wish to reveal them. If individuals wish not to reveal their decisions do not attempt to apply any social pressure to get them to make these decisions public.

3. Do not attempt to avoid the issues presented in the various cases by saying, for example, "I'd try other means." For purposes of these exercises other means are ruled out.

4. Focus some attention in the small group discussions on the origin of the various values implicit in your decisions. You might, as a starting point, consider how your parents would respond to these cases. Would their decisions be similar or different from yours? Do not settle for "conditioning" as an answer. If you wish to discuss the development of these values in terms of conditioning, focus on specific reinforcement contingencies, the rewards and punishments received, which may have led to the development of these various values.

5. Devote some attention to the concept of change. Would you have responded in similar fashion five years ago? If not, what has led to the change? Would you predict similar responses five or ten years from now? Why? Why not?

    This concept of change is also significant in another respect. Focus attention on the changes or possible changes that might occur as a result of your acting in accordance with any of the decisions. That is, is the teacher who neglects his students for two years the same individual he was two years ago? Can he ever be that same individual again? How is he different? If we accept the notion, even in part, that how we act or behave influences what we are, how does this relate to the decisions we make on these issues?

6. Consider the concept of acceptance. How willing is each group number to accept the decisions of others? Are you accepting of your own decisions? Why? Why not? Would you be pleased if your children would respond in the same way you did?

7. Note that there are two questions posed after each case: What *should* you do, What *would* you do? The distinction between the two questions is crucial and is particularly significant when your answers for the two questions are different. When answers for the *should* and the *would* questions differ, try to analyze the intrapersonal dynamics. How do you account for the difference? Is there intrapersonal conflict? Are these differences the result of changes you are going through? How pleased-displeased are you with the differences in answers?

THE CHILDREN'S HOSPITAL

You have been put in charge of raising money for your town's new children's hospital—a hospital that is badly needed. There are a number of crippled children who are presently wearing heavy braces and who must walk with crutches. These children, you reason, would be very effective in influencing people to give to the hospital fund. As a conclusion to a program of speeches by local officials and entertainment you consider having these children walk through the audience and tell the people how desperately they need this hospital. An appeal by these children, you feel, would encourage many of the people to make donations which they would not make if a more reasoned and logical appeal was presented. You know from past experience that other available means of persuasion will not be effective.

1. What should you do?

2. What would you do?

PRESENTING ANOTHER FACE

You know that the way in which people dress greatly influences the way in which they are perceived. Your regular—that is, preferred—clothes are jeans and a sweat shirt. You wear this just about every day for every occasion and you resent wearing suits and dresses. Tomorrow you have a job interview and you have been told that the personnel director favors those who present a conservative image, here operationalized as wearing a suit or dress. You really would like this job and yet you wonder if you should present this false face.

1. What should you do?

2. What should you do if this change in appearance required the removal of a religious symbol you normally wear?

3. What would you do?

4. What would you do if this change in appearance required the removal of a religious symbol you normally wear?

BECOMING A STAR

You are being tested for the lead role in an important new movie. You very much want this part since you know that it will make you a major star, something you have worked extremely hard to achieve. The old stories you have heard about "couch casting" now become a reality. The producer has indicated that the part is yours should you agree to become sexually familiar. The contracts would not be drawn up for at least a week or two. During this time you would be expected to move in with the producer. After the contracts are signed both you and the producer know that you become a free agent. This is presented to you as a business arrangement; no long-term emotional commitments or attachments are expected or desired by the producer. If you do not agree to the producer's terms the part will go to someone else.

1. What should you do (if the producer were a person of the preferred sex)?

2. What should you do (if the producer were a person of the unpreferred sex)?

3. What would you do (if the producer were a person of the preferred sex)?

4. What would you do (if the producer were a person of the unpreferred sex)?

ROLLING THE LOG

You are a politician and want a particular bill passed. You are at the same time actively fighting the passage of another bill. You were recently confronted by the proponents of the bill you are fighting with the proposition that if you support their bill they will support yours. The bills are about equal in importance and in implications—though yours, you feel, is for the good and their's for the bad. You know that your support will result in the passage of their bill and that their support will result in the passage of your bill.

1. What should you do?

2. What would you do?

SCHOLARSHIP COMPETITION

You are competing with a fellow student for a full scholarship to law school. Both of you need the scholarship and both of you seem to deserve it equally—your grades, service to the school and community, law board scores, and so on are about the same. Unfortunately, there is only one scholarship to be awarded. The committee charged with selecting the winner is a most conservative group and would vote against candidates should they find out anything about their personal lives of which they would disapprove. You have recently learned that your competitor is an ex-convict. You could easily leak this information to the committee in which case you would surely get the scholarship. No one (not even the members of the committee) would know that you were the source of this information.

1. What should you do?

2. What would you do?

TEACHER PROMOTION

You are a college teacher in a large university and feel that you deserve to be promoted. Your chairperson, however, has told you that you will not be promoted unless you agree to serve on a number of different committees all of which you feel are unnecessary. If you serve on these committees it will mean that you will have very little time to devote to your students and to the preparation for the classes you are teaching. The promotion, contingent upon serving on these committees for a least one year but probably two, would mean a considerable increase in salary which you could surely use. You do not want to neglect your students for this period of time and yet you want the promotion.

1. What should you do?

2. What would you do?

unit 14

Systems of Ethics

Wallace's Ethical Basis of Communication
McCroskey's Ethical Obligations
Keller and Brown's Interpersonal Ethic for Communication
Weinberg's Effective Time-Binder
  A Tentative Theory of Interpersonal Communication Ethics

Objectives

Upon completion of this unit, you should be able to:

1. explain the four principles which, according to Wallace, should govern free speech
2. explain McCroskey's four major obligations of the communicator
3. explain Keller and Brown's interpersonal ethic
4. explain Weinberg's time-binding as a universal ethic
5. take a tentative stand on the usefulness-uselessness of each of the four systems of ethics presented here
6. formulate a tentative theory of the ethics of interpersonal communication

Ever since man began to communicate it is probable that guidelines were set down for the proper use of this powerful skill. We have no single answer to the question, "What ethical principles should govern communication?" But we do have answers and it is to these that we should direct some attention. Each individual must build his or her own ethical system. We cannot simply take the ethical system of another and make it our own—at least most of us cannot. What we need to do is to consider several different systems and perhaps, with these as a basis, formulate our own. It is toward this end that four different ethical systems are presented here—more in the nature of a stimulus for thought than as rigid guidelines.

WALLACE'S ETHICAL BASIS OF COMMUNICATION

Karl Wallace, in "An Ethical Basis of Communication," postulates certain principles or guidelines for ethical communication. These guidelines, says Wallace, are not external to communication; rather, "communication carries its ethics within itself. Communication of any kind is inseparable from the values which permeate a free and democratic community."

Wallace's ethic is based on the essential values of a free and democratic society. According to Wallace, these values include the dignity and worth of the individual, equality of opportunity, freedom, and the opportunity of an individual to grow and develop to the limits of his or her capacity. On the basis of these four democratic values, Wallace suggests four "moralities," four principles which he feels should govern speech communication behavior.

1. "A communicator in a free society must recognize that during the moments of his utterance he is the sole source of argument and information." This calls for communicators having a thorough knowledge of their topic, an ability to answer any relevant questions, and an awareness of the significant facts and opinions.

2. "The communicator who respects the democratic way of life must select and present fact and opinion fairly." The communicator must, in Wallace's words, "preserve a kind of equality of opportunity among ideas." Put differently, this principle calls upon the communicator to provide the hearer with an opportunity to make fair judgments.

3. "The communicator who believes in the ultimate values of democracy will invariably reveal the sources of his information and opinion." The communicator must assist the audience in evaluating any prejudices and biases which might be inherent in the sources by revealing them to the audience.

4. "A communicator in a democratic society will acknowledge and will respect diversity of argument and opinion." The ethical communicator, according to this principle, should be able to admit the weight of the opposing argument and evidence if he or she intends to ethically defend an opposing position. This principle calls for a "tolerance of dissent."

These guidelines, according to Wallace, are applicable to all communications (interpersonal, public, and mass) and to all communicators in a free and democratic society.

There are a number of difficulties in putting this system into operation. What constitutes a "thorough knowledge of the topic" and "an ability to answer relevant questions" is not easy to determine. Similarly, what constitutes a fair presentation of facts and opinions, a full presentation of (all) sources of information, and a respect for diversity of argument and opinion, is equally difficult to determine. Yet the four principles seem to provide some guidance in this most difficult area.

MC CROSKEY'S ETHICAL OBLIGATIONS

Unlike Wallace, James McCroskey argues that ethics lies outside communication proper; the techniques of persuasion, for example, are neither moral nor immoral; they are amoral. Each communicator, according to this view, must evaluate what is right and what is wrong, and the final test of ethics must rest on the intent of the communicator. Having said this, however, McCroskey notes that speakers in a free society have four major obligations: to speak, to speak well, to remain silent, and to listen.

Each individual within a free society has the obligation, not merely the right, to speak—that is, to stand up for what is felt to be right and to speak against injustice. A free society cannot long exist if its citizens do not raise their voices in support of justice and against injustice.

However, simply speaking is not enough. We are, according to McCroskey, obligated to learn to speak well, to exercise all the power we can to persuade our fellows in favor of what is right and against what is wrong. Much like a doctor has an obligation not merely to practice medicine but to practice it well, citizens in a free society must practice their communicative arts well.

Much as we should speak when we are aware of the rightness and the wrongness of various matters, we should also remain silent when we know that we are wrong or when we are not certain that we are right. When we advocate a particular point of view we must be certain that we are doing it in the best interests of our audience. If we are not sure of our position or motives then our obligation is to remain silent.

Lastly, McCroskey argues that we have an obligation to listen. Without securing relevant information we have little chance of making decisions which are intelligent and based on the best knowledge available. If we do not accept the responsibility for securing information we may easily and unwittingly become the pawns of those who would attempt to manipulate and use our support for their, perhaps, unjust ends. Although selective perception is a rather universal tendency, McCroskey argues that we must consciously fight this tendency.

There are often many difficulties for the individual attempting to live up to these four seemingly simple obligations. Our own self-interests may cause conflicts with what we feel is the right thing to do for others. Do we speak out against an injustice when it may cost us our job? Do we hire a qualified minority group member to work for us when it may cause a strike or boycott? How can we know when we have fulfilled the responsibility of speaking well? Who is to determine that we have maximized our abilities to communicate? How can we be sure that we are right? How certain must we be before speaking out? How much information must we expose ourselves to as responsible members of a free society?

These are not easy questions to answer. Nor are these obligations easy to meet. "But," concludes McCroskey, "who ever said that things that are worthwhile are easy?"

KELLER AND BROWN'S INTERPERSONAL ETHIC FOR COMMUNICATION

For the most part, traditional approaches to ethics have focused on the message. They have concerned themselves with, for example, falsification of evidence, lying, distortion of facts and figures, and extreme emotional appeals. To Paul Keller and Charles Brown, these message aspects, although important, are not the only factors to consider in developing an ethic for communication.

Keller and Brown propose an interpersonal ethic for communication, an ethical perspective that focuses on the speaker and the hearer and their attitudinal and behavioral responses to each other. In this system communication is ethical (or perhaps, more correctly, communicators are ethical) when there is acceptance of the responses of others. Assume, for example, that a hearer does not agree with something for which you have argued. Although you have presented what to you is incontrovertible evidence and argument, the hearer remains adamant in his or her contradictory belief. Your communications, according to this position, are ethical to the extent that they are accepting of this hearer's freedom of choice to agree or not to agree.

Communications are unethical to the extent that they restrict the hearer's freedom of choice: when they are hostile to disagreement, or when they attempt to force compliance instead of allowing individuals the freedom to choose according to their own system of values, opinions, and beliefs.

This point of view is based on the democratic value that "conditions be created and maintained in which the potential of the individual is best realized." The assumption, based on this value which leads to the formulation of the ethical perspective of Keller and Brown, is that people will best be able to realize their potential when they are psychologically free, when they are not afraid to disagree, when their beliefs, opinions, and values are accepted rather than rejected.

The crucial questions to consider in this system, then, are "How does the speaker respond to the listener's responses?" and "How does the listener respond to the speaker's responses?" The speaker is communicating ethically "if he reacts in such a way as to enhance the self-determination within the other." The speaker is communicating unethically "if he reacts in such a way as to inhibit the self-determination forces within the other."

Keller and Brown's system is particularly interesting because it lends an ethical dimension to matters not normally considered questions of ethics. For example, the instructor who will tolerate no disagreement and will belittle students who disagree is, according to this system, unethical. Consequently, group members who sulk and withdraw whenever they do not get their way are likewise unethical in their communications. The instructor and the group members are guilty of unethical behavior since they are acting in a manner which inhibits rather than enhances the self-determination and freedom of choice of the other.

This system also raises the question of how we can operationalize the processes by which an individual's self-determination is enhanced. To what extent does disagreement (verbal or nonverbal restrict an individual's freedom? How does one behave so that an individual feels free, unafraid to disagree, and accepted? How do we disagree with someone and still conform to the principles set forth in this system of interpersonal ethics?

WEINBERG'S EFFECTIVE TIME-BINDER

Of all the animals in creation only humans have the ability to bind time; only we can pass on from one generation to the next the knowledge we have acquired so that one generation can literally build on the knowledge of the previous generation. By our ability to use symbols we have been able to bind time, to learn from previous generations all that they have learned and to transmit to future generations all that we have learned.

If, then, we live, develop, and progress largely through our receiving and sending symbols, our chances for survival or for a better life depend upon the effectiveness with which we use these symbols and hence our time-binding ability. From this comes a cross-cultural ethical standard—that is, an ethical standard applicable to all cultures at all times. The ethic is simply this: the use of symbols or communication is ethical to the extent that it leads to the development of effective time-binding and effective time-binders. Any communication, any form of government, any custom, any societal rules or regulations are good (that is, ethical) to the extent that they encourage effective time-binding and bad (that is, unethical) to the extent that they discourage effective time-binding.

The effective use of our symbolizing ability and the ethical use of it need to be distinguished. Clearly there are many effective communicators who are unethical and many ethical communicators who are ineffective. Politicians may effectively deceive constituents, religious leaders may effectively mislead followers, teachers may effectively present false information to students. But these communicators, despite their effectiveness, are unethical time-binders since they have lessened the chances for the growth and development of their hearers who are dependent upon effective time-binding.

According to Harry Weinberg, one cannot effectively delude others without having this delusion feed back on oneself. The human nervous system is designed to work as a whole and any attempt to divide it (for instance, by lying to others but supposedly not to ourselves) causes psychological problems for the individual. The way we act, in large part, determines what and who we are. We cannot act one way yet purport to be entirely different people; that is, we cannot do this without causing psychological conflicts.

Weinberg's ethical system is cross-cultural; it applies to all cultures equally—unlike the previously discussed systems which are based on the assumption of a democratic society. The time-binding ethic is cross-cultural because the nervous systems of all people are essentially the same. People depend, for effective growth and development, on the effectiveness of their symbol-using abilities. When these abilities are warped or destroyed—as in cultures where false knowledge or superstition are accepted or even encouraged—the survival mechanism essential to time-binding is also destroyed.

Put in the form of a precept, this ethical theory states: "So act as to make thyself a better time-binder; so act as to enable others to use their time-binding capacities more effectively." This is then a double-edged theory; it focuses both on the individual (as in *intra*personal communication) and on the individual's behavior and interaction with others (as in *inter*personal communication).

Exactly what communications lead to effective time-binding is not always easy to determine. We can sometimes examine the facts or interview the individuals involved and determine, to some extent at least, the degree to which the communications encouraged effective time-binding. At other times, however, it is not possible to do this. Numerous plans are currently being offered towards an amelioration of the economic problems we are now facing, for example. But by what means can we determine the extent to which these communications lead to effective or ineffective time-binding?

Sources

The four systems of ethics considered in this unit may be found in greater depth in the following: Karl Wallace, "An Ethical Basis of Communication," *Speech Teacher* 4(1955):1–9; James McCroskey, *An Introduction to Rhetorical Communication*, 2d ed. (Englewood Cliffs, N.J.: Prentice-Hall, 1973); Paul W. Keller and Charles T. Brown, "An Interpersonal Ethic for Communication," *Journal of Communication* 18(1968):73–81; and Harry L. Weinberg, *Levels of Knowing and Existence: Studies in General Semantics* (New York: Harper & Row, 1959). For additional systems of ethics see the articles in James W. Gibson, *A Reader in Speech*

Communication (New York: McGraw-Hill, 1971). This reader contains articles by George Rice, "The Right to be Silent," Wayne Flynt, "The Ethics of Democrative persuasion and the Birmingham Crisis," and Robert L. Scott, "Justifying Violence—The Rhetoric of Militant Black Power." Articles by Haiman and by Borman, cited in Units 12 and 13, and by Keller and Brown, discussed in this unit are also included.

Experiential Vehicle

A TENTATIVE THEORY OF INTERPERSONAL COMMUNICATION ETHICS

Formulate here what might be called, "My Tentative Theory of the Ethics of Communication." Formulate a theory that you feel is reasonable, justified, internally consistent, and consonant with your own system of values. Construct your theory so that it incorporates at least all of the situations presented in the previous two exercises. That is, given this statement of ethical principles another individual should be able to accurately predict how you would behave in each of the situations presented in these cases.

After constructing your tentative theory, examine the ways in which it differs from the theories discussed in this unit, namely:

1. Wallace's Ethical Basis of Communication

2. McCroskey's Ethical Obligations

3. Keller and Brown's Interpersonal Ethic for Communication

4. Weinberg's Effective Time-Binder

PART TWO
MESSAGES AND MESSAGE RECEPTION

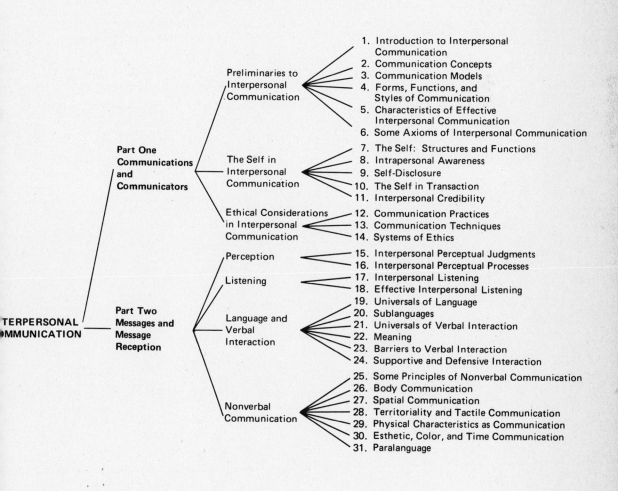

INTERPERSONAL COMMUNICATION

Part One
Communications
and
Communicators

Preliminaries to
Interpersonal
Communication

1. Introduction to Interpersonal Communication
2. Communication Concepts
3. Communication Models
4. Forms, Functions, and Styles of Communication
5. Characteristics of Effective Interpersonal Communication
6. Some Axioms of Interpersonal Communication

The Self in
Interpersonal
Communication

7. The Self: Structures and Functions
8. Intrapersonal Awareness
9. Self-Disclosure
10. The Self in Transaction
11. Interpersonal Credibility

Ethical Considerations
in Interpersonal
Communication

12. Communication Practices
13. Communication Techniques
14. Systems of Ethics

Part Two
Messages and
Message
Reception

Perception

15. Interpersonal Perceptual Judgments
16. Interpersonal Perceptual Processes

Listening

17. Interpersonal Listening
18. Effective Interpersonal Listening

Language and
Verbal
Interaction

19. Universals of Language
20. Sublanguages
21. Universals of Verbal Interaction
22. Meaning
23. Barriers to Verbal Interaction
24. Supportive and Defensive Interaction

Nonverbal
Communication

25. Some Principles of Nonverbal Communication
26. Body Communication
27. Spatial Communication
28. Territoriality and Tactile Communication
29. Physical Characteristics as Communication
30. Esthetic, Color, and Time Communication
31. Paralanguage

unit 15

Interpersonal Perceptual Judgments

Types of Judgments
Three Principles of Perception
Bases for Judgments
Accuracy in Interpersonal Perception
    Perceiving Others
    Perceiving a Stranger

Objectives

Upon completion of this unit, you should be able to:

1. define *interpersonal perception*
2. distinguish between *static* and *dynamic judgments*
3. define and supply at least one example of each of the three principles of perception
4. define and supply at least one example of each of the three bases for judgment
5. explain the influence of the following variables on accuracy in interpersonal perception: age, sex, intelligence, cognitive complexity, popularity, personality characteristics, effects of training
6. recognize the bases for our own judgments of people

TYPES OF JUDGMENTS

Static judgments refer to those characteristics of another person that are relatively unchanging. Judgments of such characteristics as race, occupation, age, or nationality would be examples of static judgments, since these characteristics are relatively enduring. We often also make judgments about an individual's habitual response to specific situations. For example, such statements as "He's a soft touch when anyone needs help," or, "She drives carefully," or, "He eats well," represent static judgments. Similarly, we make judgments concerning an individual's general behavior without regard to specific situations. Examples include the statement that an individual is quick tempered, that he or she is extroverted, or that he or she is mercenary. We also make numerous general sociometric judgments. These are judgments concerning relations among people, for example, "He loves her," "She hates her brother," or "The children are afraid of their father." All of these are "static judgments" since they refer to lasting or habitual characteristics.

Dynamic judgments, on the other hand, refer to the characteristics of other people that change more rapidly. One type of dynamic judgment would concern the specific response of an individual, for example, "He wants to leave the party," "She is having a good time," or "He is tired." These are judgments concerning a specific situation at a specific time. Judgments of affect would also be of the dynamic type. We can, for example, judge the moods of different people ("He is afraid," "She is happy," "He is in love"). A final type is what Mark Cook calls "regulation" judgments. These judgments refer to the behavior of people in social situations. For example, when we are in a group we do not talk when someone else is talking (at least not usually). When that person has finished we may make a "regulation judgment" that it is proper for us to talk now. We also make judgments about the type of social situation we are in. Consequently, we regulate the topics and the language that might be appropriate or inappropriate. At a family dinner we would probably not talk about the same things or speak in the same way as we would in a locker room. These social-type judgments allow us to regulate appropriate behavior.

THREE PRINCIPLES OF PERCEPTION

Psychologists once thought that if one wanted to understand perception all one had to do was study the stimuli being perceived. If these stimuli were analyzed fully and accurately enough, perception would be explained. The role of the perceiver in the process of perception was ignored.

Few psychological processes are that simple, and perception is no exception. In order to understand perception we need to understand some of the principles or "rules" that perceptual processes seem to follow. The three noted here seem among the most important for interpersonal communication: subjectivity, stability, and meaningfulness.

Subjectivity

Perception is an active rather than a passive process. We do not perceive the world unfiltered and in pure form; rather, we actively interact with the world as we perceive it. To a great extent we actually create the perceptions we have. Consequently, we will often perceive what we expect to perceive or what we want to perceive.

In perceiving people we do not simply perceive their individual bits of behaviors; we perceive some structured whole. In interpersonal perception, then, our expectations and our wants or needs will be particularly important. We may, for example, have been told that Jack is honest and warm and that Bill is dishonest and cold. If we then observe the exact same behaviors of these two individuals we would probably perceive them in very different ways depending upon our previous conceptions of what these people are like.

"Beauty is in the eye of the beholder," the old saying goes, and in terms of perception theory it clearly is. That is why the same individual can be perceived as ugly by one person and as beautiful by another, why the same person can be perceived as humorous by one and as "sick" by the other, why the same person can be perceived as "encouraging students to use their full potential" by one and as "unrealistic in his or her demands" by another.

Stability

In order to better understand the concept of *stability* (or invariance), focus on an object at least twenty feet away, say a picture or a book or a person. Now walk toward that object until you are a foot or less away. Physicially, of course, the object did not change in size; it also did not change in size psychologically, despite the fact that the size of the image on the retina changed drastically as you approached it. Psychologically, we adjust our perceptions because we "know" from past experiences that things do not change in size as we get closer. We know how to adjust our perceptions of size on the basis of the retinal image, distance, and object size.

In interpersonal perception we function in a very similar way. We perceive various behaviors of a friend as that friend is talking with a group of people. Naturally, this friend has never acted in this exact way before; no behaviors are ever repeated exactly. We do not focus our attention on the specific bits of behaviors but on those aspects which are more or less unchanging, for example, his or her purposes, motivations, values. Consequently, our perception of these behaviors is relatively stable; we see the behavior of our friend as being consistent with our previous conceptions.

Assume, for a moment that you know several people who seem constantly to be praising themselves. At every turn they tell you how great they are. You might then label them as "egomaniacs" or "egocentrics." Now notice what effect that label will have on your perception of the future behaviors of these individuals. Upon seeing them again, the easiest way to structure your perception and make sense of it is to categorize it as egomaniacal. In doing this you are assuming that there is a certain stability to people's behavior and that there is a certain degree of invariance.

Meaningfulness

One of the best ways of appreciating the principle of meaningfulness is to view a film of a dream sequence that is—at least at the time of viewing—without any meaning. Things seem to happen without cause and without expected effect. We sit there and wonder what we are seeing. We have difficulty perceiving this kind of presentation because the assumed meaningfulness of people is absent.

Generally, we assume that people are sensible and that their behaviors stem from some logical antecedent. We assume, in other words, a certain degree of predictability in other people's behavior. We assume that they will be consistent from one occasion to another, or at least relatively so.

If you are sitting in a classroom and a student raises her hand you perceive her to have a question. Logically, of course, there could be any number of reasons for a student's hand being up. If that same behavior were evidenced at a football game or while swimming or while cooking you would perceive the raised hand as having a different meaning. Thus we attribute to the behavior a meaning that is sensible in the context in which it occurs.

In any interpersonal perception experience these three principles of subjectivity, stability, and meaningfulness will operate with varying degrees of influence. And people differ in the extent to which they are subjective or the extent to which they seek stability or meaningfulness. These principles, although always present, influence the interpersonal perception process in different ways and to different extents depending upon the perceiver and the perceived.

BASES FOR JUDGMENTS

The judgments that we make about other people are based on behaviors (or appearance) of the individual and some rule or rules that link that behavior with some type of judgment. For example, we see a person with thick glasses and conclude that he or she is studious. To make that judgment ("studious"), however, we must have somewhere in our perceptual system a rule which would go something like this: "Persons who wear thick glasses are studious."

The question we need ask now is how we acquire the rules we have, that is, how did the rules develop. Generally such rules are derived from experience, analogy, and/or authority.

Rules from Experience

One of the most obvious ways to formulate rules about people and their characteristics is from experience. This experience may be derived from our own personal interactions or it may be from the interactions of others that we observe either in reality or in fiction (radio, television, movies, novels).

Rules from Analogy

Another way of formulating rules is on the basis of analogy. We assume that person X will respond in a particular way because person Y, who is similar to person X, has responded in this way. Such analogies are perhaps most often formed on the basis of one's own behavior but are also formed on the basis of the behavior of one's friends, one's family, and one's heros.

Thus, for example, if I as a teacher were to assume the role of mediator with a group of arguing students I might then infer that another teacher would also assume the role of mediator given a similar situation. My implicit rule might be something like: "Teachers, when with a group of arguing students, will assume mediator roles." Very often when we are trying to predict how another individual will react we attempt to reason by analogy and ask, "What would I do in this situation?" The assumption here is that other people act as we do.

Rules from Authority

When we were growing up we learned a great many rules from our parents about other people and about the ways in which they behave. Depending upon the orientation of the family, these rules might have been in the form of traditional stereotypes about various racial, religious, and national groups or perhaps in the form of suggested modes of behavior. For example, we might have learned that "all foreigners are untrustworthy," "all Americans are materialistic," "all Italians are religious," and so on. Or we might have learned such rules as, "people who study hard will achieve success," or, "honest people will come out ahead in the long run," and so on.

In many instances (and probably in most), our judgments are made on the basis of some complex system of rules derived from all three sources rather than from just one. Thus, for example, you may see a person from your home town and make some kind of judgment. That judgment, however, might be based on rules derived from your experience with home town people, from an analogy with your own behavior or general response tendency, or from something you learned when you were young or something you read or heard from an authoritative source.

It is not possible to examine a judgment and discover the specific basis for the rules that were used to formulate that judgment. But by being aware of the ways in which such rules are formed, we are in a better position to examine the judgments we make, and to evaluate and perhaps revise them.

ACCURACY IN INTERPERSONAL PERCEPTION

Children can tell what a person is really like, even though adults might have difficulty.

Women are just naturally better judges of people than men.

He or she is so popular with everyone; he or she must be an excellent judge of people.

After going on an encounter weekend we should be able to judge people more accurately.

These and perhaps various other types of statements reflect our concern with accuracy in interpersonal perception. Some of these statements seem logical on the basis of our experience. Some seem logical because of some rule of analogy—we went on an encounter weekend, improved our accuracy, and therefore conclude that encounter improves perception accuracy for people in general. Some seem logical because some authority told us so.

Actually much experimental research, clearly synthesized by Mark Cook, has been directed at testing these and similar statements to determine the characteristics of persons who are particularly accurate in interpersonal perception. Some of the more prominent factors or variables are noted here.

Age

Contrary to the popular notion that children can tell what a person is really thinking or really like, accuracy of interpersonal perception increases with age rather than decreases. For example, it has been found that judgments of emotion from facial and vocal cues as well as sociometric judgments increase in accuracy with age.

Sex

The popular notion that women are more accurate interpersonal perceivers than men has some—but not overwhelming—support. Differences on the basis of sex have not been found in most studies. In the few studies that have found differences, women have performed at a slightly better level than men.

Intelligence

Generally, the more intelligent the person the better he or she is at accurately judging other people. This variable of intelligence is probably closely related to that of cognitive complexity.

Cognitive Complexity

Individuals who have a great number of concepts for describing people—that is, those who have greater "cognitive complexity" or who are "cognitively complex"—are generally better at judging others than are those of less cognitive complexity. These cognitively complex individuals differentiate more finely and will not group people together as much as will those with less cognitive complexity.

Popularity

It is generally assumed that people who are popular and socially favored have achieved their standing because they are accurate judges of people. A number of studies have sought to investigate this but no definite conclusions seem warranted. At times, of course, accurate perception may prove a hindrance to popularity if this skill enables the individual to see all the faults in others. On the other hand, if it gives an individual better insight into other people, then it probably functions to improve social relationships.

Personality Characteristics

A great deal of research has focused on the personality characteristics of accurate perceivers. Are accurate perceivers more sociable or less sociable, more empirically oriented or less empirically oriented, more independent or more dependent? Here there is much confusion. Generally the personality characteristics of accurate judges include sociability, toughmindedness, empiricism, nonconformity, independence, strong will, and dominance. When the sex of the judge is controlled, however, a somewhat different picture emerges. "The picture of the good male judge that emerges," says Cook "is rather unexpected. The good male judge of males is described as a rather insensitive aggressive person while the good male judge of females is described as very ineffectual. The good female judges are described slightly more favorably."

Effects of Training

It is generally assumed that training will increase one's ability at almost anything. We seem to have an undying faith in the ability of individuals to be educated to the point where they can do just about anything. With interpersonal perception, however, training has not been found to be effective, at least not generally. Interpersonal perception has been improved when judges were given immediate knowledge of results, but T-groups and clinical training, for example, have not resulted in improved interpersonal perception. It should be noted that such training does provide people with a host of new labels and terms, and this makes it appear that their accuracy has improved. Actually, however, it has not. Or so say the experimental studies.

Sources

A thorough summary of this area is contained in Mark Cook's *Interpersonal Perception* (Baltimore: Penguin, 1971) on which I relied heavily for the entire unit. A more thorough and scholarly presentation of this area is by Renato Tagiuri, "Person Perception," in *The Handbook of Social Psychology*, edited by G. Lindzey and E. Aronson, 2d ed. (Reading, Mass.: Addison-Wesley, 1969) 3:395–449. Standard reference works in this area include Michael Argyle, *Social Interaction* (London: Methuen, 1969) and Renato Tagiuri and Luigi Petrullo, eds., *Person Perception and Interpersonal Behavior* (Stanford, Cal.: Stanford University Press, 1958). A brief but insightful account of interpersonal perception is provided by Albert Hastorf, David Schneider, and Judith Polefka in *Person Perception* (Reading, Mass.: Addison-Wesley, 1970).

Experiential Vehicles

PERCEIVING OTHERS

List the name of the person in this class who you would most like to:

1. have a date with

2. go into business with

3. have dinner with

4. have meet your family

5. discuss your inner feelings with

6. work on a class project with

7. have at a party

8. have as a group leader

9. borrow money from

10. room with

11. drive cross-country with

12. be happy with

13. be sad with

14. be locked in a jail cell with

15. go camping with

Class members should discuss their results as a whole. Specifically, consider the following:

1. What cues did the people give that led you to feel as you did about them?
2. What quality of the person named led you to select him or her for that purpose?
3. Think of (but do not verbalize) the persons with whom you would least like to do the fifteen things listed. Why? That is, what cues did these people give that led you to feel as you did about them?
4. What quality of the person thought of led you to reject him or her for that purpose?
5. For which purposes do you think other people would select you? What qualities do people see in you that would lead them to select you for one or more of these fifteen items?

PERCEIVING A STRANGER

The purpose of this exercise is to explore the bases you use in perceiving and judging people you see for the first time.[1] Since we all make judgments of people upon seeing them, we need to investigate the ways and means we use in making these judgments.

A stranger (someone you have not seen before) will be brought into class. Look the stranger over and answer the questions that follow. For this phase of the exercise no interaction between you and the stranger should take place. Use the number "1" to mark your answers.

[1]This exercise, though in a somewhat different form, was suggested by James C. McCroskey, Carl E. Larsen, and Mark L. Knapp in their *Teacher's Manual* for *An Introduction to Interpersonal Communication* (Englewood Cliffs, N.J.: Prentice-Hall, 1971).

After this you will be able to interact with the stranger for five or ten minutes. Ask him or her any questions you wish though none can be directly related to the questions asked on the following pages. The stranger should answer any questions posed as fully as he or she thinks necessary. The stranger should not, however, answer any questions that relate directly to the questions posed on the following pages. After this interaction, again answer the questions, this time using "2" to mark your answers.

After these answers have been recorded the stranger or the instructor will go over each of the questions, specifying which answers the stranger thinks are most appropriate.

Discussion should focus on at least the following: .

1. Which judgments were static judgments? Which were dynamic judgments?
2. Explain how rules from experience, analogy, and/or authority influenced your perceptions of the stranger.
3. Explain how the principles of subjectivity, stability, and meaningfulness operated in your perceptions of the stranger.

Instructions

Before interaction answer the questions by placing the number "1" in the appropriate space. After interaction answer the questions by placing the number "2" in the appropriate space.

The stranger would most likely:

1. read

    _____ *The Best of Mad*
    _____ *War and Peace*
    _____ *The Sensuous Man/Woman*
    _____ *Knots*
    _____ *Slaughterhouse Five*

2. see

    _____ a James Bond movie
    _____ a romantic movie
    _____ a western
    _____ a comedy
    _____ an erotic movie
    _____ a foreign film

3. participate in

    _____ football
    _____ tennis

_____ golf
_____ skiing
_____ none of these

4. listen to

_____ classical music
_____ rock music
_____ country/western music
_____ popular music

5. watch on television

_____ a situation comedy
_____ the news
_____ an educational show
_____ a detective show
_____ a sports show
_____ a soap opera

6. prefer to be

_____ alone
_____ in a crowd
_____ with one person

7. go to

_____ a rock concert
_____ an art museum
_____ a baseball game
_____ an opera
_____ a play
_____ a movie

8. look for in a mate

_____ intelligence
_____ looks
_____ personality
_____ money

9. study

_____ sciences
_____ languages

_____ music/art/drama
_____ business
_____ communications
_____ social sciences

10. subscribe to

_____ *Playboy/Playgirl*
_____ *National Geographic*
_____ *Time/Newsweek*
_____ *Popular Mechanics*
_____ *Good Housekeeping*

11. behave

_____ as an extrovert
_____ as an introvert
_____ as an ambivert

12. act

_____ very aggressively
_____ very unaggressively
_____ fairly aggressively
_____ fairly nonaggressively

13. be

_____ very energetic
_____ very lazy
_____ fairly energetic
_____ fairly lazy

14. behave in most situations

_____ very emotionally
_____ very rationally
_____ fairly emotionally
_____ fairly rationally

15. be generally

_____ very happy
_____ very unhappy
_____ fairly happy
_____ fairly unhappy

Also, what is the stranger's:

Age _____

Occupation _____

Educational level reached _____

Marital status _____

Financial status _____

Describe the stranger's personality in two, three, or four adjectives:

How does the stranger feel now? Explain.

unit 16

Interpersonal Perceptual Processes

Primacy-Recency
Self-Fulfilling Prophecy
Perceptual Accentuation
Implicit Personality Theory
Consistency
Stereotyping
  Perception and the Self: A Model of Perceptual Space
  Perception and Significant Others: Interpersonal Perceptual Processes
   in Operation

Objectives

Upon completion of this unit, you should be able to:

1. define *primacy* and *recency*
2. explain the influence of primacy-recency on interpersonal perception
3. define the *self-fulfilling prophecy*
4. explain the influence of the self-fulfilling prophecy on interpersonal perception
5. define *perceptual accentuation*
6. explain the influence of perceptual accentuation on interpersonal perception
7. define an *implicit personality theory*
8. state at least three propositions that are part of your own implicit personality theory
9. explain the influence of an implicit personality theory on interpersonal perception

10. define *consistency*
11. explain the influence of consistency on interpersonal perception
12. define *stereotype*
13. explain the influence of stereotyping on interpersonal perception
14. recognize the different ways in which you perceive and are perceived by others

Interpersonal perception is an extremely complex affair. Perhaps the best way to explain some of these complexities is to examine at least some of the psychological processes involved in interpersonal perception.

PRIMACY-RECENCY

Assume for a moment that you were enrolled in a course in which half the classes were extremely dull and half the classes were extremely exciting. At the end of the semester you are to evaluate the course and the instructor. Would the evaluation be more favorable if the dull classes constituted the first half of the semester and the exciting classes constituted the second half of the semester or if the order were reversed? If what comes first exerts the most influence, we have what is called a *primacy effect*. If what comes last (or is the most recent) exerts the most influence, we have a *recency effect*.

In an early study on the effects of primacy-recency in interpersonal perception Solomon Asch read a list of adjectives describing a person to a group of subjects and found that the effects of order were significant. A person described as "intelligent, industrious, impulsive, critical, stubborn, and envious" was evaluated as more positive than a person described as "envious, stubborn, critical, impulsive, industrious, and intelligent." The implication here is that we utilize early information to provide us with a general idea as to what a person is like, and we utilize the later information to make this general idea or impression more specific. Numerous other studies have provided evidence for the effect of first impressions. For example, in one study subjects observed a student (actually a confederate of the experimenter) taking a test. The task of the subject was to estimate the number of questions the student got right and to predict how well he would do on a second trial. The confederate followed two different orders. In one order, the descending order, the correct answers were all in the beginning. In the ascending order, the correct answers were toward the end. In each case, of course, there were the same number correct and incorrect. Subjects judged the descending order to contain more correct responses. They also estimated that students in the descending order would do better on a second trial and judged them to be more intelligent.

SELF-FULFILLING PROPHECY

Perhaps the most widely known example of the self-fulfilling prophecy is the *pygmalian effect,* now widely popularized. Basically, teachers were told that certain pupils were expected to do exceptionally well—that they were late bloomers. However, the names of these students were selected at random by the experimenters. The results were not random. Those students whose names were given to the teachers actually did perform at a higher level than did the other students. In fact, these students even improved in I.Q. scores more than did the other students.

Eric Berne in *Games People Play* and Thomas Harris in *I'm O.K., You're O.K.* both point out the same type of effect but in a somewhat different context. These transactional psychologists argue that we live by scripts which are given to us by our parents and that we essentially act in the way in which we are told to act. Much like the children who were expected to do well, we all, according to transactional psychology, live by the scripts given to us as children.

Consider, for example, people who enter a group situation convinced that the other members will dislike them. Almost invariably they are proven right; the other members do dislike them. What they may be doing is acting in such a way as to encourage people to respond negatively. Or similarly, when we enter a classroom and prophesize that it will be a dull class, it turns out, more often than not, to be a dull class. Now it might be that it was in fact a dull class. But it might also be that we defined it as dull and hence made it dull; we made a prophecy and then fulfilled it.

PERCEPTUAL ACCENTUATION

"Any port in a storm" is a common enough phrase which in its variants appears throughout our communications. To many, even an ugly date is better than no date at all. Spinach may taste horrible but when you are starving, it can taste like filet mignon. And so it goes.

In what may be the classic study on need influencing perception, poor and rich children were shown pictures of coins and later asked to estimate their size. The poor children estimated the size as much greater than did the rich children. Similarly, hungry people perceive food objects and food terms at lower recognition thresholds (needing fewer physical cues) than people who are not hungry.

In terms of interpersonal perception, this process, called *perceptual accentuation,* leads us to see what we expect to see and what we want to see. We see people we like as being better looking than people we do not like; we see people we like as being smarter than people we do not like. The obvious counterargument to this is that we actually prefer good-looking and smart people—not that people whom we like are seen as being handsome and smart. But perhaps that is not the entire story.

As Zick Rubin describes it, male undergraduates, for example, participated in what they thought were two separate and unrelated studies; it was actually two parts of a single experiment. In the first part each subject read a passage; half the subjects were given an arousing sexual seduction scene to read, and half were given a passage about seagulls and herring gulls. In the second part of the experiment, subjects were asked to rate a female student on the basis of her photograph and a self-description. As might be expected, the subjects who read the arousing scene rated the woman as significantly more attractive than did the other group. Further, the subjects who expected to go on a blind date with this woman rated her more sexually receptive than did the subjects who were told that they had been assigned to date someone else. How can we account for such findings?

Although this experiment was a particularly dramatic demonstration of perceptual accentuation, this same general process occurs every day. We magnify or accentuate that which will satisfy our needs and wants. The thirsty person sees a mirage of water, the sexually deprived person sees a mirage of sexual satisfaction, and only very rarely do they get mixed up.

IMPLICIT PERSONALITY THEORY

We each have a theory of personality. Although we may not be able to verbalize it, we nevertheless have the rules or systems that constitute a theory of personality. More specifically, we have a system of rules that tells us which characteristics of an individual go with which other characteristics. Consider, for example, the following brief questions. Note the characteristic in parentheses that best seems to complete the sentence:

John is energetic, eager, and (intelligent, stupid).
Joe is bright, lively, and (thin, fat).
Jim is handsome, tall, and (flabby, muscular).
Jane is attractive, intelligent, and (likeable, unlikeable).
Mary is bold, defiant, and (extroverted, introverted).
Susan is cheerful, positive, and (attractive, unattractive).

It is not important which words you selected. And certainly there are no right and wrong answers. What should be observed, however, is that certain of the words "seemed right" and others "seemed wrong." What made some seem right was our implicit personality theory, the system of rules that tells us which characteristics go with which other characteristics. The theory tells us that a person who is energetic and eager is also intelligent, not stupid, although there is no logical reason why a stupid person could not be energetic and eager.

CONSISTENCY

There is a rather strong tendency to maintain balance or consistency among our perceptions. As so many of the current theories of attitude change demonstrate, we strive to maintain balance among our attitudes; we expect certain things to go together and other things not to go together. On a purely intuitive basis, for example, respond to the following sentences by noting the expected response.

1. I expect a person I like to (like, dislike) me.
2. I expect a person I dislike to (like, dislike) me.
3. I expect my friend to (like, dislike) my friend.
4. I expect my friend to (like, dislike) my friend.
5. I expect my enemy to (like, dislike) my friend.
6. I expect my enemy to (like, dislike) my enemy.

According to most consistency theories, our expectations would be as follows: We would expect a person we liked to like us (1) and a person we disliked to dislike us (2). We would expect a friend to like a friend (3) and to dislike an enemy (4). We would expect our enemy to dislike our friend (5) and to like our other enemy (6). All of these—with the possible exception of the last one—should be intuitively satisfying. With some reflection even the last (6) should seem logical.

Further, we would expect someone we liked to possess those characteristics that we liked or admired. And we would expect our enemies not to possess those characteristics that we liked or admired. Conversely, we would expect persons we liked to lack unpleasant characteristics and persons we disliked to possess unpleasant characteristics.

In terms of interpersonal perception this tendency for balance and consistency may influence the way in which we see other people. It is easy to see our friends as being possessed of fine qualities and our enemies as being possessed of unpleasant qualities. Donating money to the poor, for example, can be perceived as an act of charity (if from a friend) or as an act of pomposity (if from an enemy). We would probably laugh harder at a joke told by a well-liked comedian than at that very same joke if told by a disliked comedian. And so forth and so on.

STEREOTYPING

One of the most frequently used shortcuts in interpersonal perception is that of *stereotyping*. Originally, "stereotype" was a printing term that referred to the plate that printed the same image over and over again.

A sociological or psychological stereotype, then, is a fixed impression of a group of people. We all have stereotypes whether they be of national groups, religous groups, or racial groups, or perhaps of criminals, prostitutes, teachers, plumbers, or artists.

When we have these fixed impressions we will often, upon meeting someone of a particular group, see that person primarily as a member of that group. Then all the characteristics we have in our minds for members of that group are applied to this individual. If we meet someone who is a prostitute, for example, we have a host of characteristics for prostitutes which we are ready to apply to this one person. To further complicate matters, we will often see in this person's behavior the manifestation of various characteristics which we would not see if we did not know that this person was a prostitute. Stereotypes distort our ability to accurately perceive other people. They prevent us from seeing an individual as an individual; instead the individual is seen only as a member of a group.

Sources

In addition to the works cited in the previous unit, I found Zick Rubin's *Liking and Loving: An Invitation to Social Psychology* (New York: Holt, 1973) a most useful source. Much of the discussion of the perceptual processes is based on the insights provided by Rubin. The cited study by Solomon Asch is "Forming Impressions of Personality," *Journal of Abnormal and Social Psychology* 41(1946):258–290. The cited study on forming impressions of exam-taking students was conducted by Edward E. Jones, Leslie Rock, Kelley G. Shaver, and Lawrence M. Ward: "Pattern of Performance and Ability Attribution: An Unexpected Primacy Effect," *Journal of Personality and Social Psychology* 10(1968):317–340. Both of these studies are discussed by Rubin.

Experiential Vehicles

PERCEPTION AND THE SELF:
A MODEL OF PERCEPTUAL SPACE

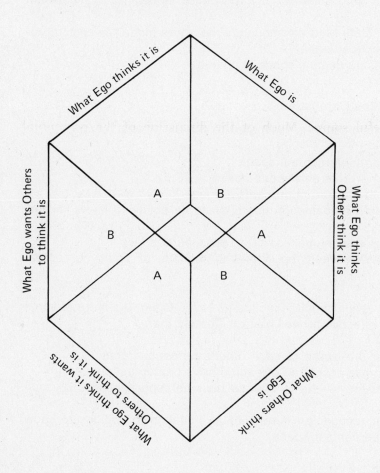

Some Structural Dynamics of the Model of Perceptual Space

1. "Perceptual space" is here conceived to involve three major components:
   a. Ego-Ego: the perception of Ego by itself[1]
   b. Ego-Other: the perception of Ego by Others
   c. Other-Ego: the perception of Others' perceptions of Ego by Ego
2. Each of these three components is divided into what is thought to be (the A sections) and what is (the B sections).
3. There is a fundamental distinction between the event (that is, the actual person, object, happening) and the perception of the event (that is, the observation of the person, object, happening).
4. All of the dimensions of the perceptual space interact; each dimension influences and is influenced by each other dimension.
5. Each dimension (and consequently the entire model) is in a constant state of change.
6. No dimensional state (and consequently the entire model) is ever reproduced in an identical manner.
7. Each individual's perceptual space is unique.

Some Communication Corollaries

Intrapersonal communication is facilitated to the extent that:

1. Ego is aware of its perceptual space
2. Ego is accepting of its perceptual space
3. Ego is willing to change its perceptual space
4. Ego recognizes a fundamental limitation to its ability to know its perceptual space
5. Ego recognizes the uniqueness of its perceptual space
6. similarity exists between the A and B sections of Ego's perceptual space

Interpersonal communication is facilitated to the extent that intrapersonal communication is effective as well as to the extent that:

7. Ego and Other are aware of each other's perceptual space
8. Ego and Other are accepting of each other's perceptual space
9. Ego and Other are willing to change their perceptual spaces of each other
10. Ego and Other recognize a fundamental limitation to abilities to know each other's perceptual space

[1]"Ego" is used for "self."

11. Ego and Other recognize the uniqueness of each other's perceptual space
12. Ego and Other have similar perceptual spaces
13. Ego and Other share their individual perceptual spaces with each other

Intrapersonal Communication Inventory

Fill in all sections of the model as completely and as honestly as you can. Certain sections of the model will no doubt be more difficult than others to complete. Make the best educated guesses that you can.

Entry Analysis
Try to form clusters of those aspects of your perceptual space for which you have similar responses. For example, which aspects of your perceptual space do you readily accept? Which do you have most difficulty accepting? What do these clustered aspects have in common? Can you label these clusters? For this analysis refer to the intrapersonal communication corollaries.

    Examine the relative frequency of the terms you used to fill in the six areas. Are some terms used more often than others? What does this frequency analysis suggest? On the basis of this entry analysis would you revise the entries you made in your perceptual space model? Make whatever revisions you think valid.

Behavioral Analysis
Try to relate each of the entries you made to your own specific behaviors. For example, assume that an entry in "What Ego thinks it is" was "reticent." Identify those of your specific behaviors which might be indicative of reticence.

    Are some entries more difficult to link to behaviors than others? Why do you suppose this is so?

    On the basis of this behavioral analysis would you revise the entries you made in your perceptual space model? Make whatever revisions you think valid.

Intrapersonal Analysis
Examine your perceptual space in relation to each of the corollaries pertaining to intrapersonal communication. Specifically, for each of the corollaries consider: 1) to what extent you agree/disagree with each of the corollaries, and 2) to what extent your particular perceptual space is facilitative of intrapersonal communication? That is, to what extent do you feel that you are aware of your perceptual space? To what extent are you accepting? And so on. Here it is particularly important that you look at

each entry you made in your model separately. Try to specifically identify those aspects of your perceptual space of which you are or are not aware, accepting, willing to change, and so forth.

Interpersonal Communication Inventory

Phase One
Interact with several people about your perceptual space. It will probably be most effective if you: 1) not reveal your own perceptions, 2) not reveal your satisfaction or dissatisfaction with any responses, 3) interact with some persons who know you well and with some who know you only little, and 4) interact with persons of different ages, sex, and background.

In your interactions ask them to be specific regarding both the entries to be made and the behavioral basis for their choices.

After all the relevant data has been collected examine the entries with specific attention to the areas of general agreement among the persons interviewed and the areas of disagreement. On what basis might you account for the similarities? On what basis might you account for the differences?

Compare these responses to the "educated guesses" you made before these interactions. Examine the areas of accurate and inaccurate guesses. Which person's responses were more accurately guessed? On what basis might you account for this?

On the basis of these interactions would you revise the entries you originally made in your perceptual space model? Make whatever revisions you think valid.

Phase Two
With one other person discuss your perceptual space models in relation to the corollaries pertaining to interpersonal communication. Specifically, for each of the corollaries consider: 1) to what extent you agree/disagree with each of the corollaries, and 2) to what extent your perceptual spaces are facilitative of interpersonal communication? That is, to what extent are each of you aware of each other's perceptual spaces? To what extent are each of you accepting of each other's perceptual spaces. And so on.

PERCEPTION AND SIGNIFICANT OTHERS: INTERPERSONAL PERCEPTUAL PROCESSES IN OPERATION

All six interpersonal perceptual processes pertain to the ways in which we make judgments about people on the basis of insufficient evidence. These judgments, then, are inferential rather than factual statements about others. Of course, we never do have ALL the evidence and because of this it is extremely important that our judgments be based on an accurate reading of at least the insufficient evidence. Since we will not stop making almost instant judgments of people, we should at least make these judgments as logically as possible.

This exercise is designed to increase our awareness of the ways in which the six perceptual processes considered in this unit operate in us and to raise questions pertaining to the logic of our judgments. The exercise may be completed in small groups of five or six students or with the entire class. Each member is supplied with a number of index cards. From the following Group Categories list, the group leader or instructor should select one and ask that each student write down five or six judgments they might make about members of this group. Students should not attempt to write down "logical" or "intellectually motivated" responses but rather should write down the judgments they would probably make upon meeting or hearing about a member of this group. No names should be put on these cards and no attempt should be made to discover the author of any particular card. The cards should be collected and read aloud by the group leader or instructor.

Discussion should center on the ways in which judgments are made and the ways in which the six perceptual processes discussed in this unit operate. Specifically, attention should be focused on the following:

1. the role of primacy and recency in the formation of judgments about these groups
2. the operation of the self-fulfilling prophecy
3. the influence of perceptual accentuation
4. the nature of our implicit personality theory and the influence it exerts on our judgments of these groups
5. the operation of our tendency to maintain or establish consistency or balance
6. the role of stereotyping

After judgments for this group are considered, another group category is selected and the process is repeated.

Group Categories

Alcoholics	Comedians
Automobile mechanics	Communists
Bartenders	Construction workers
Blacks	Convicts
Cartoonists	Delivery men
Catholics	Doctors
Chefs	Dress designers
Children	Drug addicts
Cocktail waitresses	Evangelists

Farmers
Homosexuals
Interior decorators
Jews
Lawyers
Lesbians
Movie stars
Musicians
Nurses
Opera singers
Pimps
Policemen
Politicians
Professors
Prostitutes
Protestants

Psychoanalysts
Psychologists
Religious leaders
  (priests, ministers, rabbis)
Rock singers
Stewardesses
Telephone operators
Television repairmen
Textbook authors
Theatre critics
Thieves
Truck drivers
Unmarried men
Unmarried women
Whites
Women's Liberationists

unit 17

Interpersonal Listening

Interpersonal Listening
The Nature and Importance of Listening
Listening and Feedback
   Feedback in Communication

Objectives

Upon completion of this unit, you should be able to:

1. define *listening*
2. explain the importance of feedback to listening
3. explain the five characteristics of effective feedback
4. explain the role of feedback in communication accuracy

There can be little doubt that we listen a great deal. Upon awakening we listen to the radio. On the way to school we listen to friends, to people around us, and perhaps to screeching cars, singing birds, or falling rain. In school our listening day starts in earnest and we sit in class after class listening to the teacher, to comments by other students, and sometimes even to ourselves. We listen to friends at lunch and return to class to listen to more teachers. We arrive home and again listen to our family and friends. Perhaps we then listen to records, radio, or television. All in all we listen for a good part of our waking day.

THE NATURE AND IMPORTANCE OF LISTENING

Numerous studies have been conducted to determine the percentage of our communication time devoted to listening as compared with speaking, reading, and writing. In one study, for example, it was found that adults in a variety of occupations spent approximately 70 percent of their day in one of the four communication activities. Of that time, approximately 42 percent was spent in listening, 32 percent in talking, 15 percent in reading, and 11 percent in writing. Listening percentages for students are even higher.

That we listen a great deal of the time, then, can hardly be denied. Whether we listen effectively or efficiently, however, is another matter. Although we might occasionally complain about having to study writing in elementary school, in high school, and again in college we would probably not deny its usefulness. Despite occasional problems in such courses, most people would admit that improvement in writing is both necessary and possible. With listening, however, our attitudes are different. For some reason we do not feel that it is necessary to improve our listening or that it is even possible. If you search through your college catalog you will find numerous courses designed to improve writing skills. And, of course, you will even find courses designed to improve your tennis, golf, and fencing abilities. Yet you will probably not find a single course in listening, despite its importance and its pervasiveness. The one exception to this general rule is found in music departments, where courses in listening to music will be offered. If it is useful to teach "music listening," would not a similar concern for language and speech be logical? It seems to be assumed that because we listen without a great deal of effort, we open our ears something like we open a drain. But this view, as we shall see, is far from accurate.

In actual practice most of us are relatively poor listeners, and our listening behavior could be made more effective and more efficient. Given the amount of time we engage in listening, the improvement of that skill would seem well worth the required effort. And it does take effort. Listening is not an easy matter; it takes time and energy to listen effectively.

By listening we mean *an active process of receiving aural stimuli*. Contrary to popular conception, listening is an *active* rather than a passive process. Listening does not just happen; we must make it happen. Listening takes energy and a commitment to engage in often difficult labor.

Listening involves *receiving* stimuli and is thus distinguished from hearing as a physiological process. The word "receiving" is used here to imply that stimuli are taken in by the organism and are in some way processed or utilized. For at least some amount of time, the signals received are retained by the organism.

Listening involves *aural* stimuli, that is, signals (sound waves) received by the ear. Listening therefore is not limited to verbal signals but encompasses all signals sent by means of fluctuations in air—noises as well as words, music as well as prose.

Make special note of the fact that there is nothing in this definition that implies that listening as a skill is limited to formal speaking situations, such as when a public speaker addresses a large audience. Listening is a skill that is of crucial importance in interpersonal and in small group communication, as well as in public speaking.

LISTENING AND FEEDBACK

The concept of *feedback* is crucial to an understanding of listening as an active process. Feedback refers to those messages sent from listeners and received by speakers which enable speakers to gauge their effects on their receivers. If speakers are to learn the effects of their messages and if they are to adapt their messages more effectively, then listeners must be trained to send these messages of feedback to speakers. Here are some guides for effective use of the feedback mechanism in interpersonal communication. Effective feedback is immediate, honest, appropriate, clear, and informative.

Effective Feedback Is Immediate

The most effective feedback is that which is most immediate. Ideally, feedback is sent immediately after the message is received. Feedback, like reinforcement, loses its effectiveness with time; the longer we wait to praise or punish, for example, the less effect it will have. To say to the child that he will get punished when Daddy comes home probably does little to eliminate the undesirable behavior simply because the punishment or feedback comes so long after the behavior.

Effective Feedback Is Honest

Feedback should be honest. To say this is not to provide license for overt hostility or cruelty. It is to say, however, that feedback should not merely be a series of messages which the speaker wants to hear and which will build up his or her ego. Feedback should be an honest reaction to a communication.

Feedback concerning one's understanding of the message as well as one's agreement with the message should be honest. We should not be ashamed or afraid to admit that we did not understand a message, nor should we hesitate to assert our disagreement.

We can, of course, consistently give speakers the feedback they want. You can shake your head, indicating understanding, as the teacher pours forth some incomprehensible dribble and nod agreement with his or her equally incomprehensible theories. This may make the teacher feel that you are intelligent and clever. But note the effect that this kind of behavior has: It reinforces the behavior of the teacher. It will lead that teacher to continue addressing classes with this same incomprehensible dribble. In effect, you have told the teacher that he or she is doing a good job by your positive feedback. The same is true with any speaker in any type of communication situation.

The quality of teaching and in fact of all the communicative arts are in large part a reflection of the listeners; we are the ones who keep the levels of communication where they are.

Effective Feedback Is Appropriate

Feedback should be appropriate to the general communication situation. For the most part we have learned what is appropriate and what is not appropriate from observing others as we grew up. And so there is no need for spelling out what is and what is not appropriate. We should recognize, however, that appropriateness is a learned concept; consequently, what is appropriate for our culture is not necessarily appropriate for another culture. Thus for students to stamp their feet when a teacher walks in might signal approval or respect in one culture but might signal hostility in another.

We should also note that feedback to the message should be kept distinct from feedback to the speaker. We need to make clear, in disagreeing with speakers, for example, that we are disagreeing with what they are saying and not necessarily rejecting them as people. We may dislike what a person says but like the person saying it. When students say that a class session is boring, they are not saying that they dislike the teacher personally, but merely that they disliked the class session.

Effective Feedback Is Clear

Feedback should be clear on at least two counts. It should be clear enough so that speakers can perceive that it is feedback to the message and not just a reflection of something you ate that didn't agree with you. Second, the feedback should be clear in meaning; if it is to signal understanding then it should be clear to the speaker that that is what you are signaling. If you are disagreeing then that, too, should be clear.

Effective Feedback Is Informative

The feedback you send to speakers should convey some information; it should tell them something they did not already know.

In any classroom there are always some students who sit with the same expression on their faces regardless of what is going on. You could lecture on the physics of sound or you could show a stag film and their expression would remain unchanged—or at least relatively so. These people communicate no information and serve only to confuse the speaker.

Similarly, to always respond in the same way conveys no information. To communicate information responses must be, in part at least, unpredictable. If speakers are able to completely predict how you will respond to something they say then your response conveys no information and does not serve any useful feedback function.

The importance of listening can hardly be denied. We spend most of our communication time in listening, and we probably learn more from listening than from any other means. In interpersonal communication, listening and feedback are so closely related that we cannot be said to listen effectively if immediate, honest, appropriate, clear, and informative feedback is not given.

Sources

On the nature of listening and for numerous studies see, for example, Larry L. Barker, *Listening Behavior* (Englewood Cliffs, N.J.: Prentice-Hall, 1971) and Carl Weaver, *Human Listening: Processes and Behavior* (Indianapolis: Bobbs-Merrill, 1972). Perhaps the classic in the area is Ralph Nichols and Leonard Stevens, *Are You Listening?* (New York: McGraw-Hill, 1957). On listening and feedback the chapter by Kathy J. Wahlers in Barker's *Listening Behavior* was most helpful. Listening from the point of view of auditory attention is covered in Neville Moray's *Listening and Attention* (Baltimore: Penguin, 1969). Ella Erway's *Listening: A Programmed Approach* (New York: McGraw-Hill, 1969) covers the nature of listening, its importance, and the ways in which it can be improved.

Experiential Vehicle

FEEDBACK IN COMMUNICATION

The purpose of this exercise is to illustrate the importance of feedback in communication. The procedure is to have a listener at the blackboard and a speaker prepared to communicate under various different conditions.

The object of the interactions is for the speaker to communicate to the listener instructions for reproducing a diagram. The different conditions under which this task is attempted should enable you to investigate the importance of feedback in communication.

First Condition

The speaker is given a diagram which is neither too complex nor too simple. With his or her back to the listener, the speaker must communicate instructions for reproducing the diagram. The listener is not allowed to speak.

Second Condition

The speaker is given another diagram and must tell the listener how to reproduce it. This time the speaker may observe what the listener is doing and may comment on it. The listener is not allowed to speak.

Third Condition

The speaker is given a third diagram and must tell the listener how to reproduce it. The speaker may again observe what the listener is doing and may comment on it. This time, however, the listener may ask any questions he or she wishes of the speaker. Members of the class should see the diagrams.

Discussion should center on the accuracy of the drawings and the confidence the listeners had in their attempts at reproducing the diagrams. Which is the most accurate? Which is the least accurate? To what extent did the feedback, first visual and then both visual and auditory, help the listener reproduce the diagram?

In the following conditions, how would the lack of feedback influence the communication interactions:

1. A trial lawyer addressing a jury

2. A teacher lecturing to a class of students

3. A used car salesperson trying to sell a car

4. An amorous lover with the loved one

5. A typist typing a letter

unit 18

Effective Interpersonal Listening

Obstacles to Effective Listening
Guides to Effective Listening
  Sequential Communication

Objectives

Upon completion of this unit, you should be able to:

1. list and explain the five obstacles to effective listening
2. list and explain the five guides to effective listening
3. identify and explain the three basic processes in sequential communication

In any attempt to improve our own interpersonal listening behavior we need to consider the reasons why we do not listen as effectively as we might (the obstacles to effective listening) and the means we might use to improve our listening effectiveness (the guides to effective listening).

OBSTACLES TO EFFECTIVE LISTENING

Listening is at best a difficult matter. Yet it may be made easier, more pleasant, and more efficient if some of the obstacles or barriers to effective listening were eliminated. Although there are many which could be identified, five general classes of obstacles are considered here.

Prejudging the Communication

Whether in a lecture auditorium or in a small group of people there is a strong tendency to prejudge the communications of others as uninteresting or irrelevant to our own needs or to the task at hand. Often we compare these communications with something we might say or with something that we might be doing instead of "just listening." Generally, listening to others comes in a poor second.

By prejudging a communication as uninteresting we are in effect lifting the burden of listening from our shoulders. If we have already determined that the communication is uninteresting, for example, then there is no reason to listen. So we just tune out the speaker and let our minds recapture last Saturday night.

All communications are, at least potentially, interesting and relevant. If we prejudge them and tune them out we will never be proven wrong. At the same time, however, we close ourselves off from potentially useful information. Most important, perhaps, is that we do not give the other person a fair hearing.

Rehearsing a Response

For the most part we are, as Wendell Johnson put it, our own most enchanted listeners. No one speaks as well or on such interesting topics as we do. If we could listen just to ourselves, listening would be no problem.

Particularly in small group situations but also in larger settings the speaker may say something with which we disagree; for the remainder of that speaker's time we rehearse our response or rebuttal or question. We then imagine his or her reply to our response and then our response to his or her response and so on and on. Meanwhile, we have missed whatever else the speaker had to say—perhaps even the part that would make our question unnecessary or irrelevant or which might raise other and more significant questions.

If the situation is a public speaking one, and the speech is a relatively long one, then perhaps it is best to jot down the point at issue and go back to listening. If the situation is a small group one then it is best to simply make mental note of what you want to say and perhaps keep this in mind by relating it to the remainder of what the individual is saying. In either event the important point is to get back to listening.

Filtering Out Messages

I once had a teacher who claimed that whatever he could not immediately understand was not worth reading or listening to; if it had to be worked at it was not worth the effort. I often wonder how he managed to learn, how he was intellectually stimulated if indeed he was. Depending on our own intellectual equipment, many of the messages that we confront will need careful consideration and in-depth scrutiny. Listening will be difficult but the alternative—to miss out on what is said—seems even less pleasant than stretching and straining our minds a bit.

Perhaps more serious than filtering out difficult messages is filtering out unpleasant ones. None of us want to be told that something we believe in is untrue, that people we care for are unpleasant, or that ideals we hold are self-destructive. And yet, these are the very messages we need to listen to with great care. These are the very messages that will lead us to examine and reexamine our implicit and unconscious assumptions. If we filter out this kind of information we will be left with a host of unstated and unexamined assumptions and premises that will influence us without our influencing them. That prospect is not a very pleasant one.

Inefficiently Using the Thought-Speech Time Differential

It should be obvious that we can think much more quickly than a speaker can speak. Consequently, in listening to someone our minds can process the information much more quickly than the speaker can give it out. At conventions it was especially interesting to listen to Ralph Nichols, a nationally known expert on listening. Unlike most speakers, Nichols would speak very rapidly. At first, his speech sounded peculiar because it was so rapid. Yet it was extremely easy to understand; our minds did not wander as often as they did when listening to someone who spoke at a normal speed. I would not recommend that we all speak more rapidly since there are various side-effects which are difficult to control. But it is important to realize that in listening there is a great deal of time left over; only a portion of our time is used in listening to the information in the messages.

Given this state of affairs, we are left with a number of possibilities—from letting our mind wander back to that great Saturday night to utilizing the time for understanding and learning the message. Obviously, the latter would be the more efficient course of action. With this extra time, then, we might review concepts already made by the speaker, search for additional meanings, attempt to predict what the speaker will say next, and so on. The important point is that we stay on the topic with the speaker and not let our thoughts wander to distant places from whence they will not return.

Focusing Attention on Language or Delivery

For many people in communication, having studied language and style for so long, it is difficult for them not to concentrate on the stylistic peculiarities of an individual. In hearing a clever phrase or sentence, for example, it is difficult to resist the temptation to dwell on it and analyze it. Similarly, it is difficult for many not to focus on various gestures or particular aspects of voice. Focusing on these dimensions of communication only diverts time and energy away from the message itself. This is not to say that such behaviors are not important but only that we can fall into the trap of devoting too much attention to the way the message is packaged and not enough to the message itself.

GUIDES TO EFFECTIVE LISTENING

Listening ability—like speaking, reading, and writing abilities—can be improved. As in the case of these other abilities, there are no easy rules or simple formulas. There are, however, some guidelines which should be of considerable value if followed.

Listen Actively

Perhaps the first step to listening improvement is the recognition that it is not a passive activity; it is not a process which will happen if we simply do nothing to stop it. We may hear without effort but we cannot listen without effort.

Listening is a difficult process; in many ways it is more demanding than speaking. In speaking we are in control of the situation; we can talk about what we like in the way we like. In listening, however, we are forced to follow the pace, the content, and the language set by the speaker.

Perhaps the best preparation for active listening is to act like an active listener. This may seem trivial and redundant. In practice, however, this may be the most often abused rule of effective listening. Students often, for example, come into class, put their feet up on a nearby desk, nod their head to the side, and expect to listen effectively. It just does not happen that way. Recall, for example, how your body almost automatically reacts to important news. Almost immediately you assume an upright posture, cock your head to the speaker, and remain relatively still and quiet. We do this almost reflexively because this is how we listen most effectively. This is not to say that we should be tense and uncomfortable but only that our bodies should reflect the active mind.

Listen for Total Meaning

In listening to another individual we need to learn to listen for total meaning. The total meaning of any communication act is extremely complex, and we can be sure that we will never get it all. However, the total meaning is not only in the words used. The meaning is also in the nonverbal behavior of the speaker. Sweating hands and shaking knees communicate just as surely as do words and phrases.

Along with the verbal and nonverbal behaviors we should also recognize that the meaning of a communication act lies also in what is omitted. The speaker who talks about racism solely in the abstract, for example, and who never once mentions a specific group is communicating something quite different from the speaker who talks in specifics.

Listen with Empathy

It is relatively easy to learn to listen for understanding or for comprehension. But this is only a part of communication. We also need to *feel* what the speaker feels; we need to empathize with the speaker.

To empathize with others is to feel with them, to see the world as they see it, to feel what they feel. Only when we achieve this will we be able to fully understand another's meaning.

There is no fast method for achieving empathy with another individual. But it is something we should work toward. It is important that we see the teacher's point of view, not from that of our own, but from that of the teacher. And equally it is important for the teacher to see the student's point of view from that of the student. If students turn in late papers, teachers should attempt to put themselves in the role of the students to begin to understand the possible reasons for the lateness. Similarly, if teachers fail papers because they are late, students should attempt to put themselves in the role of teachers and attempt to understand the reason for the failure.

So often we witness the behavior of others which seems, to us at least, foolish and ridiculous. We see, for example, a child cry because he or she lost money. From our point of view the amount lost is insignificant and it therefore seems foolish to cry over it. What we need to do, however, is to see the situation from the point of view of the child—to realize that the amount of money is not insignificant to the child and that perhaps the consequences of losing the money are extremely serious. Popular college students might intellectually understand the reasons for the depression of the unpopular student but that will not enable them to emotionally understand the feelings of depression. What popular students need to do is to put themselves in the position of the unpopular student, to role play a bit, and begin to feel his or her feelings and think his or her thoughts. Then these students will be in a somewhat better position to "really understand," to empathize.

Listen with an Open Mind

Listening with an open mind is an extremely difficult thing to do. It is not easy for us, for example, to listen to arguments against some cherished belief. It is not easy to listen to statements condemning what we so fervently believe. It is not easy to listen to criticisms of what we think is just great.

In counseling students one of the most difficult tasks is to make them realize that even though they may dislike a particular teacher they can still learn something from him or her. For some reason many people will attempt to punish the people they dislike by not listening to them. Of course, if the situation is that of teacher and student, then it is only the student who suffers by losing out on significant material.

We also need to learn to continue listening fairly even though some signal has gone up in the form of an out of place expression or a hostile remark. Listening often stops when such a remark is made. Admittedly, to continue listening with an open mind is a difficult matter yet here it is particularly important that listening does continue.

Listen Critically

Although we need to emphasize that we should listen with an open mind and with empathy it should not be assumed that we should listen uncritically. Quite the contrary. We need to listen fairly but critically if meaningful communication is to take place. As intelligent and educated citizens, it is our responsibility to critically evaluate what we hear. This is especially true in the college environment. While it is very easy to simply listen to a teacher and take down what is said, it is extremely important that what is said is evaluated and critically analyzed. Teachers have biases too; at times consciously and at times unconsciously these biases creep into scholarly discussions. They need to be identified and brought to the surface by the critical listener. Contrary to what most students will argue, the vast majority of teachers will appreciate the responses of critical listeners. It demonstrates that someone is listening.

Sources

The obstacles to effective listening covered here are also covered in a number of books on listening such as those listed in Unit 17. Similarly, the guides to effective listening presented here are also considered in other texts in different ways. A useful overview is Ralph Nichols' "Do We Know How to Listen? Practical Helps in a Modern Age," *Speech Teacher* 10(1961):118–124. This article contains ten suggestions for improving listening. Most of the suggestions for improving listening such as those presented here as well as those presented in other texts owe their formulation to the work of Ralph Nichols. See, for example, Ralph Nichols and Leonard Stevens, *Are You Listening?* (New York: McGraw-

Hill, 1957). Another useful and informative source is Wendell Johnson's *Verbal Man* (New York: Colliers, 1969). For serial (or sequential) communication read William V. Haney, "Serial Communication of Information in Organizations," *Communication: Concepts and Processes,* Joseph A. DeVito, ed., revised and enlarged edition (Englewood Cliffs, N.J.: Prentice-Hall, 1976) and Haney's *Communication and Organizational Behavior: Text and Cases,* 3rd ed. (Homewood, Ill.: Irwin, 1973).

Experiential Vehicle

SEQUENTIAL COMMUNICATION

This exercise is designed to illustrate some of the processes involved in what might be called "sequential communication," that is, communication that is passed on from one individual to another.

This exercise consists of both a visual and a verbal part; both are performed in essentially the same manner. Taking the visual communication experience first, six subjects are selected to participate. Five of these leave the room while the first subject is shown the visual communication. He or she is told to try to remember as much as possible as he or she will be asked to reproduce it in as much detail as possible. After studying the diagram the first subject reproduces it on the board. The second subject then enters the room and studies the diagram. The first diagram is then erased and the second subject draws his or her version. The process is continued until all subjects have drawn the diagram. The last reproduction and the original drawing are then compared on the basis of the processes listed below.

The verbal portion is performed in basically the same way. Here the first subject is read the statement once or twice or even three times; the subject should feel comfortable that he or she has grasped it fully. The second subject then enters the room and listens carefully to the first subject's restatement of the communication. The second subject then attempts to repeat it to the third subject and so on until all subjects have restated the communication. Again, the last restatement and the original are compared on basis of the processes listed below.

Members of the class not serving as subjects should be provided with copies of both the visual and the verbal communications and should record the changes made in the various reproductions and restatements.

Special attention should be given to the following basic processes in sequential communication.

1. *Omissions.* What kinds of information are omitted? At what point in

the chain of communication are such omissions introduced? Do the omissions follow any pattern?

2. *Additions.*   What kinds of information are added? When? Can patterns be discerned here or are the additions totally random?

3. *Distortions.*   What kinds of information are added? When? Are there any patterns? Can the types of distortions be classified in any way? Are the distortions in the directions of increased simplicity? Increased complexity? Can the sources or reasons for the distortions be identified?

Nonverbal Communication

Verbal Communication

At George Campbell College a new student union was recently erected. The college raised the $2.5 million for the building from alumni funds, students fees, and various fund-raising activities such as dances, ski trips, and book sales. But it fell to the students to raise the money necessary to maintain the union, a rather large four-story building. So the students formed a drag racing club with each club or organization on campus being allowed to enter one car. They plan to charge $5 admission and expect 6000 people to attend. At this rate they would be able to raise $30,000 each year which would be somewhat in excess of the estimated $25,000 needed to run the union. There are already 17 entries from both academic and social organizations and the event promises to be an even greater financial success than everyone originally hoped.

unit 19

Universals
of Language

Vocal-Auditory Channel
Broadcast Transmission and Directional Reception
Specialization
Semanticity
Rapid Fading
Interchangeability
Arbitrariness
Duality of Patterning
Total Feedback
Discreteness
Displacement
Productivity
Cultural or Traditional Transmission
Reflexiveness
Prevarication
Learnability
   Human and Nonhuman "Language" Systems
   Word Coinage

Objectives

Upon completion of this unit, you should be able to:

1. define the following terms: *vocal-auditory channel, broadcast transmission* and *directional reception, specialization, semanticity, rapid fading, interchangeability, arbitrariness, duality of patterning, total feedback, discreteness, displacement, productivity, cultural or traditional transmission, reflexiveness, prevarication, learnability*
2. identify those features that make human language superior to animal languages

3. identify those characteristics that are present or absent from the communication system of at least one nonhuman "language"
4. explain the reasons words are created

Perhaps the best way to understand language and verbal interaction is to focus on those characteristics that are universal—those characteristics that all human languages possess in common. These characteristics or universals define what language is, how it is constructed, and what its potentials and limitations are. In all we shall distinguish sixteen such universals, following the work of the linguist Charles Hockett.

VOCAL-AUDITORY CHANNEL

To say that human language is vocal-auditory means that its signals are combinations of sounds produced by the respiratory system and received by the auditory system. Not all signals so produced, however, consitute language; paralinguistic features, such as volume, intonation, and vocal quality, are not included in the domain of language proper.

That human language makes use of the vocal-auditory channel is an obvious but not a necessary fact. Gestural or tactile systems could conceivably evolve to a point where they would serve many of the communicative functions now served by the vocal-auditory channel. In fact, they have not; these nonverbal systems serve primarily to supplement the messages of the vocal-auditory channel. The advantage that this channel provides should be clear if one imagines what communication limited to other channels would be like. With a gestural system, for example, communication in the dark, or around corners, or when working with our hands, or with someone not looking directly at us would be impossible. Tactile systems are even more limiting.

BROADCAST TRANSMISSION AND DIRECTIONAL RECEPTION

This feature follows from the nature of the channel used. Broadcast transmission points to the public nature of language; sounds are emitted and can be received by anyone within earshot, by enemies as well as by friends. Directional reception refers to the fact that the emitted sounds serve to localize the source; upon hearing a sound one can detect its location. Although it is true that one can whisper so that others will not hear, or "throw" one's voice so that receivers will not be able to tell where the sounds originate, in general, human language can be heard by anyone, regardless of the intended receiver, and indicates the location of the source.

SPECIALIZATION

A specialized communication system, according to Hockett, is one whose "direct energetic consequences are biologically irrelevant." Human language serves only one major purpose—to communicate. It does not aid any biological functions. On the other hand, a panting dog communicates information as to its presence and perhaps about its internal state. But the panting itself serves the biological function of temperature regulation. The fact that communication accompanies or results from this behavior is only incidental.

SEMANTICITY

As already indicated, language signals refer to things in the real world; they have referents. Not all signals have such referents, of course; it would be difficult, for example, to find the referents of such terms as *mermaid* or *or*. Yet for the most part, language symbols have some connection, however arbitrarily established, with the real world.

RAPID FADING

Speech sounds fade rapidly; they are evanescent. They must be received immediately after they are emitted or else not received at all. Although mechanical devices now enable sound to be preserved much as writing is preserved, this is not a characteristic of human language. Rather, these are extralinguistic means of storing information, aiding memory, and so forth. Of course, all signals fade; written symbols and even symbols carved in rock are not permanent. In relative terms, however, speech signals are probably the least permanent of all communicative media.

INTERCHANGEABILITY

Any human being can serve as both sender and receiver—the roles are interchangeable. Human beings are *transceivers*. Exceptions to this property are not in the nature of language but in the nature of certain individuals. The person who cannot speak or hear obviously cannot exchange roles as can most individuals. These limitations are not a function of language but of certain physiological or psychological dysfunctions of the individual. Similarly, infants cannot function as both senders and receivers in the same way as adults. This, too, is not a function of language but of the maturational level of the individual. In some languages of the world there are different codes for men and women: certain words are restricted to males and others to females. This, too, is not so much a linguistic as it is a cultural feature. Both men and women are capable of using the other's code; when directly quoting a member of the opposite sex, for example, the appropriate code is used. The restriction is imposed by society, not by language.

ARBITRARINESS

Language signals are arbitrary; they do not possess any of the physical properties or characteristics of the things for which they stand. The word *wine* is no more tasty than the word *sand*, nor is the latter any less wet.

Opposed to arbitrariness is *iconicity*. Iconic signals do bear resemblance to their referents. A line drawing of a person is iconic in representing the body parts in proper relation to each other. But it is arbitrary in representing the texture and thickness of the anatomical structures.

Both arbitrariness and iconicity are relative. For example, a line drawing is more arbitrary than is a black and white photograph, which is more arbitrary than a color photograph. Paralinguistic features (volume, rate, rhythm) are more iconic than are the features normally classified as belonging to language. Rate, for example, may vary directly with emotional arousal and hence would be iconic. But the sound of the word *fast* is not actually fast.

DUALITY OF PATTERNING

Human language is composed of two levels: the level of the smallest differentiating, but meaningless, elements (called cenemes) and the level of the smallest meaningful combinations of these elements (called pleremes). In human language cenemes correspond to phonemes (roughly, individual sounds) and pleremes to morphemes (roughly, the smallest meaningful combinations of sounds).

According to Hockett, it is characteristic of systems possessing significant duality of patterning to have a relatively small number of cenemes and an extremely large number of possible pleremes. Human language clearly evidences significant duality in this sense; there are relatively few phonemes but a great many morphemes.

TOTAL FEEDBACK

This feature enables senders to receive their own messages. Speakers receive what they send primarily by auditory feedback, although kinesthetic and proprioceptive feedback can also be involved. This is not to say that the sources receive their messages in the same way as do receivers or that they receive all and only what the receivers do. Because the senders also hear their voices through bone conduction, as well as by ear, they sound different to themselves than they do to others.

DISCRETENESS

This universal can probably best be explained by first noting its opposite: continuousness. A continuous signal contains no sharp divisions; vocal volume is probably a good example. In reality there is no sharp break between loud and soft, for example, but only gradual changes. A discrete system, on the other hand, does contain sharp divisions. For example, the sounds /t/ and /d/ differ in the feature of voiceness (the vibration or lack of vibration of the vocal cords). By pronouncing "time" and "dime" while holding your hand against your throat, you will notice that there is vibration of the vocal cords on "dime" but not on "time." Although voiceness is, in reality, a continuous variable, the sound is heard as either /t/ or /d/ and not as one midway between /t/ and /d/, regardless of how much voicing is used.

DISPLACEMENT

Human language can be used to talk about things which are remote in both time and space; one can talk about the past and the future as easily as the present. And one can talk about things one has not, does not, and will not ever perceive—about mermaids and unicorns, about supernatural beings from other planets, about talking animals. One can talk about the unreal as well as the real, the imaginary as well as the actual.

PRODUCTIVITY

Utterances in human language, with only trivial exceptions, are novel; each utterance is generated anew. The rules of grammar have already imposed certain restrictions on the way in which sentences may be generated, so complete productivity, in regard to form at least, does not exist. One can, however, talk about a vast number of different things and can even coin new words for new ideas and concepts. Whether human language imposes any restrictions on what can be communicated is an interesting, though probably unanswerable, question.

CULTURAL OR TRADITIONAL TRANSMISSION

The form of any particular human language is traditionally transmitted. The child raised by English speakers learns English as a native speaker, regardless of the language of his or her biological parents. The genetic endowment pertains to human language in general rather than to any specific human language.

REFLEXIVENESS

Human language can be used to refer to itself. That is, we can use language to talk about people and events in the world, but we can also use language to talk about language itself—much as we are doing right now. Language used to talk about language is referred to as *metalanguage*.

PREVARICATION

As a consequence of sematicity, displacement, and productivity, speakers of human languages can lie. In any system that does not possess these three features lying would be impossible. Although animal lovers are fond of telling about their pets who try to fool them, it appears that "lying" is extremely rare in animals.

LEARNABILITY

Any human language can be learned by any normal human being. It might be added that this is only true at particular times in the life of the human. One cannot learn a language as a native after a certain age. This feature is best interpreted to refer to the equal learnability of all human languages—no one language should present any greater difficulty for a child than any other language.

These sixteen features or univerals do not, of course, exhaust the characteristics of language. Taken together, however, they should serve to clarify how human language is made up, and what some of its potentials and limitations are. Further, these features, taken together as a definition of human language, should enable you to distinguish human language from all other communication systems, whether these are animal systems, such as the language of the bee or the dolphin, or man-made systems, such as the language of semaphore, chess, or mathematics.

Sources

For universals of language I relied on the work of Charles F. Hockett, particularly his "The Problem of Universals in Language," in J. H. Greenberg, ed., *Universals of Language* (Cambridge, Mass.: M.I.T. Press, 1963) and "The Origin of Speech," *Scientific American* 203(1960):89–96. The concepts of language universals are most thoroughly surveyed in Greenberg's *Universals of Language.* Most of the material, however, presumes a rather thorough knowledge of linguistics.

Portions of the material in this unit were adapted from my *The Psychology of Speech and Language: An Introduction to Psycholinguistics* (New York: Random House, 1970).

Experiential Vehicles

HUMAN AND NONHUMAN "LANGUAGE" SYSTEMS

On the basis of your knowledge concerning animal and artificial language systems, working in groups of five or six, fill in the accompanying chart. Indicate in the appropriate spaces whether the system definitely has ($\sqrt{}$), definitely does not have (X), or might have (?) the designated feature. Be prepared to discuss the reason(s) for your decisions.

WORD COINAGE

Although language and culture are closely related and although the language closely reflects the culture, there often seem to be concepts important to a culture or a subculture for which the language does not provide a convenient one word label.

Sometimes slang or "substandard" forms fill this void, for example, *youse* or *you all* for "you" (plural) or *screw* for "prison guard." Sometimes words are created because of some social issue, for example, *Ms.* for a form of address for women regardless of marital status or *ecdysiast* for "stripper."

In order to gain greater insight into the relationship between language and culture/subculture and in order to become more familiar with the dimensions and functions of words, perform the following exercise in groups of five or six.

1. Create a new word for some concept that is important to the culture or to a particular subculture and for which a single word label is not available.
2. Define this word as would a dictionary and identify its part(s) of speech.
3. List its various inflectional forms and definitions.
4. Provide two or three examples of how the word would be used (sentences in which the word is used).
5. Justify the coinage of this new word considering, for example, why this word is needed, what void it fills, what it clarifies, what its importance is, what its effects might be should it be used widely, and so forth.

	Bee language	Dog language	Dolphin language	Chimp language	Instru-mental music language	Computer language
Vocal-auditory channel						
Broadcast transmission and directional reception						
Rapid fading						
Interchangeability						
Total feedback						
Specialization						
Semanticity						
Arbitrariness						
Discreteness						
Displacement						
Productivity						
Duality of patterning						
Cultural transmission						
Reflexiveness						
Prevarication						
Learnability						

Key:
Definitely has it (√).
Definitely does not have it (X).
Might have it or might not have it (?).

unit 20

Sublanguages

Language as a Social Institution
Functions of Sublanguages
Kinds of Sublanguages
  Five Sublanguages
  Forms of Address

Objectives

Upon completion of this unit, you should be able to:

1. define *sublanguage, subculture, codifiability, cant, jargon, argot,* and *slang*
2. explain the functions of sublanguages
3. explain the relationship between the frequency of synonyms for a concept and the importance of that concept to a culture or subculture
4. Identify how sociological variables influence the form of address used

LANGUAGE AS A SOCIAL INSTITUTION

Language is a social institution designed, modified, and extended (some purists might even say distorted) to meet the ever-changing needs of the culture or subculture. As such, language differs greatly from one culture to another and, equally important though perhaps less obvious, from one subculture to another.

Subcultures are cultures within a larger culture and may be formed on the basis of religion, geographical area, occupation, sexual orientation, race, nationality, living conditions, interests, needs, and so on. Catholics, protestants, and Jews; New Yorkers, Californians, and mountain folk; teachers, plumbers, and musicians; homosexuals and lesbians; blacks, Chinese, and American Indians; Germans, Italians, and Mexicans; prisoners, suburbanites, and "ghettoites"; bibliophiles, drug addicts, and bird watchers; diabetics, the blind, and ex-convicts may all be viewed as subcultures depending, of course, on the context on which we focus. In New York, for example, New Yorkers would obviously not constitute a subculture but throughout the rest of the world they would. In the United States as a whole protestants would not constitute a subculture (though Catholics and Jews would). In New York City, on the other hand, Protestants would constitute a subculture. Blacks and Chinese would be subcultures only outside of Africa and China. As these examples illustrate, the majority generally constitutes the culture and the various minorities generally constitute the subcultures. Yet this is not always the case. Women, although the majority in our culture, may be viewed as a subculture primarily because the society as a whole is male oriented. Whether a group should be regarded as a subculture or a culture, then, would depend upon the context being considered and the orientation of the society of which these groups are a part.

Each individual belongs to several subcultures. At the very least they belong to a national, a religious, and an occupational subculture. The importance of the subcultural affiliation will vary greatly from one individual to another, from one context to another, from one time or circumstance to another. For example, to some people in some contexts an individual's religious affiliation may be inconsequential and his or her membership in this subculture hardly thought of. When, on the other hand, the individual wishes to marry into a particular family this once inconsequential membership may take on vast significance.

Because of the common interests, needs, or conditions of individuals constituting a subculture, sublanguages come into being. Like language in general, sublanguages exist to enable members of the group to communicate with each other. And, again like language in general, there are various regional variations, changes over time, and so on. There are, however, other functions that sublanguages serve and these functions constitute their reason for existence. If they did not serve these several functions they would soon disappear. It should not be assumed, of course, that all sublanguages must serve all the functions noted.

FUNCTIONS OF SUBLANGUAGES

One of the most obvious facts about language and its relation to culture is that concepts that are important to a given culture are given a large number of terms. For example, in our culture money is extremely important; consequently, we have numerous terms denoting this concept: *finances, funds, capital, assets, cash, pocket money, spending money, pin money, change, bread, loot, swag,* and various others. Transportation and communication are other concepts for which numerous terms exist in our language. Without knowing anything about a given culture we could probably make some pretty good guesses as to the important concepts in that culture by simply examining one of its dictionaries or thesauruses. With sublanguages, the same principle holds. Concepts that are of special importance to a particular subculture are given a large number of terms. Thus one function of sublanguages is to provide the subculture with convenient synonyms for those concepts which are of great importance and hence are spoken about frequently. To prisoners, for example, a prison guard—clearly a significant concept and one spoken about a great deal—may be denoted by *screw, roach, hack, slave driver, shield, holligan,* and various other terms. Heroin, in the drug subculture, may be called *H, Harry, smack, Carga, joy powder, skag, stuff,* or just plain *shit.*

A related function of sublanguages is to provide the subculture with convenient distinctions that are important to the subculture but generally not to the culture at large—and thus distinctions that the general language does not make. For example, the general culture has no need for making distinctions among various drugs—all may be conveniently labeled *drugs.* But to members of the drug subculture it is essential to make distinctions which to outsiders may seem unimportant or even trivial. The general culture, for example, does not distinguish between "getting stoned" and "on a high." Yet to the members of the drug subculture these are two different states that need to be distinguished. Put differently, sublanguages serve to increase the *codifiability* of the general language. Codifiability refers to the ease with which certain concepts may be expressed in a language. Short terms are of high codifiability; long expressions are of low codifiability. All languages and sublanguages seem to move in the direction of increasing codifiability. As a concept becomes important in a culture or subculture the term denoting it is shortened or some other simpler expression is adopted to denote it; thus *television* becomes *TV, motion pictures* becomes *movies,* and *lysergic acid diethylamide* becomes *LSD* or simply *acid.* The expression "turn on" is the drug subculture's highly codifiable term for the general culture's low codifiable expression "to take a drug or participate in some experience which alters one's awareness." Similarly, it is much easier to say "lid" than "an ounce of marijuana" and "dex" than "dextroamphetamine capsules."

Sublanguages also serve as means of identification. By using a particular sublanguage, speakers identify themselves to hearers as members of that subculture—assuming, of course, that hearers know the language being used. Individuals belonging to various nationality-based subcultures will frequently drop a foreign word or phrase in the conversation to identify themselves to their hearers. Similarly, homosexuals and ex-convicts will at times identify themselves by using the cant of their subculture. When the subcultural membership is one that is normally hidden, as is the case of homosexuals and ex-convicts, the clues to self-identification are subtle. Generally, they are only given after the individuals themselves receive some kind of positive feedback which leads them to suspect that the hearer also belongs to the subculture in question or that the hearer is at least sympathetic. In a similar vein, the use of sublanguages also functions to express to others one's felt identification with that subculture. For example, blacks may address each other as brother and sister when meeting for the first time. The use of these terms by blacks as well as the frequent use of foreign expressions by members of various national groups communicates to others that the speaker feels a strong identification with the group.

Sublanguages also enable members of the subculture to communicate with one another while in the presence of nonmembers without having their conversation completely understood. Under certain situations, of course, the sublanguage may mark the individual as a member of a particular subculture and so he or she would refrain from using the sublanguage. This is often the case among criminals when in a noncriminal environment. At other times, however, the use of a sublanguage does not lead to an individual's identification as a subculture member, and the sublanguage serves the useful purpose of excluding nonmembers from the class of decoders.

A less obvious function of sublanguages, though a particularly important one, is that they serve to provide the group with a kind of identity and a sense of fraternity. Because ex-convicts all over the country know the same sublanguage they are, in a sense, bound together. Obviously, the more the subculture has a need to band together the greater the importance of a specialized language.

KINDS OF SUBLANGUAGES

"Sublanguage" has been used here as a general term to denote a variation from the general language that is used by a particular group or subculture existing within the broader, more general culture. But there are different kinds of sublanguages and these should now be distinguished.

Cant is the conversational language of a specific subculture which is generally understood only by members of that subculture. *Jargon* is the technical language of a particular subculture; it is the "shop talk" of the group. *Argot* is the cant and the jargon of a particular subculture, generally an "underworld" or criminal subculture such as forgers, bank robbers, thieves, and the like. *Slang* is a more general term denoting the language used by special groups (for example, different social or age groups) which is not considered proper by the general society. Slang may be viewed as consisting of those terms from the argot, cant, and jargon of the various subcultures which are known by the general population.

With the passage of time and an increased frequency of usage, slang terms enter the general language as socially acceptable expressions. When this happens new terms are needed and are therefore coined by the subcultures. The old terms are then dropped from the sublanguage since they now serve none of the functions for which they were originally developed.

This is just one of the ways by which new words enter the language and by which sublanguages are kept distinct from the general language.

Sources

For sublanguages see H. L. Mencken's *The American Language* (New York: Knopf, 1971). Mencken's chapter on "American Slang" is surely a classic work and, it should be added, a most interesting one at that. Much interesting research relevant to sublanguages is reported in the various works on sociolinguistics, for example, Joshua A. Fishman's *The Sociology of Language* (Rowley, Mass.: Newbury House, 1972) and Dell Hymes' *Foundations in Sociolinguistics: An Ethnographic Approach* (Philadelphia: University of Pennsylvania Press, 1974). One of the most insightful essays is that by Paul Goodman, "Sublanguages," in *Speaking and Language: Defence of Poetry* (New York: Random House, 1971). The theory and research on forms of address are thoroughly covered in Roger Brown, *Social Psychology* (New York: Free Press, 1965).

Experiential Vehicles

FIVE SUBLANGUAGES

Presented below are a few brief lexicons of some sublanguages. Note how these terms serve the functions discussed in this unit and how many of them are in the process of passing into the general language.

Assuming that you might like to test your knowledge of the various sublanguages, these lexicons are presented as matching quizzes. Write the number of the sublanguage term (left column) next to the letter of the corresponding general language term (right column).

CRIMINAL TALK

1. maker, designer, scratcher, connection
2. paper, scrip, stiff
3. jug stiff, cert
4. beat, sting, come-off
5. buttons, shamus, fuzz
6. mark, hoosier, chump, yap
7. poke, leather, hide
8. cold poke, dead skin
9. gun, cannon, whiz
10. boosters
11. booster box
12. bug
13. dinah, noise
14. double
15. gopher
16. hack
17. soup, pete
18. jug heavy
19. stiffs
20. heavy rackets

a. bank burglar
b. false key
c. rackets involving violence
d. forger
e. wallet
f. a parcel with a trap side for hiding stolen merchandise
g. burglar alarm
h. an iron safe
i. forged check
j. pickpocket
k. dynamite
l. forged bank check
m. shoplifters
n. watchman
o. policeman
p. negotiable securities
q. pickpocket victim
r. nitroglycerine
s. empty wallet
t. picking a pocket

PRISONER TALK

1. fish
2. kite
3. drum
4. to slam off
5. to gut
6. sleeping time
7. college
8. greenhouse
9. Cupid's itch
10. big noise
11. screw, roach, hack, slave driver, shield
12. frocker, goody, psalmer
13. croacker, cutemup, pill punk, salts, iodine
14. scraper, butcher
15. leather, young horse
16. water
17. chalk
18. beagle, dog, balloon
19. pig
20. soup jockey

a. prison waiter
b. prison chaplin
c. prison barber
d. a new prisoner
e. to escape from jail
f. prison guard
g. prison doctor
h. roast beef
i. meat
j. letter smuggled out of jail
k. venereal disease
l. prison
m. soup
n. sausage
o. cell
p. to die
q. milk
r. prison morgue
s. a short sentence
t. warden

GAY TALK

1. auntie
2. bring out
3. bull dyke
4. butch
5. camp
6. chicken
7. closet queen
8. come out
9. cruise
10. drag queen
11. fag hag
12. to be on the fence
13. to drop one's pins
14. leather bars
15. mother
16. gay
17. number

a. burlesque of one's own homosexuality
b. to introduce someone to homosexuality
c. one who wears the clothes of the opposite sex
d. to let others know that one is homosexual
e. one who engages in homosexual activity but does not consider himself homosexual
f. homosexual
g. to enter the gay life
h. masculine homosexual woman
i. old homosexual, generally effeminate
j. effeminate male homosexual

18. queen
19. trade
20. whore

k. to be undecided between heterosexuality and homo-sexuality
l. masculine appearing homo-sexual, male or female
m. to search for a sexual partner
n. a young boy
o. one who introduces another to the gay life
p. a promiscuous homosexual
q. homosexual bars whose customers are motorcycle riders who wear leather clothes and jeans
r. a casual sexual partner
s. a male homosexual who does not actively participate in the gay social life
t. a heterosexual who prefers to socialize with gays

MOUNTAIN TALK

1. a-fixin'
2. doin's
3. fetch
4. put out
5. aim
6. smart
7. book read
8. lollygag
9. crick
10. biggety
11. plumb
12. shed of
13. poke
14. red
15. skittish
16. gander
17. parts
18. smack-dab
19. fur piece
20. gully-washer

a. hard rain
b. bag
c. look at
d. getting ready to do something
e. get rid of
f. hurt
g. clean up
h. function or event
i. loaf or loiter
j. nervous
k. bring
l. stiffness
m. a great distance
n. angry
o. geographical area
p. intend, plan
q. exactly, on the dot
r. completely
s. educated
t. snobbish, stuck up

DRUG TALK

1. smack, H, Harry, Carga, joy powder, skag, stuff, shit
2. head
3. joint, stick
4. flip
5. acid
6. poppers, snappers
7. straight
8. stoned
9. trip
10. narc, narco
11. spaced out
12. zero
13. guide
14. acidhead
15. Bernice, C, candy, coke, dust, flake, snow
16. lift off
17. freakout
18. boo, tea, grass, bush, hay, hemp, jive, pot, weed, Mary Jane
19. ups, uppers
20. downs, downers

a. get high
b. ineffective dosage of drugs
c. a regular user of LSD
d. LSD experience
e. lysergic acid diethylamide
f. user of psychedelic drugs
g. narcotics agent
h. bad LSD experience
i. marijuana
j. depressants
k. one who watches over an individual on an acid trip
l. marijuana cigarette
m. high on marijuana
n. high on LSD
o. cocaine
p. stimulants
q. someone who does not take drugs
r. amyl nitrate
s. become psychotic
t. heroin

FORMS OF ADDRESS

For each of the following persons indicate the form of address you would use in speaking to them *and* the form of address you would expect them to use in speaking to you.

Use the following shorthand:

TLN — title plus last name
FN — first name
TFN — title plus first name
T   — title

	You to Them	*Them to You*
1. Your college professor	_____	_____
2. A fellow student	_____	_____
3. A younger child	_____	_____
4. Your doctor/dentist	_____	_____

	You to Them	Them to You
5. Your employer	_____	_____
6. Your employee	_____	_____
7. Your high school teacher	_____	_____
8. Your uncle/aunt	_____	_____
9. Your nephew/niece	_____	_____
10. Your grandfather/grandmother	_____	_____
11. Your state senator	_____	_____
12. The college president	_____	_____
13. Your minister/priest/rabbi	_____	_____
14. Your parents' friend	_____	_____
15. Burt Reynolds/Sophia Loren	_____	_____
16. A street bum	_____	_____
17. A millionaire	_____	_____

On what bases were your decisions made, that is, what sociological variables influenced your decisions?

unit 21

Universals of Verbal Interaction

The Principle of Immanent Reference
The Principle of Determinism
The Principle of Recurrence
The Principle of Contrast and the Working Principle of Reasonable
   Alternatives
The Principle of Relativity of Signal and Noise
The Principle of Reinforcement/Packaging
The Principle of Adjustment
The Principle of the Priority of Interaction
The Principle of the Forest and the Trees
   The Case of *Waldon* v. *Martin and Company*

Objectives

Upon completion of this unit, you should be able to:

1. distinguish between *immanent reference* and *displacement*
2. define and explain the principle of determinism
3. define *recurrence* in verbal interaction
4. explain the principle of contrast and the working principle of reasonable alternatives
5. explain the relativity of signal and noise
6. explain reinforcement/packaging
7. explain the way the principle of adjustment operates in interpersonal communication
9. explain the principle of the forest and the trees as it applies to the analysis of communication interactions

10. identify the operation of the universals of verbal interaction in the verbal interactions of others
11. identify at least three or four instances of your own behavior in which these universals were operative

Perhaps the most common and the most sophisticated means of communication is that of verbal interaction: talking and listening. The best way to approach this area is to focus on those characteristics or features that are present in all verbal interactions regardless of their specific purpose, their particular context, or their unique participants. There are nine principles of verbal interaction, but rather than being limited to specific kinds or types of verbal interactions these principles are universal. They are, in effect, generalizations which are applicable to any and all verbal interactions.

Universals such as these are significant for at least two major reasons. First, they provide a rather convenient summary of essential principles of verbal interaction. In effect, they define what constitutes a verbal interaction: what is its nature, and what are its essential aspects. Second, these universals provide us with a set of principles for analyzing verbal interactions. These principles should prove useful for analyzing any interaction which is primarily or even partially linguistic. These universals provide us with a set of questions to ask about any verbal interaction.

The nine principles, or universals, are taken from one of the most interesting research studies in the entire area of language. Three researchers (Robert Pittenger, Charles Hockett, and John Danehy) pooled their talents to analyze in depth the first five minutes of a psychiatric interview. Each word, phrase, and sentence; each intonation, pause, and cough were subjected to an incredibly detailed analysis. At the conclusion of this research the authors proposed nine "findings" (principles) which they felt would be of value to future students and researchers attempting to understand and analyze verbal interactions.

THE PRINCIPLE OF IMMANENT REFERENCE

It is true that human beings have the ability to use what Leonard Bloomfield called "displaced speech" and what Charles Hockett labels "displacement": Human language may make reference to the past as well as to the future; humans can talk about what is not here and what is not now. Nevertheless, all verbalization makes some reference to the present, to the specific context, to the speaker, and to the hearer(s). All verbal interactions, in other words, contain immanent references.

In attempting to understand verbal interaction, then, it is always legitimate to ask such questions as, "To what extent does this communication refer to this particular situation?" "To what extent does this communication refer to the speaker?" "In what ways is the speaker commenting on the hearer(s)?"

The answers to such questions may not be obvious. In many instances, in fact, the answers may never be found. Yet these questions are potentially answerable and thus always worth asking.

THE PRINCIPLE OF DETERMINISM

All verbalizations are to some extent determined; all verbalization is to some extent purposeful. Whenever something is said, there is a reason. Similarly, when in any interactional situation nothing is said, there is a reason. Words, of course, communicate and there are reasons why the words used are used. But silence also communicates and there are reasons why silence is used. Watzlawick, Jackson, and Beavin, in their *Pragmatics of Human Communication*, put it this way: one cannot *not* communicate. Whenever we are in an interactional situation, regardless of what we do or say or don't do or say, we communicate. Words and silence alike have message value; they communicate something to other people who in turn cannot *not* respond and are therefore also communicating.

Consequently, it is always legitimate in analyzing interactions to ask the reasons for the words as well as the reasons for the silence. Each communicates and each is governed by some reason or reasons; all messages are determined.

THE PRINCIPLE OF RECURRENCE

In our interactions individuals will tell us—not once but many times and not in one way but in many ways—about themselves—who they are, how they perceive themselves, what they like, what they dislike, what they want, what they avoid, and so on.

Whatever is perceived as important or significant to an individual will recur in that person's verbal interactions; he or she will tell us in many different ways and on many different occasions what these things are. Of course, they will rarely be communicated in an obvious manner. People who find themselves in need of approval do not directly ask others for approval. Rather, they go about obtaining approval responses in more subtle ways, perhaps asking how others like their new outfit, perhaps talking about their grades on an examination, perhaps talking about how they never betray a confidence, and so on.

THE PRINCIPLE OF CONTRAST AND THE WORKING PRINCIPLE OF REASONABLE ALTERNATIVES

For any signal to communicate information, two prerequisites are necessary. First, receivers must not know with certainty which signal will be communicated. Second, receivers must be able to recognize the signal they do receive.

If to every question I asked you said yes, and I knew that to every future question I would ask you would also say yes, your responses would not communicate any information to me. And of course there would be no point in my continuing to ask you questions. I would already know your answer. Your answers, and in fact all your messages, communicate information only when they cannot be predicted with certainty.

The second requisite is more obvious. If I am to receive information from you I must be able to recognize the signals you are sending. If, for example, you send signals in a language I do not understand, then I cannot recognize them and they will communicate no information to me.

My recognition of a particular signal is dependent upon my ability to discern both what that signal is and what that signal is not. If I am to receive information from a signal I must know what that signal is as well as what that signal contrasts with. My understanding of the signal "cat" rests on my ability to recognize the /k/ sound as well as to recognize that that sound is not /r/ or /p/ or /m/.

In short, in understanding and in analyzing verbal interactions we need to ask not only what the signals were but what were the reasonable alternatives that could have been used; why did the sender use the signals instead of the possible alternatives.

THE PRINCIPLE OF RELATIVITY OF SIGNAL AND NOISE

What is a signal and what is noise in any given communication is relative rather than absolute. If we are interested in hearing a particular story and the speaker, in narrating it, breaks it up by coughing, we might become annoyed because the coughing (noise) is disturbing our reception of the story (signal). But suppose this individual seeks some form of medication and in his or her interactions with the doctor coughs in a similar way. To the doctor this coughing might be the signal; the coughing might communicate an important message to the doctor. Similarly, when listening to a stutterer tell a story we may focus on the story, which would be the signal. The stuttering would be the noise interfering with our reception of the signal. But to the speech pathologist the stutters are the signals to which he or she attends and the story might be the noise.

The point is simply this: What is signal to one person and in one context might be noise to another person in another context.

THE PRINCIPLE OF REINFORCEMENT/PACKAGING

In most interactions messages are transmitted simultaneously through a number of different channels. We utter sounds with our vocal mechanism but we also utilize our body posture and our spatial relationships at the same time to reinforce our message. We say no and at the same time pound our fist on the table. One channel reinforces the other. The message is presented as a "package."

The extent to which simultaneous messages reinforce each other or contradict each other, then, is extremely important in understanding human communication. The same verbal message when accompanied by different nonverbal messages is not the same message and cannot be responded to in the same way.

THE PRINCIPLE OF ADJUSTMENT

Communication may take place only to the extent that the parties communicating share the same system of signals. This is obvious when dealing with speakers of two different languages; one will not be able to communicate with the other to the extent that their language systems differ.

This principle takes on particular relevance, however, when we realize that no two persons share identical signal systems. Parents and children, for example, not only have different vocabularies to a very great extent but even more importantly, have different denotative and especially different connotative meanings for the terms they have in common. Different cultures and subcultures, even when they share a common language, often have greatly differing nonverbal communication systems. To the extent that these systems differ, communication will not take place.

THE PRINCIPLE OF THE PRIORITY OF INTERACTION

This principle simply states that in understanding and in analyzing verbal interactions we must begin with the interaction, with the behavior. Only when we begin here can we effectively go on to deal with such questions as purpose, motivation, mental processes, and so forth.

This does not mean that questions of purpose and motivation are meaningless or even that they are of less importance than questions focusing on more objective areas. However, we need to first fully analyze the actual interaction behavior and only then can we legitimately deal with the various mental concepts.

THE PRINCIPLE OF THE FOREST AND THE TREES

This last principle is included as a warning, as a cautionary note. The previous principles have mostly focused attention on microscopic analysis, that is, on a detailed dissection of the verbal interaction. And certainly this is a valid way of approaching verbal language.

Yet it must not be forgotten that any interaction is more than the sum of its parts. It is a whole that cannot be fully understood from an analysis only of its parts, much like the forest is more than the individual trees. There is a possible danger, then, in concentrating solely on the trees and this principle calls this to our attention.

Sources

The nine universals of verbal interaction are taken from Robert E. Pittenger, Charles F. Hockett, and John J. Danehy's *The First Five Minutes: A Sample of Microscopic Interview Analysis* (Ithaca, N.Y.: Paul Martineau, 1960). Also in this area see Eric H. Lenneberg, "Review of *The First Five Minutes,*" *Language* 38(1962):69–73. For additional material on expressive language see Robert E. Pittenger and Henry Lee Smith, Jr., "A Basic for Some Contributions of Linguistics to Psychiatry," *Psychiatry* 20(1957):61–78 and Norman A. McQuown, "Linguistic Transcription and Specification of Psychiatric Interview Material," *Psychiatry* 20(1957): 79–86. On methods of analysis see Frederick Williams, "Analysis of Verbal Behavior," and Mervin D. Lynch, "Stylistic Analysis," in Philip Emmert and William D. Brooks, eds., *Methods of Research in Communication* (New York: Houghton Mifflin, 1970).

Experiential Vehicle

THE CASE OF *WALDON v. MARTIN AND COMPANY*

The purpose of this experience is to enable you to better understand the universals of verbal interaction covered in this unit. All students should first carefully read the case presented.

Six people should be selected—hopefully from volunteers—to role play the six characters involved in this case. Each person should develop his or her role as he or she feels the person would probably act.

All others should pay close attention to the drama as it unfolds. After about five minutes or so try to jot down examples of the universals of verbal interaction. Write down the phrases or sentences used by the role players that illustrate the various universals of verbal interaction. Space for this is provided following the details of the case.

Recently, a popular national magazine specializing in "the new and the different" ran an article which asked the reader's help in "conducting a scientific experiment on visual perception." Briefly, the article advised the readers to cut out "the specially treated card" inserted in the magazine, dissolve the card in menthanol (CH_3OH), drink the mixture, and focus on some bright object such as the sun or a powerful lamp. The readers were assured that if they did this they would have reactions "never experienced before," that they would be able "to see with amazing accuracy and clarity," and that they would "have insights into themselves and the world at large impossible to attain in any other way." The reader was then advised to write down any comments or reactions on a specially prepared form in the magazine and send it to the author, Professor I. C. Kleerly.

One week after the publication of this issue, Mr. and Mrs. William Waldon brought suit against Martin and Company, publishers of the magazine. Their son Robert, a high-school student of sixteen who was interested in chemistry, had tried the experiment and almost died. (Methanol or wood alcohol is a poisonous liquid formed in the distillation of wood and now generally made synthetically by the catalytic reaction of carbon monoxide and hydrogen under pressure. It is used chiefly as a solvent or antifreeze.) The Waldons seek to have the magazine banned and to recover damages.

The attorney for the Waldons argues that the publishers, in allowing this article to be published, clearly demonstrated a lack of a responsible and ethical editorial policy and thereby pose a threat to society. Although it is not now known, it is likely that other readers have attempted or will attempt the experiment with similar results. Any magazine which encourages its readers to take a poisonous substance without specifying that it is in fact poison should be prevented from publishing. Robert Waldon is now in the hospital with severely damaged intestines and throat burns which can never be healed completely. There is some question as to whether he will survive. For damages incurred as a result of this article the Waldons seek $1 million. They also seek to have the current issue of the magazine taken off the stands and the magazine forbidden to publish any longer.

The attorney for Martin and Company points out that the article was clearly presented in the nature of a satire on scientific experiments. The name of the author alone should have made this clear. No person, they assumed, would be naive enough to think that this was a valid scientific study. As of this time no one else has even written a letter of complaint. The magazine is clearly addressed to "adults only" (largely because of the nude pictures). No magazine, they argue, can attempt to prevent people who should not be reading the magazine in the first place from harming themselves. The publisher does not and in fact cannot pass judgment on the scientific accuracy of the articles appearing in its magazines. Furthermore, the magazine has already made commitments for publishing articles and advertisements for another year. If prevented from doing so, the result would be financial disaster not only for the publishing company and its stockholders but for its 200 employees as well. Lastly, the attorney argues that any such attempt to prevent publication of the magazine would be in violation of the company's right of free speech. The magazine is totally owned by Martin and Company which in turn is totally owned by Terrie Shore and Linda Blass, two sisters.

Both attorneys feel that this matter can be settled out of court and have invited the principals to meet for discussion. These include:

Ms. Margaret Waldon, mother of Robert
Mr. Raymond Waldon, father of Robert
Ms. Patricia Realyo, attorney for the Waldons
Ms. Terrie Shore, part owner of Martin and Company
Ms. Linda Blass, part owner of Martin and Company
Mr. James Basmanian, attorney for Martin and Company

1. The Principle of Immanent Reference

2. The Principle of Determinism

3. The Principle of Recurrence

4. The Principle of Contrast and the Working Principle of Reasonable Alternatives

5. The Principle of Relativity of Signal and Noise.

6. The Principle of Reinforcement/Packaging

7. The Principle of Adjustment

8. The Principle of the Priority of Interaction*

9. The Principle of the Forest and the Trees*

*These two principles should be discussed as they apply to the discussion of the first seven principles. They are useful when we analyze communications by means of the first seven principles or in fact by means of any set of principles.

unit 22

Meaning

The Triangle of Meaning
Denotation and Connotation
Measuring Meaning
   I, You, and He and She Talk
   Meanings in People
   Classification
   Association

Objectives

Upon completion of this unit, you should be able to:

1. define *meaning, denotation,* and *connotation*
2. Reproduce and explain Richards' triangle of meaning
3. explain the basic theory of semantic differentiation, classification, and association as methods of measuring meaning
4. utilize the methods of semantic differentiation, classification, and association to measure meaning

The most important aspect of speech and language is meaning. Were it not for the need to communicate meaning from one person to another there would be no speech, no language. Here we consider some of the aspects of meaning as viewed in Richards' triangle of meaning, two types of meaning (connotation and denotation), and some ways to measure meaning.

THE TRIANGLE OF MEANING

One of the most insightful characterizations of meaning is that provided by I. A. Richards. This "triangle of meaning" provides an excellent introduction to the entire area of meaning in speech and language.

    Suppose that you were to ask me what I mean by a college education. I might answer in any number of ways: (1) I might say that a college

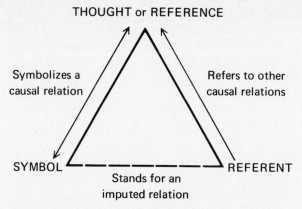

THOUGHT or REFERENCE

Symbolizes a
causal relation

Refers to other
causal relations

SYMBOL

REFERENT

Stands for an
imputed relation

Figure 22.1 *The Triangle of Meaning* (*Source*:
C. K. Ogden and I. A. Richards, *The Meaning of
Meaning* [New York: Harcourt Brace Jovano-
vich, 1923], p. 11.)

education is the accumulation of approximately 125 credits in various
subjects with a concentration in one or more of these subjects over a
period of approximately four years. 2) I might say that a college education can be the most enjoyable and most profitable experience any person could have. 3) Instead of saying anything, I might take you to a
college and let you observe the college education process, insofar as that
is possible.

In each of these instances "meaning" was interpreted differently. In
the first, where I defined a college education in terms of credits, I interpreted "meaning" to refer to the words "college education." In the
second, where I told you my feelings about a college education, I interpreted "meaning" to refer to my own feelings about college. In the third,
where we observed the process of a college education, I interpreted
"meaning" to refer to the actual thing or referent. These three aspects
are illustrated in Richards' triangle of meaning presented in Figure 22.1.

Focus first on the point of the triangle. On the bottom left is the
symbol, a word or phrase or sentence. In this view of meaning the
symbol refers objectively to the thing it symbolizes. At the apex is the
thought or reference. This refers to the thought which the speaker has
of the concept, in this case the thoughts about college education. At the
bottom right is the referent, the actual object or process or event talked
about, in this case the process of college education. The three answers
to the question of what I mean by a college education each focused on
one of these aspects of meaning. The definition focused on the symbol,
the expression of feelings on the reference, and the observation on the
referent.

Focus next on the relationships illustrated by the sides of the triangle. Between the symbol and the reference there is a causal relationship in both directions. In using the term "college education," it causes various thoughts or references in the mind of the listener which are similar to those in the mind of the symbol user. Also, the thought or reference about college education will cause the individual to use certain symbols or words.

Between the referent and the reference the causal relationship goes only from the referent to the reference. By observing a particular object (referent) it causes us to have certain thoughts or references about the object. But thinking about an object does not cause it to appear; hence, the arrow does not go from reference to referent.

The relationship between symbol and referent is perhaps the most important of the relationships. Note that between the symbol and the referent there is no direct causal relationship. The relationship between symbol and referent must go through the thought or reference. Put differently, the symbol does not refer directly to the referent; there is nothing inherent in the symbol that will lead us to find a particular referent, nor is there anything in the referent that will lead us to find a particular symbol (assuming, of course, that we had not already learned the words for the thing).

This relationship is also important because it illustrates that meanings are in the thoughts or references that people have and not in the referents themselves. There is nothing four-legged about the word *horse;* there is nothing sweet in the word *sugar.*

Richards' triangle of meaning deals with denotative meaning, that is, with symbols that refer objectively to the events, objects, or persons named. But denotation is only one aspect or type of meaning. The other is connotation. Both of these types of meaning need to be explored in more detail.

DENOTATION AND CONNOTATION

In order to best explain these two types of meaning let us take as an example the word *death*. To a doctor this word might simply mean, or denote, the time when the heart stops. Thus to the doctor this word may be an objective description of a particular event. On the other hand, to the dead person's mother (upon being informed of her son's death) the word means much more than the time when the heart stops. It recalls to her the son's youth, his ambitions, his family, his illness, and so on. To her it is a highly emotional word, a highly subjective word, a highly personal word. These emotional or subjective or personal reactions are the word's connotative meaning. The denotation of a word is its objective definition. The connotation of a word is its subjective or emotional meaning.

Some words are primarily and perhaps even completely denotative. Words like *the, of, a,* and the like are perhaps purely denotative; no one seems to have emotional reactions to such words. Other words are primarily denotative, such as *perpendicular, parallel, cosine, adjacent,* and the like. Of course, even these words might have strong connotative meanings for some people. Words such as *geometry, north* and *south, up* and *down,* and *east* and *west*—words which denote rather specific directions or areas—often produce strong emotional reactions from some people. For example, the student who failed geometry might have a very strong emotional reaction to the word even though to most people it seems a rather unemotional, objective kind of word. Other words, such as derogatory racial names and curse words, are primarily connotative and often have little denotation meaning. The very simple point that is trying to be made here is just that words may vary from highly denotative to highly connotative. A good way to determine the word's connotative meaning is to ask where it would fall on a good-bad scale. If "good" and "bad" do not seem to apply to the word then it has little, if any, connotative meaning for you. If, however, the term can be placed on the good-bad scale with some degree of conviction, then it has connotative meaning for you.

Another distinction between the two types of meaning has already been implied. The denotative meaning of a word is more general or universal, that is, most people agree with the denotative meanings of words and have similar definitions. Connotative meanings, however, are extremely personal and few people would agree on the precise connotative meaning of a word. If this does not seem correct try to get a group of people to agree on the connotative meaning for words such as *religion, God, democracy, wealth,* and *freedom.* Chances are very good that it will be impossible to get agreement on such words. But, before, attempting to test this out, read on about methods for measuring meaning.

The denotative meaning of a term can be learned from a good dictionary. When we consult a dictionary it is the denotative meaning for which we are looking. The dictionary would tell us, for example, that *south* means "a cardinal point of the compass directly opposite to the north, the direction in which this point lies" and so on. Connotative meaning, on the other hand, cannot be found in a dictionary. Instead it must be found in the person's reactions or associations to the word. To some people, for example, *south* might mean poverty, to others it might mean wealth and good land investment, to still others it might recall the Civil War or perhaps warmth and friendliness. Obviously, no dictionary could be compiled for connotative meanings simply because each person's meaning for a word is different.

Denotative meaning differs from connotative meaning in yet another way. Denotative meanings are relatively unchanging and static. Although definitions of all words change through time, denotative meanings generally change very slowly. The word *south*, for example, meant (denotatively) the same thing a thousand years ago that it does now. But the connotative meaning changes rapidly. A single favorable experience in the south, for example, might change completely one's connotative meaning for the word. With denotative meaning, of course, such changes would not occur.

MEASURING MEANING

Although there are many ways to measure meaning we discuss only three such methods here. These particular ones should prove interesting and useful in terms of understanding the role of meaning in interpersonal communication. All three methods, of course, are ways of measuring connotative meaning.

Classification

In classification a group of words are selected and are given to subjects to group into various classes. If a list of twelve words is given, the subjects group together the words that seem similar to each other and may form two, three, four, five or however many word groups seem to be logical. After all subjects have done this, a matrix similar to that presented in Figure 22.2 is drawn and in the boxes are put the number of people who have the two words in the same group. In this way the similarity in meaning among various words can be measured. Those words which are put into similar groups by many people are judged as more closely related in meaning than are those words which are put into the same classes by only few people.

As an example consider the following list of words:

dog
metal
hate
gold
lion
flower
glass
wisdom
love
doctor

	Dog	Metal	Hate	Gold	Lion	Flower	Glass	Wisdom	Love	Doctor
Dog		0	1	9	20	12	0	6	11	16
Metal			4	20	2	5	20	0	1	2
Hate				2	4	0	2	14	18	4
Gold					2	5	20	2	6	5
Lion						14	0	4	4	12
Flower							1	2	7	6
Glass								2	0	1
Wisdom									11	9
Love										10
Doctor										

Figure 22.2 *A Simplified Classification Matrix*

Many people would group dog and lion together since they are both animals. Doctor will also be in many of these groups because all three words may be designated as "animal." Hate and love will probably be put together frequently since they are both emotions and into some of the classes wisdom will be put. Metal and glass will be put into the same class often also. Inspecting the matrix we see, for example, that dog and lion (grouped together by 20 persons) are very close in meaning whereas lion and gold (grouped together by only 2 persons) are very different in meaning.

Classification, then, enables us to see the similarity or difference in words as perceived by a group of persons. Comparisons may also be made between groups of subjects. For example, males might group the words differently from females; children might group the words differently from older people, and so on.

Semantic Differentiation

Perhaps the most popular of all the methods of measuring meaning is that of *semantic differentiation.* In this procedure a word is rated on selected bipolar, seven-point scales. The scales are of three types or meaning dimensions. The evaluative dimension uses such scales as good-bad, sad-happy, valuable-worthless, and bitter-sweet. The potency dimension uses such scales as strong-weak and light-heavy. The activity dimension uses such scales as hot-cold, active-passive, and fast-slow. By using such scales, meanings may be indexed 1) for different concepts by the same subject, 2) for the same concepts by different subjects, or 3) for various concepts by the same subjects at different times (for example, before and after therapy or before and after taking a specific course or before and after hearing a specific communication).

As an example, take the concept "college education" as rated by, say, a typical college graduate. It might look something like Figure 22.3.

Notice a few things about this scale. First, all the evaluative scales, all the potency scales, and all the activity scales are not together. It is best to mix them up. Notice also that the positive ends of the scales are mixed up too; some are on the right and some are on the left. In this way we attempt to prevent a subject from simply marking down the line without really giving any attention to the scales. Each scale should be a separate and independent judgment.

If we number the scales, using 7 for the positive end and 1 for the negative end, we can add the various judgments and get summary figures. For example, taking the evaluative dimension as an example we have the scales good-bad, sad-happy, valuable-worthless, and bitter-sweet. On the good-bad scale this subject rated "college education" 5, on the sad-happy scale it was rated 3, on the valuable-worthless it was rated 5, and on the bitter-sweet it was rated 4 (note that we are considering the positive ends, good and happy, as 7 and the negative ends, bad and sad, as 1).

COLLEGE EDUCATION

Good	___ :	___ :	X :	___ :	___ :	___ :	___	Bad
Sad	___ :	___ :	X :	___ :	___ :	___ :	___	Happy
Strong	___ :	X :	___ :	___ :	___ :	___ :	___	Weak
Light	___ :	___ :	___ :	___ :	X :	___ :	___	Heavy
Hot	___ :	___ :	___ :	___ :	X :	___ :	___	Cold
Active	___ :	X :	___ :	___ :	___ :	___ :	___	Passive
Valuable	___ :	___ :	X :	___ :	___ :	___ :	___	Worthless
Bitter	___ :	___ :	___ :	X :	___ :	___ :	___	Sweet
Fast	___ :	___ :	___ :	___ :	___ :	___ :	X	Slow

Figure 22.3 *An Example of a Semantic Differential*

This totals 17 on the evaluative dimension. Note that this score means little if anything unless we compare it to something. We might, for example, compare it with the ratings of other students or perhaps with ratings of students in different colleges or studying different majors. Or perhaps we might test the difference between males and females. Or we might study this one individual's changes over time—say from freshman to senior year.

Association

Another method for measuring connotative meaning is that of *word association,* perhaps the oldest of the methods. Word association is used to find the meaningfulness of a word. The procedures are relatively simple. If we are using a large group of subjects, such as an entire class, we might simply read out a list of words, one at a time, and give the subjects 30 seconds to write down as many word associations as they can think of for each word. The assumption here is that the more associations there are to a word the more meaningful that word is. For example, think of all the associations you might have for words like *love* or *money* and how few associations you would have for words such as *joget* or *langen.*

Another way to utilize word association measurement is to have a large group respond to a list of words one at a time with only the first word that comes to mind. In scoring this we simply count the number of different associations for the various words. Note that with this method we should get many different associations for meaningless "words" (for example, *joget* and *langen*). It would be rare for two people to respond to such novel "words" with the same response. On the other hand, we should get far fewer different responses to very meaningful words such as *love* or *money.* Many people will have similar or identical associations to such meaningful words.

We might also look at word associations as the meaning of the word. We might argue (as some theorists have done) that the meaning of a word is the associations it evokes.

Sources

The area of meaning is covered in the works on semantics and General Semantics. The triangle of meaning owes its formulation to the work of I. A. Richards. See C. K. Ogden and I. A. Richards, *The Meaning of Meaning* (New York: Harcourt Brace Jovanovich, 1923). Articles contained in Paul A. Eschholz, Alfred F. Rosa, and Virginia P. Clark's *Language Awareness* (New York: St. Martins, 1974) and my *Language: Concepts and*

Processes (Englewood Cliffs, N. J.: Prentice-Hall, 1973) should provide an excellent overview of the area of semantics and meaning. Discussions of the methods of measuring meaning are generally clouded in an enormous amount of jargon; none of the accounts seems appropriate as introductory reading. The material is covered thoroughly, however, in Stephen A. Tyler's *Cognitive Anthropology* (New York: Holt, Rinehart, and Winston, 1969) and Danny D. Steinberg and Leon A. Jakobovits' *Semantics* (Cambridge: Cambridge University Press, 1971).

Experiential Vehicles

I, YOU, AND HE AND SHE TALK

The way in which we phrase something will often influence the way in which something is perceived. This is especially true when we are dealing with and talking about people. We do not talk about ourselves as we do about the people we are with or about the people we know but are not with.

Recognizing this simple language habit, Bertrand Russell, the British philosopher and mathematician, proposed a conjugation of "irregular" verbs. One example he used was:

I am firm.
You are obstinate.
He is a pig-headed fool.

The *New Statesman* and *Nation* picked up on this and offered prizes for contributions in the style of these irregular verbs. One of the best ones was:

I am sparkling.
You are unusually talkative.
He is drunk.

Twenty sentences that are phrased in the first person follow. Using Russell's lead, conjugate these irregular verbs.

1. I speak my mind.

2. I believe in what I say.

3. I take an occasional drink.

4. I like to go to the movies.

5. I sometimes bet on a horse.

6. I smoke.

7. I like to talk with people about people.

8. I form impressions of people only after long acquaintance.

9. I study.

10. I am frugal.

11. I respect authority.

12. I like to eat a good meal.

13. I am a creative thinker.

14. I am concerned with what other people do.

15. I have been known to get upset at times.

16. I like to watch television.

17. I am concerned with my appearance.

18. I like conveniences.

19. I am open-minded.

20. I will put off certain things for a few days.

MEANINGS IN PEOPLE

Ten sets of semantic differential scales, headed by various concepts, are presented. Rate each of these 10 concepts as you see them.

After the ratings are completed, small groups of five or six, or the class as a whole, should discuss the meanings of the words as they are defined in a dictionary (the denotation) and as they are defined by the ratings on these scales (the connotation).

From this experiece (the collection of the data and the ensuing discussion) the following should be clear:

1. Disagreement over the meaning of a word usually centers on the connotative meaning rather than on the denotative meaning.
2. Connotative and denotative meanings are very different aspects of a word's total meaning.
3. People are different and hence define words differently.
4. Different people can use the same word but mean very different things by it.
5. Meanings are not in words but in people.

LOVE

Good	___:___:___:___:___:___:___	Bad
Pleasant	___:___:___:___:___:___:___	Unpleasant
Ugly	___:___:___:___:___:___:___	Beautiful
Weak	___:___:___:___:___:___:___	Strong
Active	___:___:___:___:___:___:___	Passive
Sharp	___:___:___:___:___:___:___	Dull
Large	___:___:___:___:___:___:___	Small
Light	___:___:___:___:___:___:___	Heavy
Hot	___:___:___:___:___:___:___	Cold

COLLEGE

Good ____:____:____:____:____:____:____	Bad
Pleasant ____:____:____:____:____:____:____	Unpleasant
Ugly ____:____:____:____:____:____:____	Beautiful
Weak ____:____:____:____:____:____:____	Strong
Active ____:____:____:____:____:____:____	Passive
Sharp ____:____:____:____:____:____:____	Dull
Large ____:____:____:____:____:____:____	Small
Light ____:____:____:____:____:____:____	Heavy
Hot ____:____:____:____:____:____:____	Cold

CHILDREN

Good ____:____:____:____:____:____:____	Bad
Pleasant ____:____:____:____:____:____:____	Unpleasant
Ugly ____:____:____:____:____:____:____	Beautiful
Weak ____:____:____:____:____:____:____	Strong
Active ____:____:____:____:____:____:____	Passive
Sharp ____:____:____:____:____:____:____	Dull
Large ____:____:____:____:____:____:____	Small
Light ____:____:____:____:____:____:____	Heavy
Hot ____:____:____:____:____:____:____	Cold

SEXUAL BEHAVIOR

Good ____:____:____:____:____:____:____	Bad
Pleasant ____:____:____:____:____:____:____	Unpleasant
Ugly ____:____:____:____:____:____:____	Beautiful
Weak ____:____:____:____:____:____:____	Strong
Active ____:____:____:____:____:____:____	Passive
Sharp ____:____:____:____:____:____:____	Dull
Large ____:____:____:____:____:____:____	Small
Light ____:____:____:____:____:____:____	Heavy
Hot ____:____:____:____:____:____:____	Cold

RELIGION

Good	___:___:___:___:___:___:___	Bad
Pleasant	___:___:___:___:___:___:___	Unpleasant
Ugly	___:___:___:___:___:___:___	Beautiful
Weak	___:___:___:___:___:___:___	Strong
Active	___:___:___:___:___:___:___	Passive
Sharp	___:___:___:___:___:___:___	Dull
Large	___:___:___:___:___:___:___	Small
Light	___:___:___:___:___:___:___	Heavy
Hot	___:___:___:___:___:___:___	Cold

WOMEN'S LIBERATION

Good	___:___:___:___:___:___:___	Bad
Pleasant	___:___:___:___:___:___:___	Unpleasant
Ugly	___:___:___:___:___:___:___	Beautiful
Weak	___:___:___:___:___:___:___	Strong
Active	___:___:___:___:___:___:___	Passive
Sharp	___:___:___:___:___:___:___	Dull
Large	___:___:___:___:___:___:___	Small
Light	___:___:___:___:___:___:___	Heavy
Hot	___:___:___:___:___:___:___	Cold

GAY LIBERATION

Good	___:___:___:___:___:___:___	Bad
Pleasant	___:___:___:___:___:___:___	Unpleasant
Ugly	___:___:___:___:___:___:___	Beautiful
Weak	___:___:___:___:___:___:___	Strong
Active	___:___:___:___:___:___:___	Passive
Sharp	___:___:___:___:___:___:___	Dull
Large	___:___:___:___:___:___:___	Small
Light	___:___:___:___:___:___:___	Heavy
Hot	___:___:___:___:___:___:___	Cold

MUSIC

Good	___:___:___:___:___:___:___	Bad
Pleasant	___:___:___:___:___:___:___	Unpleasant
Ugly	___:___:___:___:___:___:___	Beautiful
Weak	___:___:___:___:___:___:___	Strong
Active	___:___:___:___:___:___:___	Passive
Sharp	___:___:___:___:___:___:___	Dull
Large	___:___:___:___:___:___:___	Small
Light	___:___:___:___:___:___:___	Heavy
Hot	___:___:___:___:___:___:___	Cold

TELEVISION

Good	___:___:___:___:___:___:___	Bad
Pleasant	___:___:___:___:___:___:___	Unpleasant
Ugly	___:___:___:___:___:___:___	Beautiful
Weak	___:___:___:___:___:___:___	Strong
Active	___:___:___:___:___:___:___	Passive
Sharp	___:___:___:___:___:___:___	Dull
Large	___:___:___:___:___:___:___	Small
Light	___:___:___:___:___:___:___	Heavy
Hot	___:___:___:___:___:___:___	Cold

PARENTS

Good	___:___:___:___:___:___:___	Bad
Pleasant	___:___:___:___:___:___:___	Unpleasant
Ugly	___:___:___:___:___:___:___	Beautiful
Weak	___:___:___:___:___:___:___	Strong
Active	___:___:___:___:___:___:___	Passive
Sharp	___:___:___:___:___:___:___	Dull
Large	___:___:___:___:___:___:___	Small
Light	___:___:___:___:___:___:___	Heavy
Hot	___:___:___:___:___:___:___	Cold

CLASSIFICATION

Instructions
Sort the words listed below into groups on the basis of similarity of meaning. Form as many groups as you wish and place as many words in a group as you wish. All words should be considered nouns.

baseball
football
boxing
tennis
swimming
ice hockey
cycling
poker
horse racing
wrestling

	Baseball	Football	Boxing	Tennis	Swimming	Ice hockey	Cycling	Poker	Horse racing	Wrestling
Baseball	▨									
Football		▨								
Boxing			▨							
Tennis				▨						
Swimming					▨					
Ice hockey						▨				
Cycling							▨			
Poker								▨		
Horse racing									▨	
Wrestling										▨

Fill in the data for the number of persons who grouped the terms together in the accompanying matrix. Did different people have very different groupings? Were males very different from females in the way in which they grouped these terms? Do the results shown in the matrix accord with common sense and what you know the meanings of these words to be? Explain.

ASSOCIATION

Instructions
In the spaces provided write down as many word associations as you can for each of the words. You should be allowed 30 seconds for each word. It is particularly important that equal time be given to each of the words.

1. necktie

2. brain

3. gojey

4. sun

5. artist

6. neglan

7. baby

8. byssus

9. banker

10. knot

11. earthquake

12. battle

Rank the words in order from the word with the most associations down to the word with the least associations. Does this listing accord with your common sense ideas of the meaningfulness of the various words?

Next, the first word written down by each subject should be analyzed. Count the number of different words given for each of the 12 stimulus words. If all goes as predicted, you should find that the words for which there were many word associations had few different first associates and the words which had few word associations should have had many different first associates.

unit 23

Barriers to Verbal Interaction

Polarization
Intensional Orientation
Fact-Inference Confusion
Allness
Static Evaluation
Indiscrimination
   Reflections on Words and Things
   E-Prime
   Facts and Inferences

Objectives

Upon completion of this unit, you should be able to:

1. define *polarization, intensional orientation, fact-inference confusion, allness, static evaluation,* and *indiscrimination*
2. identify examples of these six misevaluations in the media
3. identify examples of these six misevaluations in your own communications

Although communication may break down at any point in the process from sender to receiver, perhaps the most obvious site of breakdown is in the actual messages. Breakdowns, of course, may occur in both intrapersonal and interpersonal communication and the breakdowns noted here are applicable to both forms of communication.

POLARIZATION

Polarization refers to the tendency to look at the world and to describe it in terms of extremes—good or bad, positive or negatve, healthy or sick, intelligent or stupid, rich or poor, and so on. It is often referred to as the "fallacy of either-or" or "black and white." Although it is true that magnetic poles may be described as positive or negative and that certain people are extremely rich and others are extremely poor, the vast majority of cases are clearly in the middle, between these two extremes. Most people exist somewhere between the extremes of good and bad, healthy or sick, intelligent or stupid, rich or poor. Yet there seems to be a strong tendency to view only the extremes and to categorize people, objects, and events in terms of these polar opposites.

This tendency may be easily illustrated by attempting to fill in the polar opposites for such words as the following:

tall	$\longrightarrow$	_____
heavy	$\longrightarrow$	_____
strong	$\longrightarrow$	_____
happy	$\longrightarrow$	_____
legal	$\longrightarrow$	_____

Filling in these opposites should have been relatively easy and quick. The words should also have been fairly short. Further, if a number of people supplied opposites we would find a high degree of agreement among them.

Now, however, attempt to fill in the middle positions with words meaning, for example, "midway between tall and short," "midway between heavy and light," and so on. These midway responses (compared to the opposites) were probably more difficult to think of and took more time. The words should also have been fairly long or phrases of two, three, four, or more words. Further, we would probably find rather low agreement among different people completing this same task.

It might be helpful to visualize the familiar bell-shaped curve. Few items exist at either of the two extremes, but as we move closer to the center, more and more items are included. This is true of any random sample. If we selected a hundred people at random we would find that their intelligence, height, weight, income, age, health, and so on would, if plotted, fall into a bell-shaped or "normal" distribution. Yet our tendency seems to be to concentrate on the extremes, on the ends of this curve, and ignore the middle which contains the vast majority of cases.

With certain statements it is legitimate to phrase them in terms of two values. For example, this thing that you are holding is either a book or it is not. Clearly the classes of book and not book include all possibilities. And so there is no problem with this kind of statement. Similarly, we may say that the student will either pass this course or will not pass it, these two categories including all possibilities.

We create problems, however, when we use this basic form in situations in which it is inappropriate, for example, "the politician is either for us or against us." Note that these two possibilities do not include all possibilities; the politician may be for us in some things and against us in other things, or he or she may be neutral. During the Vietnam War there was a tendency to categorize people as either hawk or dove, but clearly there were many people who were neither and many who were probably both—hawks on certain issues and doves on others.

What we need to beware of is implying and believing that two extreme classes include all possible classes, that an individual must be a hawk or a dove and that there are no other alternatives. "Life is either a daring adventure or nothing," said Helen Keller. But for most people it is neither a daring adventure nor nothing but rather something somewhere in between these two extremes.

INTENSIONAL ORIENTATION

Intensional orientation (the *s* in intensional is intentional) refers to the tendency to view people, objects, and events in terms of the way in which they are talked about or labeled rather than in terms of the way they actually exist and operate.

Extensional orientation, on the other hand, is the tendency to first look to the actual people, objects, and events and only after this, to their labels. It is the tendency to be guided by what we see happening rather than by the label used for what is happening.

Intensional orientation is seen when we act as if the words and labels are more important than the things they represent, when we act as if the map is more important than the territory. In its extreme form intensional orientation is seen in the person who, afraid of dogs, begins to sweat when shown a picture of a dog or when hearing people talk about dogs. Here the person is responding to the labels, to the maps, as if they were the actual thing or territory.

Intensional orientation may be seen clearly in the results of the numerous studies on prestige suggestion. Basically, these studies demonstrate that we are influenced more when we assume that the message comes from a prestigious personality than when it comes from an average individual. Such studies have shown that if given a painting, we will evaluate it highly if we think it was painted by a famous artist. But we will give it a low evaluation if we think it was produced by a little-known artist. Other studies have focused on our agreement with dogmatic statements, our judgments of literary merit, our perception of musical ability, and so on. In all of these studies the influencing factor is not the message itself—that is, the painting, the piece of literature, the music—but the name attached to it. Advertisers, of course, have long known the value of this type of appeal and have capitalized on it quite profitably.

One of the most ingenious examples of intensional orientation requires that you role play for a minute and picture yourselves seated with a packet of photographs before you. Each of the photographs is of a person you have never seen. You are asked to scratch out the eyes in each photograph. You are further told that this is simply an experiment and that the individuals whose pictures you have will not be aware of anything that has transpired here. As you are scratching out the eyes you come upon a photograph of your mother. What do you do? Are you able to scratch out the eyes as you have done with the pictures of the strangers or have you somehow lost your ability to scratch out eyes? If, as many others, you are unable to scratch out the eyes you are responding intensionally. You are, in effect, responding to the map (in this case the picture) as if it were the territory (your own mother).

In a study conducted not long ago Philip Goldberg claimed that women were prejudiced against women. Specifically, he found that women felt that articles written by men were more authoritative and more valuable than identical articles with feminine by-lines. This result was found for messages in "traditionally masculine fields," such as law and city planning, as well as in "traditionally feminine fields," such as elementary school teaching and dietetics. Again this is a clear example of intensional orientation, of our tendency to look at the label (in this case the by-line) and to evaluate the territory (in this case the actual article) only through the label.

In a letter addressed to Ann Landers a young lady wrote that she was distressed because her parents reacted so negatively to the idea of her fiance becoming a nurse. Ann Landers offered some comfort but added, "But I do feel that they ought to call male nurses something else." This is a rather classic example of intensional orientation.

An experiment conducted with stutterers should further illustrate this notion of intensional orientation. Early research has found that stutterers will stutter more when talking with persons in authority than with subordinates. Stutterers will stutter very little when talking with children or when addressing animals, for example, but when it comes to teachers or employers they stutter a great deal. Another finding on stuttering is that of adaptation. This refers to the fact that as a stutterer reads a particular passage he or she will stutter less and less on each successive reading. In this experiment the researcher obtained from the stutterers the names of the persons to whom they had most difficulty speaking. At a later date the researchers had each stutterer read a passage five times. As predicted the stuttering decreased on each reading to the point where it was almost entirely absent on the fifth reading. Before the sixth reading the experimenter placed in front of the stutterer a photograph of the person the stutterer had named as most difficult to speak to, and on the sixth reading the stuttering increased approximately to the level during the first reading of the passage. Again, the individual was responding to the photograph, the label, the map, as if it were something more, as if it were the actual thing.

Labels are certainly helpful guides but they are not the things, and they should not be confused with the things for which they are only symbols.

FACT-INFERENCE CONFUSION

We can make statements about the world that we observe, and we can make statements about what we have not observed. In form or structure these statements are similar and could not be distinguished from each other by any grammatical analysis. For example, we can say, "She is wearing a blue jacket," as well as, "He is harboring an illogical hatred." If we diagrammed these sentences they would yield identical structures, and yet we know quite clearly that they are very different types of statements. In the first one we can observe the jacket and the blue color. But how do we observe "illogical hatred?" Obviously, this is not a descriptive statement but an inferential statement. It is a statement that we make not only on the basis of what we observe but on the basis of what we observe plus our own conclusions.

There is no problem with making inferential statements; we must make them if we are to talk about much that is meaningful to us. The problem arises, then, not in making inferential statements but in acting as if those inferential statements are factual statements.

Consider, for example, the following anecdote: A woman went for a walk one day and met her friend, whom she had not seen, or heard from, or heard of, in 10 years. After an exchange of greetings, the woman said, "Is this your little boy?" and her friend replied, "Yes, I got married about six years ago." The woman then asked the child, "What is your name?" and the little boy replied, "Same as my father's." "Oh," said the woman, "then it must be Peter."

The question, of course, is how did the woman know the boy's father's name if she had not seen or heard from or heard of her friend in the last ten years? The answer, of course, is obvious. But it is obvious only after we recognize that in reading this short passage we have made an inference which, although we are not aware of our having made an inference, is preventing us from answering a most simple question. Specifically, we have made the inference that the woman's friend is a woman. Actually, the friend is a man named Peter.

This is very similar to the example used to illustrate sexism in the language. One version goes something like this: A boy and his father are in an accident. The father is killed and the little boy is rushed to the hospital to be operated on. The surgeon is called in, looks at the boy, and says, "I can't operate on this boy; he's my son." The question is, how could the boy be the surgeon's son if his father was killed in the accident? This question should not have caused any problems, but we were sensitized to making inferences on the basis of sex. Of course, the surgeon is the boy's mother. This is a particularly good example for illustrating our expectations in regard to male and female occupations. Because of our prior conditioning we almost feel compelled to qualify the term surgeon if the surgeon is female but not if the surgeon is male. Similarly, we speak of women lawyers and women doctors but of male nurses.

Perhaps the classic example of this type of fact-inference confusion concerns the case of the "empty" gun that unfortunately proves to be loaded. With amazing frequency we find in the newspapers examples of people being so sure that the guns are empty that they point them at another individual and fire. Many times, of course, they are empty. But, unfortunately, many times they are not. Here one makes an inference (that the gun is empty) but acts on the inference as if it is a fact and fires the gun.

Some of the essential differences between factual and inferential statements are summarized in Table 23.1.

Distinguishing between these two types of statements does not mean to imply that one type is better than another type. Neither is better than the other. We need both types of statements; both are useful, both are important.

The problem arises when we treat one type of statement as if it were another type. Specifically, the problem arises when we treat an inferential statement as if it were a factual statement.

Table 23.1 *Differences between Factual and Inferential Statements*

Factual Statements	*Inferential Statements*
1. may be made only after observation	1. may be made at any time
2. are limited to what has been observed	2. go beyond what has been observed
3. may be made only by the observer	3. may be made by anyone
4. may only be about the past or the present	4. may be about any time—past, present, or future
5. approach certainty	5. involve varying degrees of probability
6. are subject to verifiable standards	6. are not subject to verifiable standards

Inferential statements need to be accompanied by tentativeness. We need to recognize that such statements may prove to be wrong, and we should be aware of that possibility. Inferential statements should leave open the possibility of other alternatives. If, for example, we treat the statement, "The United States should enforce the blockade," as if it were a factual statement, we eliminate the possibility of other alternatives. When making inferential statements we should be psychologically prepared to be proven wrong. This requires a great deal of effort but it is probably effort well spent. If we are psychologically prepared to be proven wrong we will be less hurt if and when we are shown to be incorrect.

ALLNESS

The world is infinitely complex and because of this we can never say all about anything—at least we cannot logically say all about anything. And this is particularly true in dealing with people. We may *think* we know all there is to know about individuals or about why they did what they did, yet clearly we do not know all. We can never know all the reasons we ourselves do something, and yet we often think that we know all the reasons why our parents or our friends or our enemies did something. And because we are so convinced that we know all the reasons, we are quick to judge and evaluate the actions of others with great confidence that what we are doing is justified.

We may, for example, be assigned a textbook to read and because previous texts have been dull and perhaps because the first chapter was dull we infer that all the rest will likewise be dull. Of course, it often turns out that the rest of the book is even worse than the beginning. Yet it could be that the rest of the book would have proved exciting had it been read with an open mind. The problem here is that we run the risk of defining the entire text (on the basis of previous texts and perhaps the first chapter) in such a way as to preclude any other possibilities. If we tell ourselves that the book is dull it probably will appear dull. If we say a course will be useless ("all required courses are useless") it will be extremely difficult for that instructor to make the course anything but what we have defined it to be. Only occasionally do we allow ourselves to be proven wrong; for the most part we resist rather fiercely.

The parable of the six blind men and the elephant is an excellent example of an allness orientation and its attendant problems. You may recall from elementary school that the poem by John Saxe concerns six blind men of Indostan who came to examine an elephant, an animal they had only heard about. The first blind man touched the elephant's side and concluded that the elephant was like a wall. The second felt the tusk and said the elephant must be like a spear. The third held the trunk and concluded that the elephant was much like a snake. The fourth touched the knee and knew the elephant was like a tree. The fifth felt the ear and said the elephant was like a fan. And the sixth grabbed the tail and concluded that the elephant was like a rope. Each of these learned men reached his own conclusion regarding what this marvelous beast, the elephant, was really like. Each argued that he was correct and that the others were wrong. Each, of course, was correct; but at the same time each was wrong. The point this poem illustrates is that we are all in the position of the six blind men. We never see all of something; we never experience anything fully. We see part of an object, an event, a person—and on that limited basis conclude what the whole is like. This procedure is a relatively universal one; we have to do this since it is impossible to observe everything. And yet we must recognize that when we make judgments of the whole based only on a part we are actually making inferences that can later be proven wrong. If we assume that we know all of anything we are into the pattern of misevaluation called *allness*.

Students who walk into a class convinced that they cannot learn anything will probably not learn anything. And while it may be that the teacher was not very effective, it may also be that the students have closed their minds to the possibility of learning anything. Disraeli once said that "to be conscious that you are ignorant is a great step toward knowledge." That observation is an excellent example of a nonallness attitude. If we recognize that there is more to learn, more to see, more to hear, we will leave ourselves open to this additional information and will be better prepared to assimilate it into our existing structures.

STATIC EVALUATION

In order to best understand the concept of static evaluation try to write down a statement or two that makes no reference to time—that is, we must not be able to tell whether the statement refers to the past, present, or future. Write this statement down before reading on. Next, attempt to date the following quotation. Approximately when was it written?

> Those states are likely to be well administered in which the middle class is large, and larger if possible than both the other classes or at any rate than either singly; for the addition of the middle class turns the scale and prevents either of the extremes from being dominant.

These two brief exercises should illustrate an interesting dimension of the English language. It was probably extremely difficult, if not impossible, to produce a sentence which made no reference to time whatsoever. Time, in English, is an obligatory category which means that all sentences must contain some reference to past, present, or future. Our verb system is constructed in such a way that it is impossible to produce a sentence without including a reference to time in the verb. This is not true in all languages. Second, in dating the quotation, most persons would find themselves missing the actual date by at least a few hundred years. The statement was actually written by Aristotle in his *Politics* approximately 2300 years ago.

Thus while it is impossible to make statements without reference to past, present, or future it is almost impossible to tell when statements were produced. These, of course, are obvious statements about language. Yet their consequences are not often so obvious.

Often when we form an abstraction of something or someone—when we formulate a verbal statement about an event or person—that abstraction, that statement, has a tendency to remain static and unchanging while the object or person to whom it originally referred may have changed enormously. Alfred Korzybski used an interesting illustration in this connection: In a tank we have a large fish and many small fish which are the natural food for the large fish. Given freedom in the tank the large fish will eat the small fish. After some time we partition the tank with the large fish on one side and the small fish on the other, divided only by a clear piece of glass. For a considerable time the large fish will attempt to eat the small fish but will fail each time; each time it will knock into the glass partition. After some time it will "learn" that attempting to eat the small fish means difficulty and will no longer go after them. Now, however, we remove the partition and the little fish swim all around the big fish. But the big fish does not eat them and in fact will die of starvation while its natural food swims all around. The large fish has learned a pattern of behavior and even though the actual territory has changed, the map remains static.

While we would probably all agree that everything is in a constant state of flux, the relevant question is whether we act as if we know this. Put differently, do we act in accordance with the notion of change, instead of just accepting it intellectually? Do we realize, for example, that because we have failed at something once we need not fail again? Do we realize that if someone does something to hurt us that they too are in a constant state of change? Our evaluations of ourselves and of others must keep pace with the rapidly changing real world; otherwise we will be left with attitudes about and beliefs in a world that no longer exists.

T. S. Eliot, in *The Cocktail Party*, said that "what we know of other people is only our memory of the moments during which we knew them. And they have changed since then . . . at every meeting we are meeting a stranger."

INDISCRIMINATION

Nature seems to abhor sameness at least as much as vacuums, for nowhere in the universe can we find identity. Everything is unique and unlike everything else.

Our language, however, provides us with common nouns, such as teacher, student, friend, enemy, war, politician, liberal, and the like which lead us to focus on similarities. Such nouns lead us to group all teachers together, all students together, all friends together and perhaps divert attention away from the uniqueness of each individual, each object, each event.

The misevaluation of *indiscrimination*, then, is one in which we focus on classes of individuals or objects or events and fail to see that each is unique, each is different, and each needs to be looked at individually.

This misevaluation is at the heart of the common practice of stereotyping national, racial, and religious groups. A stereotype is a relatively fixed mental picture of some group which is applied to each individual of the group without regard to his or her unique qualities. It is important to note that although stereotypes are usually thought of as negative they may also be positive. We can, for example, consider certain national groups as lazy or superstitious or mercenary or criminal but we can also consider them as intelligent, progressive, honest, hard working, and so on. Regardless of whether such stereotypes are positive or negative, however, the problem they create is the same. They provide us with short-cuts which are most often inappropriate. For example, when we meet a particular individual our first reaction may be to pigeonhole him or her into some category—perhaps a religious one, perhaps a national one, perhaps an academic one. Regardless of the type of category we attempt to fit him or her into we invariably fail to devote sufficient attention to the unique characteristics of the individual before us. As college students you may resent being stereotyped by other students. Each group seems to stereotype the other quite readily while just as rapidly deploring the unfair stereotyping that goes on in a supposedly academic community.

It should be emphasized that there is nothing wrong with classifying. No one would argue that classifying is unhealthy or immoral. It is, on the contrary, an extremely useful method of dealing with any complex matter. Classifying helps us to deal with complexity; it puts order into our thinking. The problem arises not from classifying itself. It arises from our classifying, then applying some evaluative label to that class, and then utilizing that evaluative label as an "adequate" map for each individual in the group. Put differently, indiscrimination is a denial of another's uniqueness.

Sources

The barriers to verbal interaction owe their formulation to the work of the General Semanticists. I would especially recommend the following for beginners: John C. Condon, Jr., *Semantics and Communication,* 2nd ed. (New York: Macmillan, 1974); William V. Haney, *Communication and Organizational Behavior: Text and Cases,* 3d ed. (Homewood, Ill.: Richard D. Irwin, 1973); S. I. Hayakawa, *Language in Thought and Action,* 3d ed. (New York: Harcourt Brace Jovanovich, 1972).

The nature of E-prime is discussed in detail in D. David Bourland, Jr., "A Linguistic Note: Writing in E-Prime," *General Semantics Bulletin,* nos. 32 and 33, 1965/1966.

Much that appears in this unit appears in more detail in my *General Semantics: Guide and Workbook,* rev. ed. (DeLand, Florida: Everett/ Edwards, 1974). A number of the exercises are taken from this book as well. My cassette tape series *General Semantics: Nine Lectures* (DeLand, Florida: Everett/Edwards, 1971) also covers this material.

Experiential Vehicles

REFLECTIONS ON WORDS AND THINGS

In groups of five or six discuss the following two "problems."[1] Pay specific attention to the discussion of intensional orientation in the unit and to the comments of the group members which reflect this kind of orientation or point of view.

Men's fashions have changed considerably in the last decade. Men now wear their hair as long as women, use almost as much cologne as women, and may soon be wearing as much jewelry as women. Pocketbooks for men, however, have met with some resistance from men as well as from the women who influence them. But, a man, like a woman, has to carry a great many items with him, for example, wallet, handkerchief, comb, eyeglasses, cigarettes, lighter, keys, change, checkbook, pen, pad, and probably a lot more. With the trend toward tighter and pocketless pants this becomes—at best—difficult. A pocketbook seems to some to be a reasonable solution and one which many European men have adopted.

What do you think about men carrying pocketbooks? Why do you feel as you do? Can you identify those reasons which are primarily logical and those which are primarily emotional? How would you describe your feelings and attitudes in terms of intension and extension?

A recently advanced proposal argued that names, both first and last, be done away with. Instead of the traditional names, a combination letter and digit identification number was suggested as a substitute.

The advantages of this procedure, the advocates point out, is that with the tremendous increase in population the name has lost its distinctiveness—a look through any phone book of a large city will convince most people that names are not individual or distinctive as they once were. Secondly, numbers have the advantage of eliminating much of the prejudice associated with some names;

---

[1]These two problems are taken from Joseph A. DeVito, *General Semantics: Guide and Workbook,* rev. ed. (DeLand, Florida: Everett/Edwards, Inc., 1974), pp. 33, 35.

certain ethnic names, for example, are often responded to with prejudice without any consideration of the individual. Thirdly, children will no longer have to be ashamed of their names as they often are. An odd or different name, which may sound most appropriate to parents, often creates problems for the child, especially upon entering school. But most importantly, this change would simplify current identification procedures. Each person would have one distinctive number, and this would be not only a "name" but an identification number for credit cards, bank account, license plate, social security card, passport, and all similar forms.

What do you think? Why do you think you feel as you do? Can you identify those reasons which are primarily logical and those which are primarily emotional? How would you describe your feelings and attitudes in terms of intension and extension? Do you think this question is a "put on?" Why?

E-PRIME

E-prime is normal English minus the verb *to be.* The term "E'" refers to the mathematical equation, $E - e = E'$, where E = the English language and e = the verb *to be.* E', therefore, refers to normal English without the verb *to be.*

D. David Bourland, Jr. suggests that if we wrote and spoke without the verb *to be* we would more accurately describe the event. The verb *to be* often suggests that qualities are in the person or thing rather than in the observer making the statement. We often forget that these statements are evaluative rather than purely descriptive sentences. For example, we say "Johnny is a failure" and imply that failure is somehow *in* Johnny instead of in someone's evaluation of Johnny. This type of thinking is especially important in making statements about ourselves. We say, for example, "I can't learn mathematics," or "I'm unpopular," or "I'm lazy" and imply that these qualities (the inability to learn mathematics, the unpopularity, and the laziness) are *in* us. But these are simply evaluations which may be incorrect or, if at least partly accurate, may change. The verb *to be* implies a permanence which simply is not true of the world we live in.

To further appreciate the difference between statements that use the verb *to be* and those that do not, try to rewrite the following sentences without using the verb *to be* in any of its forms, that is, *is, are, am, was,* or any other variants.

1. I'm a poor student.

2. She is inconsiderate.

3. What is artistic?

4. Is this valuable?

5. Happiness is a dry nose.

6. Love is a useless abstraction.

7. Is this book meaningful?

8. Was the movie any good?

9. Dick and Jane are no longer children.

10. This class is boring.

FACTS AND INFERENCES

Carefully read the following report and the observations based on it.[1] Indicate whether you think the observations are true, false, or doubtful on the basis of the information presented in the report. Circle T if the observation is definitely true, circle F if the observation is definitely false, and circle ? if the observation may be either true or false. Judge each observation in order. Do not re-read the observations after you have indicated your judgment and do not change any of your answers.

A well-liked college teacher had just completed making up the final examinations and had turned off the lights in the office. Just then a tall, dark, broad figure appeared and demanded the examination. The professor opened the drawer. Everything in the drawer was picked up and the individual ran down the corridor. The Dean was notified immediately.

1. The thief was tall, dark, and broad.   T   F   ?
2. The professor turned off the lights.   T   F   ?
3. A tall figure demanded the examination.   T   F   ?
4. The examination was picked up by someone.   T   F   ?
5. The examination was picked up by the professor.   T   F   ?
6. A tall, dark figure appeared after the professor turned off the lights in the office.   T   F   ?
7. The man who opened the drawer was the professor.   T   F   ?
8. The professor ran down the corridor.   T   F   ?
9. The drawer was never actually opened.   T   F   ?
10. In this report three persons are referred to.   T   F   ?

[1]This experiential vehicle is taken from Joseph A. Devito, *General Semantics: Guide and Workbook,* rev. ed. (DeLand, Florida: Everett/Edwards, Inc., 1974), p. 55.

unit 24

Supportive and Defensive Interaction

Description and Evaluation
Problem Orientation and Control
Spontaneity and Strategy
Empathy and Neutrality
Equality and Superiority
Provisionalism and Certainty
  The Case of Francis Bacon College

Objectives

Upon completion of this unit, you should be able to:

1. define and distinguish between *description* and *evaluation, problem orientation* and *control, spontaneity* and *strategy, empathy* and *neutrality, equality* and *superiority,* and *provisionalism* and *certainty*
2. identify instances of these climates in the communications of others
3. identify instances of these climates in your own communications

Verbal interaction is a most peculiar process. Through our verbal interactions we may create long-time friends or long-time enemies; we may encourage openness and honesty or fear and inhibition, create bridges or barriers. More generally, we may say that through our verbal interactions we may create a supportive climate characterized by openness, the absence of fear, and a genuine feeling of equality. At the other extreme, we may also create a defensive climate characterized by threats, fear, and domination.

Jack Gibb has provided us with a most insightful analysis of supportive and defensive climates which should enable us to see the specifics that go into making these two very different classes of communication behaviors. Gibb has analyzed and divided these specifics into six categories, each of which has a supportive and a defensive dimension.

DESCRIPTION AND EVALUATION

When we perceive a communication as being a request for information or a description of some event we generally do not perceive it as threatening. We are not being challenged and have no need to defend ourselves. On the other hand, a communication that is judgmental or evaluative leads us to become defensive, to back off, and to otherwise erect some kind of barrier between ourselves and the evaluator.

Maybe we feel that whatever we do or say is going to be evaluated and so we shy away from expressing ourselves freely, fearing perhaps that we will be criticized. Despite the usefulness of negative criticism, it is still very threatening and difficult to express ourselves openly when there is a strong possibility of evaluation.

PROBLEM ORIENTATION AND CONTROL

In working with a group of individuals on a particular problem we have probably all noticed that some individuals will readily focus on the specific problem and attempt to work with the group on a cooperative basis to solve the problem or find a solution. Other individuals, however, will just as readily attempt to control the group processes, to impose their own values on the other members of the group, and to otherwise infer that they are somehow better than the other members of the group.

Problem-oriented communications will generally be met with openness, whereas control-oriented communications will be met with resistance and defensiveness. Even though the individual attempting to control our behavior may be correct in the analysis of the problems, his or her attempt to control us is resented and resisted.

SPONTANEITY AND STRATEGY

Individuals who are spontaneous in their communications, individuals who are straightforward and open about what they think, generally receive the same response—straightforwardness and openness. But in many situations we feel that certain people are hiding their true feelings —that they have some hidden plan which they are attempting to implement for some unrevealed purposes. This strategy approach leads us to become defensive and to resist any such attempts at manipulation.

Most people employ some kind of strategy in their communications. For example, you may preface your remarks in such a way as to get the listener into a more receptive mood or you may say over and over again that you are doing something for the good of someone else and are not concerned with the benefits you yourself might receive. That is, you might do things to gain the favor of the individuals with whom you interact. This is a rather common approach in communicating. Generally, of course, it is clear to the listener that you are in fact employing some kind of strategem. You clearly recognize it in the salesperson who tells you that you look just great in this new jacket. What we all forget is that our own strategems are often just as apparent and are just as often met with resistance and resentment.

EMPATHY AND NEUTRALITY

In interacting with another individual on a personal level we often reveal certain things about ourselves which we feel are extremely important. When our listener reacts neutrally we feel we have been betrayed; they are, we feel, not seeing how important these things are to us. On the other hand, when our listeners respond empathically and we can feel that they are placing themselves in our own position, we feel supported. When a friend fails a test and confides his or her worry to us we are presented with two general classes of responses. We can respond neutrally, saying in effect, so what, don't worry, you'll get over it, and so on. By saying this we are effectively denying the importance that this person attributes to failing the exam. Although we may feel that this is the way to make the person feel better, we are probably not helping in any way. On the other hand, we can respond empathically—we can try to make the person feel that we are aware of how he or she feels and that in fact we can feel his or her worry. This is not to say that we should attempt to convey this empathic feeling without actually feeling this way. This is not something which can be easily faked and if discovered would probably be resented even more than the neutral attitude.

EQUALITY AND SUPERIORITY

When we work on a problem or on some kind of task with other individuals and make it clear that we are participating equally in the experience, they are generally more apt to be open and responsible. If, on the other hand, they perceive that we feel superior to them, they are going to resent us—they will feel that their efforts are not going to be perceived as equal to ours, or that their talents or abilities are inferior. We should not deny differences in abilities or knowledge, but we should recognize clearly that when working together on a project everyone has something to contribute.

The difficulties created by the superior attitude can be seen in college classrooms where teachers attempt to make themselves equal to the students, perhaps by being on a first name basis or wearing jeans. Then comes an exercise involving some kind of self-disclosure. The teacher, as is the practice, joins one of the groups. During the discussion each of the student members reveals certain aspects of himself or herself. When it comes to the teacher, however, he or she claims a superior position. More often than not such an individual begins to be perceived as one who has merely pretended to function on an equal level but who has all the time been holding on to power to use it when convenient.

PROVISIONALISM AND CERTAINTY

We are probably all familiar with teachers who say that they want all their students to think for themselves, to develop inquiring minds, and to explore all sides of the question—to have open minds, to leave room for differences of opinion and new facts and so on. Most teachers will verbalize some such goals at some time in their classes. Such teachers are encouraging *provisionalism* among students. (Unfortunately, however, these same teachers are often in practice very dogmatic.) And when we see this in teachers' own behavior, we become resentful—and rightly so.

We resist people who know everything and who always have a definite answer to any question. Such people are set in their ways and will tolerate no differences. They have arguments ready for any possible alternative attitude or belief. After a very short time we become defensive with such people, and we hold back our own attitudes rather than have them attacked. But we open up with people who take a more provisional position, who are willing to change their minds should reasonable arguments be presented. With such people we feel equal.

One of the difficulties in dealing with these concepts of defensive and supportive climates is that precise message elements cannot be pointed to as "defensive" or as "supportive." Rather, the defensiveness or the supportiveness is something that is perceived by the listener. It is not something that is an objective aspect of the communication process, open for all to see and analyze. Another difficulty which this creates is that while a listener may perceive a defensive climate the speaker may not be aware of it. Even when the listener attempts to explain his or her reactions they may at times be written off with a comment such as, "You must be hearing things, I never said anything like that." Put differently, the defensiveness and supportiveness is not only in what is said but primarily in what is heard.

Further complications are introduced by the fact that as we become more and more defensive, our ability to accurately gauge the motives, the intentions, and the attitudes of the other participants decreases rapidly. If you are put on the defensive a great deal in one of your classes, for example, you may perceive almost any behavior of the teacher toward you as evaluative, superior, certain, and so forth. Had there been a climate of support, that same behavior might have been perceived as descriptive, equal, provisional, and so forth.

Note also that although these six categories are presented as relatively discrete entities they are actually processes that interact with one another. For instance, we may perceive particular comments as evincing superiority in certain situations, say when the individual also evinces strategy, control, and evaluativeness. But that very same comment may not be perceived as defensive and may in fact even be perceived as supportive in an atmosphere characterized by spontaneity, empathy, equality, and so on. This is why two observers or two group members in looking at the same messages may respond very differently. The categories Gibb presents are useful ways of looking at verbal interaction, but it should not be assumed that we can easily segment any interaction and label its parts with one of Gibb's twelve classes of behavior.

These categories of behavior are applicable to all interactions—in the classroom, on the playing field, in the family, in business. We can perhaps more easily see the operation of these defensive behaviors in the interactions of others but we can be certain that others can just as easily see these very same behaviors in us.

We need to see these behaviors in our own everyday interactions. If in our communications we arouse defensive behaviors then—and to that degree—we will be ineffective in achieving open, honest, and mutually beneficial interaction.

Sources

The discussion of defensive and supportive climates is based on Jack Gibb's "Defensive Communication," *Journal of Communication* 11(1961): 141–148 reprinted in Joseph A. DeVito, *Communication: Concepts and Processes*, revised and enlarged edition (Englewood Cliffs, N.J.: Prentice-Hall, 1976). An excellent analysis of the categories of defensive and supportive behaviors appears in William V. Haney, *Communication and Behavior: Text and Cases*, 3d ed. (Homewood, Ill.: Irwin, 1973).

Experiential Vehicle

THE CASE OF FRANCIS BACON COLLEGE

This exercise is designed to illustrate in specific terms the differences between supportive and defensive interactions. Three or four members should take the role of students and three or four members should take the role of faculty and argue the three issues presented in the case of Francis Bacon College.

The following procedures should be adhered to:

1. The first five minutes should be devoted to discussing the issues without specific concentration on the categories of defensive and supportive interactions. Members should try to forget the categories during this first five minutes.
2. The second five minutes should be devoted to discussing the issues defensively. Members should follow all six defensive reactions without, of course, making the discussion unrealistic.
3. The last five minutes should be devoted to discussing the issues supportively. Members should follow all six supportive reactions without, of course, making the discussion unrealistic.

After these fifteen minutes, discussion should center on at least the following:

1. Describe your feelings as you were discussing the case with defensive reactions. With supportive reactions. Was one type of reaction more natural than another?
2. Cite instances of each of the six categories of behavior discussed in the unit: description and evaluation, problem orientation and control, spontaneity and strategy, empathy and neutrality, equality and superiority, and provisionalism and certainty.
3. Under which condition (normal, defensive, supportive) was most progress made toward coming to some kind of agreement? Would the same results be found in most arguments? (Note, of course, that the suppor-

tive period came last and perhaps the groundwork for progress was already laid.)

4. Which of the six categories seems the most significant for interpersonal interactions? Explain.

5. Which of the six categories seemed easiest to portray? Most difficult? Why?

At Francis Bacon College the students have presented a petition to the Department of Communication requesting the following:

1. that the names of instructors who will be teaching each course be listed before registration

2. that course evaluation procedures be instituted and that the evaluations for each course be published and made available to all students

3. that the students participate in the hiring and firing as well as in the granting of tenure and promotion of faculty members

The students argue that they have a right to know who is teaching the course before they register for it since some teachers are simply not interested in students or in teaching, or so it seems. Course evaluations would help to provide feedback for instructors and would provide a means for communicating to other students the opinion students had about these teachers. Further, it is important that effective teachers be recognized for their work. The students also feel that since teaching is the major task of a faculty member and since they are the ones who see the teacher teach most often, they are the ones who can best evaluate his or her performance. Teachers, they argue, should not be promoted or given tenure and, in fact, should be fired if they are not effective in the classroom.

Faculty members argue just about the opposite on all three points. It is not fair to list the names of teachers who will be teaching each course since students will then enroll in the courses given by those teachers who give little work and high grades. Similarly, high teacher and course evaluations will be given to those teachers who are easy and who give good grades rather than to those who challenge the student. Most importantly, students are not qualified to evaluate effective teaching or scholarly contributions, which also figure into promotion and tenure decision. Students cannot tell, for example, if the teacher is up to date in the material he or she is covering. They cannot tell if the teacher is just paraphrasing another textbook or if he or she is synthesizing the best available information.

unit 25

Some Principles of Nonverbal Communication

Nonverbal Communication Occurs in a Context
Nonverbal Behavior in an Interactional Situation Always Communicates
Nonverbal Behavior Is Highly Believable
Nonverbal Behavior Is Frequently Metacommunicational
   Breaking Nonverbal Rules

Objectives

Upon completion of this unit, you should be able to:

1. explain the principle that holds that nonverbal communication occurs in a context
2. explain that reasons why nonverbal behaviors in an interactional situation always communicate
3. identify the reasons for assuming that nonverbal communication is highly believable
4. define *metacommunication*
5. provide at least three examples of the ways in which nonverbal behavior is frequently metacommunicational
6. cite at least three examples of unwritten nonverbal rules of behavior

Today everyone seems interested in nonverbal communication, or what is more popularly called "body language." The gimmick used in selling the books or articles is the promise that we will learn to decipher what other people are thinking simply by observing their "body language."

The cover of Julius Fast's *Body Language*, for example, shows the picture of a woman sitting in a chair with her arms folded and her legs crossed. Surrounding the woman are such questions as "Does her body say that she's a loose woman?" "Does your body say that you're hung up?" "Does his body say that he's a manipulator?" And so on. Who could resist learning this kind of information? It would be indispensable at parties and all sorts of social gatherings. Success in one's business and social life are almost assured should one just learn to read body language.

But, as anyone who has read such works knows, such significant insight is not so easy to attain. Perhaps the primary reason is simply that we do not know enough about nonverbal communication to enable the layman to make instant and accurate readings of the inner workings of the mind. And yet we have—especially in the last 10 years—learned a great deal about this nonverbal communication business.

Here we identify a few assumptions pertaining to nonverbal communication which seem valid and useful. These assumptions should provide a kind of framework through which we might better view the specifics of nonverbal communication.

The goal of such discussion is not to provide the means for personality diagnosis or for dating success or for determining when someone is bluffing in a poker game. The purposes are 1) to enable us to better understand ourselves, 2) to enable us to better understand others, and 3) to enable us to communicate more effectively.

NONVERBAL COMMUNICATION OCCURS IN A CONTEXT

Like verbal communication, nonverbal communication exists in a context and that context helps to determine to a large extent the meanings of any nonverbal behaviors. The same nonverbal behavior may have a totally different meaning when it occurs in another context. A wink of the eye to a beautiful person on a bus means something completely different from the wink of the eye that signifies a put-on or a lie. Similarly, the meaning of a given bit of nonverbal behavior will differ depending on the verbal behavior it accompanies or is close to in time. Pounding the fist on the table during a speech in support of a particular politician means something quite different from that same fist pounding in response to news about someone's death. When divorced from the context it is impossible to tell what any given bit of nonverbal behavior may mean. Of course, even if we know the context in detail we still might not be able to decipher the meaning of the nonverbal behavior. In attempting to understand and analyze nonverbal communication, however, it is essential that full recognition be taken of the context.

NONVERBAL BEHAVIOR IN AN INTERACTIONAL
SITUATION ALWAYS COMMUNICATES

This observation is true of all forms of communication, but it seems particularly important to stress it in regard to nonverbal communication. All behavior in an interactional situation is communicative. It is impossible not to behave, and consequently, it is impossible not to communicate. Regardless of what one does or does not do, one's nonverbal behavior communicates something to someone (assuming that this is an interactional setting).

Sitting silently in a corner and reading a book communicates to the other people in the room just as surely as would verbalization. Staring out the window during class communicates something to the teacher just as surely as would your saying, "I'm bored." Notice, however, an important difference between the nonverbal and the verbal statements. The student looking out the window, when confronted by the teacher's, "Why are you bored," can always claim to be just momentarily distracted by something outside. Saying, "I'm bored" however, prevents the student from backing off and giving a more socially acceptable meaning to the statement. The nonverbal communication, however, is also more convenient from the point of view of the teacher. The teacher, if confronted with the student's, "I'm bored," must act on that in some way. Some of the possibilities include saying, "See me after class," "Im just as bored as you are," "Who cares?" "Why are you bored?" and so on. All of them, however, are confrontations of a kind. The teacher is in a sense forced to do something even though he or she might prefer to ignore it. The nonverbal staring out the window allows the teacher to ignore it. This does not mean that the teacher is not aware of it or that the staring is not communicating. Rather, nonverbal communication allows the "listener" an opportunity to feign a lack of awareness. And, of course, this is exactly what so many teachers do when confronted by a class of students looking out the window, reading the newspaper, talking among themselves, and so on.

There are, however, exceptions to this general rule. Consider, for example, if the student, instead of looking out the window, gave the teacher some unmistakable nonverbal signal such as the thumb pointing down gesture. This type of nonverbal communication is not so easy to feign ignorance of. Here the teacher must confront this comment just as surely as he or she would have to confront the comment, "I'm bored."

Even the less obvious and less easily observed behaviors also communicate. The smaller movements of the eyes, hands, facial muscles, and so on also communicate just as do the gross movements of gesturing, sitting in a corner, or staring out a window.

These small movements are extremely important in interpersonal relationships. We can often tell, for example, when two people genuinely like
each other and when they are merely being polite. If we had to state
how we know this we would probably have considerable difficulty. These
inferences, many of which are correct, are based primarily on these
small nonverbal behaviors of the participants, the muscles around the
eyes, the degree of eye contact, the way in which the individuals face
each other, and so on. All nonverbal behavior, however small or transi-
tory, is significant—each has a meaning, each communicates.

NONVERBAL BEHAVIOR IS HIGHLY BELIEVABLE

For some reasons, not all of which are clear to researchers in nonverbal
communication, we are quick to believe nonverbal behaviors even when
these behaviors contradict the verbal behavior. Consider, for example, a
conversation between a teacher and a student. The student is attempting
to get a higher grade for the course and is in the process of telling the
teacher how much hard work was put into and how much enjoyment
was derived from the classes. Throughout the discussion, however, the
student betrays his or her real intentions with various small muscle
movements, inconsistent smiles, a lack of direct eye contact, and so on.
Somehow, the teacher goes away with the feeling, based on the nonverbal
behavior, that the student really hated the class. For the most part, research has shown that when the verbal and the nonverbal messages differ,
we will believe the nonverbal. In fact, Albert Mehrabian argues that the
total impact of a message is a function of the following formula: Total
Impact = .07 verbal + .38 vocal + .55 facial. This formula leaves very
little influence for verbal messages. Only one-third of the impact is vocal
(that is, paralanguage, rate, pitch, rhythm), and over half of the message
is communicated by the face.

Why we believe the nonverbal over the verbal message is not clear. It
may be that we feel verbal messages are easier to fake. Consequently,
when there is a conflict, we distrust the verbal and accept the nonverbal.
Or it may be that the nonverbal messages are perceived without conscious awareness. We learned them without being aware of any such
learning and we perceive them without conscious awareness. Thus when
such a conflict arises we somehow get this "feeling" from the nonverbal.
Since we cannot isolate its source, we assume that it is somehow correct. Of course, a belief in the nonverbal message may simply result from
our being reinforced for conclusions consistent with nonverbal behavior;
consequently, we tend to repeat that kind of judgment. Perhaps in the
past we have been correct in basing judgments on nonverbals and so
continue to rely on these cues rather than on verbal ones.

NONVERBAL BEHAVIOR IS FREQUENTLY METACOMMUNICATIONAL

All behavior, verbal as well as nonverbal, can be metacommunicational. Any given bit of behavior can make reference to communication. We can say, "This statement is false," or, "Do you understand what I am trying to communicate to you?" In each case these statements have made references to communication and are called *metacommunicational statements*.

Nonverbal behavior is very often metacommunicational. That is why this principle or assumption is noted here specifically. Nonverbal behaviors frequently function to make a statement about some verbal statement. The most obvious example of course is the crossing of the fingers behind one's back when telling a lie. We observe frequently someone making a statement and winking. The wink functions as a comment on the statement. These are obvious examples. Consider more subtle metacommunication instances. Take the first day of class as an example. The teacher walks in and says something to the effect that he or she is the instructor for the course and might then say how the course will be conducted, what will be required, what the goals of the course will be, and so on. But notice that much metacommunication is also going on. Notice that the clothes the teacher wears and how he or she wears them, the length and style of hair, the general physical appearance, the way he or she walks, the tone of voice and so on all communicate about the communication—as well as, of course, communicating in and of themselves. These nonverbal messages function to comment on the verbal messages the instructor is trying to communicate. On the basis of these cues, students will come to various conclusions. They might conclude that this teacher is going to be easy even though a long reading list was given or that the class is going to be enjoyable or boring or too advanced or irrelevant.

The metacommunicational function of nonverbal communication is not limited to its role as an adjunct to verbal communication; nonverbal communication may also comment on other nonverbal communication. This is actually a very common type of situation. For example, the individual who, when meeting a stranger, both smiles and presents a totally lifeless hand for shaking is a good example of how one nonverbal behavior may refer to another nonverbal behavior. Here the lifeless handshake belies the enthusiastic smile.

Most often, when nonverbal behavior is metacommunicational it functions to reinforce (rather than contradict) other verbal or nonverbal behavior. You may literally roll up your sleeves when talking about cleaning up this room, or smile when greeting someone, or run to meet someone you say you are anxious to see, or arrive early for a party you verbally express pleasure in attending. On the negative, though still consistent side, you may arrive late for a dental appointment (presumably with a less than pleasant facial expression) or grind your teeth when telling off your boss. The point is simply that much nonverbal communication is metacommunicational. This does not mean that nonverbal communication may not refer to people, events, things, relationships, and so on (that is, be *object* communication), nor does it mean that verbal communication may not be metacommunication. We merely stress here the role of nonverbal communication as metacommunication because of its frequent use in this role.

Sources

General introductions to nonverbal communication are plentiful. Abne M. Eisenberg and Ralph R. Smith, Jr., *Nonverbal Communication* (Indianapolis: Bobbs-Merrill, 1971) is a brief introduction to the various areas of nonverbal communication. Mark Knapp's *Nonverbal Communication in Human Interaction* (New York: Holt, 1972) surveys the same area but in greater detail and with more attention to the numerous experimental and descriptive studies. A brief collection of readings has been edited by Haig A. Bosmajian, *The Rhetoric of Nonverbal Communication: Readings* (Glenview, Ill.: Scott, Foresman, 1971). Albert Mehrabian provides a brief but insightful overview in his "Communication without Words," *Psychology Today* 2 (September 1968). A section by Mehrabian, "Nonverbal Communication," in C. David Mortensen and Kenneth K. Sereno, *Advances in Communication Research* (New York: Harper & Row, 1973) provides an excellent review of significant literature and presents four experimental studies on various aspects of nonverbal communication.

Experiential Vehicle

BREAKING NONVERBAL RULES

The general objective of this exercise is to become better acquainted with some of the rules of nonverbal communication and to analyze some of the effects of breaking such rules.[1]

Much as we learn verbal language (that is without explicit teaching) we also learn nonverbal language—the rules for interacting nonverbally. Among such "rules" we have learned might be some like the following:

1. Upon entering an elevator turn to the door and stare at it or at the numbers indicating where the elevator is until your floor is reached.
2. When sitting down in a cafeteria take a seat that is as far away from the next person as possible.
3. When sitting next to someone (or in the general area) do not invade their private space with your body or your belongings.
4. When sitting directly across from people do not stare at them (that is, directly at their eyes) for more than a second or two.
5. Members of the opposite sex should not stare at the various sexual parts of the other person's body while that person is watching you.
6. When strangers are talking, do not enter their group.
7. When talking with someone do not stand too close or too far away. You may move closer when talking about intimate topics. Never stand close enough so that you can smell the other person's body odor. This rule may be broken only under certain conditions, for example, when the individuals involved are physically attracted to each other or when one individual is consoling another or when engaged in some game where the rules require this close contact.
8. When talking in an otherwise occupied area, lower your voice so that other people are not disturbed by your conversation.
9. When talking with someone look at their eyes and facial area only occasionally. Do not stare at them nor avoid their glance completely.

[1]This exercise was suggested to me by Professor Jean Civikly.

10. When talking with someone do not touch them more than absolutely necessary. This is especially important when the parties do not know each other. Some touching is permitted when the parties are well acquainted. Touching is more permissible for women than it is for men—that is, it is more permissible for women to touch men than for men to touch women and more permissible for women to touch women than for men to touch men.

Procedure
The procedures are relatively simple. Groups of two students are formed; one student is designated as rule breaker and one is designated as observer.

The task of the rule breaker is simply to enter some situation where one or more rules of nonverbal communication would normally be operative and break one or more rules. The task of the observer is to record mentally (or in writing if possible) what happens as a result of the rule breaking.

Each group should then return after a specified amount of time and report back to the entire class on what transpired.

unit 26
Body Communication

Areas of Kinesics
Types of Movements
  Instructing Nonverbally
  Control by Nonverbal Communication

Objectives

Upon completion of this unit, you should be able to:

1. define and distinguish between *prekinesics, microkinesics,* and *social kinesics*
2. provide two or three examples of nonverbal behaviors meaning different things in different cultures
3. define and provide at least two examples of *emblems, illustrators, affect displays, regulators,* and *adaptors*
4. identify instances of the five types of movements in the behaviors of others and in your own behaviors

AREAS OF KINESICS

The field of *kinesics* or body communication can, for convenience, be divided into three major areas; *prekinesics, microkinesics, and social kinesics.* Each of these areas is interrelated and interdependent with each other area.

Prekinesics is concerned with the physiological aspects of bodily movements. Prekinesics provides a method for the description of all bodily movements, although not all of the possible bodily movements have specific meaning. For example, not all of the hand or eye movements have individual and unique meanings. Some do and some do not. Each individually produced bodily motion is termed a *kine,* on the analogy of the individual produced sound, the phone.

Microkinesics is concerned with bodily motions that communicate different meanings. In microkinesics we are concerned with analyzing kines into classes. The range of movements that are functionally important or that communicate different meanings are termed *kinemes* and are analogous to the phonemes, which define the range of speech sounds which are functionally important in the language or which communicate different meanings.

For example, in the analysis of the English sound system an aspirated [k^h] and an unaspirated [$k^=$], as in "key" and "ski," respectively, are two sounds that belong to the same /k/ phoneme. These sounds do not communicate different meanings; we could not in English find two words which differed solely on the basis of whether the [k] was aspirated or unaspirated, that is, on whether there is a puff of air expired (aspirated, as in "key") or not (unaspirated, as in "ski"). Similarly, in the analysis of bodily movements we would find that although we could distinguish eleven positions of the eyelid, not all of these function to communicate different meanings. In fact, only four positions of the eyelid have been found to communicate different meanings. Their specific meanings, however, seem to vary depending upon the context and their collocation with other linguistic features. For example, the most open position might signify anything from surprise to fear, while the almost closed position might mean anything from exhaustion to suspicion. The eleven discernible positions are kines whereas the four meaningful positions are kinemes.

The kineme, like the phoneme, is defined for a particular language community. Although, for example, aspirated [k^h] and unaspirated [$k^=$] belong to the same phoneme in English they are different phonemes in Hindi. In other cultures only two or perhaps as many as five or six positions of the eyelid might be meaningfully different.

Social kinesics, the third major area, is concerned with the role and meanings of different bodily movements. Whereas microkinesics seeks to explore the meaningful body movements, social kinesics seeks to explore the specific meanings that these movements communicate. Research in this area focuses on the general communicative function of the larger bodily gestures as well as on the relationship between the more minute movements and vocal-auditory communication.

One interesting example used by Ray Birdwhistell to illustrate the role of social kinesics is particularly appropriate here. In this study an analysis was made of leadership in group discussion. It was found that two leaders emerged in this particular discussion among nine boys. One leader spoke a great deal and had the highest percentage of initiated conversations. The other leader, however, only originated an average number of conversations but became a leader by virtue of his bodily movements, particularly those of the face and head. He literally directed and to an extent controlled the group by head and facial movements.

It is the cross-cultural studies, however, that probably provide the most provocative examples of the meaningfulness and meaning of different movements or kinemes. Weston La Barre, the cultural anthropologist, provides a number of fascinating examples. Spitting in most Western cultures is a sign of disgust and displeasure. However, for the Masai of Africa it is a sign of affection and for the American Indian it may be an act of kindness when, for example, the medicine man spits on the sick in order to cure them.

Sticking out the tongue to Westerners is an insult; to the Chinese of the Sung dynasty it served as a symbol to mock terror or to make fun of the anger of another individual; and to the modern South Chinese it serves to express embarrassment over some social mistake.

Mediterranean peoples have a number of hand gestures which communicate quite specific meanings. For example, kissing the fingers means approval, stroking the fingers on the chin signifies a lack of knowledge and concern over a particular event or statement, and forward movement of the hand with the palm downward means "don't worry," "take it slow." For other peoples these gestures have no meanings. Since there is no real relationship between the gestures and the meanings they signify, the meanings cannot be deduced simply by observing the individual kinemes.

TYPES OF MOVEMENTS

In dealing with nonverbal movements of the body, a classification offered by Paul Ekman and Wallace V. Friesen seems the most useful. These researchers distinguish five classes of nonverbal movements based on the origins, functions, and coding of the behavior: emblems, illustrators, affect displays, regulators, and adaptors.

Emblems

Emblems are nonverbal behaviors that rather directly translate words or phrases. Emblems include, for example, the O.K. sign, the peace sign, the come here sign, the hitchhiker's sign, the "up yours" sign, and so on. Emblems are nonverbal substitutes for specific verbal words or phrases and are probably learned in essentially the same way as are specific words and phrases—without conscious awareness or explicit teaching and largely through a process of imitation.

Although emblems seem rather natural to us and almost inherently meaningful, they are as arbitrary as any word in any language. Consequently, our present culture's emblems are not necessarily the same as the emblems of 300 years ago or the same as the emblems of other cultures.

Emblems are often used to supplement the verbal message or as a kind of reinforcement. At times they are used in place of verbalization, for example, when there is a considerable distance between the individuals and shouting would be inappropriate or when we wish to "say" something behind someone's back.

Illustrators

Illustrators are nonverbal behaviors that accompany and literally "illustrate" the verbal messages. In saying, "Let's go up," for example, there will be movements of the head and perhaps hands going in an upward direction. In describing a circle or a square you are more than likely to make circular or square movements with your hands. You shake your head up and down to indicate yes and from side to side when indicating no. So well learned are these movements that it is physically difficult to reverse them or to employ inappropriate ones. Try, for example, saying "yes" while shaking your head from side to side. After a few seconds you will probably notice that your head will begin to move up and down.

In using illustrators we are aware of them only part of the time; at times they may have to be brought to our attention and our awareness.

Illustrators seem more natural and less arbitrary than emblems. They are partly a function of learning and partly innate. Illustrators are more universal; they are more common throughout the world and throughout time than are emblems. Consequently, it is likely that there is some innate component to illustrators, contrary to what many researchers might argue.

Eight types of illustrators are distinguished by Ekman and Friesen:

batons: movements that accent or emphasize a particular word or phrase
ideographs: movements that sketch the path or direction of thought
deictic movements: movements that point to an object, place or event
spatial movements: movements that depict a spatial relationship
rhythmic movements: movements that depict the rhythmic or pacing of an event
kinetographs: movements that depict a bodily action, or some non-human physical action
pictographs: movements that draw a picture in the air of the shape of the referent
emblematic movements: emblems used to illustrate a verbal statement, either repeating or substituting for a word or phrase

Affect Displays

Affect displays are more independent of verbal messages than are illustrators and are less under conscious control than are emblems or illustrators.

Affect displays are the movements of the facial area that convey emotional meaning; these are the facial expressions that show anger and fear, happiness and surprise, eagerness and fatigue. They are the facial expressions that "give us away" when we attempt to present a false image and that lead people to say, "You look angry today, what's wrong?" We can, however, also consciously control affect displays, as actors do whenever they play a role.

Affect displays may be unintentional—as when they give us away—but they may also be intentional. We may want to show anger or love or hate or surprise and, for the most part, we do a creditable job. Actors are often rated by the public for their ability to accurately portray affect by movements of their facial muscles. And we are all familiar with the awkward attempt of the would-be lover to seem seductive only to appear ludicrous—a kind of Woody Allen attempting to seduce Sophia Loren.

Regulators

Regulators are nonverbal behaviors that "regulate," monitor, maintain, or control the speaking of another individual. When we are listening to another we are not passive; rather, we nod our heads, purse our lips, adjust our eye focus, and make various paralinguistic sounds such as "mm-mm" or "tsk." Regulators are clearly culture bound and are not universal.

Regulators in effect tell speakers what we expect or want them to do as they are talking—"Keep going," "What else happened?" "I don't believe that," "Speed up," "Slow down," and any number of other speech directions. Speakers in turn receive these nonverbal behaviors without being consciously aware of them. Depending on their degree of sensitivity, they modify their speaking behavior in line with the directions supplied by the regulators.

Regulators would also include such gross movements as turning one's head, leaning forward in one's chair, and even walking away.

Adaptors

Adaptors are nonverbal behaviors that when emitted in private—or in public but without being seen—serve some kind of need and occur in their entirety. For example, when you are alone you might scratch your head until the itch is put to rest. Or you might pick your nose until satisfied. In public, when people are watching us, we perform these adaptors, but only partially. And so you might put your fingers to your head and move them around a bit but you probably would not scratch enough to totally eliminate the itch. Similarly, you might touch your nose but probably you would not pursue this simple act to completion.

In observing this kind of nonverbal behavior it is difficult to tell what the partial behavior was intending to accomplish. For example, in observing someone's finger near the nose we cannot be certain that this behavior was intended to pick the nose, scratch it, or whatever. These reduced adaptors are emitted without conscious awareness.

Three types of adaptors are generally distinguished. *Self-adaptors* are not intended to communicate information to others but rather serve some personal need, for example, grooming, cleaning, excretory, and autoerotic activity.

Object adaptors are nonverbal behaviors that make use of some kind of prop—a pencil, a tie, a cigarette or pipe—but in which the prop does not serve any instrumental function. Object adaptors would not include writing with a pencil or tying a tie or smoking a cigarette; rather, they include banging the desk with the pencil or chewing on it or playing with one's tie or chewing on a pipe.

Alter adaptors include the movements learned in the manipulation of material things—in fixing a car, in changing a tire, in sewing a dress, in licking an envelop.

In many of the more popularized versions of nonverbal behavior it is to adaptors that most attention is given. Here the authors talk about people crossing their legs a certain way—which is supposed to indicate sexual invitation—or crossed in another way—which indicates introversion—or crossed still another way—to indicate aggressiveness—and so on. The attempt here is to identify nonverbal behaviors that are performed without conscious awareness and that reveal some kind of inner desires or tendencies.

Sources

Perhaps the most authoritative source for body communication is Ray L. Birdwhistell's *Kinesics and Context: Essays on Body Motion Communication* (New York: Ballantine Books, 1970). This paperback contains 28 articles by Birdwhistell on body communication plus a most complete bibliography of research and theory in this area. Another interesting source is *Approaches to Semiotics*, edited by Thomas A. Sebeok, Alfred S. Hayes, and Mary Catherine Bateson (The Hague: Mouton, 1964). This volume also contains an excellent study by Weston LaBarre, "Paralinguistics, Kinesics, and Cultural Anthropology" and articles by Alfred S. Hayes and Margaret Mead which are particularly useful for the study of kinesics. The discussion and classification of "types of body movements" is from P. Ekman and W. V. Friesen, "The Repertoire of Nonverbal Behavior: Categories, Origins, Usage, and Coding," *Semiotica* 1 (1969):49–98. Two works by Albert E. Scheflen will be found both interesting and informative: *Body Language and the Social Order* (Englewood Cliffs, N.J.: Prentice-Hall, 1972) and *How Behavior Means* (Garden City, N.Y.: Anchor Press, 1974). Portions of the discussion of the areas of kinesics were taken from my "Kinesics—Other Codes, Other Channels," *Today's Speech* 16(April 1968):29–32.

Experiential Vehicles

INSTRUCTING NONVERBALLY

The purpose of this exercise is to heighten your awareness of nonverbal communication, particularly communication with one's body.[1]

In this exercise the class is broken up into groups of five or six. One member from each group leaves the room for approximately a minute. When these "subjects" are out of the room each group is given an instruction, which they must communicate to the subject, and the nonverbal cue or cues to which they are restricted. All groups, of course, should be given the same instruction and be limited to the same nonverbal cue or cues so that the task will be equally difficult for all groups.

The first group to get the subject to comply with their instruction wins the round and gets 10 points. After the instruction is complied with the process is repeated, this time with another subject chosen from the group, another instruction, and another nonverbal cue or cues. The exercise is completed when one group wins 50 points, when time is up, or when some other point is reached.

Some sample instructions and types of nonverbal cues follow. Instructors may wish to compile their own list of instructions to insure that they have not been seen by any member of the class.

Sample Instructions

leave the room
give the teacher a pat on the back
shake hands with each member of the group
open (close) all the windows
open (close) the door
bring into the class someone who is not a member of the class
write the time on the board

[1]This exercise was adapted from one developed by my students in interpersonal communication.

320

find a red pen
raise your hand
clap hands
sit on the floor
put your shoes on the wrong feet
get a drink of water
hold up a notebook with the name of the school on it
comb your hair

Nonverbal Cues

vocal (but nonverbal) cues
hand and arm movements
eye movements (but not head movements)
head movements
the entire body
tactile cues
manipulation of the objects in the room
leg movements (including feet movements)

CONTROL BY NONVERBAL COMMUNICATION[2]

Write the letters of a phrase or statement on pieces of typing paper or cardboard, one letter on each piece. Shuffle them randomly, and distribute one to each student. (Select a phrase or statement that contains as many letters as there are students.)

Tell the students to form a phrase or statement without talking or writing anything. The students should attempt to arrange themselves so that the letters they are carrying spell out the phrase or statement.

After the phrase or statement is formed, consider the following:

1. Did anyone emerge as leader?

[2]This exercise is adapted from one developed by my students in Small Group Communication.

2. What nonverbal behaviors were used by the leader to direct or control the behavior of the group members?

3. Did others attempt to take charge? When? In what way? With what nonverbal behaviors did they indicate a desire to take charge?

4. Were some members turned off? How did they signal this nonverbally?

5. How did you feel being directed by other people without any talking?

unit 27
Spatial Communication

Proxemic Dimensions
Proxemic Distances
  Spatial Relationships I and II

Objectives

Upon completion of this unit, you should be able to:

1. define *proxemics*
2. define the following: *postural-sex identifiers, sociofugal-sociopetal orientation, kinesthetic factors, touch, vision, thermal factors, smell,* and *loudness*
3. identify and explain the four proxemic distances
4. give examples of the kinds of communications that would take place in each of the four proxemic distances
5. explain at least five messages communicated by different seating arrangements

Edward T. Hall, in the study he calls "Proxemics," has provided much new and significant insight into nonverbal communication by demonstrating how messages from these different channels may be analyzed and by relating them to the spatial dimensions of communication. More formally, in "A System for the Notation of Proxemic Behavior," Hall has defined *proxemics* as the "study of how man unconsciously structures microspace—the distance between men in the conduct of their daily transactions, the organization of space in his houses and buildings, and ultimately the layout of his towns."

Like verbal behavior, proxemic behavior communicates; space speaks just as surely and just as loudly as do words. Speakers who stand close to their listener, with their hands on the listener's shoulders and their eyes focused directly on those of the listener, clearly communicate something very different from the speaker who sits crouched in a corner with arms folded and eyes to the floor.

Like verbal and kinesic behavior, proxemic behavior is learned without any conscious or direct teaching by the adult community. Children are merely exposed to certain spatial relations which they internalize unconsciously, much as children seem to acquire the particular codes of speech or body motion.

PROXEMIC DIMENSIONS

The best way to explain proxemics is to briefly present the eight general classes of proxemic behaviors and their more specific categories as systematized by Hall.

Postural-sex identifiers refer to the posture and sex of the communication source and receiver. Hall has divided this class into six possible categories: man prone, woman prone, man sitting or squatting, woman sitting or squatting, man standing, woman standing.

Sociofugal-sociopetal orientation, referring to the physical directness of the communication, specifies the relationship of one person's shoulders to the other person's shoulders. These positions are categorized on a nine-point scale, ranging from face-to-face communication in which the shoulders of both parties are parallel, through the situation in which the shoulders of the two parties form a straight line, to the situation in which there is back-to-back communication and the shoulders are again parallel. The nine positions are: parallel face-to-face, 45° angle, 90°, 135°, 180°, 225°, 270°, 315°, and parallel back-to-back communication.

Kinesthetic factors refer to the closeness of the two persons involved in communication and the potential that exists for the holding, grasping, or touching of each other. The four major categories are: within body contact distance, within touching distance with the forearm extended, within touching distance with the arm extended, and within touching distance by reaching. More specific degrees of closeness which lie between any two of these four major classes—for example, just outside body contact distance—might also be recorded.

Touch, referring to the amount and type of physical contact between the two parties, is quantified along a seven-point scale: caressing and holding, caressing and feeling, extended holding, holding, spot touching, brushing or accidental touching, and no contact.

Vision, the extent of visual contact between the two persons, is divided into four categories: sharp, focused looking at the other person's eyes; clear, focused looking at the person's face or head; peripheral, looking at the person in general but not focused on the head; and no visual contact.

Thermal factors, the amount of body heat of one person perceived by the other, are categorized into four types: detection of conducted heat, detection of radiant heat, probable detection of some kind of heat, and no detection of heat.

Loudness, or vocal volume, is described on a seven-point scale: silent, very soft, soft, normal, somewhat above normal, loud, and very loud.

Smell is categorized into five types: detection of differentiated body odor, detection of undifferentiated odor, detection of breath odor, probable detection of some odor, and no detection.

These categories may appear at first to be somewhat rigid or too finely delineated. In analyzing proxemic behavior, however, adjacent categories can be combined to form more general ones or, if additional distinctions are needed, the categories may be further divided. Hall has presented this system as a *tentative* strategy for analyzing proxemic behaviors.

PROXEMIC DISTANCES

One of the earliest references to space as communication occurs in the Gospel of Luke (14:1–11):

> When thou are invited to a wedding feast, do not recline in the first place, lest perhaps one more distinguished than thou have been invited by him. And he who invited thee and him, come and say to thee, "Make room for this man"; and then thou begin with shame to take the last place. But when thou art invited, go and recline in the last place; that when he who invited thee comes in, he may say to thee, "Friend, go up higher!" Then thou wilt be honored in the presence of all who are at table with thee. For everyone who exalts himself shall be humbled, and he who humbles himself shall be exalted.

This brief passage illustrates one of the concepts or meanings that space communicates, namely status. We know, for example, that in a large organization status is the basis for determining how large an office one receives, whether that office has a window or not, how high up the office is (that is, on what floor of the building), and how close one's office is to that of the president or chairperson.

In interpersonal communication space is especially important, although we seldom think about it or even consider the possibility that it might serve a communicative function. Edward Hall, for example, distinguishes four distances which he claims define the type of relationship permitted. Each of these four distances has a close phase and a far phase, giving us a total of eight clearly identifiable distances.

In *intimate distance,* ranging from the close phase of actual touching to the far phase of 6 to 18 inches, the presence of the other individual is unmistakable. Each individual experiences the sound, smell, and feel of the other's breath.

The close phase is used for lovemaking and wrestling, for comforting and protecting. In the close phase the muscles and the skin communicate while actual verbalizations play a minor role. In this close phase whispering, says Hall, has the effect of increasing the psychological distance between the two individuals.

The far phase allows us to touch each other by extending our hands. The distance is so close that it is not considered proper in public and because of the feeling of inappropriateness and discomfort (at least for Americans) the eyes seldom meet but remain fixed on some remote object.

Each of us, says Hall, carries around with us a protective bubble defining our *personal distance,* which allows us to stay protected and untouched by others.

In the close phase of personal distance (from 1.5 to 2.5 feet) we can still hold or grasp each other but only by extending our arms. We can then take into our protective bubble certain individuals—for example, loved ones. In the far phase (from 2.5 to 4 feet) two people can only touch each other if they both extend their arms. One person can touch the other by extending his or her arms fully to the point where the two people can touch only if both extend their arms. This far phase is the extent to which we can physically get our hands on things and hence it defines, in one sense, the limits of our physical control over others.

Even at this distance we can see many of the fine details of an individual—the gray hairs, teeth stains, clothing lint, and so on. However, we can no longer detect body heat. At times we may detect breath odor but generally at this distance etiquette demands that we direct our breath to some neutral corner so as not to offend (as the television commercials warn us we might do).

This distance is particularly interesting from the point of view of the body odor and the colognes designed to hide it. At this distance we cannot perceive normal cologne or perfume. Thus it has been proposed that the cologne has two functions: First, it serves to disguise the body odor or hide it; and second, it serves to make clear the limits of the protective bubble around the individual. The bubble, defined by the perfume, simply says you may not enter to the point where you can smell me.

At the *social distance* we lose the visual detail we had in the personal distance. The close phase (from 4 to 7 feet) is the distance at which we conduct impersonal business, the distance at which we interact at a social gathering. The far phase (from 7 to 12 feet) is the distance we stand at when someone says, "Stand away so I can look at you." At this level business transactions have a more formal tone than when conducted in the close phase. In offices of high officials the desks are positioned so that the individual is assured of at least this distance when dealing with clients. Unlike the intimate distance, where eye contact is awkward, the far phase of the social distance makes eye contact essential—otherwise communication is lost. The voice is generally louder than normal at this level but shouting or raising the voice has the effect of reducing the social distance to a personal distance. It is at this distance that we can work with people and yet both not constantly interact with them and not appear rude. At certain distances, of course, one cannot ignore the presence of another individual. At other distances, however, we can ignore the other individual and keep to our own business.

This social distance requires that a certain amount of space be available. In many instances, however, such distances are not available; yet it is necessary to keep a social distance, at least psychologically if not physically. For this we attempt different arrangements with the furniture. In small offices in colleges for example, professors sharing an office might have their desks facing in different directions so that each may keep separate from the other. Or they may position their desks against a wall so that each will feel psychologically alone in the office and thus be able to effectively maintain a social rather than a personal distance.

In the close phase of *public distance* (from 12 to 15 feet) an individual seems protected by space. At this distance one is able to take defensive action should one be threatened. On a public bus or train, for example, we might keep at least this distance from a drunkard so that should anything come up (literally or figuratively) we could get away in time. Although at this distance we lose any fine details of the face and eyes we are still close enough to see what is happening should we need to take defensive action.

At the far phase (more than 25 feet) we see individuals not as separate individuals but as part of the whole setting. We automatically set approximately 30 feet around public figures who are of considerable importance, and we seem to do this whether or not there are guards preventing us from entering this distance. This far phase is of course the distance from which actors perform on stage; consequently, their actions and voice will have to be somewhat exaggerated.

These four distances, according to Hall, correspond quite closely to the four major types of relationships: intimate, personal, social, and public.

Sources

For spatial communication the work of Edward T. Hall is perhaps the most well known and the most insightful. The discussion of proxemic dimensions comes from his "A System for the Notation of Proxemic

Behavior," *American Anthropologist* 65(1963):1003–1026. The discussion of proxemic distances comes from his *The Hidden Dimension* (New York: Doubleday, 1966). Hall's first popular work on spatial communication and perhaps still one of the most famous is *The Silent Language* (New York: Doubleday, 1959). Robert Sommer also deals with spatial communication, but from a somewhat different point of view. Particularly interesting are his *Personal Space: The Behavioral Basis of Design* (Englewood Cliffs, N.J.: Prentice-Hall, 1969) and *Design Awareness* (San Francisco: Rinehart Press, 1972). The Experiential Vehicles on seating positions are based on the work of Sommer summarized in *Personal Space.*

Experiential Vehicles

SPATIAL RELATIONSHIPS—PART I

Below are presented diagrams of tables and chairs. Imagine that the situation is the school cafeteria and that this is the only table not occupied. For each of the eight diagrams place an X where you and a friend of the same sex would seat yourselves for each of the four conditions noted.

1. Conversing, for example, to talk for a few minutes before class

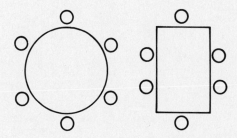

2. Cooperating, for example, to study together for the same exam or to work out a math problem

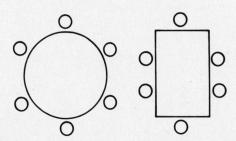

3. Co-acting, for example, to study for different exams

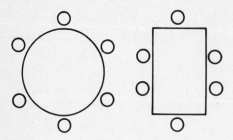

4. Competing, for example, to compete against each other in order to see who would be the first to solve a series of puzzles

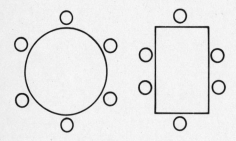

For Discussion

1. Why did you select the positions you did?
2. Explain the differences in the opportunity for nonverbal interaction which the different positions chosen allow.
3. How do these different positions relate to verbal communication?
4. Would you have chosen the same positions if the other person were of the opposite sex? Explain.
5. Compare your responses with the responses of others. How do you account for the differences in seating preferences?
6. Are there significant differences in choices between the round and the rectangular tables? Explain.

SPATIAL RELATIONSHIPS—PART II

Below are presented diagrams of tables and chairs. Imagine that the situation is the school cafeteria and that this is the only table not occupied.

In the space marked X is seated the person described above the diagram. Indicate by placing an *X* in the appropriate circle where you would sit.

1. A young man/woman to whom you are physically attracted and whom you would like to date but to whom you have never spoken

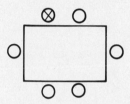

2. A person whom you find physically unattractive and to whom you have never spoken

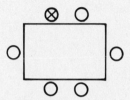

3. A person you dated once and had a miserable time with and whom you would never date again

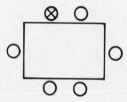

4. A person you have dated a few times and would like to date again

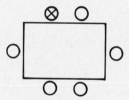

5. An instructor who gave you an "F" in a course last semester which you did not deserve and whom you dislike intensely

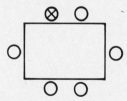

6. Your favorite instructor who you would like to get to know better

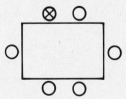

For Discussion

1. Why did you select the positions you did? For example, how does the position you selected enable you to better achieve your purpose?

2. Assume that you were already seated in the position marked X. Do you think that the person described would sit where you indicated you would (assuming the feelings and motives are generally the same)? Why? Are there significant sex differences? Significant status differences? Explain.

3. What does the position you selected communicate to the person already seated? In what ways might this nonverbal message be misinterpreted? How would your subsequent nonverbal (and perhaps verbal) behavior reinforce your intended message? That is, what would you do to insure that the message you intend to communicate is in fact the message communicated and received?

This exercise is based on studies conducted by Robert Sommer and reported in *Personal Space: The Behavioral Basis of Design* (Englewood Cliffs, N.J.: Prentice-Hall, 1969).

unit 28

Territoriality and Tactile Communication

Territoriality
Tactile Communication
  Touch Communication

Objectives

Upon completion of this unit, you should be able to:

1. define *territoriality*
2. define *tactile communication*
3. give examples of the operation of territoriality from your own experience
4. explain at least three functions frequently served by tactile communication

Both *territoriality*—a possessive or ownership-like reaction to an area of space or to particular objects—and *tactile communication*—communication by touch—are closely related to proxemic communication. Analysis and understanding of these concepts are greatly aided by insight into proxemics.

TERRITORIALITY

One of the more interesting concepts in ethology (the study of animals in their natural surroundings) is that of *territoriality*. For example, male animals will stake out a particular territory and consider it their own.

They will allow prospective mates to enter but will defend it against entrance by others, especially other males of the same species. Among deer, for example, the size of the territory signifies the power of the deer, which in turn determines how many females he will mate with. Less powerful deer will be able to hold onto only small parcels of land and consequently will mate with only one or two females. This is a particularly adaptive measure since it ensures that the stronger members of the society will produce most of the offspring. When the "landowner" takes possession of an area—either because it is vacant or because he gains it through battle—he marks it, for example, by urinating around the boundaries.

These same general patterns are felt by many to be integral parts of human behavior. Some researchers claim that this form of behavior is innate and is a symptom of man's innate aggressiveness. Others claim that territoriality is learned behavior and is culturally based. Most, however, seem to agree that a great deal of human behavior can be understood and described as territoriality regardless of its possible origin or development.

If we look around at our homes we would probably find certain territories that different people have staked out and where invasions are cause for at least mildly defensive action. This is perhaps seen most clearly with siblings who each have (or "own") a specific chair, room, radio, and so on. Father has his chair and mother has her chair. Archie and Edith Bunker always sit in the same chairs and great uproars occur when Archie's territory is invaded. Similarly, the rooms of the house may be divided among members of the family. The kitchen, traditionally at least, has been the mother's territory. Invasions from other family members may be tolerated but are often not welcomed and at times they are resisted. Invasions by members not of the immediate family, from a sister-in-law, mother-in-law, or neighbor, for example, are generally resented much more.

In the classroom, where seats are not assigned, territoriality can also be observed. When a student sits in a seat that has normally been occupied by another student, the regular occupant will often become disturbed and resentful and might even say something to the effect that this is his or her seat.

Like animals, humans too mark their territory, though generally not with urine. In a library, for example, you may mark your territory with a jacket or some books when you leave the room. You expect this marker to function to keep others away from your seat and table area. Most of the time it works. When it does not work there is cause for conflict.

Similarly, mild conflict is seen when an individual takes a seat very close to someone else in a place that is not crowded and where a more distant seat would be possible. We seem to resent this invasion of our privacy, of our territory. In elevators the individuals will in all probability take areas that provide them with the maximum distance from each other. And when that distance is not maintained annoyance can easily be read on the faces of the invaded parties. In driving a car, tailgating is resented because it is dangerous but also, it seems, because it represents an invasion of one's territory; somehow we feel that the area 10 or 15 feet behind us is ours and other cars should not encroach upon it.

The territory of humans (like that of animals) communicates status in various different ways. Clearly the size and location of the territory indicates something about status. A townhouse on Manhattan's East Side, for example, is perhaps the highest status territory for home living in the country; it is large and at the same time located on the world's most expensive real estate. Auntie Mame, for example, lived at 1 Beekman Place, perhaps the most expensive part of New York's East Side. Status is also signaled by the unwritten law granting the right of invasion. High status individuals have a right (or at least more of a right) to invade the territory of others than vice versa. The boss of a large company, for example, can invade the territory of a junior executive by barging into his or her office but the reverse would be unthinkable. Similarly, a teacher may invade the personal space of a student by looking over his or her shoulder as the student writes. But the student cannot return the invasion.

TACTILE COMMUNICATION

Touch is perhaps the most primitive form of communication. In terms of sense development, it is probably the first to be utilized; even in the womb the child is stimulated by touch. Soon after birth the child is fondled, caressed, patted, and stroked by the parents and by any other relative who happens to be around. The whole world wants to touch the new infant. Touch becomes for the child a pleasant pastime and so he or she begins to touch. Everything is picked up, thoroughly fingered, and put into the mouth in an attempt to touch it as closely as possible. The child's favorite toys seem to be tactile ones—cuddly teddy bears, teething rings, and even pieces of blankets. Much in the same way as children touch objects in the environment, they also touch themselves; children play with toes and fingers, nose and lips, and ears and genitals. At some point, children are stopped from picking their noses and playing with their genitals. No reason is given other than the admonition, "Don't do that," or a gentle slap on the hands. As children mature and become sociable, they begin to explore others through touch, though again there are certain parts that are forbidden to touch or have touched by others.

Touching as a form of communication can serve any number of functions. In fact, one would be hard pressed to name a general function of communication which could not be served by tactile communication. Special note, however, should be made of two major functions normally served by tactile communication.

Perhaps the most obvious is a sexual one. Touch seems to be the primary form of sexual interaction. From fondling one's genitals as a child, to kissing, to fondling another individual, to sexual intercourse, touch plays a primary role. Men shave or grow beards, women shave their legs and underarms, and both use body oils and creams to keep their skin smooth in conscious or subconscious awareness of the powerful role of touch as a form of communication.

Touch also serves a primary role in consoling another individual. For example, we put our arms around people, hold their head in our hands, hold their hands, or hug them in an attempt to empathize with them more fully. It seems like an attempt to feel what the other person is feeling by becoming one with them—perhaps the ideal in empathic understanding. Try to console someone, even in role playing, when you are not allowed to touch them and you will see how unnatural it seems and how difficult it is to say the appropriate words.

In almost all group encounter sessions touch is used as a supportive gesture. Generally, we do not touch people we dislike (except in fighting with them). Otherwise, we only touch people we like and so the very act of touching says, "I like you," "I care about you," "I want to be close to you," and so on.

Touching implies a commitment to the other individual; where and how we touch seems to determine the extent of that commitment. To shake someone's hand, for example, involves a very minor commitment. Our culture has, in effect, defined hand shaking as a minor social affair. But to caress someone's neck or to kiss someone's mouth implies a commitment of much greater magnitude.

The location, amount, and intensity of tactile communication is also culturally determined, at least in part. For example, Southern Europeans will touch each other a great deal more than will Northern Europeans or Americans. Women seem to be allowed to touch more and to be touched more than men. For example, it has been shown that females are touched more often than are males by same sex friends, different sex friends, mothers, and fathers. This seems true even for infants; girls between 14 and 24 months, for example, are touched more than boys of the same age. Similarly, mothers touch both male and female children more than do fathers who, in fact, hardly touch more than the hands of their children.

Touching ourselves, of course, also communicates. Lily Tomlin in her role as Ernestine the telephone operator touches herself a great deal in an attempt to communicate a certain egocentric personality which, together with the power of the telephone company, can even call on the president and make trouble. In real life we are all familiar with the individual who is constantly fixing his or her hair—to the point where we feel like screaming and perhaps sometimes do.

Although we have learned somewhere that certain ways of touching oneself are forbidden, at least in public, there are still people who pick their nose, scratch their head, stick their fingers in their ears, or scratch their genitals or anus without the least concern for those around who might not care to witness this exercise in self-gratification.

Sources

On territoriality read Robert Ardrey, *The Territorial Imperative* (New York: Atheneum Press, 1966). This is a fascinating book on man's territorial behavior. Also relevant here is the work of Edward Hall cited in the unit on spatial communication.

On tactile communication see, for a broad overview, L. K. Frank's "Tactile Communication," *Genetic Psychology Monographs* 56(1957):209–255. For an interesting account of the potentials and the applications of tactile communication, see Frank A. Geldard, "Body English," *Psychology Today* 2(1968):42–47. Perhaps the most thorough discussion is Ashley Montague's *Touching: The Human Significance of the Skin* (New York: Harper & Row, 1971).

Experiential Vehicle

TOUCH COMMUNICATION

For this exercise the group is broken up into dyads, preferably formed by persons not well acquainted with each other. When in these dyads, members should talk with each other about anything that comes to mind for two or three minutes. After this short interaction each member should complete the attached set of scales marked, "Other". Each member should rate the other person on the scales provided using as a basis for the rating the very short interaction and any other cues received at other times. After completing the scales they should be put out of sight. Do *not* show these scales to the other person.

OTHER

friendly	___:___:___:___:___:___:___	unfriendly
warm	___:___:___:___:___:___:___	cold
aggressive	___:___:___:___:___:___:___	unaggressive
strong	___:___:___:___:___:___:___	weak
tense	___:___:___:___:___:___:___	relaxed
calm	___:___:___:___:___:___:___	excitable
intimate	___:___:___:___:___:___:___	remote
emotional	___:___:___:___:___:___:___	rational
graceful	___:___:___:___:___:___:___	awkward
personal	___:___:___:___:___:___:___	impersonal

Members should next attempt to communicate the following several emotions solely through tactile means. In order to insure that messages are communicated by touch, receivers should keep their eyes closed and sources should keep their mouths shut. Adhere generally to the following procedures: A member randomly selects an emotion from the list and by touching the other person tries to communicate it. After the emotion is guessed the members should change roles of source and receiver and continue in this alternating style until all emotions are communicated. Keep some kind of record of the relative ease/difficulty in communicating these emotions by touch, for example, the number of errors the receiver made before correctly guessing the emotion that the source intended to communicate.

Emotions

Anger
Love
Hate
Fear
Determination
Nervousness
Satisfaction

After all the emotions have been communicated fill out the second set of scales for your partner. Do *not* look at the previous ratings and do *not* show these to the other person.

OTHER

friendly	___:___:___:___:___:___:___	unfriendly
warm	___:___:___:___:___:___:___	cold
aggressive	___:___:___:___:___:___:___	unaggressive
strong	___:___:___:___:___:___:___	weak
tense	___:___:___:___:___:___:___	relaxed
calm	___:___:___:___:___:___:___	excitable
intimate	___:___:___:___:___:___:___	remote
emotional	___:___:___:___:___:___:___	rational
graceful	___:___:___:___:___:___:___	awkward
personal	___:___:___:___:___:___:___	impersonal

Analysis

Feeling Analysis
How did you feel about doing this exercise before you began? Did your feelings about it change after having completed it? What accounted for the change?

Examine your own feelings about the exercise as a whole. Discuss these feelings with your partner. Were your feelings similar? Different? To what do you attribute the similarities and differences in feelings?

Tactile Communication of Emotions

Examine the relative success-failure in communicating these several emotions. How successful were you as source? As receiver?

Who was more responsible for the successes? For the failures? (That is, were the successes-failures more a function of the source's ability-inability to communicate or of the receiver's ability-inability to guess correctly?)

Were certain emotions easier to communicate than others? Which ones? Why do you suppose this was true?

Changing Perceptions as a Function of Touch Communication

Examine the two sets of scales with special attention to the differences. Was the second rating more polarized? (That is, were the ratings on the second set of scales more toward the extreme than those of the first set of scales?) Less polarized? Why? Which set was more positive? Why?

The Role of Tactile Communication

Record here what you feel are some of the functions of tactile communication. These functions need not be limited to those covered in this exercise.

unit 29

Physical
Characteristics
as Communication

Body Type
Hair
Skin Color
Odor
  Body Type

Objectives

Upon completion of this unit, you should be able to:

1. define *endomorphy, mesomorphy,* and *ectomorphy*
2. identify some of the expectations you have about different body builds
3. identify at least three messages that hair might communicate
4. identify at least two messages that skin color might communicate
5. identify at least two messages that body odor might communicate

To say that each person is physically unique is perhaps too obvious. With the exception of identical twins, each of us has a set of physical characteristics which distinguish us from every other individual. Some of us are short, others tall; some of us are fat, others skinny; some of us are muscular, others of us are flabby.

BODY TYPE

Physically, however, we can probably describe some of the major characteristics of physique in males and to a lesser extent in females, under three general headings: 1) endomorphy, the fatty dimension; 2) meso-morphy, the muscular dimension; and 3) ectomorphy, the skinny dimen-sion. We might then attempt to classify any given body in terms of the degree to which it possessed each of these three dimensions. Each body would be described by a three digit number. The first number would describe the endomorphic dimension, the second the mesomorphic dimen-sion, and the third the ectomorphic dimension. An extremely fat indi-vidual, for example, the fat man or woman of the circus, would be described as 7-1-1 indicating that he or she is high on endomorphy but low on the other two dimensions. Mr. America, Hercules, and Atlas would be described as 1-7-1—all muscle. The thin man or woman of the circus would be 1-1-7—just skin and bones. Of course few persons are at these' extremes. We might attempt to illustrate this by estimating the body types of persons who most of us have seen. Johnny Carson, for example, might be described as 2-5-4 whereas Merv Griffin might be described as 3-4-2. Joe Namath might be described as 3-6-1 whereas Mick Jagger might be 1-3-6. These, of course, are simply estimates that illustrate the con-cept; they are not accurate measurements. These three-digit numbers, then, represent one's *somatype*, or the degree to which a person is fat, muscular, and skinny. Male examples are used here because these body types were formulated on the basis of studies of the male body.

Try to picture the following individuals as they are described; try to see their physical characteristics or, better still, attempt to draw them.

Person 1. This man is dominant, confident, impetuous, domineering, enterprising, adventurous, competitive, determined, and hot-tempered.

Person 2. This man is dependent, contented, sluggish, placid, affable, tolerant, forgiving, sociable, generous, soft-hearted.

Person 3. This man is tense, anxious, withdrawn, cautious, serious, introspective, suspicious, cool, precise.

If your responses were consistent with those of others to whom similar tests were given, you probably pictured Person 1 as high on mesomorphy, as having a rather muscular build. Person 2 was probably pictured as high in endomorphy, as rather short and fat. Person 3 was probably pictured as high in ectomorphy, as relatively tall and thin.

There is considerable debate over the relationship between personality characteristics, such as those listed above, and somatype. Much research does seem to indicate a rather strong relationship between body build and personality. The further question and the inevitable one is to what this relationship can be ascribed. Is it genetic? Are persons born with tall skinny bodies also born with certain personality traits, such as tenseness, withdrawnness, and so on. Is the relationship cultural? Are persons who are fat expected to be affable, sluggish, tolerant, forgiving, and so on, and do they therefore take on these characteristics which everyone seems to think they possess anyway? This question has not been settled. What is clear is that people have certain reactions to different body types; the body types communicate something to us. We expect the fat person to be sociable, generous, and affable. We expect the muscular individual to be dominant, confident, impetuous, and hot-tempered. We expect the skinny person to be tense, precise, cool, and suspicious. At least in general we seem to have these expectations. Whether or not our judgments are well founded, we do seem to make inferences about people's personality from merely looking at their body build. And just as we have expectations of others based on their body build, they will have expectations of us based on our body build. Further, if these stereotypes are strong enough—and in many cases they seem to be—we will have expectations about ourselves based on our body build. The fact that these characteristics, these stereotypes, are so common across large sections of the population attests to the importance of body build in nonverbal communication.

It should also be noted that because of these different perceptions we will also have different perceptions of the same actions when they are performed by persons of different body build. For example, if a man at a dance sits in the corner with his head down and his arms clasped in front of him we would probably read different things into it if he were fat, or muscular, or skinny.

HAIR

For the past decade or so hair has achieved particular prominance. Haircuts for men used to be not only cheap but also routine clippings, which were done without any real fanfare by some ordinary-looking barber in a rather unattractive, drab store. Everyone got essentially the same kind of haircut, with some slight variation introduced from time to time or from season to season. For the most part these routine operations were performed as quickly and as economically as possible. Today, large numbers of the male population no longer have their hair cut; rather, they have it styled. They go not to a barber but to a hair stylist, not to a barbershop but to a salon or "hair treatment" parlor.

There seems to be a whole new set of attitudes concerning men's hair. A few years ago, stylish men had long hair. Shoulder length for college students was ideal, and the longer it was the better. This was especially true during the early years of the style, because it indicated that this person had been one of the first to start wearing this style. Older men were caught in a bind. Should they imitate the youth, let their hair grow long, and join the "revolution" and at the same time perhaps cause problems in the office where long hair might not be appreciated. Or should they continue to cut their hair short and thereby assert that they were no longer young, no longer up with the changing styles, no longer "in."

Together with the length issue was that of the natural versus the groomed look. Some people just let the hair grow anyway it wanted to and rarely attempted to change its course by combing or brushing. Others took great pains to keep their hair as neat as possible and took great pride in combing it and running their fingers through it.

The length and style of a man's hair communicates something about him which he may want others to perceive. In letting one's hair grow *or* in cutting it the individual is making statements about his personality, motivation, orientation, frame of reference, and so on. These "statements," are not always interpreted as the individual might wish and are not interpreted in the same way by every observer. Thus one person might have in the early days let his hair grow long to assert his "independence from society" but it may have been interpreted differently by different people. His mother may have seen it as a conscious attempt to go against her wishes, his girlfriend may have seen it as a statement against the "establishment," his employer may have seen it as an indication of general unrealiability. Though we each may observe the same object we each interpret and evaluate it differently.

When questioned about their long hair many men simply say, "I let it grow for no reason, I just don't get it cut." In terms of communication this is not a very acceptable answer. That "nothing never happens" is perhaps worth recalling. To do something or not to do something is governed by some reason and consequently says something. And in turn that something will be responded to in some way.

Only a few years ago there occurred a rise in black consciousness which was communicated, at least in part, by the new hairstyles that blacks, both males and females, wore. The Afro became the sign of the liberated black man and woman; no longer would hair be "processed" or slicked back to look like the hair of white people. To many people, such hair styles clearly distinguished between the liberated and the unliberated. This message was tempered somewhat when the Afro became "stylish" and whites as well as blacks wore it. At first an identification with black liberation was communicated; later, it was more a message of style than of social consciousness.

Body hair also communicates. To the young male, his chest hair may communicate maturity and manliness. And so he may open his shirt as far as necessary to show this body hair so that these qualities of maturity and manliness may be communicated to others. Women will shave their legs and underarms and dye facial hair because our society has labeled such hair unattractive and unfeminine. On men, facial hair may mean masculinity; on women it may mean embarrassment and all sorts of problems of bleaching, shaving, waxing, and so on.

SKIN COLOR

The color of a person's skin also communicates. Most obviously it communicates race—black, white, yellow, and red are the obvious classifications. But we also make use of color distinctions for general background heritage, as when we distinguish the dark Mediterranean types from the blond Nordic types. Similarly among blacks, distinctions are made in terms of lightness or darkness of the skin. Jamaican blacks are seen as quite different from African blacks.

Skin color may also communicate something about the individual's life-style. A dark tan in the winter in the northern part of the country is a status symbol that is worn with special pride, and great care is taken to make sure that the tan stays as long as possible. Bronzing creams and sun tan machines are for some people indispensible communication aids.

ODOR

Although little research has been conducted on the communicative function of odor it should be clear to anyone with a nose that smell communicates a great deal.

The person who is trying to appear sophisticated and who pours on cheap perfume or cologne communicates something different from the person who has not changed clothes in weeks and just reeks of body odor and sweat. Everyone communicates something different by the odor they carry around.

Body odor, advertisements tell us, is to be avoided, covered up, and bombarded with Right Guard, Ultra Ban 5000, Brut, or whatever else is on the market. So we cover it up. Our underarms are doused with the stuff for fear that we will offend. At first it seemed that our underarms were the only target of these manufacturers. But our feet smell too, and they therefore need protection least we cause our friends to faint when we take off our shoes at some elegant restaurant. Still this was not the end. The success of the sweaty underarm and the smelly foot led the manufacturers to look around for other parts of the anatomy where nature needed help. Through television, women were told in a soft whisper—the interesting difference between public television whispering and private face-to-face whispering is apparently not perceived by many viewers—that underarm odor was not their real problem. Their real problem area was the vagina, where, it was suggested, odor would be more than offensive—it would be downright immoral. The American woman now seems totally odor free or, at least, she now gives off an acceptable smell. But we have been fooled before, and it sems only a matter of time before manufacturers concoct a means to sell a spray for another part of our offending bodies.

At times, people take great pride in smelling as they do. And with good reason. Many people, for example, like the smell of body odor and positively reinforce those who smell of body odor. Others have been positively reinforced for heavy perfume and so they continue to use it.

Sometimes odor communicates something about people that they wish to say but are somehow too embarrassed to communicate in that way. The people who wish their friends to know how energetic they are might walk into a room smelling of sweat; this communicates to others that they are energetic, athletic, healthy, active, youthful, and so on. That it also communicates that they might be slobs seems to them at least, a minor price to pay for communicating all these positive virtues.

Sources

The discussion of body type is based on the famous and much criticized work of W. H. Sheldon. See, for example, his *Atlas of Man: A Guide for Somatyping the Adult Male at All Ages* (New York: Harper & Row, 1954). The exercise on body type comes from J. B. Cortes and F. M. Gatti, "Physique and Self-Description of Temperament," *Journal of Consulting Psychology* 29 (1965): 408–414. Perhaps the best summary of findings on physical characteristics is provided by Mark Knapp, *Nonverbal Communication in Human Interaction* (New York: Holt, 1972).

Experiential Vehicle

BODY TYPE

Instructions

Fill in each blank with a word from the suggested list following each statement. For any blank (three in each statement), you may select any word from the list of twelve immediately below. A word that fits you exactly may not be in the list, but select the words that seem to fit you most closely.

1. I feel _____, _____, and _____ most of the time.

   calm, anxious, cheerful, contented, relaxed, confident, tense, impetuous, complacent, reticent, energetic, self-conscious

2. When I study or work, I seem to be _____, _____, and _____.

   efficient, enthusiastic, reflective, placid, sluggish, competitive, leisurely, meticulous, precise, determined, thoughtful, cooperative

3. Socially, I am _____, _____, and _____.

   outgoing, affable, tolerant, gentle-tempered, considerate, awkward, affected, soft-tempered, argumentative, shy, talkative, hot-tempered

4. I am rather _____, _____, and _____.

   active, warm, domineering, introspective, forgiving, courageous, suspicious, cool, sympathetic, serious, soft-hearted, enterprising

5. Other people consider me rather _____, _____, and _____.

   generous, adventurous, withdrawn, dominant, optimistic, affectionate, reckless, detached, sensitive, kind, cautions, dependent

6. Underline the *one* word out of the three in each of the following lines that most closely describes the way you are:

   a. assertive, relaxed, tense
   b. hot-tempered, cool, warm
   c. withdrawn, sociable, active
   d. confident, tactful, kind
   e. dependent, dominant, detached
   f. enterprising, affable, anxious

unit 30
Esthetic, Color, and Time Communication

Esthetic Surroundings
Color
Time
   Esthetic, Color, and Time Communication

Objectives

Upon completion of this unit, you should be able to:

1. explain how different surroundings might influence perceptions
2. explain the arbitrariness of color symbolism
3. explain at least three messages that one's treatment of time might communicate

Esthetic, color, and *time* communication, although not researched and studied like the other forms of nonverbal communication, need to be considered since they each communicate a great deal.

ESTHETIC SURROUNDINGS

That the decorations or surroundings of a particular place exert influence on us should be obvious to anyone who has ever entered a hospital with its sterile walls and furniture, or a museum with its imposing columns, glass-encased exhibits, and brass plaques.

    Even the way in which a relatively ordinary room is furnished exerts considerable influence. Perhaps the best way to explain this is to describe an insightful study on this question. In this study Abraham Maslow and

Norbett Mintz attempted to determine if the esthetic conditions or surroundings of a room would influence the judgments people made in these rooms. Three rooms were used; one appeared beautiful, one average, and one ugly.

The beautiful room, for example, had large windows, beige walls, indirect lighting, and furnishings that made the room seem attractive and comfortable. Paintings were on the walls, a large Navajo rug covered the floor, and drapes were on the windows. The average room was a professor's office with two mahogany desks and chairs, a metal bookcase, metal filing cabinet, and shades on the windows. The ugly room was painted a battleship gray. Lighting was provided by an overhead bulb with a dirty torn shade. The room was furnished to give the impression of a janitor's storeroom in horrible condition. The ash trays were filled and the window shades torn.

Students rated ten art prints in terms of fatigue/energy and displeasure/well-being in the three different rooms. As predicted, the students rated the prints in the beautiful room to be more energetic and to evidence more well-being. Those judged in the ugly room were rated as evidencing fatigue and displeasure, while those judged in the average room were perceived as somewhere between those two extremes.

In a follow-up study Mintz selected two of the subjects from the previous experiment and used them as "examiners." For a period of three weeks these two subjects tested other subjects for one hour per day, each alternating every day between the beautiful and the ugly room. After each hour the "examiners" were asked to rate the prints again, supposedly for measures of reliability.

It was found that the ratings of the prints were similar to that found in the first experiment. The subjects still rated the prints as more energetic and evidencing more well-being when in the beautiful room than when in the ugly room. Further, these results were consistent over the three weeks. The subjects did not adjust to the surroundings over time. The experimenter also tested the time spent by the "examiners" in testing their subjects. It was found that the testing in the ugly room was completed faster than that in the beautiful room in 27 out of 32 times.

General observational conclusions show that the subjects did not want to test in the ugly room, became irritable and aggressive when they had to test in that room, and felt that time seemed to move more slowly when in the ugly room.

The implications of this type of finding seem extremely important. We are forced to wonder, it seems, if the ghetto child studying in the tenement is able to derive the same benefits as the middle-class student studying in his or her own room. Can workers in an unappealing factory ever enjoy their job as much as workers in pleasant offices? What about prisons? Is aggressive behavior in prisons in part a function of the horrible surroundings prisoners are forced to live in? Is the higher crime rate in depressed areas, in part at least, a function of the "ugliness" of the surroundings?

Questions such as these are not easy to answer but they should be asked by any student of nonverbal communication.

COLOR

Henry Dreyfuss in his *Symbol Sourcebook* reminds us of some of the positive and negative meanings associated with various colors. Some of these are presented in Table 30.1.
Dreyfuss also notes some cultural comparisons for some of these colors. For example, red in China is a color for joyous and festive occasions whereas in Japan it is used to signify anger and danger. Blue, for the Cherokee Indian, signifies defeat but for the Egyptian it signifies virtue and truth. In the Japanese theatre blue is the color for villains. Yellow

Table 30.1 *Some Positive and Negative Messages of Colors*

Color	Positive Messages	Negative Messages
red	warmth passion life liberty patriotism	death war revolution devil danger
blue	religious feeling devotion truth justice	doubt discouragements
yellow	intuition wisdom divinity	cowardice malevolence impure love
green	nature hope freshness prosperity	envy jealousy opposition disgrace
purple	power royalty love of truth nostalgia	mourning regret penitence resignation

Source: Henry Dryfuss, *Symbol Sourcebook* (New York: McGraw-Hill, 1971).

signifies happiness and prosperity in Egypt but in tenth-century France yellow colored the doors of criminals. Green communicates femininity to certain American Indians, fertility and strength to Egyptians, and youth and energy to Japanese. Purple signifies virtue and faith in Egypt but grace and nobility in Japan.

Perhaps the most talked about communicative function of color is its supposed reflection of personality. Faber Birren, for example, argues that if you like red your life is directed outward, you are impulsive, active, aggressive, vigorous, sympathetic, quick to judge people, impatient, optimistic, and strongly driven by sex. If, on the other hand, you dislike red you also dislike the qualities in those people who like red, such as aggressiveness, optimism, and the like. You feel that others have gotten the better deal in life and you never feel really secure. Sexually, you are unsatisfied.

If you like blue you are probably conservative, introspective, and deliberate. You are sensitive to yourself and to others and have your passions under control. In your own communications you are cautious, your opinions and beliefs seldom change, and you question just about everything you do not understand. If you dislike blue you resent the success of others and in fact enjoy their failures. You feel that your emotional and your intellectual lives are not fulfilled. You get irritated easily and are somewhat erratic in your own behavior.

This analysis was drawn from the many comments of Faber Birren in *Color in Your World*. Analyses of your personality based on your likes and dislikes of eleven colors as well as on conflicts (liking one color and disliking another color) are readily supplied by Birren and by various other writers though there seems to be no evidence for these claims. The idea of analyzing someone's personality on the basis of color preferences seems a most intriguing idea, and yet the validity of such analyses is uninvestigated.

The messages that colors communicate about a culture's meaning are easily determined, while the personality meanings that colors reveal are quite difficult and perhaps impossible to determine.

TIME

Just as surely as color, space, gesture, or vocal inflection communicate, so does time. Though it is not often looked at as a communication-carrying signal, time talks incessantly.

Consider, for example, the students who constantly arrive late for biology class. Their previous class is next door, and so difficulty in getting to the class is not the problem. Yet, they consistently come late. (Consider what you would think if the biology teacher was always late for class.) For some reason they find themselves engaged in something else which invariably consumes more time than at first anticipated. These same students, however, are always early for their interpersonal communication class. Regardless of the reasons for being late and early, they communicate something to the instructors of both courses. To the biology teacher it might be that the students hate the class, that they are somehow disorganized, or that they have weak kidneys. To the communication teacher it might mean that they are anxious to get better acquainted with other students, that they are interested in the course, or perhaps that they have nothing else to do. Regardless of what impression the teachers get, they do get impressions.

The sense of time varies with different cultures and even with different subcultures. Edward Hall, for example, has pointed to the phenomenon of CPT—Colored People's Time. CPT is different from WPT—White People's Time. CPT is approximate where WPT is exact. Waiting is nothing to get excited about in CPT but is an affront in WPT. This concept was used not too long ago with considerable effect in an episode of "Maude," where Florida, Maude's black maid, tell's her husband that he had better pick her up at 9 P.M., not CPT but WPT—that is, exactly at nine. Some black students, for example, may be late to class or for appointments without feeling that any great tragedy has occurred. White teachers often have difficulty adjusting to this; they feel such "lateness" somehow shows disrespect or disinterest. Actually, there is no desire to communicate disrespect; it is simply due to the fact that different people run on different clocks—some clocks are exact, some clocks are approximate.

In our society it is permissible to be 5 or 10 minutes early or late for most appointments. This, of course, is a general figure. In some sections of the country there is greater latitude—as during snow storms or when the distance to be traveled is particularly long. But for the most part our culture demands considerable clock watching. In other societies time is not looked at in the same way, and there is nothing wrong with being one or even two hours "late." Appointments are not such that a specific block of time is set aside for you (as in our culture) but rather that you are expected to arrive sometime in the evening, for example, and the business or socialization will take place when you get there.

This may cause considerable problems for Americans working in foreign countries as well as for foreigners working in America. Consider, for example, someone being one or two hours late for dinner and then entering without even attempting to make an apology. Surely we would assume that we have a right to be angry. Yet, to the foreigner, nothing inappropriate—and certainly nothing to offend the host—has occurred.

Within this culture, for example, consider what arriving early or late or leaving early or late at a party might mean. At one level the time of arrival and departure might communicate something about interest or enjoyment. But such messages also communicate something about our willingness to socialize, our concern for the host, our level of frustration tolerance, our need to make a grand entrance or exit, and so on. Some persons seem particularly sensitive to the appropriateness of time while others seem totally oblivious. Some persons consistently arrive late for dinner, for example, and then wonder why they are seldom invited back. Some seem totally unaware of when to leave. Although we may look at our watch several times, yawn three or four times at strategic places in the conversation mention that there is a full day of work ahead tomorrow, and give any number of other cues, there seems to be no awareness of time with some people.

Time is especially linked to status considerations, though none seem written down in any book of etiquette. For example, the importance of being on time varies directly with the status of the individual. If the person is extremely important we had better be there on time; in fact we had better be early just in case he or she is able to see us before schedule. As an individual's status decreases, it is less important for us to be on time. Students, for example, must be on time for conferences with teachers but it is more important to be on time for deans and still more important to be on time for the president. Teachers, on the other hand, may be late for conferences with students but not for conferences with deans or the president of the college. Deans in turn may be late for teachers but not for the president. Within any given hierarchy similar unwritten rules seem to be followed in dealing with time.

This is not to imply that these "rules" are just or fair. It is only to point out that they exist. Surely teachers should not be late for appointments with students nor should deans be late for appointments with teachers. These "rules" merely state the general cultural attitude toward such violations of schedules.

Even the time of dinner and the time from the arrival of guests to eating varies on the basis of status. Among lower-status individuals dinner is served relatively early and if there are guests they eat soon after they arrive. For higher-status people, dinner is relatively late and a longer period of time elapses between arrival and eating—usually the time it takes to consume two cocktails.

Promptness or lateness in responding to letters, in returning telephone calls, in acknowledging gifts, and in returning invitations all communicate significant messages to other individuals. Such messages may be indexed on such scales as interest-disinterest, organized-disorganized, considerate-inconsiderate, sociable-unsociable, and so on.

The time people live in one place or the time a professor stays at one school or the time an individual remains with a particular doctor or lawyer or therapist also communicates something about the individual and about the particular relationship between them.

There are also times during which certain activities are considered appropriate and other times during which they are considered inappropriate. Thus it is permissible to make a social phone call during late morning, afternoon, and early evening but not permissable to call before eight or nine in the morning or during dinner time or after 11 P.M. Similarly, in making dates an appropriate amount of notice is customary. When that acceptable amount of time is given as notice, it communicates a certain recognition of the accepted standards, perhaps respect for the individual, perhaps a certain special grace.

Should any of these time conventions be violated, however, other meanings are perceived. For example, a phone call at an abnormal hour will almost surely communicate urgency of some sort; we begin to worry what could be the matter as we race toward the phone.

If, in asking for a date, the call is made the night before or even the same night as the expected date, it may communicate any number of things. Say, A calls B Saturday afternoon for a date that evening. Calling at that particular time may communicate, for example, that A had another date who cancelled, or that A knew that B would be free and so there was no need to give notice, or that A was such a catch that B would welcome A regardless of the time called, and so on. In turn, B's response or answer communicates significant meaning to A. B's acceptance might confirm A's expectation that B was free or that B would welcome A's call at any time. B's rejection, depending on the kind of ego A had, might communicate that B really wanted to date A but could not appear too eager or that B didn't really want to date A and only used the short notice as an excuse.

Any violation of accepted time schedules is determined, that is, it has a reason. As senders we may or may not be consciously aware of such reasons. As receivers we can only guess at the possible reasons based on whatever other cues are available.

Sources

The effects of surroundings are perhaps best explained in the work of Robert Sommer cited in Unit 27, Spatial Communication. The experiment on esthetic surroundings was conducted by A. H. Maslow and N. L. Mintz, "Effects of Esthetic Surroundings: I. Initial Effects of Three Esthetic Conditions Upon Perceiving 'Energy' and 'Well-Being' in Faces," *Journal of Psychology* 41(1956):247–254. Also see N. L. Mintz, "Effects of Esthetic Surroundings: II. Prolonged and Repeated Experience in a 'Beautiful' and 'Ugly' Room," *Journal of Psychology* 41(1956):459–466. On time, see Hall's *The Silent Language* (New York: Doubleday, 1959) and Edward and Mildred Hall's "The Sounds of Silence," *Playboy* 18

(June 1971):139. *The Lüscher Color Test*, translated and edited by I. A. Scott (New York: Pocket Books, 1971) and Faber Birren's *Color in Your World* (New York: Collier Books, 1962) are interesting attempts to relate various personality characteristics to one's color preferences.

Experiential Vehicle

ESTHETIC, COLOR, AND TIME COMMUNICATION

The purpose of this exercise is to explore the influence that our physical environment has on interpersonal communication. Groups of five or six are formed at random. The task of each group is to redesign your classroom so that it is more conducive to the aims of this course. Fifteen to twenty minutes should be allowed for the groups to come up with a new design. ("Redesign" should be taken to mean anything that is possible to do within the rules or restrictions imposed by the school and would include changing, adding, or removing any materials which may and can be changed, added, or removed by the group.)

After each group has planned the "new" classroom, the designs are shared with the other members of the class. From all the suggestions a composite redesigned classroom should be constructed and put into actual operation for at least a week of classes.

Before this design is put into effect, discussion should cover at least the following areas:

1. In what ways will this new design facilitate interpersonal communication? How? Be as specific as possible.
2. How would the classroom be designed if a party were to be held in it? Why? A formal lecture? Why?
3. If you could paint it any color you wanted to, what color(s) would you select? Why?
4. What time of the day would be ideal to have this class? Why?

unit 31

Paralanguage

The Structure of Paralanguage
Judgments Based on Paralanguage
  Paralanguage Communication

Objectives

Upon completion of this unit, you should be able to:

1. define *paralanguage*
2. identify three or four major classes of paralinguistic phenomena
3. explain at least three messages that variations in paralinguistic phenomena might communicate

An old exercise to increase the student's ability to express different emotions, feelings, and attitudes was to have the student say the following sentences while accenting or stressing different words: "Is this the face that launched a thousand ships?" Significant differences in meaning are easily communicated depending on where the stress is placed. Consider, for example, the following variations:

1. IS this the face that launched a thousand ships?
2. Is THIS the face that launched a thousand ships?
3. Is this the FACE that launched a thousand ships?
4. Is this the face that LAUNCHED a thousand ships?
5. Is this the face that launched a THOUSAND SHIPS?

Each of these five sentences communicates something different. Each, in fact, asks a totally different question even though the words used are identical. All that distinguishes the sentences is stress, one of the aspects of what is called *paralanguage*. Parlanguage may be defined as the vocal (but nonverbal) dimension of speech. Paralanguage refers to the manner in which something is said rather than to what is said.

THE STRUCTURE OF PARALANGUAGE

An outline of a classification offered by George L. Trager is presented in Table 31.1. More important than the specifics of this table is that paralanguage encompasses a great deal of vocal expression and can be classified and analyzed rather precisely for various different purposes.

Table 31.1 *Paralanguage: A Classification*

I. Voice Qualities	5. Belching/yawning
A. Pitch Range	B. Vocal Qualifiers
1. Spread	1. Intensity
a. Upward	a. Overloud
b. Downward	1. somewhat
2. Narrowed	2. considerably
a. From above	3. very much
b. From below	b. Oversoft
B. Vocal Lip Control	1. somewhat
1. Rasp	2. considerably
2. Openness	3. very much
C. Glottis Control	2. Pitch Height
1. Sharp transitions	a. Overhigh
2. Smooth transitions	1. slightly
D. Pitch Control	2. appreciably
E. Articulation Control	3. greatly
1. Forceful (precise)	b. Overlow
2. Relaxed (slurred)	1. slightly
F. Rhythm Control	2. appreciably
1. Smooth	3. greatly
2. Jerky	3. Extent
G. Resonance	a. Drawl
1. Resonant	1. slight
2. Thin	2. noticeable
H. Tempo	3. extreme
1. Increased from norm	b. Clipping
2. Decreased from norm	1. slight
	2. noticeable
II. Vocalizations	3. extreme
A. Vocal Characterizers	C. Vocal Segregates
1. Laughing/crying	1. Uh-uh
2. Yelling/whispering	2. Uh-huh
3. Moaning/groaning	3. Sh
4. Whining/breaking	4. (Pause)

Source: George L. Trager, "Paralanguage: A First Approximation," *Studies in Linguistics* 13(1958):1–12; George L. Trager, "The Typology of Paralanguage," *Anthropological Linguistics* 3(1961):17–21; and Robert E. Pittenger and Henry Smith, Jr., "A Basis for Some Contributions of Linguistics to Psychiatry," *Psychiatry* 20(1957): 61–78.

Although in outline form the breakdown of paralinguistic phenomena is as shown, the four major classes are: *voice qualities, vocal characterizers, vocal qualifiers,* and *vocal segregates.*

The sounds used in vocal segregates are not the same as those sounds when used in words—that is, the *sh* which means "silence!" is not the same sound as in *shed.*

The "pause" noted as a vocal segregate is classified in a somewhat different area by many contemporary researchers. This area, generally referred to as "hesitation phenomena," is concerned with all forms of hesitations, pause being only one of these.

Some of the classifications are actually continuous scales, vocal lip control may be analyzed as ranging from rasp through openness rather than simply as either rasp or open.

If we assume the validity of the proposition that nothing never happens, that all behavior serves a communicative function, then we must further assume that each of these paralinguistic features also communicates meaning. Thus the speaker who speaks quickly communicates something different from the one who speaks slowly. Even though the words might be the same, if the speed differs the meaning we receive will also differ. And we may derive different meanings from "fast talk" depending on the speaker. Perhaps in one person we might perceive fear, feeling that he or she is hurrying to get the statement over with. In another we might perceive annoyance or lack of concern, inferring that he or she speaks rapidly so that not too much time is wasted. In still another we might perceive extreme interest, feeling that the person is speaking quickly so that he or she can get to the punch line and hear our reaction.

JUDGMENTS BASED ON PARALANGUAGE

With all of the features of paralanguage we will perceive different things depending on the specifics of the situation and on the other nonverbal and verbal cues we perceive.

We are a diagnostically oriented people, quick to make judgments about another's personality based on various paralinguistic cues. At times our judgments turn out to be correct, at other times incorrect. But the number of times correct and incorrect does not seem to influence the frequency with which we make such judgments. We may, for example, conclude that speakers who speak so softly that we can hardly hear them seem to have some kind of problem. Perhaps they feel inferior —they "know" that no one really wants to listen, "know" that nothing they say is significant, and so speak softly. Other speakers will speak at an extremely loud volume, perhaps because of an overinflated ego and the belief that everyone in the world wants to hear them, that what they have to say is so valuable that they cannot risk our not hearing every word. Speakers who speak with no variation, in a complete monotone, seem uninterested in what they are saying and seem to encourage a similar disinterest from the listeners—if any are still around. We might perceive such people as having a lack of interest in life in general, as being rather bland individuals. All of these conclusions are, at best, based on little evidence. Yet this does not stop us from making such conclusions.

It is important for us to inquire into the relationship between paralanguage and impression formation. It does seem that certain voices are symptomatic of certain personality types, of certain problems, and specifically that the personality orientation leads to the vocal qualities. When listening to people speak—regardless of what they are saying—we form impressions based on their paralanguage as to what kind of people they are. Our impressions seem to consist of physical impressions (about body type perhaps and certainly about sex and age), personality impressions (they seem outgoing, they sound shy, they appear aggressive), and evaluative impressions (they sound like good people, they sound evil and menacing, they sound lovable, they have vicious laughs).

Much research has been directed to the question of the accuracy of these judgments—that is, how accurately may we judge a person on the basis of voice alone. One of the earliest studies on this question was conducted by T. H. Pear. Pear used nine speakers and had over 4000 listeners make guesses about these nine speakers. The sex and age of the speaker appeared to be guessed with considerable accuracy. However, the listeners were only able to accurately guess the occupations of the clergymen and the actor.

Other studies, perhaps taking their cue from that of Pear, pursued the investigation of the relationship between vocal characteristics and personal characteristics. Most studies suggest, in agreement with Pear, that sex and age can be guessed accurately on the basis of the voice alone. This is not to say that complete accuracy is possible with age but it does seem able to be guessed within relatively small ranges.

Some studies report that listeners can guess the occupation of the speaker whereas other studies report that they cannot. In some studies listeners have been able to match voices to photographs and to the people themselves, although other evidence suggests that this is not always possible.

One of the most interesting findings on voice and personal characteristics is that which shows that listeners can accurately judge the status (whether high, middle, or low) of speakers from hearing a 60-second voice sample. In fact, many listeners reported that they made their judgments in less than 15 seconds. It has also been found that the speakers judged to be of high status were rated as being of higher credibility than those speakers rated middle and low in status.

There is much greater agreement in the literature when we consider the question of identifying the emotional states of listeners from their vocal expression. Generally, in these studies the content of the speech is nonexistent or is held constant. Thus in a content-free situation the speaker would attempt to communicate anxiety, for example, by saying the alphabet or perhaps by reciting numbers. In the situation where the content is held constant the speakers say the same sentences (generally rather unemotional ones) for all the emotions they are to communicate.

It has been found that speakers can communicate or encode emotions through content-free speech or through content that is unrelated to the emotions, and listeners are able to decode these emotions.

A typical study would involve speakers using numbers to communicate different emotions. Listeners would have to select the emotion being communicated from a list of 10 emotions that they were given. In situations like this listeners are generally effective in guessing the emotions.

Listeners vary in their ability to decode the emotions, speakers vary in their ability to encode the emotions, and the accuracy with which emotions are guessed depends on the emotions themselves. For example, while it may be easy to distinguish between hate and sympathy, it may not be so easy to distinguish between fear and anxiety. This type of study is used as the basis for the exercise at the end of this unit.

Sources

For a classification and introduction to paralinguistic phenomena see George L. Trager's "Paralanguage: A First Approximation," *Studies in Linguistics* 13(1958):1–12 and "The Typology of Paralanguage," *Anthropological Linguistics* 3(1961):17–21. Mark Knapp's *Nonverbal Behavior in Human Interaction* (New York: Holt, 1972) provides an excellent summary of research findings. George F. Mahl and Gene Schulze likewise provide a thorough summary of the research and theory in this area. See their "Psychological Research in the Extralinguistic Area," in T. A. Seboek, A. S. Hayes, and M. C. Bateson, eds., *Approaches to Semiotics* (The Hague: Mouton, 1964). For a collection of research studies on paralanguage see Joel R. Davitz, ed., *The Communication of Emotional Meaning* (New York: McGraw-Hill, 1964). For the study by T. H. Pear see his *Voice and Personality* (London: Chapman and Hall, 1931). For a thorough review of paralanguage see (in addition to the Mahl and Schulze and Knapp) Ernest Kramer, "Judgment of Personal Characteristics and Emotions from Nonverbal Properties," *Psychological Bulletin* 60(1963) and Albert Mehrabian, *Silent Messages* (Belmont, Cal.: Wadsworth, 1971).

Experiential Vehicle

PARALANGUAGE COMMUNICATION

In this exercise a subject recites the alphabet attempting to communicate each of the following emotions:

anger
fear
happiness
jealousy
love
nervousness
pride
sadness
satisfaction
sympathy

The subject may begin the alphabet at any point and may omit and repeat sounds, but the subject may use only the names of the letters of the alphabet to communicate these feelings.

The subject should first number the emotions in random order so that he or she will have a set order to follow which is not known to the audience, whose task it will be to guess the emotions expressed.

As a variation, have the subject go through the entire list of emotions: once facing the audience and employing any nonverbal signals desired and once with his or her back to the audience without employing any additional signals. Are there differences in the number of correct guesses depending on which method is used?

For Discussion and Response

1. What are some of the differences between encoding-decoding "emotional meaning" and "logical meaning"?

This exercise is based on J. R. Davatz and L. J. Davatz, "The Communication of Feelings by Content-Free Speech," *Journal of Communication* 9(1959):6–13.

2. Davitz and Davitz found the number of correct identifications for these emotions to be as follows: anger (156), nervousness (130), sadness (118), happiness (104), sympathy (93), satisfaction (75), love (60), fear (60), jealousy (69), and pride (50). Do these figures correspond to those obtained in class? What conclusions would you draw relevant to the relative ease-difficulty of expressing the several emotions?

3. Do you think there is a positive relationship between encoding and decoding abilities in situations such as this? Is the person adept at encoding the emotions also adept at decoding them? Explain.

4. What variables might in influence encoding ability? Decoding ability?

5. What personality factors seem relevant to the encoding and decoding of emotions?

PART THREE
INTERPERSONAL INTERACTIONS AND EFFECTS

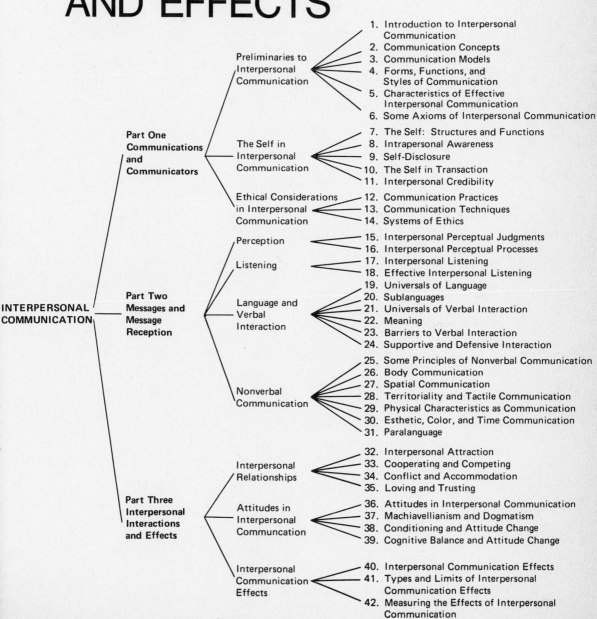

INTERPERSONAL COMMUNICATION

Part One Communications and Communicators

Preliminaries to Interpersonal Communication
1. Introduction to Interpersonal Communication
2. Communication Concepts
3. Communication Models
4. Forms, Functions, and Styles of Communication
5. Characteristics of Effective Interpersonal Communication
6. Some Axioms of Interpersonal Communication

The Self in Interpersonal Communication
7. The Self: Structures and Functions
8. Intrapersonal Awareness
9. Self-Disclosure
10. The Self in Transaction
11. Interpersonal Credibility

Ethical Considerations in Interpersonal Communication
12. Communication Practices
13. Communication Techniques
14. Systems of Ethics

Part Two Messages and Message Reception

Perception
15. Interpersonal Perceptual Judgments
16. Interpersonal Perceptual Processes

Listening
17. Interpersonal Listening
18. Effective Interpersonal Listening

Language and Verbal Interaction
19. Universals of Language
20. Sublanguages
21. Universals of Verbal Interaction
22. Meaning
23. Barriers to Verbal Interaction
24. Supportive and Defensive Interaction

Nonverbal Communication
25. Some Principles of Nonverbal Communication
26. Body Communication
27. Spatial Communication
28. Territoriality and Tactile Communication
29. Physical Characteristics as Communication
30. Esthetic, Color, and Time Communication
31. Paralanguage

Part Three Interpersonal Interactions and Effects

Interpersonal Relationships
32. Interpersonal Attraction
33. Cooperating and Competing
34. Conflict and Accommodation
35. Loving and Trusting

Attitudes in Interpersonal Communcation
36. Attitudes in Interpersonal Communication
37. Machiavellianism and Dogmatism
38. Conditioning and Attitude Change
39. Cognitive Balance and Attitude Change

Interpersonal Communication Effects
40. Interpersonal Communication Effects
41. Types and Limits of Interpersonal Communication Effects
42. Measuring the Effects of Interpersonal Communication

unit 32

Interpersonal Attraction

The Qualities of Interpersonal Attraction: Part I
Attractiveness
Proximity
Reinforcement
Similarity
Complementarity
The Qualities of Interpersonal Attraction: Part II

Objectives

Upon completion of this unit, you should be able to:

1. define *interpersonal attraction*
2. define *attractiveness* and explain its influence in interpersonal attraction
3. explain the relativity of physical and personal attractiveness
4. define *proximity* and explain the ways in which it influences interpersonal attraction
5. explain the "mere exposure" hypothesis
6. define *reinforcement* and explain how it enters into interpersonal attraction
7. define *similarity* and explain how it operates in interpersonal attraction
8. define *complementarity* and explain the ways it influences interpersonal attraction

Experiential Vehicle

THE QUALITIES OF INTERPERSONAL ATTRACTION: PART I

In order to test the principles and findings discussed in this unit, complete the following questionnaire before reading any further.

CHARACTERISTICS OF A PERSON
YOU WOULD BE MOST ATTRACTED TO:

Age   _____
Sex   _____
Height   _____
Weight   _____
General physical attractiveness   _____
Race   _____
Religion   _____
Nationality   _____
Intelligence   _____
Years of formal education   _____
Profession or professional goal   _____
Music preferred   _____
Literature preferred   _____
Political attitudes   _____
Religious attitudes   _____
Hobbies/interests   _____
City person/country person   _____
At least three major personality characteristics   _____
                                                        _____
                                                        _____

List the names of five people to whom you are very attracted:

1.

2.

3.

4.

5.

List the names of five people to whom you are not attracted:

1.

2.

3.

4.

5.

We are all attracted to some people and not attracted to others. In a similar way, some people are attracted to us and some people are not. This seems to be the universal human condition. If we were to examine the people we are attracted to and the people we are not attracted to we would probably be able to see patterns in the decisions or judgments we make. Even though many of these decisions seem subconsciously motivated, we can nevertheless discern patterns in the interpersonal choices we make.

We are all probably attracted to "a type" of person or to "types" of people. This ideal type (which differs for each person) can probably be found, in varying degrees, in each of the people we are attracted to and its opposite, in varying degrees, in each of the people to whom we are not attracted. It has been found that most people are interpersonally attracted to others on the basis of five major variables: *attractiveness, proximity, reinforcement, similiarity,* and *complementarity.*

ATTRACTIVENESS

Attractiveness comes in at least two forms. When we say, "I find that person attractive," we probably mean either 1) that we find that person physically attractive or 2) that we find that person's personality or ways of behaving attractive. For the most part we tend to like physically attractive people rather than physically ugly people, and we tend to like people who possess a pleasant personality rather than an unpleasant personality. Few would find fault with these two generalizations. The difficulty arises when we try to define "attractive." Perhaps the best way to illustrate this difficulty is to look at some old movies, newspapers, or magazines and compare the conceptions of beauty portrayed there with those popular now. Or even better, examine the conceptions of beauty in different cultures. At some times and in some cultures people who are fat (by our standards) would be considered attractive but in other cultures they would be unattractive. Where at one time fashion models were supposed to be extremely thin (remember Twiggy?) they are now allowed to have some flesh on their bones. The same difficulty besets us when we attempt to define "pleasant personality." To some people this would mean an aggressive, competitive, forceful individual whereas to others it might mean an unassuming, shy, and bashful individual.

Similarly, we would probably look for different physical and personality characteristics depending on the situation in which we were going to interact. In a classroom it might be most important to sit next to someone who knows all the answers. So regardless of this person's physical appearance, this "answer machine" is perceived as attractive. To go on a swimming date, however, we might select someone with a good body and not be too concerned with his or her intellectual abilities. When inviting someone to join a football team we might choose someone heavy and strong.

Although attractiveness (both physical and personality) is difficult to define universally (impossible is perhaps closer to the truth), it is possible to define it for any one individual for specific situations. Thus if Person A were interested in dating someone, he or she might choose someone who possessed x, y, and z characteristics. For Person A, in this situation, these are the characteristics that are considered "attractive." And in all probability, given this same person in another similar situation, he or she would again look for someone who possessed these same characteristics. That is, we seem relatively consistent in the characteristics we find "attractive."

We also have a tendency to attribute positive characterstics to people we find attractive and negative characteristics to people we find unattractive. If people were asked to predict which qualities a given individual possessed they would probably predict the possession of positive qualities if they thought the person attractive and negative characteristics if they thought the person unattractive.

PROXIMITY

If we look around at the people we find attractive we would probably find that they are the people who live or work close to us. This is perhaps the one finding that emerges most frequently from the research on interpersonal attraction. In one of the most famous studies Festinger, Schachter, and Back studied friendships in a student housing development. They found that the development of friendships was greatly influenced by the distance between the units in which the people lived and by the direction in which the units faced. The closer the students' rooms were to each other the better the chances were that they would become friends. It was also found that the students living in units that faced the courtyard had more friends than the students who lived in units facing the street: The people who became friends were the people who had the greater opportunity to interact with each other. We might add that the vast majority of marriages are between people who have lived very close to each other physically.

As might be predicted, physical distance is most important in the early stages of interaction. For example, during the first days of school proximity (in class or in dormitories) is especially important. It decreases (but always remains significant) as the opportunity to interact with more distant others increases.

The importance of physical distance also varies with the type of situation one is in. For example, in anxiety-producing situations we seem to have more need for company and hence are more easily attracted to others than when we are in situations with low or no anxiety. It is also comforting to be with people who have gone through or who will go through the same experiences. We seem especially attracted to these people in times of stress. We would also be more susceptive to being attracted to someone else if we had previously been deprived of such interaction. If, for example, we were in a hospital or prison without any contact from other people we would probably be attracted to just about anyone. Anyone seems a great deal better than no one. We are also most attracted to people when we are feeling down or when self-esteem is particularly low. If, for example, we have been put down by a teacher, friend, or parent, then we seem to have a greater need to interact with others and are more easily attracted to someone. Perhaps we assume that this person will pull us out of the state we are in.

When we attempt to discover the reasons for the influence that physical closeness has on interpersonal attraction we can think of many. We seem to have positive expectations of people and consequently fulfill these by liking or being attracted to others. If we go to a party, for example, it is a lot easier to go with the idea that the people we will meet will be pleasant ones. Since we have this expectation, we fulfill the prophecy ourselves.

Another reason is that proximity allows us the opportunity to get to know the other person, to gain some information about him or her. We come to like people we know, because we can better predict their behavior and perhaps because of this they seem less frightening to us than complete strangers.

Still another approach argues that mere exposure to others leads us to develop positive feelings for them. Just two examples of the many that could be cited to illustrate the influence of "mere exposure" should be sufficient to make the point. In one study women were supposedly participating in a taste experiment and throughout the course of the experiment were exposed to other people. The subjects were exposed to some people ten times, to others five times, to others two times, to others one time, and to others not at all. The subjects did not talk with these other people and had never seen them before this experiment. The subjects were then asked to rate the other people in terms of how much they liked them. The results showed that they rated highest those persons they had seen ten times, next highest those they saw five times, and so on down the line. How can we account for these results except by "mere exposure." Consider another study. Three groups of rats were selected at random. One group listened to recordings of Mozart for 12 hours for 52 days. Another group listened to recordings of Schoenberg for 12 hours for 52 days. A third group listened to no music at all. After these 52 days each rat was placed in a specially designed cage so that it could select the music it wished to listen to. The music selected by the rats was written by the same composer as the music that they had been exposed to for the 52-day period. Thus the rats raised on Mozart selected Mozart; the rats raised on Schoenberg selected Schoenberg. Mozart was also preferred by the rats raised without music. To make this experiment more unbelievable we should emphasize that the music the rats heard during the 52-day period was not the same as that selected by the rats in their specially designed cages; it was only written by the same composer. Again, can we account for these findings in any way other than mere exposure?

Connected to this "mere exposure" concept is the finding that the greater the contact between people, the less they are prejudiced against each other. For example, whites and blacks living in housing developments became less prejudiced against each other as a result of living and interacting together. It is interesting to speculate on the influence that architects could have on interpersonal interaction, attraction, prejudice, and the like.

The most obvious reason for the effects of proximity (which is not considered in any work on interpersonal attraction) is simply that people are basically attractive. By intertacting or being exposed to them, we find this out and are thus attracted to them. Put differently, perhaps we are attracted to people because they are attractive.

REINFORCEMENT

Perhaps the most obvious statement anyone could make about interpersonal attraction and the reasons we like or dislike people is that we like those who like us and dislike those who dislike us. Naturally there are exceptions; there are some who love people who do not love them and there are those who hate those who love them. For most of us, for most of the time, however, we like those who like us. Put in more behavioral terms, we tend to like those who reward or reinforce us. The reward or reinforcement may be social, as in the form of compliments or praise of one sort or another, or it may be material, as in the case of the suitor whose gifts eventually win the hand of the beloved.

Like most things, reinforcement too can backfire. When overdone, reinforcement loses its effectiveness and may even lead to negative responses. The people who reinforce us constantly soon become too sweet to take and we come, in short order, to discount whatever they say.

Also, if the reinforcement is to work it must be perceived as genuine and not motivated by selfish concerns. The salesperson who compliments your taste in clothes, your eyes, your build, and just about everything else is not going to have the effect that someone without ulterior motives would have. In all probability the salesperson is acting out of selfish concerns; he or she wants to make the sale. Hence this person's "reinforcements" would not lead us to be attracted to him or her since they would not be perceived as genuine.

SIMILARITY

If people could construct their mates they would look, act, and think very much like themselves. By being attracted to people like ourselves we are in effect validating ourselves, saying to ourselves that we are worthy of being liked, that we are attractive.

Generally, although there are exceptions, we like people who are similar to ourselves in color, race, ability, physical characteristics, intelligence, and so on. We are often attracted to mirror images of ourselves.

Similarity is especially important when it comes to attitudes. We are particularly attracted to people who have attitudes similar to our own, who like what we like, and who dislike what we dislike. This similarity is most important when dealing with salient or significant attitudes. For example, it would not make much difference if the attitudes of two people toward food or furniture (though even these can at times be significant) differed, but it would be of great significance if their attitudes toward children or religion or politics were very disparate. Marriages between people with great and salient dissimilarities are more likely to end in divorce than are marriages between people who are a lot alike.

Generally, by liking people who are similar to us and who like what we like, we maintain balance with ourselves. It is psychologically uncomfortable to like people who do not like what we like or to dislike people who like what we like. And so our attraction for similarity enables us to achieve psychological balance or comfort.

Agreement with ourselves is always reinforcing. The person who likes what we like, in effect, tells us that we are right to like what we like. Even after an examination it is helpful to find people who wrote the same answers we did. It tells us we were right. Notice the next time you have an examination how reinforcing it is to hear that others have put down the same answers.

Another reason we are attracted to similarly minded people is that we can predict that since they think like us they will like us as well. And so we like them because we think they like us.

We have often heard people say that the pets of people come to look and act like their owners. This misses the point. Actually, the animals do not change. Rather, the owners select pets that look and act like them at the start. Look around and test this out on people who have dogs and cats.

COMPLEMENTARITY

Although many people would argue that "birds of a feather flock to-gether," others would argue that "opposites attract." That opposites attract is the principle of complementarity.

Take, for example, the individual who is extremely dogmatic. Would he or she be attracted to others who are high in dogmatism or would he or she be attracted to those who are low in dogmatism? The similarity principle would predict that this person would be attracted to those who were like him or her (that is, high in dogmatism), while the complementarity principle would predict that this person would be attracted to those who were unlike him or her (that is, low in dogmatism). The sadist, we know, is not attracted to another sadist but is instead attracted to a masochist who in turn is attracted not to another masochist but to a sadist.

It may be found that people are attracted to others who are dissimilar only in certain situations. For example, the submissive student may get along especially well with an aggressive teacher rather than a submissive one but may not get along with an aggressive fiance or spouse. The dominant wife may get along with a submissive husband but may not relate well to submissive neighbors or colleagues.

Theodore Reik, in his *A Psychologist Looks at Love*, argues that we fall in love with people who possess characteristics which we do not possess and which we actually envy. The introvert, for example, if he or she is displeased with his or her shyness might be attracted to an extro-vert.

Conclusive evidence on the complementarity versus the similarity principle is not available. There seems some evidence to support each position. It seems that at times we are attracted to people who are similar and at other times to people who are dissimilar. Who would want complete predictability?

Sources

The area of interpersonal attraction is surveyed most thoroughly in Ellen Berscheid and Elaine Hatfield Walster's *Interpersonal Attraction* (Reading, Mass.: Addison-Wesley, 1969). I relied heavily on the review and the insights provided by Patricia Niles Middlebrook in her *Social Psychology and Modern Life* (New York: Random House, 1974). Zick Rubin's *Liking and Loving: An Invitation to Social Psychology* (New York: Holt, 1973) covers the area of interpersonal attraction in a most interesting and insightful manner. The experiments on "mere exposure" (the women in the taste experiment and the rats listening to music) are discussed by Rubin. The original references are Susan Saegert, Walter Swap, and Robert B. Zajonc, "Exposure, Context, and Interpersonal Attraction," *Journal of Personality and Social Psychology* 25(1973):234–242 and Henry A. Cross, Charles G. Halcomb, and William W. Matter, "Imprinting or Exposure Learning in Rats Given Early Auditory Stimulation," *Psychonomic Science* 7(1967):233–234. The study on friendships in college housing was conducted by Leon Festinger, Stanley Schachter, and Kurt W. Back, *Social Pressures in Informal Groups: A Study of Human Factors in Housing* (New York: Harper & Row, 1950). The most authoritative source for the "mere exposure" hypothesis is Robert B. Zajonc, "Attitudinal Effects of Mere Exposure," *Journal of Personality and Social Psychology Monograph Supplement* vol. 9, no. 2, part 2 (1968).

Experiential Vehicle

QUALITIES OF INTERPERSONAL ATTRACTION: PART II

After reading the unit return to the interpersonal attraction questionnaire at the beginning of the unit and consider the following questions relevant to your responses.

1. Concerning the characteristics of a person you would be most attracted to:

   a. Would the person whose characteristics you described be considered physically attractive? Physically unattractive? Would this person have an attractive personality? An unattractive personality?
   b. What specific characteristics did you emphasize in terms of attractiveness (physical or personality)?
   c. How similar are the characteristics you see yourself as possessing?
   d. Were the attitudinal characteristics especially important?
   e. Could instances of complementarity be identified? That is, did you list characteristics that would complement your own?

2. Concerning the persons listed as being those you are "attracted to":

   a. Are these persons attractive in terms of physical and personality characteristics?
   b. Do they live or work close to you?
   c. Do they reinforce you frequently? Socially? Materially?
   d. Are they similar to you in what they like and what they dislike? Are they similar to you in terms of physical and personality characteristics? Especially, are their attitudes toward significant issues similar to yours?
   e. Do they complement you in any way? How are they different from you? Are these differences complementary?

3. Concerning the persons you listed as being those you are "not attracted to":

    a. Are they generally unattractive? Physically? In terms of personality? What specific behaviors do you find unattractive?

    b. How does proximity enter into your choices? Do any of the persons listed live or work very close to you?

    c. Do these people reinforce you? If so, how do they do this? Why does their "reinforcement" not have the effect generally predicted?

    d. How similar-dissimilar are the persons listed to you? Physically? Intellectually? Attitudinally?

    e. In what ways are you and they complementary? That is, do these persons have characteristics which would complement your own?

4. How valuable are the five variables discussed in this unit in explaining the bases for your own interpersonal attraction? What other variables seem significant to you?

unit 33

Cooperating and Competing

Cooperating
Competing
Cooperation and Competition
  Red and Blue Game
  Orange and Green Game

Objectives

Upon completion of this unit, you should be able to:

1. define *cooperation*
2. define *competition*
3. explain how cooperation and competition relate to the five character-istics of effective interpersonal interaction (openness, empathy, sup-portiveness, positiveness, and equality)
4. state at least three differences between cooperative and competitive group processes
5. state at least five differences between cooperative and competitive group situations

In order to obtain our goals—whether they be educational, financial, social, psychological, political, physiological, or sexual—we either *coop-erate* with others or we *compete* with them. These are the two basic socially acceptable interpersonal processes for attaining goals.

COOPERATING

Perhaps the interpersonal process that is most responsible for the progress of humankind is that of *cooperation*. What we cannot do alone, we somehow manage to do in union with others. Scientists collaborating on an experiment, parents working to support the family, thieves planning to rob a bank, committee members working to get a candidate elected, a small group solving a problem, and students planning an end of the term party are all examples of cooperating.

Cooperation seems more likely to occur when the individuals involved have a positive regard for each other. Although this is not essential it does seem to help. At best, it is difficult to cooperate with people we do not like or do not respect. Cooperation seems more likely to occur, and easier to occur, when the rewards of the team effort are to be shared in some way, when each member is to get a piece of the pie. Although exactly equal sharing is not necessary to achieve cooperation, if the rewards are too unequal then cooperation may run into some snags.

Individuals in a cooperative enterprise, if they do not have positive regard for each other at the beginning, will probably develop mutually positive feelings. If such positive feelings are already present, they will probably increase. This tendency is seen very clearly in small group situations where individuals are assigned to work together on a particular project. The group members, being assigned at random, have no established friendships. During the task and especially at its end there seems to develop a strong bond among members and a high positive regard for each other. This is especially true when the outcome of the group effort is a good one or one which gets a substantial reward. When the group outcome is not a satisfying one or gets punished, the members may then look for someone to blame and negative rather than positive regard might develop.

Because of the rigid roles that people are made to play, cooperation on certain tasks seems hindered. Although this seems to be breaking down somewhat today, it still presents a considerable stumbling block to meaningful cooperation. Perhaps the clearest example of this is seen in male-female relationships. Many males, for example, cannot get themselves to cooperate in terms of cleaning the house or doing the shopping or washing the dishes or cooking the meals. The roles they have been taught to play effectively and efficiently prevent them from cooperating in this way. Similarly, many females have been taught to play the passive role in sexual encounters and so cannot be aggressive and ask the male for a date, offer to take the male to dinner, initiate love making, and so on. Again, a cooperative enterprise, such as a mutually satisfying date, may be hindered because of this rigid role playing. Learning as a function of student-teacher relationships is another example of a cooperative process. Many teachers, however, have been taught that the role they must play is that of "information dispensers" and consequently lecture to the students, expecting them to be "information receivers." And, of course, many students have been taught that this is the role they should play and become disturbed when they leave a class and do not have at least one or two pages of notes. But learning might, in some instances, best be achieved with the students teaching each other or through allowing the students to work in small groups on specific problems. But because of the rigid roles we were taught to play this possibly more useful approach is seldom allowed to develop and grow.

Cooperation encourages all of the qualities of effective interpersonal communication. The more cooperative a group, the more the members will be open and honest with each other. Because they are working on a mutually beneficial project a feeling of empathy is easier to achieve. The very nature of a cooperative effort necessitates mutual supportiveness. Through cooperating a positive attitude generally develops for oneself, for the other members of the group, and for the situation as a whole. Cooperative undertakings generally lead to high morale among group members. Lastly, a feeling of equality is encouraged. In a truly cooperative effort each member has something to contribute and each has something to learn and this, it seems, is the basis for developing or maintaining a sense of equality.

COMPETING

Perhaps the most familiar example of competition is professional or amateur sports. Baseball, football, horse racing, chess, and in fact most activities in which someone wins and someone loses are clear examples of competition. Another unambiguous example of competition is the auction sale where two or more people are bidding for the same object; one will win and the others will lose.

Competition is more relevant to interpersonal interactions when, for example, two or more people are vying for the affection of another or perhaps vying to marry a particular person. Here one will win and the others will lose. In a similar way siblings compete for the attention of their parents and relatives.

Competition as an interpersonal process is more likely to occur when there are few rewards to go around or when there is only one reward and a number of different people want it. There is competition when the demand exceeds the supply. When the parties dislike or envy or hate each other they are more likely to compete, each attempting to prove that he or she is better at something than the other. Also, competition is more likely to occur when the desired objects are to be shared unequally, as when, for example, first prize is extremely large and second prize is much less.

Competition influences and changes the attitudes of the participants, generally in a negative direction. While competing, the individuals often develop negative feelings for each other. In some ways this negative feeling allows for the mobilization of energy and perhaps helps in stimulating that extra effort necessary to win the game. If you are too positive toward your opponent, you may relax your guard and thereby give him or her an edge. Sometimes this negative feeling is long lasting and sometimes it is only temporary. Two rival store owners, each attempting to win customers, may develop a deep hostility toward each other which will last their entire lives. On the other hand, the classic example of competition being temporary is in sports, where, for example, the tennis players become friends and develop a deep respect for each other because of the way each played the game.

As we grew up we were taught, by our parents and teachers and by the mass communications we attended to, that competition was a positive good. We were told that competition was healthy and that it was what made this country great. That may be. But we should not ignore the negative consequences of competition. Competition results in a tremendous waste of energy and time. Problems of space travel are worked at by different countries individually, each jealousy guarding its secrets, its inventions, its discoveries. If they had joined in a cooperative effort, colonies would have been on the moon years ago.

By its very nature competition necessitates that there will be a loser or losers, and this naturally creates difficulties. For the would-be competitor it may create fear and anxiety; no one wants to lose. For the actual loser it means punishment of some sort, either not getting the reward (as in a horse race) or in actually losing something important (as in job cutbacks). Such outcomes are very likely to bring on self-recriminations and general despondency.

As we were probably taught that competition is a positive good, other cultures taught that competition was something negative, something to be avoided. It is particularly important to recognize that competition and the specific rewards that we compete for are influenced by the culture in which we live. For example, in our culture, say a hundred years ago, it was accepted and perhaps even encouraged for males to compete for females but not for females to compete for males. Today both males and females can compete for each other or at least the movement seems to be in that direction. But neither males nor females can compete (with social sanction) for married males and females or for young children. In other cultures where mates are chosen by the elders of the community or by the parents, sexual competition in any form would be socially condemned.

In a competitive situation openness is kept at a minimum. By being open we run the risk of revealing weaknesses which could then be attacked by our rival. And so we reveal as little as possible about ourselves—our feelings, our strengths, and our weaknesses. We make communications that we are forced to engage in as superficial as possible and perhaps omit or actually lie about anything fairly significant. Equality is, by definition, eliminated since the very object of competition is to prove one the winner and one the loser. Likewise, supportiveness, by definition, is absent since the object is to defeat the other person.

Depending on our system of values and attitudes, competition may increase positiveness for ourselves and for the actual competitive situation and, as already illustrated, for our opponent. On the other hand, it may decrease positiveness for ourselves, our opponent, and for the competition situation generally. Similarly, competition may allow us to increase our capacity for empathy since both parties are engaged in essentially the same activities with, we may assume, essentially the same attitudes. Consequently, we may be in a good position for empathic communication. However, because of the absence of openness and supportiveness, empathy may be more difficult to achieve. In terms of both positiveness and empathy then, it seems best to say, "it depends."

COOPERATION AND COMPETITION

Another way of looking at cooperation and competition is in terms of the goals of the groups. The cooperative group members have the same or similar goals, that is, the goals are homogeneous. In the competitive group, the members have different and divergent goals, that is, the goals are heterogeneous. In the cooperative situation if one member reaches or gets close to his or her goal, this action helps the other members achieving their goal. If, for example, a cooperative group is working to solve a problem and if one member solves part of it, this action brings all members closer to the goal. In the competitive situation, however, if one member reaches or gets close to his or her goal this action hinders the other members in achieving their goal. For example, if one team gets a touchdown, this action hinders the other team from attaining their goal (namely, winning the game).

Experimental research by Morton Deutsch and his colleagues yields, among other things, a number of relevant and interesting conclusions. Members in cooperative and competitive groups perceive the members' actions as being consistent with the orientation of the group. Cooperative group members see their members as cooperative whereas competitive group members see their members as competitive. In the cooperative group, more actions of the various group members will be perceived as positive than in the competitive group. This seems consistent with what has already been said about the greater positiveness of cooperation. In the cooperative situation the various actions of the members need not be repeated by other members. If one member performs a particular calculation, for example, it is not necessary for other members to do that calculation again. In competitive situations this is much less true.

Members of cooperative groups display greater helpfulness towards each other than do members of competitive groups. This is perhaps somewhat obvious but it seems to bear special mention anyway.

According to Deutsch in "An Experimental Study of the Effects of Cooperation and Competition Upon Group Processes," cooperative group situations, compared to competitive group situations, illustrate greater:

(i) coordination of efforts; (ii) diversity in amount of contributions per member; (iii) subdivision of activity; (iv) achievement pressure; (v) production of signs in the puzzle problem; (vi) attentiveness to fellow members; (vii) mutual comprehension of communication; (viii) appraisals of communication; (ix) orientation and orderliness; (x) productivity per unit time; (xi) quality of product and discussions; (xii) friendliness during discussions; (xiii) favorable evaluation of the group and its products; (xiv) group functions; (xv) perception of favorable effects upon fellow members; and (xvi) incorporation of the attitude of the generalized other.

Marvin Shaw, for example, compared cooperative and competitive groups in their ability to keep a pointer on a moving target and found that the cooperative group produced the more efficient tracking behavior. Contrary to the findings of other researchers, Shaw found that members of the competitive situation rated the task as more satisfying than did the members of the cooperative group.

Although there is a clear preference for cooperation, it should not be thought that all competition is negative. As we can see from our own cooperative and competitive experiences, some are dull and unproductive and others are exciting and rewarding.

Sources

Most useful in the preparation of this unit were the insights of David Dressler, *Sociology: The Study of Human Interaction* (New York: Knopf, 1969), Marvin Shaw, *Group Dynamics: The Psychology of Small Group Behavior* (New York: McGraw-Hill, 1971), and the writings of Morton Deutsch, for example, "An Experimental Study of the Effects of Cooperation and Competition Upon Group Process," *Human Relations* 2(1949): 199–232; "A Theory of Cooperation and Competition," *Human Relations* 2(1949):129–152; and "Conflicts: Productive and Destructive," *Journal of Social Issues* 25(1969):7–41.

Experiential Vehicles

RED AND BLUE GAME

For this exercise the class should be divided into dyads. One student is designated as Player 1 and the other student as Player 2. All players should inspect the accompanying matrix which contains the payoffs for each player, for each move. More specifically: Each player can play either RED or BLUE. (Follow this explanation by referring to the matrix.) The moves of Player 1 determine whether the payoffs come from the top two quadrants (if red is played) or the bottom two quadrants (if blue is played). The moves of Player 2 determine whether the payoffs come from the left two quadrants (if red is played) or the right two quadrants (if blue is played). Numbers before the slash are the payoffs for Player 1 and numbers after the slash are the payoffs for Player 2. If both players play BLUE, each player wins one point (+1). If both players play RED, each player wins ten points (+10). If Player 1 plays RED and Player 2 plays BLUE, Player 1 loses five points (−5) and Player 2 wins fifteen points (+15). If Player 1 plays BLUE and Player 2 plays RED, Player 1 wins fifteen points (+15) and Player 2 loses five points (−5). The maximum amount of time allowed for each decision is one minute.

MATRIX FOR RED AND BLUE GAME

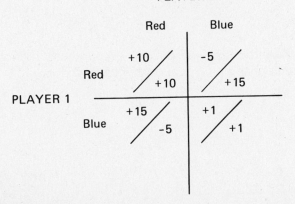

The game is played for 10 rounds and is scored on the score sheet provided. Players reveal their decisions (that is, whether they choose BLUE or RED) only after they have entered them on the score sheet. Players must also record the amount won or lost and their balance in the spaces provided.

Score sheet for Red and Blue Game

Round	Decision	Amount Won or Lost	Balance
1			
2			
3			
4			
5			
6			
7			
8			
9			
10			

Total _____

Discussion should center on at least the following:

1. How was cooperation evidenced?
2. How was competition evidenced?
3. How would the amount won or lost have differed had greater cooperation or competition been used?
4. How did your own history of conditioning influence your cooperative/ competitive behavior?
5. How does the "winner" feel?
6. How does the "loser" feel?
7. If you were playing for real stakes (for example, money, grades), how would your behavior have differed?

ORANGE AND GREEN GAME

For this exercise the class is divided into groups of nine. Each group of nine should be subdivided into three groups of three. These subgroups of three members each will act as a team with only one decision allowed among them for each round.

All players should inspect the following matrix which contains the rules of the game and the payoffs for each player, for each move. More specifically: Each team of three members may play either ORANGE or GREEN. (Follow this explanation by referring to the matrix.) If all three teams choose ORANGE, all three win three points (+3). If two teams choose ORANGE and one team chooses GREEN, the teams choosing ORANGE lose five points (−5) and the team choosing GREEN wins ten points (+10). If one team chooses ORANGE and two teams choose GREEN, the team choosing ORANGE wins five points (+5) and the two teams choosing GREEN lose ten points (−10) each. If all three teams choose GREEN, all three lose three points (−3) each. The maximum amount of time allowed for each decision is one minute.

The game is played for nine rounds and is scored on the score sheet. Players (that is, teams) reveal their decisions (whether they chose ORANGE or GREEN) only after they have entered them on the score sheet. Teams must also record the amount won or lost and their balance in the spaces provided.

For each round the three members of each team must confer among themselves and decide on ORANGE or GREEN. If necessary, the decision may have to be made by majority vote. Each team, to repeat, is allowed but one choice for each round.

For rounds three, six, and nine the three teams confer with each other for a maximum of two minutes. They may discuss mutual strategy, decisions they intend to make, or anything relevant to the playing of the game. After these two minutes, members of each team confer among themselves and must make two decisions. First, they must decide whether they will choose ORANGE or GREEN. Second, they must decide if they wish to have the amount won or lost multiplied by three (×3) or if they wish to simply receive the amount won or lost without any increases (even). The choice selected must be indicated at the time the color is chosen by circling "even," or "x3." Like the choice of color, this decision is not revealed to the other teams until all teams reveal their colors.

This exercise is an adaptation of one presented in J. William Pfeiffer and John E. Jones, *A Handbook of Structured Experiences for Human Relations Training,* vol. 3 (Iowa City, Iowa: University Associates Press, 1971).

MATRIX FOR ORANGE AND GREEN GAME

If 3 teams choose Orange, then all ⟶ +3
If 2 teams choose Orange, then ⟶ -5   and 1 team chooses Green, then ⟶ +10
If 1 team chooses Orange, then ⟶ +5   and 2 teams choose Green, then ⟶ -10
If 3 teams choose Green, then all ⟶ -3

Score sheet for Orange and Green Game

Round	Decision	Multiple	Amount Won or Lost	Balance
1				
2				
3		even ×3		
4				
5				
6		even ×3		
7				
8				
9		even ×3		

Total _____

Discussion should center on at least the following:

1. How was cooperation evidenced?
2. How was competition evidenced?

3. How can the behavior of the teams in rounds 3, 6, and 9 be best described?
4. Was there much conflict among team members over the decisions for rounds 3, 6, and 9?
5. How does the "winning" team feel?
6. How do the "losing" teams feel?
7. At what point did the teams decide to compete with each other? Why?
8. How do each of the members feel now?
9. If you were playing for real stakes, such as money or grades, how would your behavior have differed?

unit 34

Conflict
and Accommodation

Conflict
Accommodation
  Sandy
  The Case of Michael Mannix

Objectives

Upon completion of this unit, you should be able to:

1. define *conflict*
2. provide at least three examples of conflict situations
3. state at least three conditions under which conflict is likely to occur
4. define *accommodation*
5. provide at least three examples of accommodation situations
6. state at least three conditions under which accommodation is likely to occur

When cooperation and competition fail, when we cannot attain our goals through these processes, we often resort to a more extreme form of competition—*conflict*. And when conflict or fighting proves futile we may then resort to *accommodation*—a kind of cold war fight. Each of these processes are ways of dealing with situations which seem not to yield to more rational methods.

CONFLICT

A more extreme form of competition, with more significant consequences, is that of *conflict*. In its most insidious form, conflict is war between individuals or nations. The object of the game is to bring the enemy to surrender. To accomplish this anything goes. But conflict is also an everyday process.

In sports, boxing perhaps comes closest to real conflict. Although disguised as competition and supported as analogous to baseball or football, the object of boxing is to harm your opponent to the point where he will surrender or to the point where he is rendered incapacitated for 10 seconds. The greater the harm a fighter inflicts on his opponent the closer he is to winning the bout and being proclaimed a hero. Verbally abusing one another would be conflict as well. It is a kind of verbal version of the boxing ring, as, for example, in slander or libel.

Conflict is likely to occur when both parties want or perhaps need the same thing—a particular river, grazing land, a protective mountain, a desirable job, an important promotion—and the only way to secure the desired object is to beat down any other person or group intent on taking it from you. Conflict is also likely to occur when one or more parties are threatened. Perhaps the classic version of this is in the fighting of young boys where one of the boys is threatened to the point where he cannot extricate himself in a socially acceptable manner without actually fighting and so delivers the first blow. In more mature versions the same basic pattern is followed, only the threats are more subtle and more sophisticated and the consequences more lethal. Even among nations the same general pattern is followed. First, the threats are verbal; then they are physical, but on a small scale, for example, blockading ships or shooting down a plane. When the threats can no longer be ignored—for physical, psychological, or social reasons—actual conflict results.

Naturally, conflict is more likely to occur among persons who dislike or hate each other, though there is also much conflict in marriage and among supposed lovers. And this suggests another condition under which conflict is likely to occur, namely, when one party has been hurt. When this happens, he or she is often likely to hurt back. If, for example, the husband hurts the wife by not responding favorably to her advances, she in turn may attempt to hurt him. As a result he in turn may attempt to hurt her. As a result she in return may attempt to retaliate and hurt him and he again may respond in kind. The process of conflict spirals with one response serving as the stimulus for another response and so on. Each attack becomes more and more deadly, like competition.

In terms of the characteristics of effective interpersonal communication, conflict leads to increased negative regard for the opponent. At times this negative feeling is passed down from generation to generation as with warring families, tribes, or nations, for example. Generally, the more conflict, the deeper the negative regard. Again, there is a spiral effect here. The conflict leads to negative regard which leads to still more conflict and so on. Conflict like competition leads to a tremendous waste of time and energy for both sides. War, for example, is seldom profitable for the winner or the loser. Most obviously, conflict can lead to serious damage or death, physical or psychological. Even in the most ritualized of all conflict situations, the boxing ring, men have died. But they also die in gang fights and in wars.

Conflict leads us to close ourselves off from the other individual which seems a reasonable defensive strategy. It would not, for example, be to our advantage to reveal our weaknesses to our enemy who is attempting to harm us. Conflict is perhaps the opposite of supportiveness; conflict is destructiveness. We seek not to help but to destroy our opponent. In some cases conflict may lead people to develop an increased positiveness for themselves; perhaps the idea of glory due the conquering hero is still with us. But most reasonable people, it seems, would not take pride in killing. Conflict attempts to eliminate whatever equality may have been present at the start. If equality were to remain there would be a constant stalemate. By harming or thwarting or destroying the other we are in effect establishing superiority over them. Empathy, on the other hand, is perhaps increased in times of conflict. The only person who can empathize with the fighter who gets knocked cold in the first round seems to be another fighter who went through the same or similar experience. So perhaps the victim and the victor are not so far apart in their feelings.

ACCOMMODATION

When I was a teenager in New York every boy was a member of a group. Some groups were formally established into social clubs, athletic clubs, or gangs. Some had shirts and jackets while others simply "hung out" together without any formal symbols of unity. Fighting among the groups was extremely frequent. By word and by action each group was in a state of conflict with every other group.

Yet while at school, or in fact in any environment other than the street, members of the different groups would often interact and even come to like each other. But at night on the street, each returned to his own group and opposed each other.

Even as young boys, however, we realized that this fighting was not very productive. And so there were a number of alternatives open to us. Like the country that declares war on another to gain control of their territory, one alternative was to have a gang war. Although this alternative was at times attempted, it was usually too unpleasant and too unproductive to be viable. Every night it seemed a different group would win the battle but no group ever really won the war. Another alternative was to become one large gang—like a federation of states joining to form one union. But with too much previous hostility and an unwillingness to give up autonomy, this alternative never materialized. The third alternative, a kind of compromise between war and union, was usually chosen, namely an agreement to stop battling although still in conflict. This is *accommodation*.

Perhaps the clearest example of this type of interaction process is that existing between the United States and the Communist nations. It is not war and it is not peace or union; it is a cold war or accommodation. The relationship between many unions and their management might also be described as that of accommodation. On a more personal level we can see accommodation in the relationship between children and their parents. They do not understand each other; they do not agree with each other. Yet they are tired of fighting and so they agree to live together not in union but not in war either; they agree to accommodate.

Accommodation is especially likely to occur when the conflict shows no signs of ending to either party's advantage. If two groups are in battle and each knows that neither can win, it is to the advantage of both to cease hostilities and accommodate. This situation is obviously most likely to happen when both sides are about equal in strength or when each side could be wounded in equally fatal ways. When, for example, labor and management are engaged in a struggle, each can be severely hurt; thus it might be to their mutual advantage to stop fighting and accommodate. If, on the other hand, labor was much more powerful than management, labor might be unwilling to accommodate since it could profit more from the conflict and eventually win the war.

Accommodation is heavily dependent upon social reinforcement, with nations and with individuals. Millions argued for "peace with honor" in Vietnam, a perfect example of accommodation. No one won; both sides lost a great deal. But, as both sides were able to see, it would not have profited either side to continue the struggle; thus an agreement to stop the combat was established—that is, accommodation. The social reinforcement, "with honor," was essential to many; otherwise it would have been thought a loss or "peace with defeat." Two little boys fighting each other can agree to stop only if they can retain their pride. They will stop if they can stop with honor. They can, for example, agree to stop now and continue tomorrow, as many small boys do. Fortunately, when tomorrow comes neither feels much like fighting and so the matter is forgotten and off they go to play ball together. The agreement to fight tomorrow, however, is essential in allowing the boys to retain their pride and not to suffer a defeat.

Accommodation is especially prevalent in marriage relationships and in love relationships generally. One partner may do something to irritate the other—anything from squeezing the tooth paste tube in the middle (oddly enough a reported source of much trouble among people living together), to infidelity, alcoholism, or general cruelty. The other partner, like the street gangs, has a number of options. Initially, he or she might fight over it. After numerous and fruitless battles, war might be ruled out as a viable option. And so this partner agrees to live with this alcoholism or infidelity and agrees to cease hostilities. Note that the problem is not solved in this way. They still have this difference between them. Yet it does allow them to continue to interact and communicate whereas war rules out such interpersonal relations. And so they might enjoy numerous good times together because they have agreed to stop fighting over this one issue.

Such decisions may leave unsolved problems smoldering, and the hostility may manifest itself in other ways at other times, with or without conscious awareness of the connection with the original decision to accommodate. Let us say, for example, that one partner drinks and after numerous fights the couple agrees to live with this problem and to accommodate. The partner who does not drink may develop feelings of hostility toward the drinker. This may manifest itself in the nondrinker getting sexually involved with other people, with or without any conscious awareness of the connection with the alcohol problem.

Accommodation, however, can have positive effects as well. Because accommodation allows the individuals to again interact it provides them with the opportunity to develop a mutual respect for one another which in turn might lead to real cooperation. The accommodation between the United States and Russia, for example, has led to the development of increased positive regard for each other, for cooperation in science and the arts, and to a historic union in space. The real value of accommodation, then, is clearly in the fact that it allows future interaction and communication to take place.

Since it allows further interaction to take place, accommodation allows for the development of openness, empathy, supportiveness, positiveness, and equality. Accommodation does not in itself create these qualities (with the possible exception of equality which is in a sense a prerequisite for accommodation) but rather allows these to develop through the further interactions which take place. In ending the actual conflict, accommodation brings to a halt the disintegration of openness, empathy, supportiveness, and positiveness. Perhaps that is its main value.

Sources

Two recent works relating conflict to communication should be noted. Fred E. Jandt's *Conflict Resolution through Communication* (New York: Harper & Row, 1973) is a collection of *sixteen* articles, many of which are helpful in conceptualizing the role of conflict in communication and the role of communication in conflict. *Perspectives on Communication in*

Social Conflict (Englewood Cliffs, N.J.: Prentice-Hall, 1974), edited by Gerald R. Miller and Herbert W. Simons contains eight thorough and perceptive articles on communication and conflict. This work also contains a bibliography of over 500 items.

Both conflict and accommodation are considered by David Dressler, *Sociology: The Study of Human Interaction* (New York: Knopf, 1969). The *Journal of Conflict Resolution* is devoted to conflict in all its dimensions and especially to its communication dimension.

Experiential Vehicles

SANDY

Sandy is a beautiful young woman, age 21, and a senior in college. Sandy is majoring in biology and is an honor student; she plans to work toward her master's degree in biology at night while teaching high school during the day.

At this particular high school, where Sandy has applied for a job, a committee of five members plus the school principal make all the hiring decisions. After reviewing Sandy's record—outstanding in every respect—the committee asks her in for a personal interview. This is a standard procedure with this high school. In this case, however, because Sandy's records and recommendations are so outstanding, the personal interview is regarded by the members of the committee and the principal as a formality. They are clearly eager to hire Sandy. Although there are other qualified applicants, none seems as outstanding as Sandy.

At the specified time Sandy appears to meet the committee. The members look at each other in shocked amazement; it seems obvious to them that Sandy is _____.* There is just no doubt that Sandy is in fact _____.

Thinking quickly, the principal, as committee chairperson, tells Sandy that the committee has fallen behind schedule and that they will see her in 15 minutes. Sandy leaves the room and sits outside waiting to be called back in. Sandy is well aware of their reactions and knows why they asked her to wait outside. She has seen those reactions before and is not surprised. She is _____ and as she sits waiting she ponders what the committee will do.

The committee, now alone for fifteen minutes, comes quickly to the point. The applicant is _____. "What should we do?" the principal asks.

Students should role play members of the committee and reach a decision as to what they should do in regard to Sandy. The members of the committee are:

Mrs. Markham, the school principal
Mr. Ventri, the biology department chairperson
Miss Colson, teacher of physical education
Mr. Garcia, teacher of chemistry
Ms. Goldstein, teacher of Romance languages
Mr. Jackson, teacher of art

*Your instructor will fill in this space.

Approximately 15 to 20 minutes should be allowed for the discussion. After this time, the class members should discuss the interactions which took place in the role playing session in terms of conflict and accommodation. This discussion should have no rigid structure and may focus on any of the concepts considered under conflict and accommodation.

THE CASE OF MICHAEL MANNIX

Role Playing

All persons involved are aware of the following:

Norma Moore, a student, and Michael Mannix, an assistant professor, are living together on a commune near the college. Norma's mother, Diane Moore, is violently opposed to this and is attempting to have Mannix fired.

The only part of the Faculty Code which may be relevant reads as follows; "Any faculty member may be dismissed from his or her duties—with or without prior notice, with or without compensation, depending upon the decision of the appropriate committee(s)—for behavior unbecoming a professional in charge of young men and women."

You are a committee appointed by the president of the college and empowered to make any decision you feel justified. You have decided to have the principals discuss the issues and on this basis will render your decision. The remainder of the class may function as this committee, or several committees may be formed from those not participating in the role-playing session. (Each person playing a role should read only the description for his or her role.)

Michael Mannix: Assistant Professor of Communication, age 27, divorced, no children.

You came to Cicero College this past September. In one of your classes sat Norma Moore, an attractive and intelligent junior, age 19. In class and in conferences she made a number of advances and indicated quite openly that she would like to go out with you and develop a more personal relationship. At first you resisted, thinking that perhaps it was not right for an instructor to date a student. It did not take long for Norma to convince you otherwise, and you soon began to see her not as a student but as a woman you could become seriously interested in. You dated for about a month and became quite serious. Norma was living on a commune near the college and convinced you to move in with her. You did and have never been so happy. So far there has been no talk of marriage.

You are fulfilling your professional obligations and feel that you are doing well. Your classes are sucessful and you would like to continue teaching at Cicero. At the same time, however, you are determined not to alter your style of living regardless of the consequences. You are aware that other faculty members and students are talking about you and Norma. Some of the comments are extremely negative but for the most part the students and other staff members feel that you both have the right to live as you choose.

You know that Sandra Meyers, your department chairperson, has been dating a number of students. No one else seems to know about this except you. You do not, however, want to bring this up since you do not want to jeopardize her marriage, nor do you think it particularly relevant. On the other hand, such a disclosure could make the whole situation seem a bit more common and harmless than it might appear if you were the only instructor dating a student. Also, if the chairperson knew that you were aware of her dating students it might make her support your cause more directly.

Norma Moore: Junior at Cicero, age 19, single.

You pride yourself on being a free spirit. You became attracted to Michael Mannix from the first day of class and you are now in love with him. You are now living on a commune with him and various other students and for the first time in your life are really happy. You are determined that nothing interfere with your relationship with Michael. Your mother has always objected to your boyfriends and has in the past succeeded in breaking up any relationship you developed. You are determined not to let this happen again. At times you feel that you are losing Michael and would get married to make your relationship more secure. You don't think that Michael wants to get married and so you have not brought up the topic. You love your father very much and do not want to hurt him; you hope that he understands why you are living as you are.

Diane Moore: Norma's mother, age 40.

You are terribly disturbed by the way in which your daughter is living and are determined to break up this relationship regardless of what it costs you. You are President of the Alumni Association of Cicero, an influential member of the Board of Trustees, and a millionaire several times over. You will use whatever power or money necessary to break up this affair. You are determined that Professor Mannix be fired for behavior unbecoming a professional. You are convinced that when he is fired your daughter will soon forget him since her behavior in the past has been such that she becomes involved with different people for short periods of time and then quickly forgets them. You have broken up relationships in the past for her own good and are determined to do the same now. You control the entire family fortune; your husband is a convenience though you could just as well do without him and have, in fact, often considered a divorce.

Steven Moore: Norma's father, age 58.

You love your daughter and want her to be happy. You don't feel that anything is drastically wrong with the relationship. Mannix seems like a nice enough individual and if he makes Norma happy you are satisfied. You have never been a very forceful individual; your wife has always run the house and the business and you much prefer not making decisions. Your wife controls the family fortune and should she wish she could easily throw you out of the business and even divorce you. You know she has recently considered divorce. Since you are fifty-eight years old—with no particular talent or trade—you are reluctant to irritate her to the point of divorce. You like the luxury you have had since marrying Diane and do not know what you would do if she divorced you.

Robert Banyon: Dean of the Faculty, age 50.

You are shocked at the behavior of Mannix and are determined to see him fired. You realize that Diane Moore is highly influential and that she could make your life extremely pleasant or extremely unpleasant. She has already indicated that a new president of Cicero is to be selected and that she would support your candidacy if all went right with the Mannix case. You want the presidency very much. Thus your own personal convictions about what constitutes professional behavior and your own desire for additional power lead you to press for the dismissal of Mannix.

Sandra Meyers: Chairperson of the Department of Communication, age 40, married with two children.

This is the first time such a situation has come up and so you have no precedent to go on. On the one hand, it does not look good for the image of the department and the college for a professor to behave in this way and get caught. On the other hand, you feel you should support your own faculty members. You have yourself on occasion dated students but have been particularly cautious and you believe no one is aware of this. You are not aware of what the Dean of the Faculty thinks but you do know that he can make life extremely unpleasant for you should you go against his own thinking. He could dismiss you from chairing the department since chairpersons at Cicero are appointed by the Dean of the Faculty. You enjoy being chairperson and do not want to jeopardize your position.

Before rendering your decision consider the following questions relevant to conflict and accommodation as evidenced in the role playing:

1. Identify any conflict situations.

2. Identify any attempts to accommodate.

3. What conditions were present which would normally lead to conflict?

4. What conditions were present which would normally lead to accommodation?

5. What influence did the conflict and accommodation situations have on
   interpersonal communication?

unit 35
Loving
and Trusting

Loving
Trusting
   Roommate Preference

Objectives

Upon completion of this unit, you should be able to:

1. define the five dimensions or variables of love identified by Pitirim Sorokin
2. explain at least three conditions under which love is more likely to occur
3. define *trust*
4. explain the relationship of trust to predictability, self-disclosure, and anxiety
5. identify the four basic kinds of trust directly related to communication

Of all the positive interpersonal processes the two most important are *loving* and *trusting*. Although separated here, these two interaction processes may be inseparable in reality. It is difficult to visualize a truly loving relationship in which trust is absent and similarly there seems to be some love, in some form, in any trusting relationship. Love and trust seem to grow with each other and when one deteriorates so, it seems, does the other.

LOVING

Of all the types of human interaction none seems as important as loving. Cyril Bibby in his essay, "The Art of Loving," explains why *loving* and not *love* is used and in so doing gets at some of the important qualities of this interpersonal interaction process.

> So long as love is treated as a thing, to be built up mechanically by the addition of this piece of social relationship to that piece of amatory technique, it can never really flourish. To make the most of the human capacity for loving, it is necessary to treat it as an activity of the whole person, in which body and mind and emotions are all actively involved. This is not to deny the importance of social factors or of sexual techniques, but merely to put them in their proper place as aids to an essentially out-giving activity.

Loving is not an easy term to define. Unlike concepts, such as competition or cooperation, which can be defined and measured with some ease, "loving" resists such approaches. Perhaps it's the variety of things that loving means that makes definition difficult. In *How Do You Feel?* a book on varied feelings, four different approaches to loving are presented. Among the words these writers used in describing the feelings and the behaviors of loving were these: warmth, contentment, excitement, oneness, limitless, infinite, boundless, totally encompassing, lucky, faith, trust, dynamic, effort, commitment, tender, multicolored, active, healthy, energetic, courageous, forward-looking, patient, robust, openness, honesty, understanding, and fun.

Throughout these words there is a clear emphasis on activity rather than passivity. Loving is an active process. Larry Carlin in one of the essays in *How Do You Feel?* puts it this way: "When I feel loving it seems like I can't keep what's inside inside; I have to reach out, touch, embrace, hold, kiss."

Pitirim Sorokin explains love by identifying its dimensions or variables. He notes five.

1. *Intensity.* Loving feelings or behavior can vary in intensity from nothing to slight to some undefined extreme. It can vary in intensity from giving a dime to a beggar to sacrificing one's life for one's loved ones.
2. *Extensity.* Love can vary in terms of the degree to which it extends from outside the individual and may be solely a love of oneself (low extensity) or it may range to the love of all mankind (high extensity).
3. *Duration.* Like any emotion loving can vary from seconds to a lifetime.
4. *Purity.* By "purity" Sorokin means the degree to which the love is motivated by considerations for the self or by considerations for the other person. "Impure" love, in this system, refers to love motivated by selfish considerations without concern for the other person. Pure love is the love of an individual for the sake of the beloved.

5. *Adequacy.* Love may vary from the wise to the blind. In inadequate or blind love there is a huge difference between the purposes or motives in loving and the consequences. An example of inadequate or blind love might be the excessive love a father and mother have for their child which leads the child to become totally dependent upon them. Adequate or wise love, on the other hand, has consequences which are positive for the object of the love, that is, the beloved.

Love is probably the most positive, the most meaningful emotion that we can express and yet our society has placed hard and fast strictures on its expression. One can express love for one's husband, wife, boyfriend, girlfriend, parents, relatives, children, country, and religion, as well as for ideals such as freedom, truth, and honor. But left out from this list is the expression of love for the person next to us, be this person male or female, young or old, black or white.

Loving is an extremely difficult emotion to deal with in terms of the conditions conducive to its occurrence. How do you make someone love someone? What makes a person love another? These are not simple questions and so it is with considerable hesitancy that some tentative propositions are offered relative to the occurrence of love. Loving, it seems, is more likely to occur under the following circumstances.

1. *When there is mutual respect.* Both research and folk wisdom attest to the difference between loving and liking. One can be present without the other. We can like someone we do not love and we can also love someone we do not like. Yet it seems that in most situations we like and respect the person we love, with the liking and respecting coming first.

2. *When the individuals have positive self-images.* We assume here that for a person to engage in a loving relationship it is easier if he or she first has a positive self-image. If one dislikes oneself then it will be extremely difficult if not impossible to love another.

3. *When there is a sexual attraction.* Although we are here talking about love in general, including both sexual and nonsexual, it seems that there is a sexual component in any love relationship. At best, we have to want to be with someone to love them, and we choose, generally at least, not to be with people we find unattractive. And—to complete the argument—attractiveness-unattractiveness is in part sexual.

4. *When the individuals are relatively free of significant problems.* Again, although not always the case, it is difficult to love or be loving when we have nothing to eat and no prospects for getting a job, for example. If we are on the verge of being convicted and being sentenced to jail for life, it is understandable to think very little, if at all, about love and loving. We may, of course, worry about our loved ones and what will happen to them but we would not be in a very good position to

establish a new love relationship. These examples are purposely far removed from our own experiences. But consider the individual who constantly worries about and plans for his or her business. His or her available energy for love is greatly reduced. The student who thinks only about grades has little time and energy for loving.

Herbert A. Otto, one of the leaders in the human potential movement, has noted in *Love Today* the paradoxical conclusions made about communication in love. Communication in love, says Otto, is characterized by two features: "(1) confusion and lack of clarity; and (2) increased clarity and comprehension." While some lovers note the extreme difficulty in understanding what the other person means, many others note the exceptional ability they now seem to possess in understanding the other person. Related to this is Truman Capote's definition of love as not having to finish your sentences.

Ron Lunceford, in *How Do You Feel?* expresses clearly the strong desire to communicate love and the difficulties in doing so.

> The one thing I think I wish for myself is that I could express my love more. I can express my love, but sometimes I have the fear of talking about it too much. I like being loved and I like giving love and sometimes talking about it changes that feeling for me. Sometimes too it is sad for me to talk about love and loving feelings to people who don't have someone to love or anyone to love them; that's sad.
>
> I want to say sometimes to people, "Hey, you can love me and we don't have to make promises to each other." Some people can handle that and some can't. Some just need permission to express love and be open to it; sometimes it helps to begin to take that risk.
>
> But for me, I want to say, "I love you" more. I don't want anyone I love to go without knowing that.

But loving implies the taking of risks, as Lunceford mentions. We run a risk of not having our love returned or of being rejected outright. The alternative we often take is to conceal our love or perhaps never even admit it to ourselves. Communicating our love also involves a risk which is part of self-disclosure. In any love relationship mutual self-disclosure is important. As Otto says, "This helps to establish a relationship characterized by optimal personality growth for both lovers."

Much as loving relationships are helped by self-disclosure, love also encourages openness and honesty. We seem to have a need to express ourselves, to let other people know who we "really" are. And yet, perhaps because of the fear of rejection, we conceal our "true selves." In a love relationship we have someone to whom we can reveal ourselves without fear of being rejected or thought foolish. Not everything is so simple of course. In many instances it is with the people we love that we are most on guard. If, for example, we initially pretended to be particularly strong, we might conceal weakness for fear that it was our strength that made us attractive. It is often with people we love that we hide aspects of ourselves that we might readily reveal to strangers if we were sure of never meeting them again.

Empathic communication is naturally increased in any love relationship since, on the basis of our more open communication, we can understand how the other feels and would want to feel what he or she feels. In many ways, to love someone is to support them. We naturally support those we love in part because we want them to be secure and unafraid. Our supportiveness helps them and theirs helps us. Loving is an emotion which is not only good to receive but good to feel as well; it makes us feel pleased to love and consequently the positiveness we feel for ourselves as well as for the other and for the situation is increased. Normally, we love persons we respect and whom we regard as good; we like them as well as love them. If we love someone we want to become a part of him or her. This is perhaps the best way to encourage the feeling of equality.

TRUSTING

If we were able to secure conclusive proof about the outcomes of our behavior we might be able to get along without trust. But since such proof is impossible, trust must occupy an important role in our daily lives. We have no proof that our doctors are prescribing the right medicines; instead we trust them. Similarly, when we tell a friend a secret, we can only trust that he or she will not reveal it.

In these examples trust always involves some kind of risk. As a result of the trusting behavior some loss might result. Reickert, for example, notes that trust is an "ability to risk yourself, to put yourself in the hands of another, to put yourself at the service of another. . . . Trust is always a risk, a kind of leap in the dark. It is not based on any solid proof that the other person will not hurt you. If you have that kind of proof, you are dealing with a sure thing, and trust is always a gamble."

In terms of interpersonal interaction, trust involves our taking the initiative in establishing a relationship. It is, says Reickert, "to make the first step toward another, to hold out your hand, to say 'I like you' before you are sure what the other person will say in return."

As with all interpersonal processes, but perhaps especially with trust, there are various levels ranging from practically no trust at all to complete confidence. In some situations we might risk a few dollars to play a horse, trusting the tip of a friend. But we might not be willing to risk much more. Here our level of trust is rather minimal. On the other hand, we might trust someone so much that we would invest our life savings on his or her advice. Unfortunately, we are not always justified in the level of trust we place in various people.

Trust is related to respect in a most important way. Reickert notes that both respect and trust are basic to human interpersonal relationships, but that trust is a more advanced kind of relationship. When we respect someone we have a certain feeling for him or her but we do not risk anything. When we trust someone we act on the basis of this feeling and do risk losing something that is important to us.

When we say, "I don't trust that person," very often we mean that we cannot predict what that person will do in a given situation. For example, you may hand in a late term paper to a teacher. Upon receiving the paper the teacher says, "O.K." But for some reason you might say, "I don't trust this teacher." By saying this you probably mean that you cannot predict what he or she will do with this late paper. Trust, then, seems related to the predictability of another's behavior; we are more apt to trust someone whose behavior we can predict with relative accuracy. In this sense we are putting our trust in favorites—in people whose behavior we can pretty well predict—and not in people whose behavior we cannot predict.

This concept of predictability is also related to that of self-disclosure. Generally, we are more apt to trust those people who have self-disclosed to us; that is, we are more apt to trust those who have opened up to us and who have revealed something significant about themselves. We are less likely to trust those who are secretive. Very probably, we feel we are in a good position to predict the behavior of those who have self-disclosed to us and in a bad position to predict the behavior of more secretive people. This also works in reverse. We will probably be trusted by others to the degree that we have made ourselves known to them and will not be trusted by others to the degree that we have kept ourselves hidden.

As society becomes increasingly specialized and as interpersonal communication becomes more difficult, trust is going to be more and more related to roles rather than to individual people. Because we cannot possibly learn about numerous specialities, we have to rely on or trust the "experts." Similarly, as we have less and less time to get to know these experts individually, we will have to put our trust in the roles or titles rather than in the people. We will have to trust, not the individual who lives down the street and who has been healing people for 20 years, but rather the degree. Because of our past experiences we may come to trust or distrust doctors, lawyers, real estate brokers, psychologists, bankers, salesmen, professors, and so on. That is, our trust-distrust will probably become more and more linked to the roles of people rather than to the people themselves.

In terms of communication, Giffin and Patton distinguish four basic kinds of trust. First, we can have trust in a speaker. We may, for example, believe what the speaker says is true or believe he or she has our own best interests at heart. Or we may distrust the speaker. Second, we can have trust in a listener. This type of trust is especially important when we self-disclose, for example. We need to feel that the listener will be supportive and not reveal what we have said to others. Third, we can have trust in ourselves as speakers. This is a kind of self-confidence that we may feel for ourselves when in communication situations. When we have to give a speech or argue for a point of view or write an essay, we need to have trust in our own abilities to perform these behaviors well. Fourth, we can have trust in ourselves as listeners. This seems to be the area where most people do have trust in themselves; almost all of us see ourselves as effective and supportive listeners.

Trusting behavior is learned. We learn to trust or distrust someone on the basis of our previous experiences. If our trusting behavior has been rewarded (or for example, we did not lose what we risked), then we are more apt to trust on future occasions. However, if our trust was betrayed, then we would probably be reluctant to trust anyone on future occasions. Trusting behavior also seems to be influenced by the atmosphere established; this is particularly evident in the classroom situation. On the last day of a class in interpersonal communication we decided to perform an exercise in interpersonal trust. The exercise was performed as follows: Two rows of five persons each were formed. The two rows faced each other and each pair held hands firmly so that a kind of net was formed by all 10 people. One individual then ran toward this net and leapt upon it, trusting that the 10 members would hold him or her up. This generally presented no great difficulty. Although there was some risk, no great fear developed. The worst that could happen was falling to the floor. The second part involved greater risk. The person who had just jumped onto the hands of the 10 now lay on the floor under the net formed by the hands of the group. The person was to lay there until another person performed the jump. Seeing another person jump right on top of you was at first a bit scary. But again there was the trust in the group—trust that they would not allow anyone to fall on anyone else. This experience illustrates the influence that the general atmosphere has on trusting behavior. In this class not one person, neither myself nor any of the students, refused to participate in the exercise. It was clear at the start of the exercise that the group was deserving of trust and that we would not lose anything in participating. We were convinced that we were able to predict the behavior of the group members and this prediction was that they would hold up whoever jumped.

Trusting behavior leads very quickly to a decrease in anxiety. If we have trust in another individual there is little reason to be anxious. We would feel that we would not lose anything regardless of what we risked. Probably because of this we become more spontaneous. We are apt to lower our defenses, simply because we feel that we will not be hurt; we feel that we will be supported. We feel secure and hence can be ourselves. While self-disclosure will often lead to greater trust, greater trust will often lead to greater self-disclosure. If we trust someone then we risk little in self-disclosing. When our trust is confirmed we will be more likely to engage in even more self-disclosure. And here we have a healthy spiral (Figure 35.1).

Trust increases openness. When you trust someone you can be yourself, let your own hair down. A trusting relationship is a supportive one; each person gives support to the other. Empathic understanding is also

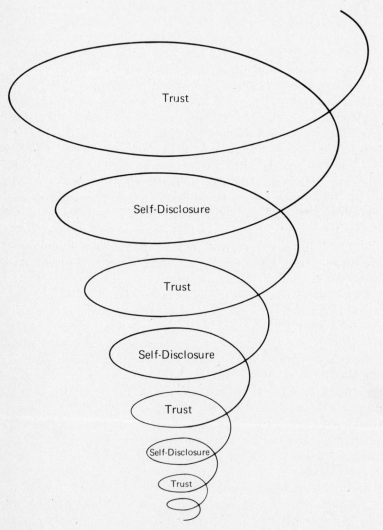

Figure 35.1 *The Relationship between Trust and Self-Disclosure*

increased, in part because of the greater self-disclosure and in part because of respect for the other. Trust is a positive kind of relationship and
also one of equality; we do not trust people we do not respect and we do
respect people we do not consider equal.

Trust in others will increase if we first have trust in ourselves. If we
do not consider ourselves worthy of trust, we would be much less likely
to put our trust in others. And with trust in ourselves comes a general
confidence in facing life. As Goethe put it: "As soon as you trust yourself,
you will know how to live."

Sources

Pitirim A. Sorokin's "Altrustic Love" and Cyril Bibby's "The Art of Love"
in *The Encyclopedia of Sexual Behavior,* edited by Albert Ellis and Albert
Abarbanel (New York: Hawthorn, 1967) were particularly helpful in defining and characterizing love and loving. *How Do You Feel?* edited by
John Wood (Englewood Cliffs, N.J.: Prentice-Hall, 1974) contains interesting articles by Ron Lunceford and Larry and Kay Carlin, both cited
here, as well as by John Wood and Bill and Audrey McGraw. All four
articles, and in fact the entire book, are worth reading. Zick Rubin's
Liking and Loving (New York: Holt, 1973) is especially insightful. Bobby
R. Patton and Kim Giffin's *Interpersonal Communication* (New York:
Harper & Row, 1974) details the relationships between trust and communication. Herbert A. Otto's "Communication in Love" in Otto, ed.,
Love Today: A New Exploration (New York: Delta, 1972) is perhaps the
best single source on love and communication. Richard Reichert's *Self-
Awareness through Group Dynamics* (Dayton, Ohio: Pflaum/Standard,
1970) provides an insightful account of both trust and respect.

Experiential Vehicle

ROOMMATE PREFERENCE

You are a student entering John Ward College, a new experimental college located on a tropical island in the South Pacific. Among the information you receive from Ward is the attached list of roommates with the following cover letter.

Enclosed are six short profiles of other entering students. In order to provide some choice in the selection of roommates each student is asked to read over the enclosed profiles and rank them in order of preference using 1 for the most preferred and 6 for the least preferred. When all preference rankings are received, roommate selection will be made. The college cannot, of course, guarantee that you will get the roommate of your first choice. However, we will try to assign roommates on the basis of personal preferences as much as we possibly can.

There are certain facts about roommates which you should be made aware of before ranking your preferences. First, the college does not segregate the sexes. You may room with a student of either sex. Second, once roommates are assigned you must stay roommates for an entire academic year and must change after the year is over. In this way each student will room with four different persons over the period of his or her stay at Ward. Third, rooms are equipped with twin beds, a screen which may be used as a partition, two desks and chairs, book-shelves, and various tables, lamps, and so forth. In addition, there is one bath-room and one kitchen. Since no dining facilities or maid service is available, students are expected to cook for themselves and to clean their own rooms.

After all students have indicated their preferences, in groups of five or six discuss your rankings. Construct a rank order of the possible room-mates for the group as a whole. After these rankings are completed, share your group's decisions with the decisions of the other groups. Discuss the rankings and the reasons for them with particular, though not exclusive, reference to the concepts of loving and trusting, as discussed in this unit.

Roommates

Mark, age 19, 6'2" tall, 190 pounds, black. Majoring in physical education with plans to become an elementary school teacher. High school average, 84. Worked as athletic director of community youth groups. Major purpose in attending college is to prepare himself to teach physical education. Active in various athletic clubs.

Martin, age 18.5, 5'10" tall, 120 pounds, white. Majoring in mathematics with plans to earn a Ph.D. and work in industry. High school average, 98. Never worked and is not active in any organizations or clubs. Major purpose in attending college is to learn mathematics.

Elizabeth, age 21, 5'5" tall, 112 pounds, white. Majoring in elementary education with plans to teach. High school average, 82. Worked as exotic dancer for two years before deciding to attend college. Major purpose in attending college is to meet a man, get married, and raise a family.

Peggy, age 18, 5'4" tall, 110 pounds, white Majoring in chemistry with plans to teach in high school. High school average 93. Worked for two summers as a camp counselor. Major purpose in attending college is to learn chemistry and to meet people. Active in the local bird-watching society.

Arnold, age 18.5, 6' tall, 170 pounds, white. Majoring in sociology with plans to become a social worker. High school average, 87. Worked for the past year for the Gay Activists Alliance and active in the gay liberation movement. Major purpose in attending college is to learn.

Carol, age 18, 5'7" tall, 128 pounds, black. Majoring in political science with plans to enter law. High school average, 93. Worked during the past year for a militant black organization and active in black liberation movement. Major purpose in coming to college is to prepare for a legal career to help oppressed people.

unit 36

Attitudes in Interpersonal Communication

Attitude, a Definition
Related Concepts
Dimensions of Attitudes
Functions of Attitudes
   The Attitude Game
   The Attitudes and Values Game

Objectives

Upon completion of this unit, you should be able to:

1. define *attitude*
2. distinguish among *attitude, belief, faith, opinion,* and *value*
3. identify and define the six dimensions of attitudes
4. identify and define the four major functions of attitudes

Central to the study of any form of communication, especially communication that seeks to influence people, is the concept of *attitude*—a tendency to respond in one way rather than in another. Unlike communication messages or noise, attitudes cannot be observed directly. We cannot see attitudes or touch them or hear them. What we do see or touch or hear are behaviors which we ascribe to the influence of attitude. So, for example, if a person constantly compliments us, asks us to go out, invites us to all sorts of activities, is always with us, and so on, we might conclude from these behaviors that this person has a favorable attitude toward us. We do not see the favorable attitude but rather we infer it exists from the behaviors that we can observe. Attitude is thus a hypo-

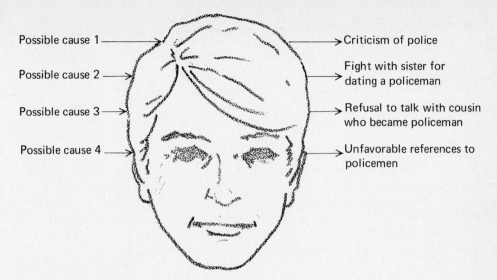

Possible cause 1 ———————→ Criticism of police

Possible cause 2 ———————→ Fight with sister for dating a policeman

Possible cause 3 ———————→ Refusal to talk with cousin who became policeman

Possible cause 4 ———————→ Unfavorable references to policemen

Figure 36.1 *Stimuli and Responses*

thetical construct. It is a useful concept which we create to simplify our descriptions and explanations of behavior.

Take the case of a young man we observed engaging in the following behaviors: 1) criticized the police for whatever they do; 2) fought with his sister because she dated a policeman; 3) refused to talk with a cousin who became a policeman; and 4) referred to policemen with the least favorable expressions he could think of. We might then attempt to explain these behaviors by postulating stimuli for each of these responses. The individual might then be seen as depicted in Figure 36.1.

In attempting to predict the possible causes for these various behaviors, we must be careful to also include the behaviors feeding back and becoming causes of themselves and of other behaviors. That is, calling policemen vulgar names may now become a stimulus for other behavior, say throwing things. This circular kind of process must also be explained. This type of analysis can get extremely complicated.

ATTITUDE, A DEFINITION

Enter the concept of attitude. Because of the tremendous complexity of behavior we need a kind of summary statement that will enable us to describe and explain (at least on one level) the behaviors we observe as well as those we cannot or have not yet observed. *Attitude* serves these functions well. By postulating a negative attitude toward policemen we can describe and to some degree explain the individual's behavior. Also, the concept of attitude will help us to predict what this individual might do on other occasions. If, for example, the individual has an unfavorable attitude toward policemen, we may then be in a better position to predict what he will do if his brother wishes to become a policeman or if a policeman performs some kind of service for him.

We may define attitude as *a predisposition to respond for or against an object*. An attitude is a *predisposition* or a kind of *readiness to respond*. The attitude is not the behavior but only a mental or internal state of readiness that we postulate. Attitudes are predispositions to respond *for or against* something. Attitudes, by definition, are evaluative; they are predispositions to respond favorably or unfavorably and, obviously, anywhere between these two extremes. Theoretically, at least, we can have neutral attitudes, fairly favorable, quite unfavorable, and extremely favorable attitudes, and, in fact, attitudes covering any possible gradation from extremely unfavorable to extremely favorable. Attitudes are predispositions to respond for or against *an object*. The word "object" is used here in its broadest sense to include things, people, situations, events, ideas, and so on. Attitudes, then, are not merely abstract evaluations but have connections to referents.

RELATED CONCEPTS

The term *attitude* is often used interchangeably with a number of other terms and at times it is confused with them. Some of the more closely related terms should be noted here so that the concept of attitude may be clarified still further. We here follow the insights provided by Cooper and McGaugh.

Belief

We have attitudes *toward* something but we have beliefs *in* or *about* an object or person or event or idea. According to Martin Fishbein, *beliefs* may be viewed as the cognitive dimension of attitude rather than the affective or emotional dimension. Whereas attitudes vary from favorable to unfavorable, beliefs vary from true to false, probable to improbable, existent to nonexistent, likely to unlikely. Thus when we have an attitude toward something we are favorable or unfavorable to it, but when we have a belief in something we believe it to be true or false, probable or improbable, and so on. Beliefs are in some ways the bases or foundations of attitudes. If we believe x, y, and z about someone, then we may develop an attitude toward him or her on the basis of these beliefs. Thus if we believe that this person steals, cheats, and beats children, then we would develop an unfavorable attitude toward this person. However, note that the process goes in the other direction as well. If we have an unfavorable attitude toward someone then we are more likely to believe negative things about this person and less likely to believe positive things. Similarly, if we have a favorable attitude toward someone we are more likely to believe positive things and less likely to believe negative things.

Given this relationship between attitudes and beliefs we can easily imagine two general ways to change attitudes and beliefs. Attempts at change may be directed at the affective component or at the cognitive component. We might attempt to develop or change an existing favorable or unfavorable attitude toward an object by appeals to the emotional dimension; on the other hand, we might attempt to change individuals beliefs about an object which in turn will lead them to change their attitudes. For example, we might change our negative attitudes toward the person mentioned earlier if we were first made to change our beliefs about him or her. So if we were made to believe that this person did not steal, did not cheat, and did not beat children, then we would have no reason for an unfavorable attitude toward him or her and might even develop a favorable attitude.

Beliefs are often used to make predictions about the future or even guesses about the past that is unknown. If we believe that Jane is the brightest kid in the world then we might predict that she will do well on her examinations and that she will get into the college of her choice and so on. Or if we believe that Jane is a drunk we might guess—information to the contrary—that when she came home late last night it was because she first stopped at a local bar. Although not all predictions are made on the basis of beliefs, the majority of our guesses seem related in some way to our system of beliefs.

Faith

Faith is a type of attitude that is primarily emotional in meaning. To have faith in someone or something, for example, is to have an emotional attachment of some sort. Faith is a kind of belief; to have faith in someone is to believe in him or her. Like belief, we also often use faith to predict the unknown. If we did not know what happened to our favorite team in some game we might predict their behavior on the basis of our faith in them. Faith is also a kind of ideology in that it is often used to explain some phenomenon. Faith, for example, may enable us to explain the cycle of life and death, the achievements and failures of people and nations, the goodness and the cruelty of humankind.

Opinion

Of all the terms considered here, *opinion* is perhaps the most frequently used; we express our opinions, we listen to the opinions of others, we read the results of opinion polls, we gauge public opinion. Opinions are perhaps best viewed as tentative conclusions regarding some object, person, or event. Opinions are tentative and thus change rather quickly. Attitudes on the other hand are relatively enduring. In fact, many writers make this enduring quality an essential part of the definition of attitude.

When opinion is used in the phrase "public opinion," we are in a sense speaking of a general or collective mind with a given opinion or more concretely, the opinion of the majority or at least a large portion of the people.

Value

Value refers objectively to the worth of an object or subjectively to the perceived worth of an object. Some would argue that value is inherent in an object and hold, for example, that a Rembrandt painting is inherently valuable and would be so even if there were no people to evaluate it. Others, however, would argue that value is in the observer's evaluation rather than in the object and that the Rembrandt is valuable because millions of people perceive it to be of value.

In one sense, a value is an organized system of attitudes. If, for example, we have a cluster of favorable attitudes pertaining to various issues relating to freedom of speech, for example, then we might say that one of our values is that of free speech.

In another sense, a value is an organizing system for attitudes. If we have a particular value, say financial success, then this will give us guidelines for developing and forming attitudes. Thus we will have favorable attitudes toward high-paying jobs, marrying into a wealthy family, and inheriting money because of the value we place on financial success. Values also provide us with guidelines for behavior; in effect, they direct our behavior so that it is consistent with the achievement of the values or goals we have.

DIMENSIONS OF ATTITUDES

In order to more fully understand the nature and the operation of attitudes we need to appreciate the various dimensions. Daniel Katz distinguishes six such dimensions or ways in which attitudes may vary or differ from one another.

Intensity

The *intensity* of an attitude is its strength, that is, the degree to which we are for or against an object. Intensity applies to both directions of the favorable-unfavorable continuum. A highly intense attitude may be one that is extremely unfavorable or one that is extremely favorable. An attitude of low intensity might be described as fairly favorable or fairly unfavorable, or perhaps as somewhat favorable or somewhat unfavorable. In terms of communication and attitude change, the more intense an attitude is the more difficult it will be to change and the more the individual holding the attitude will resist change. If you are madly in love with someone it is going to take a great deal of persuasion to get you to change your mind. On the other hand, if you are somewhere around neutral in your feelings, just a few words might sway you one way or the other.

Specificity or Generality

Attitudes may vary from highly specific to extremely general. We may, for example, have a favorable attitude toward Mick Jagger as a singer, a rather specific attitude. On the other hand, we might have a favorable attitude toward all humankind, to all students, to all women, to all men or whatever—that is, the attitude may be extremely general.

Degree of Differentiation

Each attitude consists of a number of items or cognitions or beliefs and the *degree of differentiation* refers to the number of these items or beliefs. Some attitudes are more complex than others; that is, some attitudes have many beliefs (high in differentiation) and others are simple, having few beliefs (low in differentiation).

For example, my favorable attitude toward Barbara may be based on such beliefs as the following: she is charitable, she is willing to help others, she is a hard worker, she always has something nice to say about other people, she is an excellent conversationalist, she is friendly to me, and so on. This attitude, based on many beliefs, is relatively complex or high in differentiation. If I had a favorable attitude toward a particular politician because he or she promised to lower the taxes on gasoline and if this was the only belief which led to my favorable attitude, then this would be a relatively simple attitude and one low in differentiation.

Complex attitudes are more resistant to change. To alter a complex attitude it is necessary to change a number of the underlying beliefs or cognitive items. A simple attitude is generally easier to change since fewer items need to be changed before the attitude itself will change.

Number and Strength of Its Linkages to a Related Value System

Some attitudes are tied very closely to an elaborate value system while other attitudes seem rather unrelated to any such system. For example, a parent might have a favorable attitude toward allowing children to eat when they want rather than at specified times. If this is linked closely to a value system of general permissiveness or concepts of freedom then this attitude is going to be very difficult to change. On the other hand, if this was simply an isolated attitude unrelated to any value system it would probably be less resistant to change.

Centrality

Attitudes also vary in terms of *centrality*, that is, the degree to which the value system (of which the attitude is a part) is related to the person's self-concept. Attitudes that are more central will be more resistant to change than attitudes that are less central. For example, parents may have an unfavorable attitude toward the use of drugs by their children, and this attitude may be related to a value system that is very close to their self-concepts, to the way they see themselves and their roles as parents. When this is the case, that is, when attitudes are central, they will be very resistant to change. On the other hand, if this attitude was less central (that is, not closely related to self-concept) it would be easier to change.

Action Component

Although all attitudes are defined as predispositions to respond, the relationship to actual behavior varies greatly from one attitude to another. One attitude, for example, may lead me to act in accordance with it while another attitude may not motivate me to engage in the behavior at all. For example, my favorable attitude toward helping the poor motivates me to give money to charities. On the other hand, my unfavorable attitude toward a cluttered desk does not motivate me to clean it.

FUNCTIONS OF ATTITUDES

Daniel Katz has distinguished four functions of attitudes which are important to consider in any attempt to understand how attitudes operate and why they operate as they do.

Utilitarian

Some attitudes are directed at objects that will enable us to reach our goals (in which case they are favorable) or to avoid undesirable goals (in which case they are unfavorable). *Utilitarian* attitudes, as the term implies, are formed on the basis of the perceived usefulness-uselessness of the object to the individual.

Typical utilitarian attitudes of college students might be, for example, favorable attitudes toward high grades, scholarships, admission to graduate school, athletic prowess and popularity with peers. Unfavorable attitudes might be directed toward low grades, unpopularity, conservatism, and meaningless courses. These attitudes are utilitarian in that they are directed at objects which can help or hinder the individual in his or her attainment of goals.

Utilitarian attitudes are generally formed on the basis of associations. For example, if the mother satisfies the child's hunger need, the child will develop favorable attitudes toward the mother, toward the food, and perhaps toward the general situation in which this need is satisfied. We have a favorable attitude toward high grades because high grades have been associated in the past (and we predict will be associated in the future) with social reinforcement, entrance into the school of our choice, and so on.

Utilitarian attitudes are formed on the basis of the rewards and the punishments that we receive. For example, if upon studying we are positively reinforced, for example, by a social reward, then studying will become positive for us—that is, we will develop favorable attitudes toward studying. If, on the other hand, studying was punished, say by peer criticism as it often is in high school, then we might develop unfavorable attitudes toward studying.

Ego Defensive

Many of our attitudes are developed to protect our rather sensitive egos. At times such attitudes might protect us from the real or imagined dangers which we face in the outside world and at other times they may protect us from discovering something about ourselves which might be ego deflating. If we are unpopular with our peer group we might develop attitudes that will protect our egos from this kind of realization; we might, for instance, develop unfavorable attitudes toward these members, considering them generally inferior, stupid, immoral, dull, or whatever. By putting this group down we evaluate ourselves (in our own minds at least) and in this way protect our egos.

Thus *ego-defensive attitudes* are not created in response to an object in the outside world and its relationship to our goals, as is the case with utilitarian attitudes. They are created in response to some inner need or conflict. Consequently, such ego-defensive attitudes may be destructive rather than constructive. For example, if we develop negative attitudes toward this peer group with whom we are unpopular, then we do not confront the issue of our own unpopularity with other people but rather take refuge in the idea that these people are dull, or whatever other designation is handy and ego protecting.

Value Expressive

Some attitudes express the values we hold and thus help us to articulate to ourselves and to others the kind of person we are or wish ourselves to be.

For example, I see myself as a progressive instructor. Consequently, I have a number of attitudes which are appropriate expressions of this "progressive teacher" value. For example, I have favorable attitudes toward maintaining office hours for students, preparing thoroughly for classes, grading papers as soon as they are turned in, keeping on top of the new developments in the field, and so on. These attitudes reflect to some extent my own self-image.

We all see ourselves differently. But regardless of how we see ourselves we maintain attitudes that are expressions of the values we believe in. If we value freedom of expression, then we would have unfavorable attitudes toward censorship and laws limiting free expression and favorable attitudes toward whatever is positively related to this freedom of expression value.

Knowledge

Many of our attitudes help us to give meaning to the world by providing us with standards against which various objects and actions may be measured. For example, if we have a negative attitude toward a particular form or forms of education then this attitude will be useful by providing us with a frame of reference into which we may fit new knowledge about this type of education.

Similarly, we may have a favorable attitude toward a certain philosophy. This may provide us with the standard against which we can evaluate or judge new courses of action or evaluate decisions which have to be made.

Attitudes may serve any or all of these functions, singly or in combination; a single attitude may serve one function or all four at the same time.

The importance of appreciating these different functions is two-fold. First, by recognizing these four functions we will be in a better position to understand our own attitudes—how they are developed, how they are maintained, and, to some extent, the usefulness-uselessness of them to our own self-image and our own goals. Some attitudes are unproductive and in fact destructive and these need to be examined and altered. Perhaps a prerequisite is the understanding of the functions our attitudes now serve.

Second, attitudes serving different functions will not be susceptible to the same forces of change. Should we, for example, attempt to change someone's attitude, the way it will change, the appeals it will be responsive to, the resistance we will run into, and the chance for success will in large measure depend on the function that the attitude is now serving. An attitude serving important ego-defensive needs, for example, will be highly resistant to change and will obviously not respond to the same kinds of appeals as would an attitude that serves primarily a knowledge function.

Sources

Attitudes are covered in most social psychology texts in considerable detail. On the dimensions and functions of attitudes see "The Functional Approach to the Study of Attitudes" by Daniel Katz, *Public Opinion Quarterly,* 24(1960). I relied heavily on this article for the discussion of the dimensions and the functions of attitudes presented here. Perhaps the most comprehensive work on attitudes is that of William J. McGuire, "The Nature of Attitudes and Attitude Change" *The Handbook of Social Psychology,* 2d ed., edited by Gardner Lindzey and Elliot Aronson, vol. 3 (Reading, Mass.: Addison-Wesley, 1969).

Excellent collections of articles on attitude are *Readings in Attitude Theory and Measurement,* edited by Martin Fishbein (New York: Wiley, 1967) and *Attitudes,* edited by Marie Jahoda and Neil Warren (Baltimore, Md.: Penguin, 1966). Joseph B. Cooper and James L. McGaugh's "Attitudes and Related Concepts," used here extensively, is reprinted in Jahoda and Warren's *Attitudes.*

Experiential Vehicles

THE ATTITUDE GAME

This game is played in a group of approximately six people. The procedure is as follows: One member is selected through some random means to be the first subject. If the group members do not know each other, the subject should introduce himself or herself with a brief talk (no more than one or two minutes). After this introduction the group members, one at a time, attempt to guess the objects toward which the subject has a favorable attitude. Proceeding clockwise, the group members each guess a favorable attitude of the subject until one member guesses incorrectly. Naturally, the subject should respond honestly to the various guesses of the group. When an incorrect guess is made, the guessing stops. The group then focuses on the reasons for their success or failure to guess accurately. The individual who is the subject should lead this discussion and should attempt to discover what cues he or she gives off which led the group members to guess as they did. At any point the subject may conclude the discussion and ask that the group go on to another person. The subject's wishes should be respected and another member should be chosen, again in some impartial manner.

The same general procedure may be repeated to deal with unfavorable attitudes, positive values, and negative values. Ten or fifteen minutes should be reserved so that the group as a whole might discuss and evaluate the game. DO NOT READ ANY FURTHER UNTIL THE GAME HAS BEEN PLAYED.

After completing the game the group members should focus on at least some of the following questions:

1. How brave were the group members in guessing meaningful and significant attitudes and values?
2. How honest was each player in telling the group members whether they were right or wrong?
3. To what extent did the group members make the subject feel that they

were really interested in his or her attitudes and values? How did they indicate this interest or disinterest?

4. To what extent are the members of this group homophilous? Heterophilous? Are there specific areas of similarity and difference?
5. Do you feel you know anyone better as a result of this exercise? Explain.

THE ATTITUDES AND VALUES GAME

The purpose of this exercise is to explore the nature of attitudes and values in more specific and more personal terms than is possible in any reading.

Groups of six or seven persons should be formed; members may or may not be familiar with each other. It is best to have all members either familiar with each other or all members unfamiliar with each other rather than to have groups composed of some members who know each other and other members who do not know anyone. The exercise may be effectively played with the entire class as one group.

Each member of the group should complete the accompanying attitude and value form as honestly as possible. Each member should respond to the questions with those attitudes and values which are most important to him or her.

The papers should be collected, shuffled randomly, and read aloud to the group by one member. The first objective is for members to attempt to guess the person whose form was read. After all forms are read, discussion should focus on some or all of the following areas:

1. To what extent do these attitudes and values reveal something of the individual? To what extent do they enable one to predict other attitudes and values? Test this by actually making some predictions.
2. What functions do these attitudes and values serve (using a system such as that described in this unit, that is, utilitarian, ego defensive, value expressive, knowledge)?
3. To what extent are these attitudes and values resistant to change?— that is, how difficult would it be to change these attitudes and values? What types of appeals would be most effective in trying to change these attitudes and values? Why?
4. Do any of those attitudes and values create dissonance? How is this dealt with?
5. Can the origin of these attitudes and values be determined?—that is, how did the individual come to hold these attitudes and values?
6. How do those attitudes and values differ from those that would be expressed by the parents of the group members? Test this by asking some parents.
7. Was it easier to guess the forms of some people rather than others? Why?

8. Do you feel you know anyone better as a result of this exercise? Explain.

Attitudes and Values Form

1. Among those objects toward which I have favorable attitudes, some of the most important are:

    a.

    b.

    c.

2. Among those objects toward which I have unfavorable attitudes, some of the most important are:

    a.

    b.

    c.

3. Among those objects for which I have high positive value, some of the most important are:

    a.

    b.

    c.

4. Among those objects for which I have high negative value, some of the most important are:

    a.

b.

c.

unit 37

Machiavellianism and Dogmatism

Machiavellianism
Dogmatism
  Individual and Group Decision Making

Objectives

Upon completion of this unit, you should be able to:

1. define *Machiavellianism*
2. provide at least two examples of the atypical behavior of high Machs
3. define *dogmatism*
4. explain at least three ways in which the dogmatic individual deals with communication differently from the nondogmatic individual

One of the best ways to understand attitudes and attitude change in interpersonal communication is to examine extremes. Two such extremes in attitude and behavior are considered here, *Machiavellianism* (manipulation to control people) and *dogmatism* (closed-mindedness).

MACHIAVELLIANISM

Of all the manipulators throughout history the name of Niccolo Machiavelli (1469–1527) stands out. In *The Prince*, Machiavelli provided an in-depth analysis of political power, how it is secured and how it is maintained. Because of the cynicism and the detachment with which he wrote *The Prince*, "Machiavelli" has come to mean control without concern.

In interpersonal communication *Machiavellianism* refers to the techniques or tactics by which control is exerted by one person over another. A great deal of research has been directed at analyzing Machiavellianism in people.

Much of this research has utilized a test in which subjects are asked to respond to various items on a scale ranging from much agreement, through neutral, to much disagreement. Items include, for example, "There is no excuse for lying," "The best way to handle people is to tell them what they want to hear," and "One should take action only when it is morally right."

Richard Christie has noted some general characteristics of "high Machs"—people who exhibit a high degree of Machiavellianism. Machiavellianism is generally not concerned with moral issues, at least not as we normally think of them. Interpersonally, high Machs are rather uninvolved, detached, and cool. High Machs become involved in the art of manipulation and seem to enjoy it and engage in it almost for its own sake. They are, in other words, more concerned with the means of conning another individual than with the ends to be achieved with this conning. Lastly, and contrary to what some might assume, Machiavellians are not at all pathologically disturbed. Since they must be cool and detached and must function effectively in the real world, they have an undistorted view of the world and at times are overly logical in their interactions with others.

In one experiment Christie and Geis worked with groups of three college students. One student had scored high on the Machiavellian (Mach) test, one scored low, and one scored near the middle. The three members were seated around a table where 10 one-dollar bills were placed. Their instructions were to divide up the money among any two of them in any way they wished. The only restriction was that no deals be made to include the third person in the payoff. The results showed that the high Machs won significantly more money than the middle or low Machs. Even children have been found to perform differently depending on their Mach score. In one case, children were divided into high, low, and middle Machs (on the basis of an adaptation of the Mach test suitable for children). The high and low Machs were used as subjects while the middle Machs were used as "targets." All the children were given an unpleasant-tasting cracker to eat. After eating it the subjects (high and low Machs) were asked to try to convince the targets (middle Machs) to eat another cracker. For each cracker they persuaded a child to eat they would receive a nickle. As predicted, the high Machs were significantly better than the low Machs at persuading the children to eat these quinine-soaked crackers.

In another study, when high Machs were caught cheating—in a specially rigged experiment—they resisted confessing more than did the low Machs. They also engaged in more direct eye contact with the accusing instructor than did the low Machs.

Machiavellians do not always perform at higher levels than low Machs. Christie and his colleagues have found that for high Machs to perform at significantly better levels than low Machs, three conditions are helpful. First, when the interaction is face-to-face high Machs have a decided advantage. Machiavellians are particularly effective in influencing attitudes and behavior when they are in face-to-face contact. Second, high Machs perform better when there is room for improvisation. If a high Mach is restricted to pushing buttons or marking items on a test he or she is not likely to do any better than a low Mach. But when there is an opportunity for free behavior he or she will usually perform at a more effective level. Third, the high Mach is more influential when emotions can be brought into play and when the consequences of an action are serious. If high Machs participate in an experiment where they could merely win points they will be less effective than if they could win money.

DOGMATISM

We have probably all said at one time or another that such and such a person is dogmatic; "There is no sense arguing with him; he's too dogmatic," or perhaps, "she'll never change her beliefs and agree with us; she's too dogmatic." On the other hand, there is the open person with whom there is sense in arguing because he or she will evaluate the information fairly and if found satisfactory will change his or her beliefs.

This concept of *dogmatism* or *closed-mindedness* is significant in interpersonal communication primarily because these people treat communications very differently. Closed-minded people are heavily dependent upon reinforcement for their reactions to information. They will evaluate information on the basis of the rewards and the punishments they receive. We all do this to some extent; the closed-minded person, however, does this to a greater degree than do most people. The open-minded person is better able to resist the reinforcements of other people and outside situations.

All communications contain immanent reference; all communications are to an extent ego reflexive; all communications say something about the speaker as well as about taxes, crime, pollution, or whatever. In dealing with this inevitable message duality, the closed-minded person has difficulty separating the information about the source or speaker from the information about the world. The open-minded person, on the other hand, can accept or reject the information about the world and either accept or reject the information about the speaker independently of each other. Throughout the course of a semester's class, for example, a professor will say many things, advocate various ideas and criticize others. The closed-minded listener will have difficulty evaluating what the professor says about these ideas from what he or she thinks of the professor and similarly will have difficulty separating what he or she thinks of the professor from what he or she thinks of the ideas. It becomes a rather confused mass of information. The open-minded individual, on the other hand, can accept or reject the professor or any of the ideas after evaluating each separately.

Assume that a conservative wishes to obtain information about liberalism or for some reason has a need to obtain such information. If this individual is closed-minded, it is likely that this information will come from conservative sources writing or speaking about liberalism. Closed-minded people will rarely put themselves into the position of obtaining information from sources that will contradict their existing belief system. Thus when closed-minded individuals seek information relevant to their belief systems, that information will more likely be secondhand and particularly from the hand of a source sharing their belief systems. Whereas closed-minded people will fear obtaining information from firsthand sources which might contradict their own belief systems, open-minded people will not have this fear and will consult the best available sources whether they be in or out of sympathy with their own belief systems.

Closed-minded people see the world as generally threatening. Because of this perceived threat, they become anxious and unable to deal with the relevant information independent of the source (as already noted). Consequently, they come to rely very heavily on authority. They do not evaluate information themselves, but allow the authority to evaluate it for them. Then all there is to do is accept the authority's conclusions. Open-minded people, on the other hand, see the world as nonthreatening, even friendly. They are not anxious and hence may evaluate information calmly and rationally. Although they do not ignore authority they do not accept what an authority says uncritically.

In terms of interpersonal relationships, closed-minded people will evaluate others according to the similarity-dissimilarity of others' belief systems with their own. They evaluate positively those people who have similar belief systems and negatively those people who have dissimilar belief systems. Closed-minded people become friends with people who are of the same religion, same race, and same political persuasion. Open-minded individuals do not use similarity of belief systems or homophily as the measure of interpersonal relationships.

These two types are extremes. Few people are completely closed and few people are completely open. The vast majority of people exist somewhere in between these two extremes. The important issue to see is that we are all to some extent closed-minded and to the extent that we are we prevent meaningful interpersonal interaction.

The extremes of Machiavellianism and dogmatism are conceptualized and investigated as deviations from the "normal" in human behavior. But all persons are in part Machiavellian and in part dogmatic. Perhaps a knowledge of this will help in our interpersonal communications.

Sources

For an interesting overview of Machiavellianism see Richard Christie, "The Machiavellis Among Us," *Psychology Today* 4 (November 1970):82–86. More detailed treatments are provided in Richard Christie and Florence Geis, *Studies in Machiavellianism* (New York: Academic Press, 1970) and Florence Geis and Richard Christie, "Machiavellianism and the Manipulation of One's Fellow Man" in *Personality and Social Behavior*, edited by David Marlowe and K. J. Gergen (Boston: Addison-Wesley, 1970).

For dogmatism, see Milton Rokeach, *The Open and Closed Mind* (New York: Basic Books, 1960), especially, "A Fundamental Distinction between Open and Closed Systems," (written with Frank Restle) and "The Measurement of Open and Closed Systems." For a measuring instrument see Franklyn Haiman, "A Revised Scale for the Measurement of Open Mindedness," *Speech Monographs* 31(June 1964):97–102. A good review is provided by Ralph Vacchiano, Paul Strauss, and Leonard Hochman, "The Open and Closed Mind: A Review of Dogmatism," *Psychological Bulletin* 71, no. 4 (1969).

Experiential Vehicle

INDIVIDUAL AND GROUP DECISION MAKING

The purpose of this exercise is to explore the differences between individual and group decisions and the ways in which group decisions are influenced.

The States Problem should be completed first. The procedures are as follows: Each person should rank the states in order of their size using 1 for the largest state, 2 for the next largest state and so on down to 20 for the smallest state of this group. (These 20 states are the 20 largest of the United States.)

After each person has completed his or her rankings, groups of five or six should be formed at random. Each group should then compile a group ranking for the 20 states utilizing all the insight from all the members. Again, 1 should be used for the largest state, and so on.

The object of the States Problem is 1) for each individual to obtain a better score than his or her group and 2) for the individual's group to have a better score than the other groups.

The scoring procedure is based on error points and these are computed as follows: First, each individual's error score should be computed. This is done by subtracting the ranking you gave each state from the correct rankings without regard to sign. (Your instructor will supply you with the correct rankings.) For example, if you gave Utah a ranking of 5 and the correct ranking is 12 then there is an error score of 7 points. Similarly, there would be an error score of 7 points if you ranked Utah 12 and the correct ranking was 5 because we are disregarding positive and negative signs. Compute your individual error score by subtracting your rankings from the correct rankings for all 20 states and adding up the error points. This sum constitutes your error score. Obviously, a low error score is a good one and a high or large error score is a bad one. Record your error score here _____.

Second, compute the group's error score by following the same procedures, that is, subtract the group's rankings from the correct ones for all 20 states and add them. This sum is the group's error score. Record that score here _____.

If your score is lower (that is, better) than the group's score then you have won this round of the game.

Next compare your group's error score with the error score of the other groups. If your group's error score is lower (that is, better) than the other groups, you have won this second round.

The Countries Problem should be completed next. The procedures are the same except for the formation of the groups.

Rank the countries in order of their size using 1 for the largest, 2 for the next largest, and so on down to 20 for the smallest country in this group. After each person has completed his or her rankings, groups should be formed. This time the groups should be formed, not at random, but on the basis of the scores received in the previous game. More specifically, groups should be formed of those persons who got better scores than their groups; other groups should be formed of those who did not get better scores than their groups. Thus those who received lower (that is, better) scores than their group should form groups of about five or six persons. Those who had poorer scores than their groups should also form groups of five or six persons.

The object of this exercise is again for the individual to have a better score than his or her group and for the individual's group to have a better score than the other groups.

Utilize the same scoring procedure as was used in the States Problem. Record your error score here _____. Record your group's error score here _____.

States Problem

Rank the following states in order of their size, using 1 for the largest, 2 for the next largest, and down to 20 for the smallest of this group.

_____	Alaska	_____	Nevada
_____	Arizona	_____	New Mexico
_____	Calfornia	_____	North Dakota
_____	Colorado	_____	Oklahoma
_____	Idaho	_____	Oregon
_____	Kansas	_____	South Dakota
_____	Minnesota	_____	Texas
_____	Missouri	_____	Utah
_____	Montana	_____	Washington
_____	Nebraska	_____	Wyoming

Countries Problem

Rank the following countries in order of their size, using 1 for the largest, 2 for the next largest, and down to 20 for the smallest of this group.

_____ Argentina	_____ Nigeria
_____ Brazil	_____ San Marino
_____ Denmark	_____ Saudi Arabia
_____ Egypt	_____ Syria
_____ France	_____ Tonga
_____ Italy	_____ Turkey
_____ Iceland	_____ USSR
_____ India	_____ USA
_____ Japan	_____ Venezuela
_____ Kenya	_____ Yugoslavia

After completing both the States Problem and the Countries Problem respond individually to the following questions:

1. Was there a manipulator or manipulators in either of your groups? Who?

2. By what means did this person manage to manipulate the group? Be as specific as possible.

3. Were there any instances where members were confronted with criticisms for attempting to fool the group? How was this done? What were the responses to this confrontation?

4. Were there dogmatic individuals in your group? Who?

5. On what basis do you consider them dogmatic? Point to specific behaviors of the individual which led you to say that he or she was dogmatic.

6. Were there people who had difficulty separating the messages from the sources? Explain.

7. Were the manipulative and dogmatic behaviors easier to see in the first group or in the second group? Why?

Return to your original groups and bring up for discussion whatever you feel would be meaningful and valuable to discuss. Keep in mind the five characteristics of effective interpersonal communication: openness, empathy, supportiveness, positiveness, and equality.

unit 38

Conditioning and Attitude Change

The Operation of Conditioning
Principles of Behavior Control
  Conditioning Behavior

Objectives

Upon completion of this unit, you should be able to:

1. define *conditioning, positive reinforcement, negative reinforcement,* and *punishment*
2. explain how conditioning principles may account for the development, maintenance, and change of attitudes
3. specify the five principles of behavior control

Perhaps the branch of psychology most often in the popular news is that of behaviorism. The techniques of conditioning and reinforcement as applied to learning, behavior problems, and social planning are by now familiar to most. For our purposes, however, some of the basics of conditioning need to be considered before its relationship to attitude and attitude change may be discussed.

THE OPERATION OF CONDITIONING

Operant behavior—that form of behavior which is peculiarly human, unlike reflexive behavior—is behavior that is dependent upon its consequences. If the behavior is rewarded its strength and frequency or likelihood of occurrence will increase. If the behavior is punished or ignored then its strength and frequency will decrease and the behavior may be extinguished or eliminated.

Behavior may be rewarded in two general ways. First, and perhaps the method most familiar, is by positive reinforcement, which is what we normally think of when we talk about reward. Positive reinforcement is simply the presentation of a positive or rewarding stimulus. For example, if after pressing a lever we present the rat with food, we are positively reinforcing the lever-pressing behavior. We can also reward through negative reinforcement. If, for example, a person is equipped with earphones through which a painful sound is passed, and if upon his or her performing the desired behavior we shut the sound off for 10 seconds, we are engaged in negative reinforcement. Notice that shutting off the sound—more formally, the removal of an aversive stimulus—is rewarding for the individual in a way similar though not identical to that of positive reinforcement. Punishment is simply the presentation of an aversive or unpleasant stimulus or the removal of a pleasant stimulus. Thus, for example, we may punish a child by spanking or by taking away candy.

According to behaviorists, most of our behaviors are learned through this system of reinforcement. We learn to respond to other people in the way we do because we have in the past been reinforced for some behaviors and punished for other behaviors. Similarly, we learned to smoke, for example, through reinforcement (probably social) when we were younger. Alternatively, we unlearn behaviors through the same basic means. Smoking behavior, for example, may be unlearned by making punishment contingent upon it and reward contingent upon nonsmoking behavior.

The theories of operant conditioning may be utilized to explain how attitudes are developed and how they are maintained. Take a simple issue, such as eating popcorn. Eating popcorn was accompanied by hunger satisfaction which is rewarding or positively reinforcing and so the popcorn comes to have a positive meaning for the individual. On future occasions—for example, when we are hungry—we would be more likely to reach for the popcorn because this has in the past been associated with reward. On the other hand, if the popcorn made us violently ill, that is, if it were punishing, then our tendency to reach for the popcorn would be lessened or perhaps extinguished entirely. On the basis of the consequences of the behavior we develop favorable or unfavorable attitudes—favorable attitudes if the consequences were positive or rewarding and unfavorable attitudes if the consequences were negative or punishing. Thus we would have a predisposition to reach for or not reach for the popcorn because of its previous consequences and this predisposition we choose to call *attitude*.

It is often said that children are not born with prejudices but must learn them from their parents. A prejudice may be viewed as a negative attitude toward a class of people which is unrealistic and not based on any concrete evidence. It is an irrational attitude. Consider how this type of attitude or prejudice might develop in a child. The child comes home from nursery school and tells the parents about this new child whose skin was a different color and whose eyes did not look like everyone else's. Immediately the child is told how bad these other children are and how they should not be associated with. Notice that this relatively simple kind of expression of prejudice in effect tells the child that negative consequences will follow or that rewards will be withdrawn if this child is played with. Because of this kind of teaching the child now has a predisposition to respond against another child of a different skin color and this predisposition we simply call an unfavorable attitude.

Perhaps the most difficult type of attitude to account for in operant terms is that which we normally term moral behavior. Take the situation of a student who is caught with a term paper he or she did not write. The instructor discovers that another student wrote the paper and attempts to get the name of the paper writer from this student. Even when faced with all sorts of unpleasant consequences the student refuses to tell on his or her friend. Even if the instructor were to offer a reward for telling (say, letting the student off with no penalty), he or she opts to take the punishment and remain silent. On the surface it would seem that this type of behavior defies what has already been said about behavior being governed by its consequences. With somewhat more analysis, however, we can see that this type of behavior is similar to that of the popcorn or even to the rat pressing the lever. Even in this situation there are rewards and punishments but here they are internalized. By not telling on his or her friend the student gets rewarded through the social reinforcement of his or her peers and also avoids the punishment that would be received if he or she had told. To the student the peer group reinforcement is the more powerful. In a similar manner we may engage in behavior that has immediate unpleasant consequences—for example, studying on a warm Saturday night when everyone else is on a date—in order to get a positive reinforcement at a later time—perhaps in the form of a good grade and possible social reinforcement as well. The ability to delay our rewards is dependent in great part on maturity. Children have great difficulty in delaying rewards; they are not satisfied to be told they can have ice cream tomorrow or even in an hour. They want it when they want it and that is that.

Behavior theory, as the name implies, deals with behavior; hypothetical constructs such as attitude are not dealt with as such. However, behavior theory allows us to account for the behavior, that is, the predisposition to engage in a certain form of behavior, whose motivation we call attitude.

PRINCIPLES OF BEHAVIOR CONTROL

We also want to know how behavior is controlled through this system of rewards and punishments. Perhaps the best way to explain the operation of behavior conditioning principles is to specify the steps necessary to alter the behavior of an individual. Let us assume, then, that we wish to stop a particular behavior, say smoking. There are five basic steps to be followed.

Specify the Behavior to Be Learned or Unlearned

This principle may seem unnecessary except that it emphasizes *behavior*. In applying the principles of conditioning we are dealing with behavior, not with internal emotions. We do not attempt to extinguish anxiety; we do attempt to extinguish nail biting or foot stamping. The behavior in our example is smoking behavior; that is what we are attacking, not any symptoms or causes of the behavior but the behavior itself—the puffing and inhaling to be exact.

Establish and Apply the Reinforcers

To control behavior we manipulate the consequences of the behavior. To learn a particular bit of behavior we use reinforcement; to unlearn behavior we use punishment. Now the question arises as to what is reinforcing. David Premack has suggested a relatively simple but ingenious method for determining what is a reinforcer. The theory, called variously the *Premack principle* or the *differential probability hypothesis*, states that high frequency behaviors may be used to reinforce low frequency behaviors. If, for example, telephoning behavior is extremely frequent, then that behavior may be used to reinforce other behavior which is normally less frequent, for example, studying behavior. The application of the principle requires that telephoning behavior be allowed only as a reward for engaging in the less rewarding (or less immediately rewarding) studying behavior. The specific application of the reward will depend on the individual case. For example, if you cannot seem to study for more than one hour at a time then it is the short period of time that needs to be increased. Thus in the beginning you may allow yourself one telephone call for each hour of studying. After this period is no longer such a strain, increase it to one hour and a quarter and only after that time allow yourself the phone call. In this way you will be able to increase the time you engage in normally "undesirable" behaviors.

With punishment we generally know what works and what will not work. At times the punishment needs to be extreme whereas at other times it may be relatively mild. For example, you may make a "contract" with yourself which goes something like this: for every cigarette I smoke I will send $5 to the American Cancer Society. Assuming you stick to this contract you will stop smoking or go broke in very short order. I smoked almost three packs of cigarettes a day for 15 years. When I decided to stop I chose a somewhat more drastic punishment which I applied three times: For every cigarette I smoked I would stick my fingers down my throat until I threw up. I must confess that this was not the most pleasant experience and yet it did get me to stop smoking, at least for a time. At that time I stopped for six months and then went back to smoking. The reason for the failure of this application was that I allowed myself to cheat. It is very easy to cheat ourselves; we are such easy marks. At any rate, I cheated by concluding that cigars were not in the original contract I made with myself and so I smoked cigars. As many cigarette smokers who attempt cigars know, they are relatively unsatisfying if you do not inhale. And so for about a month I inhaled about 20 cigars a day. The house smelled so bad that guests would refuse to enter. Of course, it was not difficult for me to cheat myself one step further and conclude that the evil of cigarettes was far less than that of cigars. With cigars not only was I going to lose my health but my friends as well. And so I went back to cigarettes and smoked for four years until the second and last conditioning. In some cases it is possible to be your own contingency manager and to monitor, yourself, the contract you make with yourself. At other times it is not so easy, as I learned. The only real change I made in the procedure was to have someone else monitor the no smoking agreement and to apply the punishment. In this case it was electric shock administered as I held a cigarette in my mouth. After approximately five hours of this treatment (spread over five days) and discussion pertaining to my reasons and rationalizations for smoking I was "cured." I still consider myself a smoker—rather like the alcoholic who has ceased drinking—but one who does not smoke. At the time of this writing it has been approximately two years since I had a cigarette.

Recognize that the Situation Has Stimulus Properties and Utilize This to Advantage

If a rat is repeatedly shocked in a maze it will attempt to avoid the maze. This is not a particularly profound discovery on the part of the rat but it is a useful one. The maze takes on stimulus properties of the original stimulus, the shock. Because of this we need to structure our learning situations so that the stimulus properties of the situation will work for rather than against us. Consider, for example, instructors who use the classroom as a place for discussion of personal problems and then expect the students to work when told to do so. The classroom, in this situation, has become the stimulus for reading the newspaper, playing tic-tac-toe, or just daydreaming. Instructors who think they can turn the situation around at whim are fools and should be told so. Notice how effective instructors do utilize the stimulus properties of the situation to advantage. Many students have difficulty studying because of the failure to properly utilize the stimulus properties of the situation. The student who wants the situation to stimulate studying behavior needs to study and only study in the same place. If this is a desk then one should do nothing else at that desk but study. When one wishes to read a magazine or make a phone call one should sit somewhere else. In this way studying behavior will be stimulated by sitting at the desk. Similarly, many people have difficulty sleeping because they do things other than sleep in bed.

Smoking behavior is often situational: Our smoking behavior is often triggered by various situations. For example, having coffee after eating stimulates smoking behavior in most smokers as does having a drink at a bar; important phone conversations also stimulate smoking behavior. Situations that stimulate the behavior that we wish eliminated should be avoided, especially at the beginning of the period when we are modifying behavior.

This issue is closely related to the perceived rewarding value of the actual smoking behavior. For example, smokers will say that smoking relaxes them, but we know that physiologically smoking does not relax the body; it tenses it. Actually, the smoking is closely related to relaxing but in itself has nothing to do with it. The smokers among the readers should imitate the act of taking a drag on a cigarette. Notice how deep we breathe when we smoke. It is this deep breathing that is relaxing and because it is associated with the smoking we perceive the smoking to be relaxing.

Reinforce Immediately

Reinforcers lose their effectiveness over time. Teachers who return examinations or papers after weeks of time should be made to realize that the effects of their reinforcement or punishment are much less than they would be if the papers were returned after only a short time. The mother who says to the child that he or she will be punished when father gets home does nothing to extinguish the undesirable behavior because the time between the actual behavior and the reinforcement is too long. If we wish the reinforcer to have its maximum effect it must be applied immediately. It should in fact be the next thing in time after the behavior itself.

One instructor attempting to teach students about teaching and especially about teacher-student communication equipped the student teachers with a receiving set so that as they gave their sample lectures he was able to reinforce immediately.

At times, of course, the desired behavior does not manifest itself, and we simply do not have the time to wait for it. What we do in this case is to reinforce successive approximations of the desired behavior. This procedure is called *shaping behavior*. If we are teaching a pigeon to make the classic S-shape design, we reinforce any movement in the desired direction until the complete S is formed.

With smoking behavior the punishment must come immediately after the cigarette is taken or even while the cigarette is being held. If we wait until a whole pack is smoked, for example, then the effectiveness of the punishment is going to be minimal.

Introduce Uncertainty

One of the more interesting aspects of conditioning is that constant reinforcement does not work as effectively as intermittent reinforcement. For example, if the pigeon is reinforced every time it presses the lever the frequency of its lever-pressing behavior will be less than if it is reinforced only intermittently. Ideally, the time of the reinforcement and the form of the reinforcement should be somewhat unknown to the individual whose behavior we are trying to shape or mold.

If, for example, we are shocked for every fifth puff on a cigarette, this will be less effective in curbing smoking behavior then if we were shocked on a quasi-random schedule, even if this averages one shock for every five puffs. The reason is simple enough: If we know that we will be shocked on every fifth puff we will be able to enjoy the first four and so the association between the behavior and the punishment is not established. But if we do not know when the shock will come then we will be apprehensive on each puff and the association between the smoking and the shock will be more firmly established. When we are our own contingency manager we cannot apply this principle but it is most useful when we are attempting to control another's behavior.

Sources

For conditioning, the works of B. F. Skinner are essential. Particularly valuable are the recent *Beyond Freedom and Dignity* (New York: Knopf, 1971) and *About Behaviorism* (New York: Knopf, 1974). Arthur W. Staats' *Complex Human Behavior* (New York: Holt, Rinehart and Winston, 1963) and *Learning, Language, and Cognition* (New York: Holt,

Rinehart and Winston, 1968) clarify much of the research and theory relating to conditioning. The five principles of behavior control are taken from my "The Teacher as Behavioral Engineer," *Today's Speech* 16(February 1968):2–5. For Premack's principle see David Premack, "Toward Empirical Behavior Laws: I. Positive Reinforcement," *Psychological Review* 66(1959).

Experiential Vehicle

CONDITIONING BEHAVIOR

This exercise is performed by the entire class with three or four people as subjects. Subjects leave the room now. These "subjects" should not read any further since it is best to have subjects who are at least somewhat naive with regard to the nature of the experiment.

The exercise is designed to illustrate some of the processes and some of the effects of conditioning.

When these subjects are out of the room, the class should decide on some type of behavior which they will attempt to reinforce and thereby strengthen or increase its frequency or likelihood of occurrence. There are many forms of behavior that might be appropriately conditioned in the classroom. Examples of both verbal and nonverbal behaviors would include the following: a type of word, for example, plural nouns, verbs of action, nouns, pronouns, positive words, negative words, or self-reference words; a type of statement, for example, statements that make reference to the past, statements that make reference to the future, statements beginning with "I," statements that begin with "the" or "a," or statements that include proper names; or physical behaviors, which include staying near the window or door, staying close or far away from the class members, or walking or moving around.

Once the type of behavior to be reinforced is chosen, the type or types of reinforcers to be used must be selected. Saying the word "good" or "O.K." or applauding or patting the subject on the back might be used. In a classroom situation, however, it seems best to use a simple verbal reinforcer, such as "good." Facial expressions, of course, should complement the verbal reinforcer.

Because in a class meeting we do not have a great deal of time for this exercise, the subject should be instructed to emit a class of behaviors of which the behavior to be reinforced is a part. For example, if the behavior to be reinforced is plural nouns, then we might ask the subject to give us a list of words, one at a time. We would then of course reinforce the plural nouns and ignore the others.

A recorder should be appointed to make note of all instances of both the desired behavior and the undesired behavior. For example, if the behavior to be reinforced is plural nouns, the recorder might make a list of "x's" for each word emitted by the subject and "√'s" for the plural nouns. In this way we will be able to see if the frequency of plural nouns increased as a resut of the reinforcement.

When the subject is brought into the room he or she is instructed to engage in some behavior, say a list of words to keep with our previous example. When the subject emits the desired behavior, that is, a plural noun, only then should he or she be reinforced with our saying "good." The entire class should do this. All members will have to be extremely alert so that all plural nouns are reinforced and are reinforced immediately.

A special attempt should be made to remain absolutely quiet while the behaviors which are not to be reinforced are being emitted. For example, by laughing at other terms we might be reinforcing behavior we do not wish to reinforce.

After five or ten minutes the session should be stopped. The process should be repeated with a different subject, this time retaining or changing the behavior to be conditioned and the type of reforcement used.

After the class has attempted to condition two or three subjects, discussion and response should center on at least the following:

1. Were the subjects conditioned? Did the frequency of the reinforced behavior increase? Explain.

2. Were the subjects aware of what was going on? Did this make a difference in the effectiveness of the conditioning?

3. Are certain people easier to condition than others? How about you?

4. Are certain behaviors easier to condition than others? Explain this in reference to your own behaviors, habits, mannerisms.

5. Are certain reinforcers more effective than others? Explain this in relation to the reinforcers which seem to work to influence your own behaviors.

6. What are the real-life counterparts of this type of conditioning process? In school? In the home? With peers?

unit 39

Cognitive Balance and Attitude Change

The Nature of Cognitive Balance
Cognitive Dissonance
  The Related Attitudes Game

Objectives

Upon completion of this unit, you should be able to:

1. define the concept of *balance* as it applies to attitude
2. state the conditions under which attitudes are balanced and unbalanced
3. define *cognitive dissonance*
4. state the conditions necessary for dissonance to develop
5. state the possibilities for dissonance reduction—that is, in what ways dissonance may be reduced
6. explain how dissonance operates in forced compliance, decision making, exposure to information, and social support

Instead of concentrating solely on the behavior, *consistency* or *balance theory* "goes into the mind" and attempts to explain some of the cognitive dynamics involved in the process of attitude change. The fundamental assumption of all balance theories—and there are a number of different variations—is that there is a universal tendency to maintain homeostasis, psychological balance, or consistency. *Balance* might best be defined as a state of psychological comfort in which all the attitude objects in our minds are related as we would want them to be or as we would psychologically expect them to be. Imbalance or inconsistency, then, is a state of psychological discomfort in which the attitude objects in our minds are not related as we would want or expect them to be.

THE NATURE OF COGNITIVE BALANCE

Let us say that we positively evaluate Peter and Patricia and that we negatively evaluate Neil and Nancy. Our minds would be balanced under the following conditions:

1. if Peter liked Patricia/if Patricia like Peter
2. if Neil liked Nancy/if Nancy liked Neil
3. if Peter and Patricia liked us
4. if Neil and Nancy disliked us
5. if Neil and Nancy disliked Peter and Patricia/if Peter and Patricia disliked Neil and Nancy

We expect people we like to like us (3) and expect people we dislike to dislike us (4). Similarly, we expect people we like to like each other (1) and expect people we dislike to like each other (2). Further, we expect people we like to dislike people we dislike (5). With a little reflection these should be intuitively satisfying.

From these examples we can deduce the states of imbalance:

6. if Peter disliked Patricia/if Patricia disliked Peter
7. if Neil disliked Nancy/if Nancy disliked Neil
8. if Peter and Patricia disliked us
9. if Neil and Nancy liked us
10. if Neil and Nancy liked Peter and Patricia/if Peter and Patricia liked Neil and Nancy

The assumption in all balance theories is that when our attitudes are in a state of balance we are psychologically comfortable and are not motivated to change our attitudes or our behaviors. On the other hand, when we are in a state of imbalance or inconsistency, we are psychologically uncomfortable and are motivated to change our attitudes and our behaviors. (It should be noted that some theories argue that given a state of imbalance, attitude change is automatic. Other theories claim that given a state of imbalance, we must be motivated to change our attitudes; it is not automatic.)

Let us take one of the imbalanced examples and attempt to predict the type of changes that would bring this imbalanced condition into a state of balance: "If Peter disliked Patricia." Visualizing our minds as boxes with a positive side for favorable attitude objects and a negative side for unfavorable attitude objects, we might diagram this as follows (the line between the two attitude objects is the expressed relationship which in this case is negative, Peter *dislikes* Patricia):

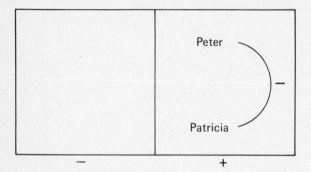

Figure 39.1 *Attitudes in an Unbalanced State*

We should now consider what kinds of changes would bring this model into balance. Obviously, if Peter changed his attitude toward Patricia and liked her it would bring the model into balance. But this is an alternative over which we do not always have control, although we sometimes do convince ourselves that one person likes or dislikes another simply to suit our own needs. Generally, however, the choices open to us are 1) to change our attitude toward Peter or 2) to change our attitude toward Patricia. If one of them (but not both of them) were evaluated negatively, we would be in a state of psychological comfort and balance. This change may seem very mechanical and unrealistic when viewed in terms of the diagram and the clear-cut divisions between positive and negative. But the general procedure or process by which attitudes are changed does not seem much different from the situation as depicted here. We might change our attitude toward Peter and explain it in any number of ways, for example, if Peter does not like Patricia then he is the one who has problems. Or we might change our attitude toward Patricia and reason that if Peter does not like her there must be something wrong with her.

This process is perhaps seen most clearly when we are confronted with a neutral attitude object, that is, an object about which we do not feel very positive or very negative. However, when a positive or a negative bond is created between this neutral object and an object toward which we do have a definite attitude then we change our attitude from neutral to either positive or negative depending upon which would produce a balanced state. For example, if Bill No. 75, about which we feel neutral, is introduced and supported by a politician toward whom we feel positive then we would soon feel positive toward the bill, perhaps reasoning that if this politician supports it it must have merit. In this case then, we have a positive bond between two positively evaluated objects. This is similar to situation (1), Peter liking Patricia. On the other hand, if the politician was someone toward whom we had a negative attitude then we would develop a negative attitude toward the bill, reasoning that this incompetent politician could not possibly support anything worthwhile. Here we are creating a positive bond between two negatively evaluated objects, similar to situation (2), Neil liking Nancy.

In order to explain this consistency approach more clearly we shall explain one of the balance theories in greater depth. The theory to be considered here is that of *cognitive dissonance* which is perhaps the most interesting of all the theories in social psychology today. It is also the most general and the most applicable to interpersonal communication.

COGNITIVE DISSONANCE

The theory of *cognitive dissonance* was formulated by Leon Festinger and originally presented in his *A Theory of Cognitive Dissonance*. Since then there have been thousands of studies conducted to test the implications and the predictions of cognitive dissonance.

"Dissonance" and "consonance" refer to relationships between elements, cognitions, or "knowledges" about oneself, about other people, or about the world. Elements or cognitions may be beliefs, attitudes, feelings, behaviors, desires, and so on. In our examples the elements were, for example, "Peter likes Patricia" or "Neil and Nancy dislike us."

Dissonance (similar to imbalance) and consonance (similar to balance) exist when there is a relation between two elements. The relation is dissonant when *the obverse of one element follows from the other element.* Two elements, A and B, are dissonant if, given A, non-B would be expected to follow. For example, A might be "I like Peter" and B might be "Peter does not like me." Given that I like Peter (A) it would follow that Peter likes me (which is the obverse of B). Hence this relation would be dissonant. Or take an example aluded to earlier. As a smoker I had the following cognitions: (A) smoking is unhealthy and (B) I am a heavy smoker. Given A, it would be more logical if non-B followed. That is, given the fact that I know smoking is unhealthy my being a heavy smoker would not follow. Hence this relationship was dissonant.

On the other hand consider the following relations: (A) I like Peter, and (B) Peter likes me. Given A, B would logically follow; hence this relationship is consonant. Similarly, consider these two relationships: (A) Smoking is unhealthy and (B) I no longer smoke. Given A, B would be logical to follow and hence this is a state of balance or consonance.

Consonance, then, exists when, given one element, the other would be psychologically or logically expected.

When we are in a dissonant state there is pressure to reduce the dissonance and restore consonance; there are a number of alternatives to accomplish this. Obviously, if there is a great deal of dissonance there will be much pressure to reduce it; if there is little dissonance there will be little pressure to reduce it.

Explaining the alternative modes of dissonance reduction will be simplified if we worked through an example. Suppose that I am a skydiver and that I very much enjoy this experience. But I know that it is dangerous and so the two elements (I skydive, skydiving is dangerous) are dissonant. Now, what are my alternatives to reduce the dissonance?

First, I could change the behavior, that is, I could stop skydiving and that would eliminate the dissonance. Similarly, the person who smokes and yet knows that smoking is unhealthy can reduce the dissonance by stopping the behavior. But, as any smoker knows, this is not always easy. The typical unrequited love story presents a dissonant relationship to the person who loves but is not loved in return. To change the behavior and get himself or herself to not love may not be possible, and so he or she may have to eliminate changing behavior as one alternative to reducing dissonance.

A second method to reduce dissonance is to change the environmental element. This is often the most difficult of all alternatives. In the case of my skydiving it would involve making skydiving safe or at least less dangerous. Similarly, for the smoker it would involve making smoking healthy or at least not unhealthy. For the lover it would involve getting the other person to love in return. At best these are extremely difficult to accomplish. Of course, there are situations when changing the environment is not out of the question, as it is in the examples given. We might for example be riding in a car with bad brakes. Our two elements are (A) I ride in this car and (B) this car has bad brakes and is therefore dangerous. Here it is quite possible to change the environment and get the brakes fixed, reducing the danger, and eliminating the dissonance.

A third alternative to reduce dissonance is to acquire new elements. As a skydriver I might read about the numerous precautions being taken to make skydiving safe and perhaps read about how dangerous automobile travel is or about how people are dying every day and have never had the thrill of skydiving. As a smoker the person might read about the biased nature of the research linking smoking to cancer or perhaps rationalize that smoking has enabled him or her to accomplish a great deal of work by relieving tension. The lover might attempt to find faults with the loved one. These new elements would reduce the dissonance perhaps to the point where it would no longer be uncomfortable.

In order to see the relevance of cognitive dissonance to interpersonal communication we should examine the four situations Festinger notes as applicable to the theory: forced compliance, decision making, exposure to information, and social support.

Forced Compliance

Dissonance is created when our public behavior contradicts our private attitudes. Such a situation might be brought about by the individual being promised a reward for compliance or by being threatened for non-compliance. But the amount of dissonance created will vary with the nature of the reward or threat. Consider, for example, a situation used in one of the many experiments designed to test dissonance. Subjects participated in an extremely boring experiment. After they participated in this boring experience they were asked to lie to subjects who were waiting to participate in the same experiment and to tell them that the experiment was interesting. Some subjects received $20 for this lying whereas other subjects received only $1. In which group would more dissonance be created? The measure of the amount of dissonance was taken to be the amount of attitude change that took place after the lying; thus after completing the experiment the subjects rated the experiment in terms of how interesting it was, then they lied to the other subjects, and then they again rated the experiment. The results of the experiment showed that the group that was paid $20 changed their attitudes very little and thus were judged to have experienced little dissonance. The subjects who were paid only $1, however, changed their attitudes a great deal (now feeling that the experiment was not so boring) and were judged to have experienced much dissonance. This seems quite logical after some reflection. The subjects who were paid $20 were able to justify their lying; they had received a significant reward for a relatively minor lie. But the subjects who were paid only $1 could not justify their behavior because the reward was too small.

In another study students were offered rewards for writing essays advocating shorter summer vacations, a position with which they did not agree. The group receiving the greatest reward showed the least attitude change in the direction of shorter summer vacations whereas the group receiving the smallest reward showed the most attitude change and hence the greatest dissonance. Again, their reward was not sufficient to justify taking a position contrary to that which they really believed.

This procedure of forced compliance with the resulting attitude change is obviously something many hucksters and charlatans have long known. One of the most obvious techniques of persuaders is to get you to verbally agree with them or to try their product even if it means it will be at an initial loss to them. The product is generally offered for a minimal amount or at times given free. The object here is to get you to use the product and by the mere fact that you have used it you will develop a more positive attitude toward it and hence will be more likely to use it in the future.

Decision Making

Dissonance is created after making any decision, according to the theory. The reasoning is that any decision involves the acceptance of one alternative and the rejection of one or more other possible alternatives. In accepting A, for example, we also accept all the negative features of A and of course we reject all the positive features of B, C, D, and so on. For example, suppose you are going to buy a stereo and are deciding between a Pioneer and a Maranz. In selecting the Pioneer you are also accepting its negative features and rejecting (by not buying) the positive features of the Maranz. Because of this, dissonance is created after making decisions. The closer the items and the harder the decision, the more dissonance will be created. If, for example we are offered two prizes but may select only one to keep, we would experience much dissonance if the prizes were about equal in value; we would experience little dissonance if one item was valuable and the other worthless.

In one experiment new car buyers were investigated and were found to read more advertisements of the car they had finally bought and less advertisements of the car they had considered but not bought. The reasoning here is that the advertisements for the car they had bought would provide support for their decision and would reduce the dissonance. If they had read advertisements for the car they were going to buy but did not buy, they would in effect be told that they had made the wrong decision. Hence their dissonance would be increased rather than decreased.

Exposure to Information

When we experience dissonance we may attempt to reduce it by seeking new information. We expose ourselves to information which will decrease our dissonance as in reading the advertisements for the car that we purchased and avoiding ads for the car we did not buy.

The way in which we expose ourselves to information is particularly important in our interpersonal relationships. Take for example people who ask us how they look. They want to be told they look great. Similarly, a new pair of pants or a new jacket brings on a kind of "tell me what you think" attitude. But in doing this they are really attempting to expose themselves to dissonance-reducing information. They are expecting us to tell them that they look great, that the pants or jacket look fine, and so on. In fact, we often expose ourselves to those people who are normally complimentary so that our dissonance may be reduced.

As a smoker I used to avoid the commercials by the American Cancer Society or the Heart Association. I did not want to be reminded that smoking was dangerous and uncomfortable for others. And at the same time I would actively dwell on advertisements depicting the pleasures of cigarette smoking. Now, however, my behavior is reversed. I actively seek out the commercials against smoking as a kind of reinforcement and avoid the ads for cigarettes. Even my decision to stop smoking created dissonance. By not smoking I have given up the pleasures of smoking; consequently, I experience dissonance. My behavior with the different kinds of advertisements is clearly directed at reducing the dissonance. Even in reading this unit and especially these examples of smoking, the reader who smokes will experience a great deal of dissonance, the reader who stopped smoking will derive reinforcement, and the reader who has never smoked will wonder why there's all the fuss about smoking.

Social Support

The social group is a powerful influence on both the creation of cognitive dissonance and on its reduction. If a group disagrees with us, finds us unpleasant, or ignores us this will create dissonance in us. On the other hand, if the group supports us dissonance will be reduced.

Not all groups or group members produce dissonance equally. The credibility of the group members is significant in the amount of dissonance produced. If members are of high credibility then they are able to produce a great deal of dissonance by disagreeing with us. On the other hand, if they are of low credibility, their disagreeing with us would produce only slight dissonance. Another factor is the number of members who disagree with us. The greater the number of members who disagree with us, the greater the amount of dissonance that will be created. The cohesiveness of the group is also significant. If the group is very cohesive then it will have much more influence in producing or in reducing dissonance than if the group was not a very cohesive one. In fact, one of the important functions that peer groups serve is the reduction of dissonance for its members. When parents do not understand their son or daughter he or she can always go to the peer group who will give the social support necessary to reduce the dissonance created by parental disagreements.

When there is dissonance resulting from disagreement with a social group there are three major ways of reducing it. One way is to change one's attitude so that it is in agreement with that of the group. This is the route taken by many young people who are afraid to be loners or who are afraid that the group might withdraw its support from them because of disagreements. A second way is to change the opinions of those who disagree. When confronted by the disagreement of the group we might at first attempt to change their opinions so that they will be consistent with ours and so that dissonance will be reduced. This method is rather like changing the environment discussed earlier. Third, we might attempt to make the group members somehow different from us so that they now have little effect in producing dissonance. We might attribute to the group some undesirable trait; we might say, for example, that they disagree with us because they are prejudiced or because they are mercenary or immature. When these undesirable traits are attributed to them, their attitudes and opinions are given less importance.

Cognitive dissonance is only one of the many balance theories of attitude change. It was selected for discussion because it seems to be the most widely applicable. It should not be thought that there are no problems with the theory of cognitive dissonance. All theories have problems. Yet the theory seems to provide an amazing degree of insight into the processes of interpersonal communication.

Sources

A summary of the theories of consistency in attitude change are summarized in my *The Psychology of Speech and Language: An Introduction to Psycholinguistics* (New York: Random House, 1971). The original work on cognitive dissonance is Leon Festinger's *A Theory of Cognitive Dissonance* (Stanford, Cal.: Stanford University Press, 1957). Extensions of the theory and additional experimental evidence is provided by J. W. Brehm and A. R. Cohen in their *Explorations in Cognitive Dissonance* (New York: Wiley, 1962).

An assessment of consistency theories of attitude change is provided by William J. McGuire, "The Current State of Consistency Theories" and "Cognitive Consistency and Attitude Change," both in Martin Fishbein, ed., *Readings in Attitude Theory and Measurement* (New York: Wiley, 1967). A recent and excellent overview and analysis is provided by Patricia Middlebrook, *Social Psychology and Modern Life* (New York: Knopf, 1974).

Experiential Vehicle

THE RELATED ATTITUDES GAME

Attitudes toward or against an object are seldom unrelated to other attitudes. An individual probably does not hate dogs and love all other animals. Rather, he or she probably has a generally favorable or unfavorable attitude toward animals and then more specific attitudes toward various classes of animals. Similarly, the person who has a favorable attitude toward animals is probably unfavorable toward hunting wild animals and toward wearing wild animal fur. This same person may then have a favorable attitude toward efforts of ecologists to preserve the natural environment and an unfavorable attitude toward pollution, littering, and so on. Thus one attitude is often related to another attitude which in turn is then related to another attitude and so on.

The object of this game is to explore the degree to which attitudes are related, and it is played like "twenty questions." Groups of approximately six persons are formed. One person is selected to be the first subject, and the subject thinks of one of his or her attitudes. It is generally best that the subject write the attitude down without showing it to the group. In this way there will be no arguments later on. The subject then identifies the area which the attitude is in. That is, rather than animal-vegetable-mineral, the general area is identified—for example, political, social, religious, economic, educational, psychological. The group members may then ask a maximum of 20 questions which may be answered by the subject with only "yes" or "no." The object is to guess the attitude the subject has written down.

The game should continue until all members have had a chance to be subjects or until the members feel that they have understood the concepts sufficiently. Discussion and response should then focus on some of the following questions:

1. We may predict that the attitudes that were the most difficult to guess

were also the ones that somehow did not seem to fit into the general orientation of the individual subject. Was this true?

2. Why would dissonance-producing attitudes be more difficult to guess than consonance-producing attitudes? Why would dissonance-producing attitudes be less likely to be selected by the subjects for guessing? Were any dissonant attitudes used?

3. A pool of inconsistent attitudes should be collected by each group and then shared with the entire class. Why are these attitudes inconsistent with other attitudes? What would the parents of these members say about these attitudes? (Do *not* settle for an easy answer to these questions.)

unit 40

Interpersonal Communication Effects

Importance of Communication Effects
Difficulties in Determining Effects and Causes
    Self-Concept: Part II
    Positive Words

Objectives

Upon completion of this unit, you should be able to:

1. state at least three reasons why the study of communication effects is important
2. state how the "obstinate" audience differs from the passive audience
3. explain at least three major difficulties in determining communication effects and causes

Because we are here not only concerned with our own interpersonal communications but with communication analysis as well, the question of communication effects needs to be considered.

IMPORTANCE OF COMMUNICATION EFFECTS

In the physical sciences it is relatively easy to isolate the effect of any given element or chemical. Generally, all else is kept constant while a chemical is added to one test tube and not added to the other. The effect of the chemical can then be studied by observing what happens to the elements in the tube or by any number of appropriate methods available to the chemist. Of course there are interactions which must be accounted for and other difficulties. But generally speaking, it is relatively easy for the laboratory scientist to observe effects.

For the behavioral scientist observing and measuring effects is perhaps one of the most difficult aspects of the field. So difficult is it that many have simply given up and have argued that we do not have to understand communication effects to understand interpersonal communication itself. Unfortunately, difficulties cannot be dismissed so easily. This situation is very much like the situation in linguistics some years ago. Meaning was extremely difficult to study; the linguist simply did not have any appropriate methodology for studying meaning and so it was claimed that meaning was outside of linguistics and that linguistics was only concerned with sounds and sentences and not with the meaning of these sounds and sentences. The situation is similar in interpersonal communcation. An understanding of communication effects is essential because communication is not a simple linear process. Communication is not something that goes from source to receiver, from source to receiver, from source to receiver. Rather communication is transactional; communication is a process that feeds back onto itself. The effects of any given communication, then, may turn around and become causes of further communications. For example, if you are speaking, the effects of your communications on me are capable of being observed by you. You may be able to see my smiling face or my bored expression or my look of intense interest, and so on. These expressions are part of the effects of your communications and these effects in turn will serve as stimuli to influence you in what you next communicate. The effects, in other words, are in turn causes of communications. Another reason for being concerned with effects is that communication exists for the most part to have some effect on an individual. We speak so that others will do as we wish or believe as we want them to or for any number of other reasons. But all the reasons involve some kind of effect. We anticipate and plan for effects. Consequently, the effects are significant since they influence our strategy or plan for communicating.

We might also mention that communication effects are important to understand because they are the bases from which we develop principles of effective and ineffective communication. We may perhaps develop a particular strategy for communicating. If that strategy proves effective—that is, if it produces the desired effect—we may incorporate that strategy into our arsenal of principles of effective interpersonal communication. On the other hand, if the strategy proves ineffective then we need to revise our plans. But we can only do this when we know what the effects of communication are.

In short, then, communication effects are important to understand and analyze because they influence our communications in progress, they influence our communication strategy or plan, and they influence the development of principles for effective communication.

Consider the following not uncommon situations:

1. As a result of reading an individual's speeches and seeing this person on television, you vote for this person for a seat in the assembly.
2. Your friend tells you about a date with a particular individual and you become anxious to date this individual yourself.
3. After reading the brief synopsis in *TV Guide* you decide to watch a particular program.
4. The advertisements have said that Crest fights cavities and so you buy it.
5. You hear that some people risked their lives to save a young child and your respect for them increases.
6. You applaud after viewing the first act of a play.
7. You studied hard and received an "A" on your examination.
8. You decide to register for another course in interpersonal communication after having had a month or so of this course.
9. You look over various record albums, remember that friends recommended one in particular, and you buy it.
10. You continue reading this unit.

Obviously hundreds of such examples could have been given. These few, however, should illustrate the broad range of effects that communication might have. We do not vote for a candidate or want a date or decide to watch a TV program for no reason; we do these things at least in part because of the communications we have encountered.

Before pursuing this question of effects we need to offer at least two qualifications. First, any bit of behavior or any cognitive change is brought about by a number of differnt factors. No matter how brilliant or how thorough our analysis may be, we will never be able to determine all the causes of any given effect. So we cannot know exactly what part communication contributed to any given effect. We do know that communication makes a difference but we cannot always be sure what that difference is or with what other causes the communication may have interacted.

Second, we need to get a clearer idea of the nature of the audience or receiver. In the early years of communication theory, during World War I when the world was so frightened by even the thought of propaganda, the audience was viewed as a rather passive mass into which communications would be poured and out of which would come the desired effects. The audience was seen as uncritical, never passing judgment on any of the ideas contained in the communications. It was an unselective audience which took in all and only that which the communicators wanted it to take in. This view of the audience was overly simplistic and unrealistic. It pictured the audience as mindless bodies ready to do as the communicator bid. This view was not too different from the view many had of the "audiences" of "brainwashing" who we felt were helpless to resist the directives of their captors.

Our present view of the audience is 180° removed from this early view. Today we see the audience of communication as "obstinate," as Raymond Bauer put it. The audience is critical and selective, and this is true, I think, for an interpersonal receiver as well as for a mass audience. It is not a passive but an active part of the communication process and performs not only receiver functions but source functions as well. This obstinate audience sends out information, just like a source does, and this information or feedback is effective in altering the messages of the source.

Thus in viewing communication effects we must recognize that effects are not easy to separate and that when a message is received by an audience that audience works actively with the message, making the message received very different from the message sent. It selects what it feels is useful and rejects what it feels is useless. The same message, received by very different audiences, will in effect be different messages.

DIFFICULTIES IN DETERMINING EFFECTS AND CAUSES

The student of interpersonal communication who attempts to study effects needs first to recognize at least some of the difficulties involved in determining communications effects and causes.

Discovering Long-Range Effects

Although many communications have effects that are immediate or that at least occur close enough in time to the actual communication for us to connect the two, there are many instances in which the communication does not have any observable immediate effect but does have an effect after a considerable lapse in time. For example, you may have a talk with a friend now without seeming to experience any great effects from it. Yet years later, when you are in a different situation, the message of that talk might affect your behavior and your attitudes greatly. Similarly, you may sit in a course in small group communication without being noticeably affected, at least not immediately. A year later, however, you may find yourselves appointed leader of a task-oriented group and all the seemingly abstract concepts and experiments may come back to exert considerable influence on your present behavior.

This type of delayed effect presents problems for anyone concerned with attempting to discover and analyze communication effects. If we attempt to discover communication effects and do not find any, we *cannot* conclude that there were no effects. Significant effects may manifest themselves months or even years later.

Isolating the Message

Communications are being received every second of our lives; with our eyes we are talking in all sorts of visual messages; with our ears we are hearing noises from other people, from radio, from television, from cars; with our skin we are constantly perceiving tactile messages. In short, we are always receiving messages and their impact is being recorded, at times with awareness and at times without awareness. Given this state of affairs it becomes extremely difficult to take any given effect—say a commitment to vote a particular way or a favorable attitude toward a fellow student or antagonism for a colleague—and isolate *the* message that led to this effect. Effects are always multiply determined; no effect is produced by a single cause. Similarly, no communication effect is produced by a single message. The effects of communication are often cumulative—much like the straws on the proverbial camel's back. At some point the camel may be observed to break down. Similarly, at some point the effect of communication becomes observable. The previous straws or messages were having effects but were simply unobservable. When the camel's back breaks we cannot attribute this to the one straw nor can we attribute some behavioral effect to the one preceding message. All the straws and all the messages contributed to the final effect.

Accounting for the Interaction Among Messages

Closely related to this problem of immediate and delayed effects of messages is the concept of interaction among messages. Because we are forever receiving stimuli from all our senses, any given stimulus interacts with other stimuli. Its effect, therefore, is largely dependent upon other stimuli with which it interacts. For example, if you have your hand in water of 200° and then place it in water of 100°, the 100° water will seem cold. But if your hand was first in 35° water and then in 100° water, your hand would perceive the 100° water as warm. The water is the same 100°, but your perception of it differs greatly from one situation to another. The effect that the water has depends upon past experiences. The stimulus (the water) interacts with another stimulus (for example, the water that your hand was in, the 200° and the 35° water) and its effect is dependent in part at least by the interaction with these other stimuli.

Assume that you are watching television and a commercial comes on advocating periodic heart examinations. To the viewer whose father recently died of a heart attack that message is going to be interpreted quite differently from the viewer who has not had such experiences. The commercial, in other words, interacts with previous messages stored by the individual and it therefore becomes extremely difficult to determine which effect was caused by which message. In fact, the messages interact.

Where one leaves off and another begins is extremely difficult if not impossible to determine.

Measuring Instruments

Perhaps the most obvious difficulty in discovering the effects of communication is the problem of measuring instruments. Given a message, how do we go about determining if it had an effect. Most of the time we can observe nothing happening in the receiver of any communication. Students, for example, sit in a college classroom and are, hopefully, influenced by the messages of the instructor. But often the students do nothing to indicate that these messages are having an effect.

There are many ways we can go about measuring effects. We can, in the case of college students, give tests and hope that these measure the effects of the communications they were expected to expose themselves to, for example, the instructor's lectures and the textbook readings. Or, in the case of persuasive messages, we can give the receivers attitude tests before and after the message to note if any changes took place. Or, of course, the most obvious method is simply to observe the behavior of the individuals. But, as already indicated, this is often difficult and at times impossible.

Sources

The best introduction to communication effects and one I relied on heavily is Wilbur Schramm, *Men, Messages, and Media: A Look at Human Communication* (New York: Harper & Row, 1973). For a consideration of effects from a mass communication point of view see Joseph Klapper, *The Effects of Mass Communication* (New York: Free Press, 1960). The concept of the obstinate audience is best explained by Raymond A. Bauer, "The Obstinate Audience," *American Psychologist* 19 (May 1964):319–328. A general introduction to the nature of audiences may be found in Paul D. Holtzman's *The Psychology of Speaker's Audiences* (Chicago, Ill.: Scott, Foresman, 1970) and in Theodore Clevenger's *Audience Analysis* (Indianapolis: Bobbs-Merrill, 1966).

Experiential Vehicles

SELF-CONCEPT: PART II

Following these instructions is a set of semantic differential scales, identical to the ones you filled out at the beginning of the term. Fill in these scales now.

ME

Happy	___:___:___:___:___:___	Sad
Positive	___:___:___:___:___:___	Negative
Healthy	___:___:___:___:___:___	Sick
Strong	___:___:___:___:___:___	Weak
Beautiful	___:___:___:___:___:___	Ugly
Honest	___:___:___:___:___:___	Dishonest
Good	___:___:___:___:___:___	Bad
Self-Confident	___:___:___:___:___:___	Not Self-Confident
Active	___:___:___:___:___:___	Passive
Interesting	___:___:___:___:___:___	Boring
Graceful	___:___:___:___:___:___	Awkward
Elegant	___:___:___:___:___:___	Uncouth
Pleasant	___:___:___:___:___:___	Unpleasant
Powerful	___:___:___:___:___:___	Powerless
Fast	___:___:___:___:___:___	Slow
Up	___:___:___:___:___:___	Down
Clean	___:___:___:___:___:___	Dirty
Kind	___:___:___:___:___:___	Cruel
Successful	___:___:___:___:___:___	Unsuccessful
Sociable	___:___:___:___:___:___	Unsociable
Moral	___:___:___:___:___:___	Immoral
Realistic	___:___:___:___:___:___	Unrealistic
Optimistic	___:___:___:___:___:___	Pessimistic
Brave	___:___:___:___:___:___	Cowardly
Organized	___:___:___:___:___:___	Disorganized

The scales you completed at the beginning of the term should now be recovered and compared with the scales you just completed. Examine carefully all the differences. Differences of two or three scale positions are generally significant and bear special attention.

Recall here the difficulties in determining effects and their causes, for example, the problem in discovering long-range effects, the difficulty in isolating the message, the problems in accounting for the interaction among messages, and the fallibility of the measuring instruments. With this in mind, which of the changes do you think are real and signficant changes?

It is important to recognize that changes do not just happen. Instead, they happen because of something and this something is what we should attempt to discover. Therefore, for each change you feel is significant and real attempt to determine the causes. Jot down any notes you wish here and in groups of five or six discuss these changes. Feedback from other group members concerning these changes should be free and honest and should be welcomed by each member. Again, it is wise to recall the five characteristics of effective interpersonal communication: openness, empathy, supportiveness, positiveness, and equality.

1. What is the nature of the change?

2. Why is it assumed that this change is real?

3. How is this change manifested? Do you act differently as a result of the change?

4. Do other people notice the change in you? Here feedback from the group members is especially important. (Of course, it is possible that real changes cannot be seen by this group.)

5. What were the causes of these changes? (*Note:* Look for cause*s*, not for a cause. All behavior and all changes are multiply caused.)

6. What role do you feel this course and your experiences in it played in these changes? Be as specific as possible.

POSITIVE WORDS

This exercise is performed by the entire class. One person is "it" and takes a seat in the front of the room or in the center of the circle. (It is possible, though not desirable, for the person to stay where he or she normally sits.) Going around in a circle or from left to right, each person says something positive about the person who is "it."

Note: For this exercise only volunteers should be chosen. Students may be encouraged but should not be forced to participate. Although this exercise is perhaps more appropriate to the content of the earlier units, it is best done when the students know each other fairly well. For this reason, it is put here.

Persons must tell the truth, that is, they are not allowed to say anything about the person that they do not believe. At the same time, however, all statements must be positive. Only positive words are allowed during this exercise. Persons may, however, "pass" and say nothing. No one may ask why something was said or why something was not said. The positive words may refer to the person's looks, behavior, intelligence, clothes, mannerisms, and so on. One may also say, "I don't know you very well but you seem friendly" or "You seem honest" or whatever. These statements, too, must be believed to be true.

After everyone has said something, another person becomes "it."

After all volunteers have been "it" respond to the following questions individually:

1. Describe your feelings when thinking about becoming "it."

2. How did you feel while people were saying positive words?

3. What comments were the most significant to you?

4. Would you be willing to be "it" again?

5. How do you feel now that the exercise is over? Did it make you feel better? Why do you suppose it had the effect it did?

6. What implications may be drawn from this exercise for application to everyday living?

7. Will this exercise change your behavior in any way?

After you have completed all these questions, share with the entire class whatever comments you would like to.

This exercise was suggested by Diane Shore.

unit 41

Types and Limits of Interpersonal Communication Effects

Types of Effects
Limiting Variables
   Effects of the Course

Objectives

Upon completion of this unit, you should be able to:

1. define and give examples of *cognitive effects*, *affective effects*, and *psychomotor effects*
2. diagram and explain the model of communication effects
3. explain the limiting variables of *duration, intensity, significance, time orientation, value,* and *spread* on interpersonal communication effects

To learn something, to feel something, to be able to do something are all effects of communication. But they are different types of effects. An understanding of these different types should further clarify the nature of interpersonal communication effects. Similarly, we need to look into the limiting variables, that is, those variables that qualify the type of effect and determine how one effect may differ from another effect. For example, two affective changes may be brought about by communication but one of these changes lasts a long time while the other fades in a short time. Thus this time factor, or duration, is a limiting variable. Here we consider six limiting variables: *duration, intensity, significance, time orientation, value,* and *spread.*

TYPES OF EFFECTS

Borrowing the divisions of behavior from instructional development research, we may distinguish three general classes of communication effects: *cognitive effects, affective effects*, and *psychomotor effects*.

Cognitive Effects

Cognitive effects include those consequences of communication that we might think of as intellectual or "cerebral." Perhaps the most obvious example is the acquistion of information or new knowledge. For example, by reading the next few sentences, this communication (that is, the messages that are written down on this page) should have a cognitive effect on you by providing you with information you did not have before: 1) The largest residential palace in the world is the Vatican Palace. 2) The longest sentence in Western literature was written by Victor Hugo and contains 823 words with 93 commas, 51 semicolons, and 4 dashes. 3) The country with the highest female to male ratio is the USSR having 1,171 females to every 1,000 males. 4) The most expensive car ever made was the Presidential 1969 Lincoln Continental Executive which cost a total of $500,000 to research, develop, and manufacture. 5) The largest nudist colony is located in Indiana and covers some 386 acres.

These bits of information, thanks to the *Guinness Book of World Records*, are probably new to most readers and so the messages would have an effect (assuming that the sentences were comprehended) in changing the cognitive domain.

Cognitive effects need not be limited to isolated bits of information. They would also include, for example, knowledge concerning how to apply something, how to analyze, how to synthesize, how to evaluate.

Cognitive effects would be the type emphasized in many classrooms. In fact, not so long ago it was thought that the only type of effect that education should be concerned with was the cognitive. Now it is realized that education must include not only the cognitive but the affective and the psychomotor domains as well.

It should not be thought that cognitive effects are completely separate and distinct from affective or psychomotor effects. It would be difficult if not impossible to acquire some psychomotor skill without there being at least some cognitive and/or affective dimension to it.

Affective Effects

Affective effects include those consequences of communication that we would call emotional or attitudinal or psychological. This class comprises an amazingly large number of specific types of effects.

One of the principal affective effects is that of initiating, establishing, and maintaining relationships with other human beings. In many lists of the purposes of speech or communication, this particular function is often omitted, although persuasion, propaganda, and advertising are given great attention. For some reason many teachers and researchers hesitate to talk about this kind of interpersonal communication effect, but clearly it is among the most important.

As soon as we perceive an individual we start to receive messages from this person, whether he or she is trying to communicate with us or not. The way the person dresses, the way the person stands, the way the person looks at us or avoids us—all communicate something to us. Similarly, our responses to these messages—which we cannot not make—communicate back to this person. A relationship has been at least initiated. It may even be that this relationship was initiated so that one of the parties might let the other party know that it is not a relationship that will continue. Once initiated, communication is necessary to establish a relationship, to let each person know that a relationship is desired. And of course communication is necessary if the relationship is to be maintained and developed.

Thus interpersonal relationships are started, built, and maintained through communication, and, they are broken down largely through communication. We can communicate love, affection, and passion as well as we can communicate hate, hostility, and indifference. We can promise undying love and we can swear vengeance.

The role of communication in establishing relationships is a particularly difficult one to analyze, especially in our culture. Men, for example, are not allowed to verbalize affection for each other although women can, and, of course, men may verbalize affection for women and women for men. And so affection between men is communicated nonverbally, a rough arm around the shoulder, a gentle punch on the chin, a tight squeeze of the hand or arm, and so on. Even with women, men are supposed to be less demonstrative in verbalizing affection. Women are permitted the "luxury" of stating their affection openly. Similarly, the very young and the very old are permitted to verbalize affection more than are the middle aged.

The strictures on communication that is designed to establish relationships are rigid and plentiful, and yet we all wish to and need to establish close relationship with others. Although we may at times want to be alone and actually resent encroachments on our time and space, we nevertheless wish to have at least some close relationships with other human beings.

Another affective effect is enjoyment, simple selfish enjoyment. We talk to ourselves largely for purposes of enjoyment; we sing and daydream largely for enjoyment.

Perhaps the most important class of affective effects is that of changes in our attitudes, beliefs, and values. Whenever we expose ourselves to communications we are in effect putting our existing attitudes, beliefs, and values on the line with the chance that they may be changed, modified, or even destroyed. Or they may be strengthened.

Psychomotor Effects

Perhaps the major effects of communication are behavioral ones. One obvious type of effect is that of training in a particular skill and the improvement of that skill. Through communication we might learn to fix a motor, develop a picture, or ask for a date. Our skills can be developed and changed through some instructional type of communication.

Other behavioral effects would be grouped under social behavior or etiquette. Through communication we learn how to behave in various social situations. Through a general process of reward and punishment we learn what to talk about, how to talk, and (sometimes) when to talk.

But the major type of effect is that on our general behavior—that is, on what we do. It is through communications that we eventually buy the products we buy, for example. Billions of dollars a year are put into advertising; although we sit back and say that these ridiculous commercials have no effects, they apparently do have effects. It is also largely through communications that we make a commitment to a cause and fight or march or sit in or protest.

We might view these three types of changes as steps or stages in the process of communication effects. The general process of communication and its effects may be diagrammed as in Figure 41.1.

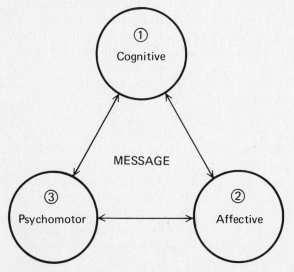

Figure 41.1 *A Model of Communication Effects*

We may begin with the assumption that a message has been sent and that it has been attended to and heard by the receiver. At Step 1 in the process of effects the message produces some kind of cognitive change in the receiver. The message might provide new information or some type of synthesis of existing information. In either case the message exerts some change in the cognitive or thinking or intellectual dimension.

At Step 2 we have some kind of affective change. The message might be enjoyed or might change some existing attitude or belief. Such affective change seems usually to be brought about on the basis of new information received at Step 1. For example, at Step 1 certain facts about a person are learned and at Step 2 the attitudes toward that person change.

Note, however, that as illustrated in Figure 41.1 Steps 1 and 2 are actually interrelated and influence each other (illustrated by the arrow going in both directions). In most instances these steps are interrelated to such an extent that it is difficult if not impossible to determine which came first.

It is important to observe that often changes at one step induce changes at another step. Thus, for example, if at Step 1 we learned certain facts about an individual and at Step 2 we change our attitude toward him or her, further changes at Step 1 might follow as a result of the Step 2 changes, for example, a revised evaluation of the individual and perhaps a decision to vote for him or her in the next election. This decision-making process (Step 1) might then again alter our affective state (Step 2). Deciding to support someone for election, for example, will often result in a more positive attitude toward that person.

At Step 3 we have psychomotor effects or behavioral change. In the example already cited this might involve such changes as talking with people who are supporting this candidate or perhaps the actual act of voting this particular ticket. Overt behavioral action (Step 3) will of course influence our cognitive (Step 1) and affective states (Step 2). If, for example, we actively campaign for someone we will as a result become more positive in our attitude toward this individual. So there is constant transaction throughout the model.

The steps as illustrated and numbered in the diagram seem to be in the order normally followed. Generally, there seems to be a cognitive change followed by an affective change followed by a psychomotor change. Needless to say, this does not always happen. In many instances affective change comes first—we enjoy something and only later come to understand it or evaluate it. And of course we might behave in a certain way first and only later come to have an affective or cognitive response to it. As with so many areas of communication, here too we need to qualify our rather simple model with the caution that interpersonal communication effects are not linear and do not always follow the same pattern.

Further, the interaction among the various steps, which should not be viewed as discrete stages but rather as fluid exchanges, makes it impossible to predict with certainty the effect any given communication message may have.

LIMITING VARIABLES

The effects of communication—that is, the changes that communication produces or leads to—need to be viewed in terms of a number of limiting variables. Any communication effect may differ from any other communication effect in at least the following ways: *duration, intensity, significance, time orientation, value* and *spread.*

Duration

At a very obvious level the changes produced by communication vary in terms of their *duration.* Effects are not usually forever; they vary in terms of durability. Although the effects could range all the way from a momentary change to a lifelong change; most changes fall in between these two extremes. For the most part we may distinguish between short- and long-term effects.

Talking with people at a party or at some social gathering usually has but short-term effects; what they say and who they are influence us during the time we are communicating with them but seldom are there lasting effects. But then that certain someone comes along and the effect is a longer lasting one. Lifetime conversions have also been brought about through interpersonal communication. A brief conversation may often determine a career pursued, a person married, a crime committed, a political course of action followed.

Important in this connection is the concept of self-motivation. Suppose that a student talks with a teacher he or she admires and decides, as a result, to become a college teacher. So the student fills out the necessary applications, gets accepted to graduate school, completes the degree, and takes a job as a college teacher—a job he or she keeps until retirement.

We my trace the decision to become a college teacher to the student's conversation with his or her own teacher. But we cannot really be certain that that conversation was the beginning. Other experiences during the student's life have prepared the student in certain ways; perhaps the conversation with the teacher was only the most clearly identifiable stimulus. Further, experiences after the conversation have had an effect. Had this student experienced numerous failures in graduate school or unpleasant experiences during the first year of teaching he or she might have changed the career decision.

Intensity

Communication effects vary in terms of *intensity* or strength. At times the effects of a communication may be relatively mild; at other times the effect may be of great intensity. We may be persuaded, for example, to switch toothpaste; behavior is changed but there is no really intense effect. For most people, the brand of toothpaste they use is relatively insignificant. On the other hand, we may be persuaded to fight in a war, to vote "guilty" in a jury deliberation, or to say "I do." For communications to result in these behaviors, their effects must be relatively intense.

The intensity of any communication effect is not necessarily obvious to any of the individuals involved. A seemingly minor incident during childhood may leave an impression so intense as to influence sexual development, ability to love, or need for approval. Similarly, a communication that brings on a seemingly intense effect, perhaps an outbreak of crying and screaming, may have little lasting effect and may, in a few hours, be all but forgotten.

Thus the intensity of any given effect is not something that can be determined by the initial impact or the observable impact, nor is it something that can be determined by the length of time for which the effect is influential. A communication may change our toothpaste-buying behavior forever not because it was necessarily intense but merely because it established a habit, which became self-perpetuating. On the other hand, a communication may lead us to kill another human being and then be forgotten.

Significance

The importance of the effect or change may vary from extremely significant to extremely insignificant. This particular variable may be looked at from many different points of view. From the point of view of the individual affected, significance may mean one thing; to the parents of a child affected, significance may mean quite another thing; and to the child's teacher, significance may mean something else again. Any given communication effect may vary greatly in significance and this significance may be defined differently by different people.

As with other variables it is not easy to tell the extent of the significance of any communication effect. For example, a president may set down a policy which seems relatively minor, a kind of insignificant formality. Years later, however, that seemingly minor statement or policy might become a doctrine that influences the entire world. Examples of this should not be hard to find in any history text.

Time Orientation

Everything happens in the present. The future can only be envisioned and the past can only be remembered. It is the present in which we live and will always live our lives—now, 10 minutes from now, 10 years from now. All our time is present time. And yet the past and the future are very real to us. We are influenced by our past and we are influenced by the way in which we see or plan for our future.

Communication effects, then, may influence us only in the present and yet may themselves refer to the past or to the present or to the future. At a very basic level we may be influenced by a communication to continue reading this page or to stop reading it or to throw the book on the floor. Thus some communications would influence our present behavior and refer to the present.

But communications may also refer to the past; they alter our view of the past, and in turn they influence us in the present and influence our expectations and plans for the future. For example, we might learn about some actions of our parents in the past or about some secret affair our boyfriend or girlfriend had in the past or about how a political leader committed certain acts before entering politics. These new bits of information change our present behaviors and perhaps our expectations and plans for the future.

Similarly, communication effects might refer to the future but they influence the present. The person who is told that he or she will die within six months will probably live a very different present from the person who is told that he or she will live another 50 years. The present behavior of college students is influenced by communications referring to the future as when, for example, they are told that better jobs are available to persons who have a college degree or to persons with a specific major.

Communications may refer to any point in time and still have an effect on present behavior, attitudes, and values.

Value

Communication may have positive effects, and it may have negative effects. Communications may influence us to live a happy and healthy life, or they may influence us to kill or hate—or anything in between.

What constitutes positive and negative is not easy to determine; probably no one answer will suffice. The military training officer who influences people to kill the "enemy" before they can turn around may view these communications and their effects as positive. To the officer such messages are designed to train an individual in survival, which is regarded as a positive good. To someone else, however, killing is not justifiable and therefore to train someone to kill can only produce a negative effect.

The difficulty of determining what is positive and what is negative must not, however, lead us to conclude that communications and their effects should not be looked upon as having a value dimension. Quite the contrary. The positive-negative dimension of communication and of any and all of its effects must always be recognized and evaluated carefully and thoroughly.

Spread

The effect of any given communication may be relatively circumscribed and limited to a particular action or particular attitude or it may be relatively wide ranging, covering general behaviors and attitudes toward numerous and different persons and objects.

For example, we might have learned when we were young about the value of working hard for what we want. Through whatever means we might imagine, we were taught that hard work was good and something we should always engage in if we wanted to succeed. Throughout our growing up we might have internalized this work ethic to the point where it now influences our behavior in almost every aspect we can think of; it influences how hard we play basketball, how hard we study, how hard we work driving a cab, and so on. The effect of these communications, then, may be said to be almost universal; that is, they have influenced us in almost everything we do.

Communication effects may also be limited. We may have been influenced to read a particular book or to watch a particular program or to date a particular individual. But after the book is read, the program over, and the date finished the effect of the communication for all intents and purposes disappears. Of course, we must at the same time recognize that we cannot easily be sure that these effects are limited. Perhaps reading the book will have a profound effect on us, the television program might convince us to major in television production, and the date might prove to be someone we eventually marry. In other instances the effects might be present but not visible or observable. We might for example be influenced to read a particular book, which we enjoy. This enjoyment or reinforcement might then make us book lovers and avid readers. Whether it would be fair to trace our new avocation to the initial communication urging us to read a particular book is something we might attempt to analyze but not something we could easily determine with certainty.

Sources

The discussion of the types of communication effects utilizes the classification of behavioral objectives instruction. Particularly valuable here is Robert J. Kibler, Donald J. Cegala, Larry L. Barker, and David T. Miles, *Objectives for Instruction and Evaluation* (Boston: Allyn and Bacon, 1974). Any recent work on behavioral objectives will provide adequate discussion of cognitive, affective, and psychomotor effects.

Discussion of the limiting variables may be found in any of the better and more recent texts on persuasion. Particularly recommended are: Gary Cronkhite, *Persuasion: Speech and Behavioral Change* (Indianapolis: Bobbs-Merrill, 1969); Erwin P. Bettinghaus, *Persuasive Communication*, 2d ed. (New York: Holt, 1973); Kenneth E. Andersen, *Persuasion: Theory and Practice* (Boston: Allyn and Bacon, 1971); and Wayne N. Thompson, *The Process of Persuasion* (New York: Harper & Row, 1975).

Experiential Vehicle

EFFECTS OF THE COURSE

The purpose of this exercise is to explore some of the effects (cognitive, affective, and psychomotor) of this course on you.

Complete the accompanying chart which asks that you list at least five cognitive, five affective, and five psychomotor effects that the course has had on you. (If this proves difficult, reread the unit.) In the right-hand columns, indicate how long you think these effects will last (duration), how intense they are (intensity), how significant they are (significance), to what time the effects refer (time orientation), of what value the effects are (value), and what type of spread they might have (spread).

These results may be discussed with the class as a whole or your instructor may simply ask that they be turned in without extensive class discussion.

	Duration	Intensity	Significance	Time	Value	Spread
Cognitive Effects 1.						
2.						
3.						
4.						
5.						

	Duration	Intensity	Significance	Time	Value	Spread
Affective Effects						
1.						
2.						
3.						
4.						
5.						
Psychomotor Effects						
1.						
2.						
3.						
4.						
5.						

unit 42
Measuring the Effects of Interpersonal Communication

Reliability and Validity
Observing the Behavior
Rating the Behavior
Measuring Interpersonal Communication Effects

Objectives

Upon completion of this unit, you should be able to:

1. define *reliability* and *validity*
2. state at least four problems that observing behavior presents to valid and reliable measurement
3. define *cloze procedure*
4. state the two purposes of cloze procedure
5. explain how cloze procedure is used
6. define *semantic differentiation*
7. state the three dimensions of meaning measured in semantic differentiation, and give at least two examples of appropriate scales for each dimension of meaning
8. explain how the semantic differential is used

RELIABILITY AND VALIDITY

In attempting to gauge or measure the effects of communications two problems should be kept in mind. These are the problems of *reliability* and *validity*.

Reliability refers to the degree of agreement that can be obtained from a number of different observers or evaluators. A measuring instrument is reliable if on repeated application it would yield the same results. For example, if you had a fever and took your temperature with a thermometer, a reliable thermometer would give you essentially the same readings on repeated applications. An unreliable thermometer would give you very different readings.

In estimating the value of a measuring instrument we are particularly concerned with the reliability. There would be little value in using an instrument that would tell the first observer one thing, the second observer something else, the third observer something still different, and so on.

The second problem is that of validity. *Validity* refers to the degree to which the observation or instrument measures what it is supposed to measure. If we are interested in temperature there would be little point in using an instrument that measures heart rate. The instrument may of course be perfectly valid for measuring heart rate. Note that the instrument for measuring heart rate, when applied to measuring temperature, might yield essentially the same scores with each application and hence be of high reliability; but it would obviously still not be valid for measuring temperature. In the physical sciences questions of validity are much easier to answer; a thermometer measures temperature in a highly valid manner. But in the behavioral sciences we work with concepts that are not so easily quantifiable and for which valid instruments are not so easy to find. For example, how can we validly measure cooperation? Competition? Persuasiveness? Teaching effectiveness?

One of the issues being debated on many college campuses is that of teacher evaluations. Generally, standardized tests are used on which students will indicate what they think of the teachers' ability to present material clearly, to encourage independent thinking, to act democratically, and so on. One of the arguments that many people raise against such instruments is that of validity, that is, do these standardized tests measure teaching effectiveness or do they measure other things—whether a teacher is well liked or disliked, or whether he or she is friendly or unfriendly, or whether the student is getting a high or a low grade.

One of the most persistent validity problems centers on intelligence tests. Some claim that they provide valid measures of intelligence. Others claim that they do not measure intelligence so much as they reflect cultural upbringing. The questions on intelligence tests, they claim, are phrased so that the middle-class child has the advantage over the lower-class child. To be valid, intelligence tests should not favor one group over another, since they claim to measure something that is uninfluenced by social class.

No instrument or observational method for measuring communication effects is completely reliable or completely valid. The perfect method or

instrument has not been devised. We have to be content with varying degrees of success. With this qualification in mind, we need to examine the two general ways of determining the effects of communication.

OBSERVING THE BEHAVIOR

As a teacher, for example, it is necessary that I attempt to gauge the effects of the communications occurring in the classroom. If someone looks bored, I may conclude that I am not having the effect that I want to have and consequently might try to change my behavior. On the other hand, if students are sitting on the edge of their seats, their eyes wide open, and perfectly quiet, I may conclude that they are concentrating on my messages and that I am having the effect I want to have. Or take the case of the advertiser. The product that the advertiser is in charge of is not doing well, and so it is decided to change the image of the product completely. Where once the image of the product was that of an old person's drink, now an attempt is being made to have it appeal to the young. After some time, the advertiser might look at the sales of the product to determine if they went up or down and perhaps look at the breakdown of the sales according to age of consumers. In each case we are focusing on the actual behavior.

This all *seems* very simple. Unfortunately, it is not so easy to ascertain the effects of communications. With these examples in mind, we need now to look into some of the reasons why observing behavior presents problems and what some of these problems are.

Observer Competency

It is generally assumed that everyone is capable of observing behavior, and certainly that is true. But not everyone is capable of observing behavior and drawing appropriate or logical inferences from their observations. Assume for a moment that I was to observe the effects of instructional directions on a student's ability to diaper a baby. If I do not know anything about diapering a baby I would have no way of gauging the effects of the instructor's message on the student. Even though I could observe the student's behavior, I would have no way of ascertaining whether he or she correctly followed the instructions.

One of the more unpleasant tasks of some teachers is to observe their colleagues in the process of teaching and to comment on their perform-ance, in effect to evaluate the effects of their messages on the students. One of the items that teachers are told to look for is the extent to which the teacher encourages original thought in the students. Another is to look for the extent to which the teacher motivates the students to learn. Now given these instructions, what does the observer look for in the

behavior of the students to determine whether they are engaging in "original thought" or whether they have been "motivated to learn." Although some observers might be able to do this, many observers would not be able to; it would be beyond their level of competency.

Observer Bias

One of the greatest problems in observing the effects of communication is that the observer will often have biases which will influence what he or she sees and the inferences drawn from what is seen. If I observe another teacher in class, I can readily see looks of boredom on the faces of the students. The interesting thing is that I do not see them on students in my own classes. Although I like to think this is due to the fact that my classes are interesting, I must realize that it may be due to the fact that I am simply not seeing what students are really expressing. Similarly, if students are talking among themselves in another class it is easy to conclude that the class is boring and that the teacher is not maintaining their interest. If that same behavior occurs in my class, it is very easy to assume that I have stimulated them so much that they simply must talk among themselves about their new-found insights. Note what happens in classes of well-liked and disliked teachers. Both teachers can do essentially the same thing and yet the inferences drawn from the behaviors may be completely different.

The Effects of Observation

One of the most familiar arguments against observation as a method of measuring or gauging the effects of communications is that the presence of the observer influences what happens. For example, a teacher who is observed, say by the chairperson of the department, is not likely to perform the way he or she normally performs. The observer, simply by being present, influences what he or she is observing. After observing one class recently, students told me that that was the first interesting class that they had had all semester. The instructor was obviously influenced by having me there and taught a class that was not at all typical. It must also be realized that the observer cannot change the situation entirely. A teacher cannot fake an ability to answer questions, for example, nor could he or she fake the ability to lecture coherently.

Interpreting Behavior

Another problem is determining what inferences we draw from the behavior that is observed. How do we interpret the behavior? For example, we observe a class in which there are numerous questions from the

students. As the teacher is lecturing, hands are waving all over the place. What do we conclude from this? Do we conclude that the class was stimulating? Confusing? So dull that the students had to say something? So incorrect that the students had to correct the teacher? Thus given the behavior, what do we make of it? At times there is little difficulty. At other times, however, such inferences are little more than guesses.

Behavioral Units

Assume that we are to observe a small group communication situation, particularly the degree to which members cooperate with one another. How do we do this? What behaviors do we focus on that will enable us to make inferences concerning cooperation? Do we look at the number of smiles? The number of times agreement is expressed? The number of times compliments are exchanged?

How would we attempt to measure the degree to which a teacher stimulates thought? What do we focus on? We can easily measure the financial success of a movie simply by counting the number of people who pay admission to see it. But how would we measure its effect on an audience? Count the number of laughs? Screams? Expressions of satisfaction?

RATING THE BEHAVIOR

At times it may be impractical or even impossible to observe the actual behavior and so we may attempt to investigate the effects of communication through some pencil and paper test or what might generally be called *rating instruments.* Two of the more popular types of rating instruments used and some of the problems they raise are noted here.

Cloze Procedure

Suppose that you wish to investigate the degree to which your message was understood by a particular audience. Such a question would be potentially significant to, for example, advertisers who wanted to test a number of different approaches to selling their product and who wanted to be sure that their messages would be understood. Or perhaps you might be interested in determining if reading this text had any effect on your understanding of additional communications-oriented messages. So here we might take two groups, one who read this text and one who did not and then test to see if there were any differences in the ability to understand messages dealing with interpersonal communication theory.

One method we might use is *cloze procedure.* "Cloze" is derived from the Gestalt notion of closure and refers to our tendency to close or complete that which is in reality incomplete. For example, it is our tendency to see an incomplete circle as a complete one simply because the concept of circle is so familiar to us. Similarly, we can easily complete such sentences as 1) ''A triangle has three angles and three ———.'' 2) ''The old ——— kissed his wife.'' 3) ''The soldier ——— the flag as it passed the reviewing stand.'' Sentences such as these are relatively easy to fill in. Note that our ability to fill in such sentences does not depend on our knowledge of triangles, old people, or soldiers—at least not entirely. A large portion of our ability to fill in the correct responses depends on our knowledge of English structure and vocabulary. For example, in the first sentence we say *sides;* note that we do not say *side.* In the second sentence we say *man,* not *men* and not *woman.* And in the third sentence we say *saluted* rather than *salute.* In the first sentence ''three'' cues us to the plural, in the second ''his'' and ''wife'' cue us to a masculine noun, in the third, ''passed'' cues us to a past tense verb.

In cloze procedure this basic principle is utilized. Generally, a passage is mutilated by deleting every nth word, every fifth word, for example. Receivers attempt to fill in the word they think belongs in the blank based on the context that remains. Every correct response counts as one cloze point.

Cloze procedure is used for two general purposes. First, it is used to measure the readability or listenability of a passage. The more correct fill-ins the easier the passage is to understand. Second, it is used as a measure of comprehension. After hearing a lecture, a portion of that very lecture might be presented to the audience in cloze procedure form. The extent to which people are able to fill in the original words is a measure of the extent to which they understood the original message.

Semantic Differentiation

Perhaps the most often used rating instrument in the entire area of communication is the semantic differential. A semantic differential consists of a series of seven-point, bipolar scales, for example:

good ———:———:———:———:———:———:——— bad

Subjects are presented with a series of scales and a concept which they are to rate on the scales. A semantic differential makes use of three general dimensions of meaning: *evaluation,* measured by such scales as good-bad, positive-negative, healthy-unhealthy; *potency,* measured by such scales as strong-weak, heavy-light; and *activity,* measured by such scales as fast-slow, active-passive, dynamic-static.

Very often the semantic differential is used as an attitude test in which case only the evaluative dimension is used. The semantic differential might be useful if we were interested in taking before and after measures of attitude; that is, we might measure a person's attitude toward "legalized marijuana" before presenting him or her with a specific message relevant to marijuana. Then the message would be presented, and then the post-test—another form of the semantic differential—would be administered. In this way we would be able to measure the type and extent of change that took place as a result of the message.

These are just two general methods for evaluating or measuring the effects of communication. We could simply design questions and do essentially what a teacher would do in designing an examination. Teachers attempt to write questions that will enable them to measure the effects of their messages on you as a student. Teachers might ask essay-type questions, which are easier to design but difficult to grade, or they might use short-answer questions, which are difficult to design but easy to grade.

Problems in Using Rating Instruments

One of the most obvious questions in using rating instruments, such as the semantic differential or in fact any pencil and paper test of attitude, is to what extent are we really measuring attitude. And once we have answered that, we need to ask to what extent attitude enables us to say something about behavior. Suppose that the person in the example used earlier responds more favorably to the concept "legalized marijuana" after hearing the message. Does this mean that his or her behavior will now be different? Does it mean that he or she will vote for legalization or that he or she will still vote against it?

We would also have to wonder to what extent people are even aware of their attitudes. To what extent can they put their attitudes down on paper. Similarly, to what extent will people be honest about their atti- tudes, especially when they concern controversial subjects?

While cloze procedure might be able to measure essentially what a comprehension test can measure, we would want to ask to what extent a receiver can gain a great deal from a message and yet not have this reflected in the score. For example, you might listen to a lecture and because of something said get a real brainstorm; then your mind wanders off and creates something which you value a great deal. Yet this would never be measured by the cloze score or by any conventional tests.

The important point is that although these instruments have high reliability, we still need to ask to what extent they measure what they say they measure. That is, to what extent are they valid? There are problems and difficulties with estimating the effects of com-

munication. Observing behavior directly has advantages and disadvantages. Similarly, using various scales and pencil and paper tests have advantages and disadvantages. What should be clear is that the effects of communication need to be assessed, despite the difficulties involved, if valid and reliable principles of communication are to be developed.

One important message is simply this: If we want to find out the effect of a particular message we should attempt to measure it and not rely on some predigested statement which tells us—or purports to tell us—what is and what is not effective.

Sources

The problems of measuring communication effects are largely the problems of determining effects of stimuli generally. Therefore any good research methodology book will provide insight into the relevant issues. Particularly recommended is Fred N. Kerlinger's *Foundations of Behavioral Research: Educational and Psychological Inquiry*, 2d ed. (New York: Holt, 1973). In this text Kerlinger also considers specific research methods, such as the semantic differential. Also see Frank S. Freeman, *Theory and Practice of Psychological Testing*, 3d ed. (New York: Holt, 1964) for specific research methods. Both the semantic differential and cloze procedure, as well as other research methods, are covered in my *The Psychology of Speech and Language: An Introduction to Psycholinguistics* (New York: Random House, 1970).

Experiential Vehicle

MEASURING INTERPERSONAL COMMUNICATION EFFECTS

This exercise is designed to provide you with some practice in attempting to measure the effects of interpersonal communications. The communications whose effects are to be measured are those that occurred in this course. More specifically, the object is to investigate the effects of the course, the instructor, and the textbook.

Semantic differential scales are provided for rating all three variables. Fill these out individually and then compute class averages for each scale for each of the three variables. After completing this, discussion should center on at least the following areas:*

1. How valid do you think these scores are? Do they "seem right?"

2. The textbook, because it is the most impersonal, is generally rated the lowest. Did this happen here? For the reason given?

*Your instructor may simply have the scales be filled out and returned without any class discussion. In either case try to be as specific and frank as possible.

3. How could the course have been improved? Be as specific as possible and try to refer to the scales in suggesting these changes.

4. How could the instructor have improved? Again, be as specific as possible.

5. How could the textbook have been improved? Again, be as specific as possible. (It would be much appreciated if the evaluations of the textbook could be sent to the publisher or to me. These reactions are important and will influence the second edition of the book. Send them to me at Queens College, Flushing, New York 11367 or to Harper & Row, Publishers, Inc., 10 East 53rd St., New York, New York 10022.)

THE COURSE

Positive	——	:	:	:	:	:	—— Negative
Active	——	:	:	:	:	:	—— Passive
Interesting	——	:	:	:	:	:	—— Uninteresting
Pleasant	——	:	:	:	:	:	—— Unpleasant
Successful	——	:	:	:	:	:	—— Unsuccessful
Realistic	——	:	:	:	:	:	—— Unrealistic
Organized	——	:	:	:	:	:	—— Disorganized
Difficult	——	:	:	:	:	:	—— Easy
Relaxed	——	:	:	:	:	:	—— Tense
Informative	——	:	:	:	:	:	—— Not Informative
Clear	——	:	:	:	:	:	—— Unclear
Good	——	:	:	:	:	:	—— Bad

Additional Comments

THE INSTRUCTOR

Positive	____:____:____:____:____:____	Negative
Active	____:____:____:____:____:____	Passive
Interesting	____:____:____:____:____:____	Uninteresting
Pleasant	____:____:____:____:____:____	Unpleasant
Successful	____:____:____:____:____:____	Unsuccessful
Realistic	____:____:____:____:____:____	Unrealistic
Organized	____:____:____:____:____:____	Disorganized
Difficult	____:____:____:____:____:____	Easy
Relaxed	____:____:____:____:____:____	Tense
Informative	____:____:____:____:____:____	Not Informative
Clear	____:____:____:____:____:____	Unclear
Good	____:____:____:____:____:____	Bad

Additional Comments

THE TEXTBOOK

Positive	____:____:____:____:____:____	Negative
Active	____:____:____:____:____:____	Passive
Interesting	____:____:____:____:____:____	Uninteresting
Pleasant	____:____:____:____:____:____	Unpleasant
Successful	____:____:____:____:____:____	Unsuccessful
Realistic	____:____:____:____:____:____	Unrealistic
Organized	____:____:____:____:____:____	Disorganized
Difficult	____:____:____:____:____:____	Easy
Relaxed	____:____:____:____:____:____	Tense
Informative	____:____:____:____:____:____	Not Informative
Clear	____:____:____:____:____:____	Unclear
Good	____:____:____:____:____:____	Bad

Additional Comments

Glossary

Listed here are definitions of the technical terms of interpersonal communication—the words that are peculiar or unique to this discipline. These definitions should make new or difficult terms a bit easier to understand. For the most part the words included here are used in this text. Also included, however, are terms which, although not used here, may be used in the conduct of a course in interpersonal communication.

A Language. The infinite set of grammatical sentences generated by the grammar of any language, for example, English, French, Bantu, Chinese. See *language*.

Abstraction. The process by which we derive a general concept from a class of objects.

Accent. The stress or emphasis that is placed on a syllable when pronounced.

Action Language. Movements of the body, for example, the way one walks, runs, sits.

Allness. The assumption that all can be known or is known about a given person, issue, object, or event.

Ambiguity. The condition in which a word or phrase may be interpreted as having more than one meaning.

Arbitrariness. That feature of human language which refers to the fact that there is no real or inherent relationship between the form of a word and its meaning. If we do

not know anything of a particular language we could not examine the form of a word and thereby discover its meaning.

Argot. A kind of *sublanguage;* cant and jargon of a particular class, generally an underworld or criminal class, which is difficult and sometimes impossible for outsiders to understand.

Associative Meaning. An approach to meaning that focuses on the word association of a term; in some views the meaning of a term is all the word associations that a subject makes to it, hence associative meaning.

Attention. The process of responding to a stimulus or stimuli.

Attitude. A predisposition to respond for or against an object.

Belief. Confidence in the existence or truth of something; conviction.

Bit of Information. That amount of information which is necessary to divide the possible alternatives in half. If, for example, you are try-

ing to guess which number will be chosen from 1 to 8, and you are told that it will not be 1, 2, 3, or 4, then one bit of information has been communicated since it reduced the number of alternatives by half.

Blindering. A misevaluation in which a label prevents us from seeing as much of the object as we might see; a process of concentrating on the verbal level while neglecting the nonverbal levels; a form of intensional orientation.

Body English. Popular term referring to tactile communication.

Body Language. A form of nonverbal communication in which messages are communicated by gestures, posture, spatial relations, and so forth; a popular term covering all aspects of nonverbal communication.

Bypassing. A misevaluation caused when the same word is used but each of the individuals gives it different meaning.

Cant. A kind of sublanguage; the conversational language of a special group which is generally understood only by members of the subculture.

Channel. The vehicle or medium through which signals are sent.

Channel Capacity. The maximum amount of information that a communication system can handle at any given time.

Chemistry-Binders. A class of life, characterized by the ability to combine chemicals in order to grow and survive; plants are chemistry-binders.

Classification. A method of semantic analysis whereby subjects group words into classes. The words are then analyzed in terms of how frequently they are put into the same classes and the type of

classes into which they are put. The analysis of the classes into which they are put provides us with a discovery procedure for semantic features. The analysis of the frequency with which words are grouped together provides us with a measure of similarity of meaning.

Classifying Abstracting. A form or type of abstracting in which one places an object, person, or event in a particular class.

Cliché. An expression that is overused and calls attention to itself; to describe a man as "tall, dark, and handsome" would be considered cliché.

Cloze Procedure. A technique for estimating the relative ease with which a message may be understood or the level of comprehension; in this process a message is mutilated by deleting every nth word and receivers fill in the words they think were deleted on the basis of the context that remains. The number of correct fill-ins is the cloze score for the passage.

Code. A set of symbols used to translate a message from one form to another.

Cohesiveness. The property of togetherness. Applied to group communication situations it refers to the mutual attractiveness among members; a measure of the intent to which individual members of a group work together as a group.

COIK. Acronym for "clear only if known," referring to messages that are unintelligible for anyone who does not already know what the messages refer to.

Communication Gap. The inability to communicate on a meaningful level because of some difference between the parties, for example,

age, sex, political orientation, religion.

Competence. The knowledge of language that a speaker has in his or her head. See *performance*. One of the dimensions of *credibility*.

Complementary Relationships. A relationship between two or more persons in which one person's behavior serves as a stimulus for a different type of behavior from the other person(s). The classic complementary relationship would be the relationship between a sadist and a masochist. Other examples of complementary relationships would be those between the dominant and the submissive, the talker and the listener, the lover and the loved. See *symmetrical relationships*.

Complementary Transaction. In transactional analysis, a transaction involving messages that are sent and received by the same ego state for each of the participants. For example, if person A is in the Parent ego state and if person B is in the Child ego state, then in a complementary transaction person A will address the Child ego state of B and B will address the Parent ego state of A. Thus complementary transaction would involve lines connecting ego states that are parallel to each other, as in the example given here:

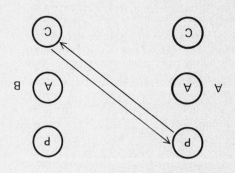

Connotation. The evaluative, potency, and activity dimensions of meaning; the associations of a word. See *denotation*.

Consonance. A psychological state of comfort created by having two elements (for example, cognitions or beliefs) one of which follows from the other. For example, consonance would exist for the following two cognitions: 1) X is healthy, 2) I engage in X.

Context of Communication. The physical, psychological, social, and temporal environment in which communication takes place.

Credibility. The degree to which a receiver perceives the speaker to be believable. See *ethos*.

Crossed Transactions. In transactional Analysis, a transaction involving a message being sent to one ego state but being responded to by another ego state. For example, if person A (in the Adult state) addresses person B's Adult but person B responds in the Child state to A's Parent state. A crossed transaction then would involve lines connecting ego states that literally cross each other. A diagram of this example would look as follows:

Cultural Transmission. See *traditional transmission*.

Date. An extensional device used to emphasize the notion of constant

and symbolized by a subscript: for example, John Smith$_{1972}$ is not John Smith$_{1976}$.

Decoder. That which takes a message in one form (for example, sound waves) and translates it into another code (for example, nerve impulses) from which meaning can be formulated. In human communication, the decoder is the auditory mechanism; in electronic communication the decoder is, for example, the telephone earpiece. See *encoder.*

Decoding. The process of extracting a message from a code, for example, translating speech sounds into nerve impulses. See *encoding.*

Delayed Reactions. Reactions that are consciously delayed while the situation is analyzed; a symbol reaction.

Denotation. Referential meaning; the objective or descriptive meaning of a word. See *connotation.*

Dialect. A specific variant of a language used by persons from a specific area or social class; dialects may differ from the "standard" language in phonology, semantics, and/or syntax, but they are intelligible to other speakers of the language.

Discreteness. That feature of human language which refers to the fact that the sounds of language (that is, the phonemes) are discrete categories of sound. Any given sound is either a particular phoneme of the language or it is another phoneme; it cannot be partly one phoneme and partly another.

Displaced Speech. Speech used to refer to that which is not present or in the immediate perceptual field.

Dissonance. A psychological state of

discomfort created by having two elements (for example, cognitions or beliefs), one of which would not follow given the other. Two such elements might be, for example: "X is harmful" and "I engage in X." These two elements represent dissonance, since given one of them the other would not follow. See *consonance.*

Duality of Patterning. That feature of language which refers to the fact that language consists of two levels: the level of individual sounds (phonemic level) and the level of individual meaningful units or morphemes (morphemic level). Duality of patterning makes it possible for a language to consist of relatively few phonemes (about 45) which can be combined in various different ways or patterns to form an extremely large number of morphemes.

Dyadic Communication. Two-person communication.

Elementalism. The process of dividing verbally what cannot be divided nonverbally, for example, speaking of body and mind as separate and distinct entities.

Empathy. The feeling of another person's feeling; the feeling or perceiving something as does another person.

Encoder. That which takes a message in one form (for example, nerve impulses) and puts it into another form (for example, sound waves). In human communication the encoder is the speaking mechanism; in electronic communication the encoder is, for example, the telephone mouthpiece. See *decoder.*

Encoding. The process of putting a message into a code, for example,

translating nerve impulses into speech sounds. See *decoding.*

Entropy. A measure of the extent of disorganization or randomness in a system. Entropy is a measure of the degree of uncertainty that a destination has about the message to be communicated by a source. Entropy is high if the number of possible messages is high and low if the number of possible messages is low.

E-Prime. A form of the language that omits the verb "to be" in all its forms. Designed to eliminate the tendency toward *projection,* that is, assuming that characteristics that one attributes to a person (for example, in "He or She is brave") are actually in that person instead of in the observer's perception.

Etc. An extensional device used to emphasize the notion of infinite complexity, since one can never know all about anything, any statement about the world or event must end with an explicit or implicit *etc.*

Ethics. That branch of philosophy which deals with the rightness or wrongness of actions; the study of moral values.

Ethos. That aspect of persuasiveness which depends on the audience's perception of the character of the speaker; to Aristotle *ethos* or ethical proof depended upon the speaker's perceived good will, knowledge, and moral character. *Ethos* is more commonly referred to as *speaker credibility.*

Evaluation. A process whereby a value is placed on some person, object, or event.

Evaluative Abstracting. A form or type of abstracting in which we form an evaluative judgment, for example, good or bad, positive or negative, pleasant or unpleasant.

Event Level. The level of atomic goings on), the level of WIGO (what is going on), an inferential level that we "construct" on the basis of what scientists tell us the world consists of: the event level is characterized by infinite complexity, constant change, and non-identity.

Experiential Limitation. The limit of an individual's ability to communicate, as set by the nature and extent of his or her experiences.

Extensional Devices. Those linguistic devices proposed by Alfred Korzybski for keeping language as a more accurate means for talking about the world. The extensional devices include the *etc., date,* and *index,* the working devices; the *hyphen* and *quotes,* the safety devices.

Extensional Orientation. A point of view in which the primary consideration is given to the world of experience and only secondary consideration is given to the labels. See *intensional orientation.*

Fact-Inference Confusion. A mis-evaluation in which one makes an inference, regards it as a fact, and acts upon it as if it were a fact.

Factual Statement. A statement made by the observer after observation, and limited to the observed. See *inferential statement.*

Feedback. Information that is fed back to the source. Feedback may come from the source's own messages (as when we hear what we are saying) or from the receiver(s) in the form of applause, yawning, puzzled looks, questions, letters to the editor of a newspaper, increased or decreased subscriptions to a magazine, and so forth.

See *negative feedback, positive feedback.*

Field of Experience. The sum total of an individual's experiences which influences his or her ability to communicate. In some views of communication, two people can only communicate to the extent that their fields of experience overlap.

First Verbal Level. The level of concrete naming and of factual and descriptive statements.

Frozen Evaluation. See *static evaluation.*

Game. A simulation of some situation with rules governing the behaviors of the participants and with some payoff for winning.

General Semantics. The study of the relationships between language, thought, and behavior.

Grammar. The set of rules of syntax, semantics, and phonology.

High-Order Abstraction. A very general or abstract term or statement; an inference made on the basis of another inference. See *level of abstraction*

Honorific. Expressing high regard or respect. In some languages certain pronouns of address are honorific and are used to address those of high status. In English such expressions as Dr., Professor, and the Honorable are honorific.

Hyphen. An extensional device used to illustrate that what may be separated verbally may not be separable on the event or non-verbal level; although one may talk about body and mind as if they are separable, in reality they may better be referred to as body-mind.

Identification. In General Semantics, a misevaluation whereby two or more items are considered as

identical; according to Kenneth Burke, a process of becoming similar to another individual; Burke sees identification as a necessary process for persuasion.

Idiolect. An individual's personalized variation of the language.

Index. An *extensional device* used to emphasize the notion of nonidentity (no two things are the same) and symbolized by a subscript, for example, politician$_1$ is not politician$_2$.

Indiscrimination. A misevaluation that is caused by categorizing people or events or objects into a particular class and responding to specific members only as they are members of the class; a misevaluation that is caused by failing to recognize that each individual is an individual and is unique; a failure to apply the *index.*

Inferential Statement. A statement that can be made by anyone, is not limited to the observed, and can be made at any time. See *factual statement.*

Information. That which reduces uncertainty. See *bit of information.*

Intensional Orientation. A point of view in which primary consideration is given to the way in which things are labeled and only secondary consideration (if any) to the world of experience. See *extensional orientation.*

Interchangeability. That feature of language which makes possible the reversal of rules between senders and receivers of messages. Because of interchangeability all adult members of a speech community may serve as both senders and receivers; persons may reproduce any linguistic message they can understand.

Interpersonal Communication. Com-

munication between or among persons, generally distinguished from mass communication and from public communication. Often used as a general term to include intrapersonal communication, dyadic communication and small group communication.

Interpersonal Conflict. A conflict between two persons; a conflict within an individual caused by his or her relationships with other people.

Intrapersonal Communication. Communication with oneself.

Jargon. A kind of *sublanguage;* the language of any special group, often a professional class, which is unintelligible to individuals not belonging to the group; the "shop talk" of the group.

Kinesics. The study of the communicative dimension of facial and bodily movements.

Language. The rules of *syntax, semantics,* and *phonology;* a potentially self-reflexive structured system of symbols that catalogs the objects, events, and relations in the world.

Learnability. That feature of language which refers to the fact that any normal human being is capable of learning any language as a first language. Learnability is dependent upon and follows from language being traditionally or culturally transmitted.

Level of Abstraction. The relative distance of a term or statement from the actual perception; a low-order abstraction would be a description of the perception, whereas a high-order abstraction would consist of inferences about inferences about descriptions of a perception.

Linguistic Determinism. A theory that holds that language determines what we do, say, and think and in fact limits what we are able to do, say, and think.

Linguistic Relativity. A theory that argues that the language we speak influences what we perceive and think. Since different languages catalog the world differently, speakers of different languages will see the world differently.

Linguistics. The study of language; the study of the system of rules by which meanings are paired with sounds.

Low-Order Abstraction. A description of what is perceived. See *level of abstraction.*

Macroscopic Approach to Communication. The focus on broad and general aspects of communication.

Mass Communication. Communication mediated by some medium, for example, television, newspapers, billboards, movies.

Message. Any signal or combination of signals that serve as *stimuli* for a receiver.

Metacommunication. Communication about communication.

Metalanguage. Language used to talk about language.

Microscopic Approach to Communication. The focus on minute and specific aspects of communication.

Model. A physical representation of an object or process.

Multiordinality. In General Semantics, a condition whereby a term may exist on different levels of abstraction.

Multivalued Orientation. A point of view that emphasizes that there are many sides (rather than only one or two sides) to any issue.

Negative Feedback. Feedback that serves a corrective function by informing the source that his or

her message is not being received in the way intended. Negative feedback serves to redirect the source's behavior. Looks of boredom, shouts of disagreement, and letters critical of newspaper policy would be examples of negative feedback.

Negative Reinforcement. The strengthening of a particular response by removing an aversive stimulus. See *positive reinforcement*.

Noise. Anything that distorts the message intended by the source. Noise may be viewed as anything that interferes with the receiver's receiving the message as the source intended the message to be received. Noise is present in a communication system to the extent that the message received is not the message sent. Noise may originate in any of the components of the communication act, for example, in the source as a lisp, in the channel as static, in the receiver as a hearing loss, in written communication as blurred type. Noise is always present in any communication system and its effects may be reduced (but never eliminated completely) by increasing the strength of the signal or the amount of redundancy, for example.

Nonallness. An attitude or point of view in which it is recognized that one can never know all about anything and that what we know or say or hear is only a part of what there is to know, say, or hear.

Nonelementalism. See *elementalism*.

Object Language. Language that is used to communicate about objects, events, and relations in the world; the structure of the object language is described in a metalan-guage; the display of physical objects, for example, flower arranging, the colors and clothes we wear.

Object Level. The nonverbal level of sense perception which we abstract from the event level; the level on which we live our lives.

Objective Abstracting. A form or type of abstracting in which we group individual units into a class of which they are all members, for example, all chapters being grouped into a book.

Olfactory Communication. Communication by smell.

Openness. See *productivity*.

Operant. A response emitted without a clearly identifiable prior stimulus; a bit of behavior controlled by its consequences.

Operant Conditioning. A process whereby reinforcement is contingent upon a particular response with the effect that the response is strengthened, or a process whereby punishment is contingent upon a particular response with the effect that the response is weakened.

Paralanguage. The vocal (but nonverbal) aspect of speech. Paralanguage consists of voice qualities (for example, pitch range, resonance, tempo), vocal characterizers (for example, laughing/crying, yelling/whispering), vocal qualifiers (for example, intensity, pitch height), and vocal segregates (for example, uh-uh meaning "no," or sh meaning "silence").

Perception. The process of becoming aware of objects and events from the senses.

Performance. The actual utterances that a speaker speaks and a hearer hears. See *competence*.

Persuasion. The process of influen-

cing attitudes and behavior.

Phonology. That area of linguistics concerned with sound.

Pictics. The study of the pictorial code of communication.

Pitch. The highness-lowness of the vocal tone.

Polarization. A form of fallacious reasoning in which only the two extremes are considered; also referred to as "black or white" or "either-or" thinking.

Positive Feedback. *Feedback* that supports or reinforces behavior along the lines it is already proceeding in, for example, applause during a speech.

Positive Reinforcement. The strengthening of a particular response by making a reward contingent upon it. The process may be visualized in three stages: 1) a response is emitted, for example, a child says "daddy"; 2) a reward is given, for example, a smile or candy or touching; 3) the response, "daddy," is strengthened, that is, it is more likely to occur under similar circumstances. See *negative reinforcement*.

Prevarication. That feature of human language which makes lying possible. This feature depends upon and is a function of displacement, openness or productivity, and semanticity.

Productivity. That feature of language which makes possible the creation and understanding of novel utterances. With human language we can talk about matters that have never been talked about before and similarly we can understand utterances that we have never heard before. Also referred to as *openness*.

Projection. A psychological process whereby we attribute character-

istics or feelings of our own to others; often used to refer to the process whereby we attribute our own faults to others.

Proxemics. The study of the communicative function of space; the "study of how man unconsciously structures microspace—the distance between men in the conduct of their daily transactions, the organization or space in his houses and buildings, and ultimately the layout of his towns."

Public Communication. Communication in which the source is one person and the receiver is an audience of many persons.

Quotes. An *extensional device* used to emphasize that a word or phrase is being used in a special sense and should therefore be given special attention.

Rate. The speed with which we speak, generally measured in words per minute.

Receiver. Any person or thing that takes in messages. Receivers may be individuals listening to or reading a message or a group of persons hearing a speech or a scattered television audience or a machine that stores information.

Redundancy. That quality of a message which makes it totally predictable and therefore, lacking in information. A message with zero redundancy would be completely unpredictable; a message of 100 percent redundancy would be completely predictable. All human languages contain some degree of redundancy built into them, generally estimated to be about 50 percent. All human messages, therefore, have some redundancy.

Reflexiveness. That feature of language which refers to the fact that human language can be used to

refer to itself, that is, we can talk about our talk, create a language for talking about language. See self-reflexiveness.

Reinforcement. The strengthening of a particular response. See positive reinforcement, negative reinforcement.

Relational Abstracting. A form or type of abstracting in which relationships among items are abstracted and represented in some kind of formula or equation or diagram; for example, the formula $a^2 = b^2 + c^2$ expressing the relationship among the sides of a right triangle is the result of relational abstracting.

Response. Any bit of overt or covert behavior.

Role. The part an individual plays in a group; an individual's function or expected behavior.

Second Verbal Level. The level of class terms and of generalizations, theories, and inferences.

Self-Acceptance. Being satisfied with ourselves, with our virtues and vices, abilities and limitations.

Self-Concept. An individual's self-evaluation; an individual's self-appraisal.

Self-Disclosure. The process of revealing something significant about ourselves to another individual or to a group, which would not normally be known by them.

Self-Reflexive Abstracting. A form or type of abstracting in which the abstraction is of itself as when, for example, we think about our thinking, love our love, fear our fear.

Self-Reflexiveness. The property of being able to refer back to itself; for example, language is self-reflexive in the sense that it can be used to refer to itself. See reflexiveness.

Semantic Differential. A device for measuring connotative meaning consisting of seven-point, bipolar scales; generally, three dimensions of meaning are measured: evaluation, potency, and activity.

Semantic Differentiation. The process of measuring meaning in a three-dimensional space consisting of evaluative, potency, and activity dimensions.

Semantic Reaction. A total reaction; a reaction of the organism-as-a-whole; a reaction that is determined by what the whole situation means to an individual.

Semantic Space. The connotative meaning of a term viewed as existing in a three-dimensional space consisting of evaluative, potency, and activity dimensions.

Semanticity. That feature of human language which refers to the fact that some words have denotations in the objective world. All human languages possess semanticity, but not all words have denotations (for example, "of," "the," and "is" do not have objective references in the real world).

Semantics. That area of language study concerned with meaning.

Semantogenic. Caused by semantics or labels; used most widely in reference to a problem or disorder whose origin may be found in the labels. For example, stuttering has been labeled semantogenic, that is, stuttering develops because some particular behavior was labeled "stuttering" according to the semantogenic theory.

Sign. Something that stands for something else and that bears a natural, nonarbitrary relationship to it, for example, dark clouds as a sign of rain. See symbol.

Signal Reaction. A conditioned response to a signal; a response to

Sign Language. Gesture language that is highly codified, for example, a hitchhiker's gesture.

Slang. The language used by special groups which is not considered proper by the general society; the language made up of the *argot*, *cant*, and *jargon* of various subcultures which is known by the general public.

Source. Any person or thing that creates messages. A source may be an individual speaking or writing or gesturing or a group of persons formulating an advertising policy or a computer solving a problem.

Space-Binders. A class of life that maintains itself by moving about in space and combining materials from various different places; animals.

Specialization. That feature of human language which refers to the fact that human language serves no purpose other than that of communication. Human language (unlike a dog's panting, for example) does not serve any biological function; it is a specialized system.

Specialized Communication System. A communication system that serves no other function than that of communication; human language is a specialized system.

Speech. Messages utilizing a vocal-auditory channel.

Speech Community. A group of persons using the same language.

Static Evaluation. An orientation that fails to recognize that the world is characterized by constant change; an attitude that sees people and events as static rather than as constantly changing.

some signal that is immediate rather than delayed. See *symbol reaction.*

Stimulus. Any external or internal change that impinges upon or arouses an organism.

Stimulus-Response Models of Communication. Models of communication that assume that the process of communication is a linear one, which begins with a stimulus which then leads to a response.

Structural Differential. A model of the abstraction process consisting of an event level, an object level, and first, second, third, and so forth, verbal levels.

Sublanguage. A variation from the general language used by a particular subculture; *argot*, *cant*, and *jargon* are particular kinds of sublanguages.

Symbol. Something that stands for something else but that bears no natural relationship to it, for example, purple as a symbol of mourning. Words are symbols in that they bear no natural relationship to the meaning they symbolize. See *sign.*

Symbol Reaction. A reaction that is made with some delay. See *signal reaction.*

Symmetrical Relationship. A relation between two or more persons in which one person's behavior serves as a stimulus for the same type of behavior in the other person(s). Examples of such relationships would include situations in which anger in one person encourages or serves as a stimulus for anger in another person or where a critical comment by one person leads the other person to respond in like manner. See *complementary relationship.*

Syntax. That area of language study concerned with the rules for combining words into sentences.

Taboo. Forbidden; culturally censored. Taboo language is that

which is frowned upon by "polite society." Themes and specific words may be considered taboo, for example, death, sex, certain forms of illness, and various words denoting sexual activities and excretory functions.

Tactile Communication. Communication by touch; communication received by the skin.

Theory. A general statement or principle applicable to a number of related phenomena.

Third Verbal Level. The level of inferences about inferences.

Time-Binders. A class of life that survives by passing information on from one generation to another, thus making knowledge cumulative; man.

Traditional Transmission. That feature of language which refers to the fact that human languages (at least in their outer surface form) are learned. Unlike various forms of animal language, which are innate, human languages are transmitted traditionally or culturally. This feature of language does not deny the possibility that certain aspects of language may be innate. Also referred to as *cultural transmission*.

Trust. Faith in the behavior of another person; confidence in another person which leads us to feel that whatever we risk will not be lost.

Two-Valued Orientation. A point of view in which events are seen or questions are evaluated in terms of two values, for example, a right and a wrong, a good and a bad. Often referred to as the fallacy of black or white or polarization.

Ulterior Transactions. In transactional analysis, an ulterior transaction is one in which more than two ego states are involved and

in which there is an unspoken or hidden agenda which is generally communicated nonverbally. For example, a woman (A) applies for a job and in her Adult state addresses a question to the personnel director (B) in his Adult state, "Do I have the job?" The personnel director, leering at her chest, responds, "What can you do besides type?" This transaction is an ulterior one and would be diagrammed as follows: (the ulterior transactions are denoted by dotted lines):

P   P

A →→ A   B
   ←

C ---- C

Undelayed Reaction. A reaction that is immediate; a signal response; a reaction made without any conscious deliberation.

Universal of Interpersonal Communication. A feature of interpersonal communication which is common to all interpersonal communication acts.

Universal of Language. A feature of language that is common to all known languages.

Value. Relative worth of an object; a quality that makes something desirable or undesirable; ideals or customs about which we have emotional responses, whether positive or negative.

Variable. A quantity that can increase or decrease; something that can have different values.

Volume. The relative loudness of the voice.